Dancing in the Wild Spaces of Love

Currents in Reformational Thought Series

Currents in Reformational Thought seeks to promote new scholarship emerging from the rich and dynamic tradition of reformational intellectual inquiry. Believing that all scholarly endeavour is rooted in and oriented by deep spiritual commitments of one kind or other, reformational scholarship seeks to add its unique Christian voice to discussions about leading questions of life and society. From this source, it seeks to contribute to the redemptive transformation and renewal of the various aspects of contemporary society, developing currents of thought that open human imagination to alternative future possibilities that may helpfully address the damage we find in present reality. As part of this work, *Currents in Reformational Thought* will bring to light the inter- and multi-disciplinary dimensions of this intellectual tradition, and promote reformational scholarship that intentionally invites dialogue with other traditions or streams of thought.

www.icscanada.edu/cprse

Robert Sweetman and Ronald A. Kuipers
SERIES EDITORS

DANCING IN THE WILD SPACES OF LOVE

A THEOPOETICS OF GIFT AND CALL,
RISK AND PROMISE

James H. Olthuis

WIPF & STOCK · Eugene, Oregon

DANCING IN THE WILD SPACES OF LOVE
A Theopoetics of Gift and Call, Risk and Promise

Currents in Reformational Thought Series

Copyright © 2022 James H. Olthuis. All rights reserved. Except for brief quotations in critical publications or reviews, no part of this book may be reproduced in any manner without prior written permission from the publisher. Write: Permissions, Wipf and Stock Publishers, 199 W. 8th Ave., Suite 3, Eugene, OR 97401.

Wipf & Stock
An Imprint of Wipf and Stock Publishers
199 W. 8th Ave., Suite 3
Eugene, OR 97401

www.wipfandstock.com

PAPERBACK ISBN: 978-1-6667-3792-9
HARDCOVER ISBN: 978-1-6667-9803-6
EBOOK ISBN: 978-1-6667-9804-3

06/06/22

Several chapters in this book have been previously published in an earlier form, although they have all been altered and revised for the present manuscript. The earlier essays appeared as follows.

Chapter 1: "Creatio Ex Amore," in Bruce Benson and Norman Wirzba, eds. *Transforming Philosophy and Religion*. Bloomington: Indiana University Press, 2008, 155–170.

Chapter 4: "Taking the Wager of/on Love: Luce Irigaray and the Caress," in B. Keith Putt, ed. *Gazing Through a Prism Darkly: Reflections on Merold Westphal's Hermeneutical Epistemology*. New York: Fordham University Press, 2009, 150–162.

Chapter 5: "Be(com)ing: Humankind as Gift and Call." *Philosophia Reformata* 58/2 (1993) 153–172.

Chapter 8: "Otherwise than Violence: Toward a Hermeneutics of Connection," in Lambert Zuidervaart and Henry M. Luttikhuizen, eds. *The Arts, Community and Cultural Democracy*. London: Palgrave Macmillan, 2000, 137–164.

Chapter 9: "Face to Face: Ethical Symmetry or the Symmetry of Mutuality?" *Studies in Religion/Sciences Religieuses* 25/4 (1996) 459–479.

Chapter 10: "Crossing the Threshold: Sojourning Together in the Wild Spaces of Love." *Toronto Journal of Theology* 11/1 (1995) 39–58.

Scripture quotations are from New Revised Standard Version Bible, copyright © 1989 National Council of the Churches of Christ in the United States of America. Used by permission. All rights reserved worldwide.

For Arvilla Ann Sipma

Love: Re-Born

CONTENTS

Series Editors' Preface · Robert Sweetman and Ronald A. Kuipers   ix
Acknowledgements   xi
Pro/epilogue: Where there is love, there is God . . .   xiii
"Love's Embrace" · Hendrik Hart   xix
"Cross Pollination" · Hendrik Hart   xxii

I. *Ex Amore*: Overflowing Love

Chapter 1 · Creatio Ex Amore   3
Chapter 2 · Theopoetics: Love on a Cosmic Scale   20
Chapter 3 · Thinking God Otherwise: Sovereignty without Sovereignty   58
Chapter 4 · Taking the Wager of/on Love: Luce Irigaray and the Caress   75

II. *Cum Amore*: Rhythmic Becoming

Chapter 5 · Be(com)ing: Humankind as Gift and Call   93
Chapter 6 · Rhythmic (Dis)Continuity: Trauma and the Uncanny   126
Chapter 7 · On the Im/Possibility of the Gift: From Derrida's Pure Giving to Irigaray's Mutual Loving   140
Chapter 8 · Otherwise than Violence: Towards a Hermeneutics of Connection   156

III. *Ad Amorem*: Zigzag Sojourning

CHAPTER 9 · Face to Face: Ethical Asymmetry or
the Symmetry of Mutuality? — 185

CHAPTER 10 · Crossing the Threshold: Sojourning Together
in the Wild Spaces of Love — 210

CHAPTER 11 · Towards a Radical Politics of Love: On the Interface
Between Personal Integrity and Societal Renewal — 230

BIBLIOGRAPHY — 251
SUBJECT INDEX — 265
SCRIPTURE INDEX — 271

SERIES EDITORS' PREFACE

BY Robert Sweetman AND Ronald A. Kuipers

CURRENTS IN REFORMATIONAL THOUGHT is an academic series designed to publish Christian scholarship that is interdisciplinary in its implications, philosophically primed in its conceptual strategies, theologically literate, and spiritually aware in its depth orientation. Sponsored by the *Institute for Christian Studies* (ICS), this series is intended to make a scholarly contribution to human flourishing in relation to ordinary human experience and understanding of the world as a servant of that experience and understanding rather than as a detached arbiter of it. The series is designed to publish work that exudes a deep spiritual awareness of the interplay of fallenness and Grace throughout the creation we inhabit, a creation made for the flourishing of its creatures in communion with its Creator. As a consequence, it seeks to publish scholarship both deeply at one with its orienting spiritual impulses, but also open to the presence of wisdom wherever it is to be found.

James H. Olthuis' studies in this volume, *Dancing in the Wild Spaces of Love: A Theopoetics of Gift and Promise* fit the bill to a tee. It is deeply philosophical in its way of setting up problems and asking questions. It is deeply conversant with signal modern and postmodern philosophical voices and perspectives. It addresses one of the central anxieties and concerns of modern philosophy after the "discovery" of the historicity of human experience: what does it mean to be a human participant in the enduring process of existence. This is, of course, a way of rearticulating the age-old problem of identity. It does its work from two philosophical vantage points, anthropological and hermeneutical, the ways-in to philosophical thinking that he has championed for so many decades at ICS in Toronto.

At the same time, this volume is deeply theological. It is wise about the project of and the challenges facing theology, attuned to some of the salient theological voices of the twentieth century, and deeply sensitive to the character of faith and religion in our culture and experience.

Finally, it is suffused with the knowledge and experience of the psychotherapist. This allows Olthuis a particular facility with the most psychoanalytically charged forms of postmodern thought, which he is able to collate with the wisdom of a therapist's observant service of persons in psychological crisis. The result is a volume that is at one and the same time a blessing to philosophers, to theologians, to psychotherapists, and indeed, in its central teaching, to all of us, for Olthuis is a philosopher of a secret that he has been gifted and called to shout to the high heavens. We creatures are loved and therefore we are. Indeed, the world comes from Love, it perdures in Love, and is headed toward Love no matter the impediments, no matter the duration, for Love is infinitely patient and ever beckoning creatures to communion. The volume represents in important ways the culmination of James H. Olthuis' career as scholar/teacher/therapist, and we are delighted to have it appear in our series.

ACKNOWLEDGEMENTS

Nothing Less than Love . . .

This book is the culmination of years of speaking, teaching, discussing, and studying in addition to years of psychotherapeutic practice. For this reason alone, it is impossible to remember and name all the people to whom I owe a word of thanks on its publication. Countless interactions, conversations, and discussions with students, colleagues, therapists, listeners, readers, friends, family have all played a role for which I am grateful. These took place not only in Canada and the United States, but in Great Britain, the Netherlands, Greece, South Africa, South Korea, Japan, and Indonesia. However, I do wish to mention a few people by name: Jeffrey Dudiak (with whom I first envisioned a project of this kind), Jamie Smith, Richard Middleton, Ken Van Wyk, Phaedon Kaloterakis, Jeff Pool, Henry Venema, Roger Smith, John Valk, Matt Bonzo, Ruthanne Crapo, Dianne Bergsma, Denise Hughes, Janet Hellmann, Steve Martin, Neal De Roo, Shane Cudney. Friends and ICS colleagues Hendrik Hart, Robert Sweetman, Calvin Seerveld, Lambert Zuidervaart, Nik Ansell, and my brother John have been pertinent discussion partners. Brian Walsh carefully read the manuscript and made helpful suggestions. Jack Caputo deserves particular mention as his pioneering work has served as a welcome challenge and counterpoint.

I am thankful to President Ronald A. Kuipers, and to ICS, that this book will be published in its Currents of Reformational Thought series. Thanks to Héctor Acero Ferrer and Emily Briggson for copyediting. I owe a special note of thanks to Dean Dettloff. Dean not only served as an invaluable assistant in the entire process, encouraging, discussing, editing; he first brought Slavoj Žižek's *Less than Nothing* to my attention. Much later, Dean said: "I think of your work as saying: 'There is nothing less than Love . . .'"

I am also most grateful to Henk Hart for his poems which so graphically portray the pathos of love in the midst of death. May they serve as an *in memoriam* of his life and witness.

I thank my grandson Jordan McIntyre for his cover painting. I love it. In his words: "The contents of this book elucidate the subject of love in all its forms; the love of others and of the community, the love of a significant other, the love between a parent and a child, the love of nature and other creatures, and God's love above and encompassing it all. It is also a jubilant invitation to 'Come dance with Me,' and celebrate this love with God. For its cover, I have tried to capture the essence of this exultant message. A circular image on a field of black, with deep greens and vibrant blues hugging the sides, the cover resembles Earth from space. Inside the picture, variegated and bright colours leap out unabashedly, as do the Matisse-inspired dancing figures, connected to each other in body and spirit. Humanity, animals, nature, in a cheerful dance, are watched over by a white dove, which radiates God's love from the sky. This jubilance even finds a way, like God's love, to spill out beyond the earthly bounds of the image into the title and author's name, a subtle glint of golden hope in the universe."

I dedicate this book to my lovely wife, Arvilla Sipma. Her love rejuvenated my life after the loss of Jean. She "believed," as she said, in the project, copyedited the manuscript, and perceptively commented. Thank you, darling.

Indeed, love makes all the difference. We only exist in love. Thanks be to God!

PRO/EPILOGUE: WHERE THERE IS LOVE, THERE IS GOD . . .

Wild Spaces

In the wild, there is love
In the between, there is promise
In the interval, there is hope
In the rupture, there is forgiveness
In the end, there is grace

This book is about Love, not only as an intense feeling of deep affection, which it is, but Love as the primordial cosmic force of All there is. It is about Love as the energy generating, driving, sustaining, redeeming the universe. All of creation lives, moves, and has its being in Love. God's *gifting* creation into existence is at the same time a *calling* for creation to participate in its becoming. The universe—existence in all its forms and with all of its creatures—is invited to join in, work with, incarnate, and pass on love. How and what happens depends on creation's response. Humankind plays a pivotal role in co-partnering with God and the family of earth's creatures in making love "real," in making the world a place of connection, cooperation, mutuality, growth, health, care, blessing, justice, peace, and joy. Making love "real" in the world is to give God a visible face in the world. "God is love," proclaims the Apostle John, and anyone who "dwells in love is dwelling in God and God in them." Indeed, God "dwells in us if we love one another," and God's "love is brought to perfection within us."[1]

Wow! God at home in us, with us!

Enacting love is doing the truth, being true to self, others, creation, and God. It calls for the faithful, everyday, non-identical repetition of love

1. 1 John 4:12, 16 (NRSV).

in new and novel ways. There is a double movement in loving: an active giving-over coupled with an expectant waiting, a risk inspired by the promise of hope. God waits, creation and all its inhabitants on tip toes awaits. As agents *of* and *for* love, we matter.

However, as human history to the present bears eloquent and bloody witness, when we miss the mark of love, and, in fear, are taken in by the forces of evil, we devise machinations of hate rather than liturgies of love. Instead of the mutual give-and-receive of the flow of Love, we fall prey to the Big Lie: it is dominate or be dominated, power-over or power-under. Instead of creation as a blessing, a warm, invigorating, inviting habitation, creation becomes a cold, alien, and comfortless expanse. The wild spaces of and for love are turned into fields of battle. Difference is taken to be opposition.

The tragic result, still so very real, is "the war of all against all": us versus them, the haves versus the have-nots, race against race, faith against faith, the battle of the sexes, nation against nation, on and on. In the process, instead of the Truth of Love's inclusivity claiming and connecting us in our difference, "we" (the dominators) claim possession of the Truth, declaring ourselves morally justified in dividing, excluding, or marginalizing all who disagree or resist. In the first part of the twentieth century, Louis-Ferdinand Céline vividly put words to the resulting widespread cultural anguish: "Not much music left inside us for life to dance to.... The truth is death. You have to choose: death or lies."[2]

In this book, I beg to differ. We do face a choice. Not between death or lies, but between love or lies. The truth is love. Life is not a lie, life is love. Life is dancing in the wild spaces of love. Graced, rhythmic, improvised, playful, faltering, mournful, celebrative dancing brings meaning and hope—even in the midst of anguish, horror, and death.

In recent years, although the call to control the other and dominate the battle-space is still often politically loud and shrill, there has been a growing chorus of postmodern voices, mortified by the killing fields and the exile of compassion, emphatically calling out for justice for the other and different. There is increasing recognition that ideological claims to possess the truth only lead to persecution of those who resist and, in fact, multiply violence and injustice. With all of this has come a renewed philosophic emphasis on the supreme importance of love. Emmanuel Levinas led the way with his plea that philosophy become once again "the wisdom

---

2. The full quote reads: "Not much music left inside us for life to dance to. Our youth has gone to the ends of the earth to die in the silence of the truth. And where, I ask you, can a man escape to, when he hasn't enough madness left inside him? The truth is an endless death agony. The truth is death. You have to choose: death or lies. I've never been able to kill myself" (Céline, *Journey to the End of the Night*, 97).

of love at the service of love."³ In modernity, philosophy (*philo-sophia*, love-of-wisdom) focused on concepts with Reason as the judge of truth. Truth ceased to be a claim made on us, and became a claim we made on behalf of our reasoned assertions. Knowledge equaled Power. Wisdom languished in the shadow of Reason and less and less was said about Love. For, as Augustine famously noted in regard to time, we may know what love is until someone asks us to explain it. Then we are soon at a loss for words. Love is an excess, beyond the powers of definition.

However, with all the new, welcome attention and focus on love as the revolutionary Event or Act that gives room to the other, fosters community, mandates protest, and brings about justice for all, not just us, one thing remains in the main unchanged. Unchanged, largely unchallenged, is the belief that structurally endemic to being human is being self-interested and self-centered. At bottom, it is said, we are first of all egocentric, opponents and rivals, in opposition to each other. To love another is to run against the grain of human nature. The best we can hope for is a curbing of self-interest and a minimizing of violence. Our only hope is failing better.

It is this encrusted belief in the fundamental oppositional/antagonistic nature of life that I call into question in this book. My wager—my faith, my hope, my trust—is that Love is the "oxygen" of this universe, the generating life-force, charging and recharging the cosmos and all that exists. It is in and through this life-current, the Love of God—inscendent in the creation, not transcendent—that we, all creatures and all matter, live and move and have our being. The way of love is a relational flow in-and-with-difference, connecting-with in coherence rather than opposing-to in antagonism. Living is breathing-in and breathing-out the *Ruah*, the Love-Breath, of the universe. The cosmos is an orchestration, a symphonic interplay of an array of processes with a host of players.

However, there is nothing automatic, insured, or guaranteed about the creational flow of love. For the gifting (by love) into existence is at the same time the *calling* (by love) to receive, participate, engender, share in, and pass on this love. How creation responds to the call makes all the difference. How we—and with us the rest of creation—dance in the uncharted, wild spaces of love is our signal calling. We are responsible for giving love shape in the world, for filling-in and filling-out what it means for each of us to be unique embodiments of love.

However, the sad reality is that in the darkness of evil, the spirit of fear can replace the *élan* of love, interrupting, stopping, betraying, poisoning the flow of love in all kinds of ways and on all kinds of levels. Time and

3. Levinas, *Otherwise than Being*, 62.

time again connections break, bonds become terrible binds, we wound or are wounded. Too often we act as if life is a zero-sum game in which we need to be in control and aggressive or we will miss out. Working together, conspiring, cooperating, breaks down, replaced by conflict, conspiracy, and catastrophe. Indeed, often we seem to be assailed on virtually every side by such troubles, imbroglios, disasters and injustices.

But is conflict, breakdown, failure, finally all there is, the last and final word? The leitmotif of this book is: No! *Life is risky, and difficult. But it is a beautiful risk, filled with promise, because Love carries all things, hopes all things, bears all things.* With-and-in the Spirit of Love, we are graced even as we are invited to join in, becoming bearers and couriers of love.

Letting love well up and flow through us as the beat, pulse, and rhythm of our lives is our challenge and blessing. Blessing because it allows us to partner with God, enacting, co-writing, co-implementing the Big Story of God's love that is the unfolding creation. Challenge because it asks us to give up the illusion of control, abandoning ourselves to God's love and trusting that Love will open the way, giving shape, pattern, identity, integrity, and grace to our lives individually and in community. Challenge because in our broken world, finding our way together is an uneasy, fretful, worrisome, pained negotiation, a journey through unpredictability, disappointment, surprise, and suffering. Instead of dancing in step with another, we too often limp and falter, mis-stepping, falling. Blessing because, in the face of suffering that makes us feel powerless and defenceless, we are not alone. God is with us.

All the chapters in this book, in one way or another, in greater or lesser detail, seek to give shape to a visioning which, hopefully insightful, is at the same time encouraging and healing, helping us dance in the wild spaces of love that is our cosmic home. This vision insists that authentic, genuine power—in contrast to power-over—is power-with, which is love.

The first group of chapters has a theopoetic, cosmological focus, proposing that the world was not created *ex nihilo* (out of nothing), as long theorized, but *ex amore* (out of love). Creation was birthed in love. Its spaces were made for dance and play, for connecting and reconnecting, for invention and adventure. The story of creation is an ongoing cosmological Love story in which the sun, moon, and stars, all creatures large and small, trees and animals, are interdependent partners. It is not only a story of Love's creative power but, due to the demonic forces of evil, by way of the *via dolorosa*, of Love's recreative power.

The second group of chapters has a more anthropological emphasis. As image-bearers of God who is love, love is who we are. It is in loving (or not loving) that we show (or betray) our humanity. As God is with-us

(Emmanuel), so we are to be-with others, *cum amore* (with love). "With-ing" (power-with rather than power-over) is our gift and calling, be(com)ing the unique selves we are through relationships with other persons (intersubjectivity), with creation and all its creatures (solidarity), and with God (spirituality). In and with the impetus of love's promise, we live-with, work-with, wrestle-with, suffer-with, celebrate-with the whole family of earth's creatures, all of creation, and God.

The third group of chapters has an ethical focus as we—individually, interpersonally, and globally—strive for health and healing for ourselves, all peoples, for all creatures, for the planet itself. We look for paths of healing, avenues of justice, and oases of refuge amidst the killing fields, abysmal poverty, trenchant racism, and global exploitation. We dance, *ad amorem* (toward love), stumbling and falling, rising and soaring, twisting and turning into the future with the hope and promise that love, outlasting death, will in the end be all-in-all. All of the chapters, it is my hope and prayer, in some small ways, give witness to my desire to follow after Jesus in the way of love. My hope and wish is that these pieces may inspire, stimulate dialogue, and hopefully contribute to our joint efforts to incarnate compassion in a suffering world.

One more observation: all of these chapters—some early, some recent, and some very new—found their origin as occasional pieces in diverse circumstances as I lived my life with one foot in the academy among philosophers and theologians and one foot in the counselling clinics of psychotherapists and psychologists. As I trust will become abundantly clear, although these studies have a clear theo-philosophic flavor, all of them bespeak a persistent psychotherapeutic concern. My thirty-plus years of psychotherapeutic practice have served as a kind of laboratory for the validity of the philosophical/theopoetic constructions, and the philosophizing has emphatically underlined the importance of developing a coherent, integrated rationale for psychotherapeutic practice. What became therapeutically increasingly apparent throughout the years is that when we are *with*-each-other, open-hearted, meeting in the middle, the flow of love connects. On such occasions, we experience a "we"—an authentic interpersonal connection beyond all doubt and argument—caught up in the being-with of love that heals. In no small way, this reality underlies my voiced conviction in this book that creation's spaces, in their wildness, need not be gaps of fear and antagonism, but can become "betweens" of and for love—openings of hope, promise, and grace.

I end this prelude on a theopoetic note with a doxological poem of the Sufi master Hafiz and two poignant poems written by a dear friend and colleague of sixty years, Henk Hart. The poems are an evocative, heart-rending, heart-touching poetic testimony of how in "Love's embrace" a person passes through the valley of the shadow of death and evil with deepened faith and renewed hope. Where there is Love, in spite of evil, we are not alone, God is with us.

The God Who Only Knows
Four Words[4]

Every
Child
Has known God,
Not the God of names,
Not the God of don'ts,
Not the God who ever does
Anything weird,
But the God who only knows four words
And keeps repeating them, saying:
"Come dance with Me."
Come
Dance

---

4. Hafiz, *The Gift*, 270.

Love's Embrace

Hendrik Hart

I

At heart,
a human life
gains without measure
in depth and scope
exposed to giving
or receiving
love,
primeval energy
of all that is.
In the embrace of Love
we
vessels of love
become aware:
irresistible energy
compels us
be centered
in all we do
in Love's embrace;
to seek for ourselves
and others
peace, justice, joy, life,
fulfillment, patience,
hope, life, and healing.
Love begins,
guides us
to set our priorities,
distribute our energies,
choose our relationships,
value our involvements.

Love fills us,
its blessed awareness
whenever and wherever we follow
step by step but irresistibly,
bids darkness recede—
light spreads.
We become driven by Spirit—
Ruah, Wind, Breath
Blows where it wills
harvesting without exception
light and life
wherever it blows.
Growing in trust
the Presence of Love
in our life
bit by bit
becomes
our presence as love
in the Presence.

II

I experienced Love
dawning forcefully
at the dark edge of the abyss
in their last journey.
The doom of death
revealed depths unknown
of Love.

III

Death!
Who are you?
fullness of evil?
part of life?
final separation
from self and other?
Why do we weep?
Death's deepest sense persists

as ineradicable persuasion:
new life emerges for us all
after our death.
Daisies bloom another spring,
so do we.
Our death is singular,
no circling cycles,
no seasons,
we die
then live forever.
The birth of Love in our life,
foretaste of eternity:
this inexpressible joy will be ours
forever.

IV

What is hereafter
after their death?
In my brain
survival beyond the end
is dead.
In my heart
a compelling reality
anticipated and celebrated
in music, in song.
Tears well up
with songs of visions of redemption,
reconciliation,
resurrection,
rebirth.
No remnants of a childish faith,
a final maturation
of our trust
of Life and Love.
In Love's world
Our tears of weeping
trickle into rivers of joy.

Cross Pollination

Hendrik Hart

In Paradise
the Tree of Life
turned deadly
At Golgotha
a cursed cross
transformed dead wood
A Man of Sorrows
hung bleeding
the soil beneath
baptized with love
Pierced hands
now bless a new creation
clap for a love tree rising
from soil soaked red with life
Come love with Me
embrace birth's pains
let forests of crosses
set deserts abloom

EX AMORE: OVERFLOWING LOVE

CHAPTER 1

CREATIO EX AMORE

—poetic prologue—

And God stepped out on space,
And She looked around and said,
"I'm lonely—
I'll make me a world."
As far as the eye of God could see
Darkness covered everything,
Blacker than a hundred midnights
Down in a cypress swamp.
Then God smiled,
And the light broke,
And the darkness rolled up one side,
And the light stood shining on the other,
And God said, "That's good!"
. . .
Then God walked around,
And God looked around
On all that She had made.
She looked at Her sun.
She looked at Her moon.
And She looked at Her little stars;
She looked on Her world
With all its living things,
And God said, "I'm lonely still."
Then God sat down
On the side of a hill where She could think;
By a deep, wide river She sat down;

> With Her head in Her hands,
> God thought and thought,
> Till She thought, "I'll make me a human!"
> Up from the bed of the river
> God scooped the clay;
> And by the bank of the river
> She kneeled Her down;
> And there the great God Almighty,
> Who lit the sun and fixed it in the sky,
> Who flung the stars to the most far corner of the night,
> Who rounded the earth in the middle of Her hand—
> This Great God,
> Like a mammy bending over her baby,
> Kneeled down in the dust
> Toiling over a lump of clay
> Till She shaped it in Her own image;
> Then into it She blew the breath of life,
> And human became a living soul.
> James Weldon Johnson[1]

IF GOD IS LOVE, and God is all in all, then without love, there is nothing, which means, as James Weldon Johnson's evocative 1927 poem "The Creation" poetically presages, that the world was not created *ex nihilo*, but *ex amore*. That is the central theme of this chapter: we would do well to replace the doctrine of *creatio ex nihilo*, with its emphasis on God's omnipotent power, with *creatio ex amore* and its accent on God's generating and regenerating love.

Although the focus of this essay is theological and philosophical, the exegetical and hermeneutical considerations of such a reconceptualization are, I suggest, so striking that I cannot resist at the outset presenting one example: Genesis 3:9. "But the Lord God called to the man and said to him, 'Where are you?'" (NRSV).

---

1. Johnson, "The Creation" in *God's Trombones*, 17–20. In this rendition, in reference to God, "she" replaces "he," and in reference to human beings, "human" replaces "man."

Traditionally, this text has generally been read—I first heard it in catechism classes more than sixty-five years ago—as an angry God taking humans to task. Beginning *ex amore*, another reading suggests itself. Looking forward, as was God's wont, to walking with Adam and Eve in the garden in the cool of the day, God is disappointed when they are nowhere to be found, and calls out: "Where are you my friends? I'm missing you."

When God locates Adam and Eve, they point fingers, assign blame, implicate the animal world, in effect accusing God, the creator of all, after which follows the curse as God's declaration of humankind's future in sin. Such a reading—with its focus on intimacy, communion, and loneliness—does, I suggest, more justice to the actual words of Genesis. In the text, God does not play the heavy hand, accusingly pointing the finger, "What have you done now?" Rather, distressed at being stood up, God cries out, "Where are you?"

Wild Spaces, Wild Times

Everything that happens, happens in time and space. When we begin *ex amore*, time and space are not neutral, empty receptacles, but God's primings—occasions and places for giving and receiving love. There is no meaningless time, only time to be full-filled in love (or impaired by hate). There is no vacuous space, only space as the abodes of love (or the haunts of evil). Created beings are called to live side by side, dwelling in enduring relations with each other.

Indeed, as I have become fond of saying, the spaces and times of creation are the wild spaces and times of love.[2] Wild, because they are uncharted and unpredictable—to venture into them is to take the beautiful risk. Spaces can turn out to be healing meadows, or they may become killing fields. Time can make for fulfilling or distressing connections. Although space can be traversed and time filled, there is no guarantee of enduring connections or healing moments.

Moreover, in regard to both space and time, if we attempt to tame the space and determine the time in order to guarantee the outcome, we may have control, manipulation, aggression, co-option, domination, subjection, bullying, intimidation—but never meeting or intimacy, never fulfillment. In the spaces and times that we are given, we are called to negotiate ways together of hope and healing.

Trading on the many African and Asian rituals in which the metaphor of the world as dance has symbolized these negotiations,[3] we are called to

2. See Olthuis, *The Beautiful Risk*, 48.
3. Moltmann, *God in Creation*, 304.

dance together in the wild spaces and times of love. Choreography is always required, with the risk of wrong moves, black-and-blue shins, not to mention hurtful tumbles, bruised egos, abused bodies, and betrayed hearts. The dance metaphor nicely links space and time in rhythmic movement. In rhythm, "space is measured in terms of time, and time in terms of space."[4]

Moreover, one of the most compelling images of the Trinity in the patristic church is that of the "sacred dance-play between three persons" known as the *perichoresis*, which literally means "dance (*choros*) around (*peri*)."[5] The celebrated Shaker song, "The Lord of the Dance" trades on these images, with the Son as the Lord of the dance inviting all of humanity to join, as Lucian stated it, in the "great dance of creation and rebirth."[6] Thirteenth-century Beguine, Mechtild of Magdeburg, talks of God as "playmate":

> I, God, am your playmate!
> I will lead the child in you in wonderful ways
> for I have chosen you.
> Beloved child, come swiftly to Me
> For I am truly in you.[7]

A timed/spaced creation is God's adventure in love, the original blessing[8] in which God both loves creation into being and desires to be loved by creation. It was God's let-there-be's of love that brought forth time and space for the great dance of creation. Eleventh-century mystic Hildegard of Bingen exclaims:

> For it was love which was the source of this creation in the beginning when God said: "Let it be!" And it was. As though in the blinking of an eye, the whole creation was formed through love.[9]

There it is: *ex amore*. Everything in creation speaks and bespeaks love, which means that it is not only *ex amore*, out of love, but also *cum amore*, with love, and *ad amorem*, to love.

Spacing and timing are the between-ings of love, which can become meetings-in-the-interval, passages of visitations of love, with-ings[10] of the

---

4. Moltmann, *God in Creation*, 306.
5. Kearney, *The God Who May Be*, 109.
6. Kearney, *The God Who May Be*, 109.
7. Woodruff, *Meditations with Mechtild of Magdeburg*, 47.
8. Fox, *Original Blessing*.
9. Fox, *Hildegard of Bingen's Book of Divine Works*, 308.
10. On with-ing, see Olthuis, *Beautiful Risk*, 48.

Spirit. Time and space are holy containers, wombs primed for love, spaces for the formation of love.

Simone Weil declared that "time is the waiting of God, who begs for our love." Upon reading this description, Emmanuel Levinas substituted "who commands our love" for "who begs for our love."[11] Time—and I include space—are the waitings of God, and at the same time, they are also the yearnings of God, gifting us for love, calling us to redeem the time.

Since the gifting God, in the beginning, *ex amore*, made the world, we, image-bearers of God, both receive and find our being *ex amore*. The question is not Shakespeare's: To be or not to be. Rather, the make-or-break question—God's question, one could say—is: To love or not to love. And in the degree that we love, we are, and in the degree we fail to love, we are not. Instead of "I think, therefore, I am"—Descartes' classic starting point—it is "I was loved, therefore, I am." Indeed, we are Love's agents in the world—in the double sense of being both agents of love and for love. To be a lover is to be caught up in the intrigue of love even as we are an active agent of that love.

Waging love, rather than waging war, is no easy matter in our world that knows so much violence and brokenness. Too often the reality is one in which we turn the spaces and times of love into killing fields and instants of terror. In a world in which compassion is in exile, the practice of compassion—redeeming time and space—is a working and a waiting in faith, living in hope and by grace, a beautiful risk, a ministry of encouragement.

We are, says the Apostle Peter, in these between times, to adopt a double strategy, waiting for, and at the same time, hastening the coming of the "kindom" of God (2 Pet 3:12). Kindom, with its connotations of partnership, family, friendship, and kindred spirits, seems more becoming to me than the more political, militaristic image of the kingdom. Waiting and hastening at the same time is not easy. With one eye fixed on Christ's coming and one eye fixed on our task in this world, we are, so to speak, cross-eyed—even if starry-eyed—witnesses. Our focus is never 20/20. We, "lovers in a dangerous time," sorely need to hold onto each other in the fellowship of faith and communion of the spirit as, in the words of Bruce Cockburn, we "kick at the darkness till it bleeds daylight."[12]

---

11. See Fuchs and Henrix, *Zeitgewinn: Messianisches Denken nach Franz Rosenzweig*, 163–83.

12. Cockburn, "Lovers in a Dangerous Time," *Stealing Fire*.

Love as Strange Attractor

In my book *The Beautiful Risk* I have further elucidated what it means anthropologically that love is who we are, rather than something we do. In this chapter I want to deepen this understanding by exploring some cosmological implications of beginning *ex amore*. If God creates *ex amore*, then creation not only lives out of love, but love is the cosmic energy of creation, one could say, the oxygen, the glue, the fire of the universe. Love is the being and becoming of created reality. Love is the oxygen of the universe without which we cannot live even though we cannot see it. At the same time, when it is not there we know it, we gasp for breath, slowly dying.

Love is the glue of the universe, the staying power that acts to hold it together in all its contingency and randomness. One of the most striking features of contemporary chaos theory is the attention it pays to the reality that in and through the open-ended, chaotic systems of nature is an emergent force that lures and evokes new patterns of novelty and surprise. This force has been designated the strange attractor. Love, I want to suggest, is not just a random effect; rather, love is the strange attractor luring creation into new life, and God is the divine attractor.[13] Indeed, Richard Middleton makes a similar claim that "not only does Genesis 1 depict a fractal universe, but it depicts a creator less like a Newtonian lawgiver and more like a strange attractor."[14]

Love is the fire, the driving force of the universe. Creation, fired by the love of God, will always tend toward the fullness of love, as the lover searches for the beloved. The spirit of love, the Divine Eros, lures creation and its creatures to participate in the creative process itself toward ever new and widening spirals of love. The cosmos in this way, speaking the language of Whitehead, has a divine aim. Creation is not only *ex amore*, but *cum amore*, and *ad amorem*.

Love measures us, not we, love. Without love's grace, imagination and vision are finally very limited, for the graceless mind proves in the end to be boring, caught in its own repetitive reverberations—shades of Levinas—in

---

13. When first preparing this essay for publication, I was pleasantly surprised that Catherine Keller has raised the same possibility: "Might we every now and then imagine Elohim as the strange attractor of the creation?" (*The Face of the Deep*, 98).

14. Middleton, *The Liberating Image*, 286. "Whereas the world rhetorically depicted in Genesis 1 is certainly ordered, patterned, and purposive . . . , this world is not mechanistically determined, as if it were governed by ineluctable, ironclad Newtonian laws. . . . The God who is artisan and maker, reflected rhetorically in the complex literary artistry of the text, does not overdetermine the order of the cosmos . . . [T]he process of creation [is] God sharing power with creatures, inviting them to participate (as they are able) in the creative process itself" (*The Liberating Image*, 285–87).

which the regime of the same conquers. Without love, we measure the other on the basis of our own insights and interests, and in so doing, there is a failure of hospitality, a hardening of arteries, a closing off, a becoming unavailable, a violation of the other. With love, there is a suffering-with—a standing-with the other, giving and forgiving.

Love is the echo before the anonymous, menacing, rumbling of "the impersonal *there is*"[15] (*il y a*), the recurrence that interrupts and breaks open any congealed or clotted identity. The law of friendship is, as Derrida demonstrates, that "one must always go before the other," that one must always die before the other.[16] When love (as well as justice) is undeconstructible, the law of friendship receives another face: Yes, one must go before the other, but meanwhile, one may go with the other. Friendship, life as a whole, is a risk, and there will be wounds and death, but life is a beautiful risk to run because it holds within it the graced possibilities of connection, not being alone, being touched by love. At the same time, it is true, I suspect, that a mark of true friendship in distinction from acquaintance relations is the frightening realization between friends that one will die before the other.

All these considerations point in one direction: the logic of creation, in its height and depth, in its human and non-human dimensions is the logic of love. If this is the case, there is an impressive case to be made for replacing our doctrine of *creatio ex nihilo* with *creatio ex amore*. *Creatio ex nihilo* emphasizes the difference, the externality, between God and creation: God the infinite transcendent creator, who brings forth the finite creaturely universe as something separate from God.

In other words, too often the difference between God and the world is radically misunderstood as the difference between two discrete entities that extrinsically relate. In this view God is a kind of master craftsperson, divine architect, mastermind who designs and creates, connecting the parts, and who thereafter, because of sin and evil, reconnects and repairs. Often this is coupled with an interventionist view of divine action in which God—who is immutable, unmoved, and unaffected by anything—from time to time miraculously intervenes.[17]

Viewing the God-creation relationship as external in this way does not do adequate justice to the biblical testimony that God is love, tending to

---

15. Levinas, *Totality and Infinity*, 190.

16. Derrida, *The Work of Mourning*, 1.

17. Thus, physicist-theologian Arthur Peacocke judges that our understanding of God as creator has been "too much dominated by a stress on the externality of God's creative acts.... We should work the analogy of God creating the world within herself. God creates a world that is in principle other than himself, but creates it within himself" ("Theology and Science" in *Cosmos as Creation*, 36).

bracket, if not abrogate, the uniquely personal and mutually participatory relationship between God and creation. As love, God cannot be related to the world in extrinsic fashion such as in deism or dualisms of any sort.

Moreover, as Catherine Keller summarizes in her provocative *The Face of the Deep*, "although the *creatio ex nihilo* has reigned largely uncontested in the language of the church since the third century ACE,"[18] more and more biblical scholars are recognizing that the Bible does not support it. Thus, Jon Levenson claims that the "overture to the Bible, Genesis 1:1–2:3, cannot be invoked in support of the developed Jewish, Christian, and Muslim doctrine *creatio ex nihilo*."[19] In fact, it needs to be noted that the Bible does not talk about a creation from nothing, but "knows only a formation of something new from something-else, something yet unhinged, unformed, some sort of marine chaos."[20]

However, the alternative to *creatio ex nihilo* need not leave us with a Plotinian emanation in which the creation is an efflux of the divine self-same—one of the alternatives that *creatio ex nihilo* was constructed to avoid. Instead of a pure dualism (God and nothing), we need a "third possibility" as Karl Barth also recognized.[21]

My "third space of beginning"[22] is *creatio ex amore*, which shifts the focus from an understanding of God who creates by omnipotent power over and periodic divine intervention in creation, to a God whose unconditional love gives birth to creation and intimately and enduringly suffers-with creation, redeeming and renewing it.

Along these lines, creation is not the demonstration of God's almighty power, but the communication of God's unfailing, unconditional love. "Creation," exclaims Jürgen Moltmann, "is not a demonstration of his boundless power, it is the communication of his love, which knows neither premises nor preconditions: *creatio ex amore Dei*. In Dante's words, 'From the Creator's love came forth in glory the world . . .'"[23]

In contrast to the *creation ex nihilo* doctrine that emerged in the third century, as Gerhard May has documented, "to express and safeguard the omnipotence and freedom of God acting in history,"[24] *creatio ex amore*

---

18. Keller, *The Face of the Deep*, 4.
19. Levenson, *Creation and the Persistence of Evil*, 121.
20. Keller, *The Face of the Deep*, 25.
21. Barth, *Church Dogmatics*, 3/1:104. However, Barth's third possibility is to demonize the chaos: "Nothingness is not nothing . . . it 'is' nothingness" with its "own being, albeit malignant and perverse" (3/3:349). See Keller's chapter on Barth in *The Face of the Deep*, 84–99.
22. Keller, *The Face of the Deep*, 12.
23. Moltmann, *God in Creation*, 76.
24. May, *Creatio Ex Nihilo*, 180.

would emphasize "the risk-taking, power-sharing character of God,"[25] passionately involved with the creation. In creating, God took the supreme risk of love, letting the other be.

The Let-There-Be's of Genesis One

The concept of an omnipotent God in splendid supremacy masterfully ordering creation does not fit the picture of creation in Genesis 1. The let-there-be's of Genesis are, Richard Middleton reminds us, not "imperatives at all, but Hebrew jussives (which have no exact counterpart in English)"; but, even as they may range "from the very strong (almost a command) to the very soft (almost a wish)," they always possess a "voluntary element."[26] "God said, 'Let the *earth put forth* vegetation, plants yielding seed etc. . . .' And it was so. The *earth brought forth* vegetation; plants yielding seed of every kind." Indeed, "the earth is *agent* of *Elohim's* creation. . . . The same again with the sea. . . . *Creation takes place as invitation and cooperation.*"[27]

William P. Brown concludes that the creative process described in Genesis "does not thereby imply a God who simply imposes order on unruly matter or creates *everything ex nihilo*," but the let-there-be's can be "read as invitations to enter into the grand creative sweep of God's designs." Indeed, "God chooses and implements noncoercive ways of creating, thereby allowing the elements to share positively in cosmogony."[28] This fits very well with Catherine Keller's suggestion that in Genesis 1 we have the impetus for a "theology of creation, in which the chaos is neither nothing nor evil; in which to create is not to master the formless, but to solicit its virtual forms. Such solicitation, when expressed as divine speech, may sound less like command than a seduction."[29] Keller talks of a *creatio cooperationis*.[30] She asks: "Does not the vibratory proximity of *ruach* upon the waters suggest that intimate co-generativity"?[31]

Richard Middleton goes even farther, surmising that the text of Genesis "depicts God's founding exercise of creative power in such a way that we might appropriately describe it as an act of generosity, even of love."[32] In the advent(ure) of creating, God put Godself at risk. God gave Godself

---

25. Middleton, *The Liberating Image*, 287.
26. Middleton, *The Liberating Image*, 265.
27. Keller, *The Face of the Deep*, 195.
28. Brown, "Divine Act and the Art of Persuasion in Genesis One," in Brown, Graham, and Kuan, *History and Interpretation*, 28, 32.
29. Keller, *The Face of the Deep*, 115.
30. Keller, *The Face of the Deep*, 117.
31. Keller, *The Face of the Deep*, 121.
32. Middleton, *The Liberating Image*, 278.

over to the adventure and risk of time and space, inviting, hoping, wooing all the family of God's creatures to participate in the creative process itself. God as love yearns for and desires another, not out of lack or need, but out of the profusion or abundance of love as self-giving and out-going. God's life as love spills over into what is other than God, birthing creation, empowering and inviting creation into a covenant partnership. Rather than being a supreme display of power, creation is a revelation of the power of love in which the Godhead becomes vulnerable, risking rebuff, refusal, and hurt. In place of power as demonstration of mastery and total control (power-over), we have the power of love as opening to the other, gifting to and calling for partnership (power-with).

Thus, in our turn away from God in the Fall, God was deeply wounded, as our previous reference to Genesis 3 reminds us, and still suffers, yearning/waiting for us to pass love on rather than hoard it. Yet the risk and vulnerability of Divine Love is at the same time its very power. Love is unstoppable; it never stops coming—reaching a particularly marvelous climax in the coming of Jesus, love incarnate. And even when we killed Christ on the cross, love was born anew in his resurrection.

God's heart of love can be wounded, it can be violated and betrayed, but it cannot be destroyed. God's love keeps on coming back. That, in fact, is the meaning of the crucifixion and Easter. God redemptively suffers with the world and its creatures to the point of death, so that all things might be made new in the power of the resurrection. Love, if there is such a thing, is indeconstructible. No matter what—even death, as Christ proved on the cross—Love can never be defeated because it keeps on coming back in resurrection power, suffering with us now and in the future until the end. Love is stronger than death—period.

—interlude—

> Without the Word of God no creature has meaning.
> God's Word is in all creation, visible and invisible.
> The Word is living, being, spirit, all verdant greening,
> all creativity.
> This Word manifests in every creature,
> Now this is how the spirit is in the flesh—the Word is
> indivisible from God.
> Hildegard of Bingen[33]

---

33. Uhlein, *Meditations with Hildegard of Bingen*, 49.

Omnipotence as Unfailing Love

Thinking of *creatio ex amore* opens, I want to suggest, new and promising ways for approaching some of the most baffling and controversial issues having to do with God's relation to creation. First is the question of omnipotence that we have just broached. Instead of speaking of God's omnipotence in terms of sheer power over any and everything—which always raises a host of haunting questions: How can an omnipotent, good God allow evil and suffering? Why does not such an all-powerful God intervene? And if God could, but does not, how are we to distinguish God from an arbitrary and sadistic despot?—we can say that God's omnipotence is the unfailing, boundless power of love, a vulnerability that can never, despite sin and evil, be defeated. Love cannot not come back. That is who God is, that is who God will be, that is who God always has been, life.

In the face of evil, with a traditional view of God's omnipotence, it is usually said with orthodoxy that God freely restricts his/her power. That, however, leaves unanswered the cluster of questions that we have just mentioned. More recently, realizing the need for a different approach, John Caputo, pointing to the *tohu wa bohu* of Genesis 1:2 argues that "God's power only extends so far, that is, up to the point of the formless void which is of itself, not from God. So God can only do so much."[34] Richard Kearney is even more blunt: "God can't stop evil. . . . God has no power over what God is not—namely, evil. . . . God is *not* omnipotent when it comes to evil. God is utterly powerless. And that's terribly important."[35]

Although I fully share Caputo's and Kearney's dissatisfaction with God's self-limitation of his/her power, it strikes me that they are still working too much with power as power-over. If, instead, we understand the power of love as power-with, another possibility suggests itself.

God's love is omnipotent in respect to evil because love outlasts evil. The power of love de-stings the sting of death, not by redeeming evil, but by redeeming from evil. Evil is/will be defeated by love because, despite everything that evil conjures up, God's infinite love does not/cannot/will not stop coming.

Inordinate Intrigue: *Ebullitio*

Secondly, traditionally, it has often been asked: Did God create out of necessity or out of freedom? However, to say that it was necessary to the Godhead

---

34. Caputo, "Olthuis's Risk: A Heretical Tribute," in Smith and Venema, *The Hermeneutics of Charity*, 46.

35. Kearney, "Philosophizing the Gift," in Smith and Venema, *The Hermeneutics of Charity*, 59.

that God create not only brings with it the suspicion that God lacked something, but it leaves little room for joy and spontaneity on God's part: God had to do it—which seems cold, impersonal, and disheartening. On the other hand, to say that God was free to create or not to create brings with it, besides a certain arbitrariness in God, the idea that creation is external to God—a kind of wonderful afterthought, an amusement for a lonely deity—that God didn't have to create—which also seems disconcerting.

In contrast, when we conceive of God as a Trinity of Love—ebullient, exuberant, passionate, bubbling or boiling over, gushing forth creatively—God's relation to creation can be framed in ways that avoid or go beyond the confines of the necessity/freedom binary. Creation begins, not as the Big Bang, but as the Bursting out of God's love. Considering the hotness of God's love, it's ebullience—*ebullitio*, boiling over, said Meister Eckhart[36]—creation was bound to be an outbursting of love. If God is love, creation will be God's self-giving love going out to the other for the sake of the other. In that way, creation is not the result of an external act of God, which God could or could not have made, but proceeds quite naturally from the heart of God's love. On the other hand, for love to be love, it needs to be spontaneous, unconditional, and gratuitous rather than necessitated, forced, or programmed.

In understanding God as love, to be God is to be the creator. This means that God's acting as creator is not something that is added to the divine essence. That is, "to be in relation to creation as the Creator, is not a relation added on to the divine essence, ancillary to God's being. To be God is to be the Creator of the world."[37] Creation's "reason," then, is hidden in the inscrutable mystery of God as self-originating and self-giving love. "While the world is the gracious result of divine freedom, God's freedom means necessarily being who and what God is. From this standpoint the world is not created *ex nihilo*, but *ex amore ex condilectione*, that is, out of divine love."[38]

In *creatio ex amore*, we have a creation that, although not a necessary emanation from God with its pantheistic overtones, is nevertheless in all its difference from God, internally, intrinsically, and intimately—as opposed to deistically, distantly, externally—connected/covenanted with

---

36. Meister Eckhart, as cited in Colledge and McGinn, "Introduction," *Meister Eckhart: The Essential Sermons, Commentaries, Treatises, and Defense*, 38–41. "The differences between *bullitio* and *ebullitio*, between the emanations of the divine Persons and the creation of the universe, were frequently highlighted by the Meister, but their inner connection was never in question" (Colledge and McGinn, "Introduction," 39).

37. LaCugna, *God for Us*, 355.

38. LaCugna, *God for Us*, 355.

God. In this way, creation is not a self-same emanation of the Godhead, but a creation of a different sort out of God's love. However, if the difference between God and creation is from the Godhead, there is just as much reason to posit that this establishes the most intimate intrinsic connection precisely in the differentiation. *Ex amore* emphasizes the connection-in-difference between God and creation.

Theologically, such a connection-in-difference points in the direction of panentheism (God-in-all and all-in-God) as an alternative to either deism or pantheism. At this point, I am resistant to describing my position as panentheism because of fears that it still be seen as yet another metaphysical construction that seeks to capture or bracket the holy mystery. At the same time, a mystical "*apophatic panentheism*," of the kind that Catherine Keller is suggesting, that "retains what all theism desires: a 'Thou' different enough and intimate enough to love and be loved"[39] is attractive. Particularly, this would be the case when the fundamental distinction between creation and Creator is heightened in intensifying the relationality, and when the "in" of panentheism would begin "to designate creation as incarnation."[40]

Levinas, at this point, afraid of any totalizing ontology, talks of the "intrigue of infinity," the "inordinate intrigue"[41] of God. Inordinate intrigue are words that seem particularly apt for the holy mystery of the omnipotence of Divine Love in *creatio ex amore*. In this understanding, if God is love, God could not be God without a bestowal of the Godself in love.

To-Be Is To-Be-Related

Another crucial advantage of talking of God as love means that we can give up our focus on God as Being, as *causa sui*, which historically (whatever the details) has developed into ontologies of maintenance, control, domination: power-over. In the world of being-as-power, suffering has no legitimate place. Pain and suffering are diminutions of being. Is this perhaps a telling reason why the philosophical idea of the impassibility of God has often, even to the present, prevailed over the biblical teaching of the suffering love of God?

Beginning *ex amore* gives legitimate place to suffering, not as a diminution of being, a suffering-from, but as suffering-with, a becoming-with, *with-ings* that comfort and heal, enriching and transforming. Love as excess seeps into life's cracks and fissures as suffering-with. We have the promise that the wounds of creation, suffering, and death will be taken

---

39. Keller, *The Face of the Deep*, 219.
40. Keller, *The Face of the Deep*, 219.
41. Levinas, "God and Philosophy," in *Basic Philosophical Writings*, 135, 146.

up in the wounds of Christ—not erased, but transformed. We are heirs of Christ, says Romans 8:17, provided we suffer with him. Love turns us to the other, not as foe, not as a diminution of being, but as enrichment, hospitality, and celebration.

When the Love of God is the Spirit of Life, creaturely life is life-with-God. For God so loved that creation came forth. Creation as the first incarnation of love. *Ex amore*. For God so loved the world that God gave us the Son. The Word became flesh in Jesus Christ for our redemption as the second incarnation. *Cum amore*. For God so loved the world that God sent us the Spirit. The Spirit of Love aflame in the hearts of God's people as a third incarnation. Such incarnations of love both in suffering-with and celebrating-with each other and the whole family of God's creatures help fill up what is lacking in the sufferings of Christ (see Col 1:27). From before the foundations of the world God destined us in love, says Ephesians, to be God's sons and daughters. For God so loved the world that in the end God will be all in all, the fourth incarnation, we could say. *Ad amorem*.

When love is the being of being, we allow space for the deep mystery of God's dance of love with the creation. We make space, then, for the Yes of Love most ancient to sound forth from before the very beginning, resounding as the norm for all of life, including the disciplines of philosophy and theology, even as it invites that we end our endeavors in doxology, in praise and thanksgiving. Emphasizing that God created because God is relational and made a creation that is at heart relational also fits well, as we noted earlier, with contemporary physics that tells us that relationality is the prime feature of the universe in which we live.

What I am saying amounts to a suggestion: What if we were to set aside our focus on God as Being, and talk of God as Love, beyond both the categories of being and non-being? Without love, nothing. Love calls into existence everything and anything that is. To-be is to-be-related. Creation is then conceived, not as *ex nihilo*, but as *ex amore*. As the creative Love that exceeds all systems, physical and metaphysical, and yet evokes such systems, God may be said to be beyond creation, the excessive. As the Love revealed and incarnated in the world, God is not-beyond. Then we can perhaps begin to move beyond our squabbles about whether talking of both the being of creation and of God is to be interpreted univocally, equivocally, or analogically.

Indeed, I am left wondering about the usefulness of any kind of infinite/finite, transcendence/immanence, archetypal/ectypal, being/non-being scheme for envisioning the creator/creation relationship. In such binaries, there is not only the pull to prefer one term as superior to the other, but even more sinister, each term gets defined in terms of the other so that an emphasis on one is taken at the expense and cost of the other. The difficulties of such binary schemes are astronomically amplified when applied to the God/creation relation because even when God is identified as infinite or transcendent or Being (in contrast to the finite, non-transcendent, non-being), God, who as creator is not a creature, is placed within a human conceptualization. Regardless of how God's infinity is explained, whether as so-called bad or good infinity, God is subjected and understood in terms of what needs to be more fully recognized as human (non)understandings. In the process, it is not only God who suffers, but the excellence of humankind, as a good creation, is eclipsed: in contrast to the infinite, the "being" of the finite is always limited, inferior, contingent.

Developing a radical ontology of love as a with-paradigm (rather than an oppositional paradigm of comparison) would, I suggest, provide new openings. "With" speaks of difference-and-connection, non-oppositional difference, without definition of one in terms of the other and without valorization of one above the other.

At the same time, I want to acknowledge that suggesting that we would be better off with love than being doesn't mean that the problem of conceptualization is solved. Being a philosopher indeed entails precisely that I need to translate the intuitions of my faith into philosophical concepts. The secret that is no secret but is revealed—God's love—can only be thought through and worked out by philosophers and theologians in terms of concepts. *Ex amore*, even as a faith response, involves conceptualization. So when I suggest that "love" is the preferable term, as other than being and different than being, when love and loving become the conditions for being and becoming, love functions as an ontological category, the condition of possibility for being itself. Love is other than being and yet the condition of being. Love, in this way, becomes, one may say, the being of being. All I can say, following Derrida, is that at these limits, speaking of the conditions from within the conditioned makes for a certain conceptual incoherence.

My argument, however, is that whereas a metaphysics of being or substance is designed to understand the world in terms interior or intrinsic to individual entities, inside-out, with relationality always an accidental property, a radical ontology of love begins as it were outside-in, from inter-relationality as the warp and woof of creation. Instead of talking in terms of being with its connotations of substance, confinement, definition, boundaries, totality, and independence, talk of love emphasizes relationality, inter-relationality, inter-subjectivity, openness, excess, infinity.

When 'being" is taken as the central concept—whether of God or of creation—love, as the dynamic source and end of being, can too easily be eclipsed or lost. It is as if being is possible without love, with love becoming the ethical imperative that we attend to once we exist as beings. In contrast, *ex amore*, we only are, we only exist, insofar as we love. *Ex amore*, God only exists, is, insofar as God loves.

God as Love is not the "being" above in the splendid isolation of *epekeina tes ousias*, but the gracious, passion-filled *inter-esse*, the being-with. God, as the *Logos* by whom all things were created, as the *Logos* Incarnate, Emmanuel (God-with-us), is the Logos of Love, the *Meta-Logos*. *Logos* as *Meta-Logos* offers a more fruitful image for moving us beyond divine aseity, with its immutable, impassible God, to a God who, as Scripture reveals, sojourns and journeys with us, lamenting, mourning, redeeming, loving.[42]

The seventeenth century mystic Angelus Silesius said: *Gott spricht nur immer Ja* (God only always says Yes). That is the yes of love, the yes of being human. Humans, with ears to hear, eyes to see, and hands to touch, are called in all they do individually and communally to say, Yes, Yes, to each other as they dance—and, when appropriate, grieve, resist, and say No—in the wild spaces and times of love.

Life—all of creation—is God-with-us: Love. "God is love, and those who abide in love abide in God, and God abides in them."[43] We, as human creatures, participate with God in the ongoing adventure of creation until Love is all in all. God lives as the mystery of love. Which means that life in all its mystery is *ex amore, cum amore, ad amorem*.

---

42. S. D. Goiten has interestingly proposed a morphological correlation between God as love and the Exodic naming of Yahweh. Comparing the Hebrew Tetragrammaton *YHWH* with certain Arabic roots, he suggests that the "I am that I am" of Exodus 3:14 may be translated as "I shall passionately love whom I love" ("*YHWH* the Passionate," 2).

43. 1 John 4:16 (NRSV).

—poetic epilogue—

The Ambience of Love
We all
Sit in his Orchestra
Some play their
Fiddles,
Some wield their
Clubs.
Tonight is worthy of music.
Let's get loose
With
Compassion,
Let's drown in the delicious
Ambience of
Love.
Sufi Master Hafiz[44]

---

44. Hafiz, *The Gift*, 186.

CHAPTER 2

THEOPOETICS: LOVE ON A COSMIC SCALE

IN THE BEGINNING . . . in the middle . . . in the end (in spite of and in resistance to evil) is Love. This, as the first chapter detailed, is my wager of faith, an adventure in Love and in God as creator: Love abundant, the Excess of Love itself, *ipsum amare*. Love overflows, generates, reaches out, embraces, sustains, transforms, redeems. All that God is and does is of, with, and for love: *ex amore, cum amore, ad amorem*.

In faith I give my heart in surrender to God. This surrender is not a giving *up*, a resignation or acquiescence, or anything of the sort. It is a giving *over* to God in hope and trust, an intimate act of commitment, faith, and prayer. "Oh, Spirit of the living God, dwell in me, revive, inspire, and energize me—all of creation—with the fire of your love, with a passion for justice, given to mercy, humble of spirit." Such a prayer gives words to a desire to be caught up in and by the awesome wonder of the Gifting of God's Love: to receive it, embody it and pass it on. We humans are co-workers with God, agents of love and for love, gifted with and called to a ministry of loving service to God, neighbor, and the entire cosmos, a "marriage of mysticism and social justice."[1] Indeed, God depends on us to enact and effectuate the creative and healing work of love. What we do or fail to do makes all the difference in whether Love—God's design and desire for the world—becomes tangible and real in our lives, in the lives of others, indeed in the life of the universe itself.

Acting as God's emissaries of love in the world requires developing and practicing a spirituality of compassion. "Be merciful, just as your Father is merciful."[2] Central to the formation and exercise of such a spirituality is giving shape to, forming, and articulating a vision *of* love *for* the world,

1. Fox, *A Spirituality Named Compassion*, iii.
2. Luke 6:36 (NRSV).

relevant to and in terms of our particular place and time in world history. Performative, liturgical "I believe in . . ." testimonies of praise give rise to "I believe that . . ." declarations of creeds and doctrines. Faith-reflection is a communal undertaking, a collaborative endeavor both giving an account of that faith even as it gives shape to an orienting perspective for living out this faith in the push and pull of daily life. Such reflections and musings are doxological in character, a first-order spiritual exercise of people speaking in praise *of* God *to* God (not talking *about* God), eager to and intent on making the love of God evident and palpable in the world. In our broken world replete with so much suffering and injustice, such faith-born visions have a transforming and healing focus.

At the same time, when the focus in faith reflection steps back from living out the faith in our daily life and shifts to thinking more deeply *about* the God we worship, and more generally about the structure and function of faith, we move into the area of theory. Since this involves second-order theoretic conceptualization with its concern with definitions, systematic consistency, and coherence, it is called theology: theo-logic.

While there is an evident reciprocity in both directions between first-order confessional utterances and theological/theoretic second-order statements, it is of foremost importance to not overlook or minimize their difference. This is because recognizing and attending to this critical difference opens a space of generosity and hospitality to consider that divergence in emphasis, conceptualization, and paradigm may be alternative ways of articulating deep solidarity, rather than fundamental disagreement.[3] Indeed, without the space which such recognition affords, any difference or disagreement on a theological level raises the spectre and intense suspicion of radical difference, inflaming the discussion—as all the accusations and acrimony which mar the history of the Christian church give baneful witness—to a fever pitch, with each side quick to impute the other as heterodox. All of which is to say: without the implicit or explicit fear that entertaining new paradigms or alternative ways of thinking opens one to charges of infidelity, paths open for theological explorations and discussions to become hospitable, more playful, more creative, and more gracious.

The difference between the testimonies of faith and theological concepts has often in the past and sometimes still in the present been obscured, concealed, or not fully recognized because both have been referred to as theology: "'primary theology' (*theologia prima*)" of praise and worship and "'secondary theology' (*theologia secunda*)'" with it focus on

---

3. See Olthuis, "Afterword: A Radical Ontology of Love" for an example of how recognizing this "space" allows recasting the Reformed tradition and Radical Orthodoxy as cohorts rather than rivals.

concepts, propositions, arguments, coherence. While in praise and prayer we talk *to* God, the danger is that wittingly or unwittingly doxological to-God-statements of prayer and praise be considered theoretical concepts detailing the nature of God. Not recognizing and emphatically insisting on the prime importance of the difference between confessing one's faith-*in* God and theory-*about* God has led to a tangle of questions which haunts theology to this day.

Historically, as theologian Catherine LaCugna observes: "Augustine, like every seminal Christian thinker, perceived the inherent incongruity entailed in the doing of theology. Only a fool would be so bold as to presume to speak authoritatively about God's ineffable mystery."[4] As she emphasizes, "both Greek and Latin traditions found ways to speak meaningfully about God without presuming to speak from the standpoint of God."[5] Theologians in the Latin tradition of the Western Church generally preferred the affirmation mode (*kataphasis*) of positive theology and the method of analogy, while the Greek tradition of the Eastern Church generally favored the denial mode (*apophasis*) of negative theology which endeavored to describe God by negating all definitions. Anselm of Canterbury, for example, set out to prayerfully prove the existence of God by juxtaposing prayer (faith is the only way to God) and argument (reason is able to prove God's existence). And Thomas Aquinas was "merely summarizing the long tradition of theology East and West when he said that we know God only from God's effects; I do not know what God is, only that God is."[6]

However, in the academy, theologians were under pressure, not only because "secondary theology often is regarded as the true theology, while primary theology is seen neither as the starting point nor context but something that may be dispensed with, something, at any rate, that is not essential to the doing of theology,"[7] but especially because theological examinations of God were led by philosophy's drive for a comprehensive conceptual grasp of God as its "object." As LaCugna suggests, negative theology's emphasis on the incomprehensibility of God can lead "to a stubborn silence that is nothing more than agnosticism," and positive theology's "analogies for the immanent Trinity can be mistaken for descriptions of God's 'inner life.'" Along these lines, as she warns, both positive and negative theology can end up as "self-sufficient methods" which "appear to control God."[8]

4. LaCugna, *God for Us*, 324.
5. LaCugna, *God for Us*, 330.
6. LaCugna, *God for Us*, 330.
7. LaCugna, *God for Us*, 357.
8. LaCugna, *God for Us*, 331.

When that happens we have various ontotheologies, metaphysical treatments of God in abstract, humanly constructed and defined concepts such as being, essence, origin, and cause. In doing so, as Heidegger[9] has detailed, metaphysics fitted God into predetermined frameworks, in effect making God a super "idealized" human person. The problem: the God whom we worship as creator and sustaining mystery of existence is "cut down to size like any object"[10] of theoretic investigation, with its focus on explanation, containment, logical consistency and comprehension. The danger: the mystery of God as the alpha and omega, the unconditional beyond whose affirming presence permeates existence, is corralled and domesticated to the point that, as Heidegger declared, you can "neither fall to [your] knees in awe nor can [you] play music and dance before this God."[11]

In response to recognizing that metaphysics has been "a power play on the part of human conceptuality,"[12] more recently there have been incisive critiques of ontotheologies,[13] as well as renewed efforts in a variety of corners to recapture and re-emphasize that (the glory and mystery of) God lies far beyond the reach of reason. Arguing that "concepts are always reductions"—or, as I prefer, concepts are *handles*, not containers or nets—"fundamentally metaphorical," LaCugna argues that "theology is not theology—*theos-logos*—unless it proceeds in the mode of praise.... Apophatic and kataphatic theology coincide and find their proper balance in doxology."[14] On the contemporary theological scene, in his own distinctive way, to offer one example, Wolfhart Pannenberg attempts to strike such a balance by proposing "analogy" and "doxology" to be opposites that simultaneously coincide.[15]

Indeed, at present, in the struggle to find appropriate ways to speak of God, a conviction is growing in various quarters, in my view with abundant cause, that theoretical attention to "ultimates,"[16] matters at the

---

9. Heidegger, "What Is Metaphysics?" in *Pathmarks*, 82–96.

10. Hector, *Theology without Metaphysics*, 13. For a pertinent discussion of "the question of metaphysics," see 2–15.

11. Heidegger, *Identity and Difference*, 72.

12. Caputo, *Radical Hermeneutics*, 185.

13. Such as Marion, *God Without Being*, and Westphal, *Overcoming Onto-Theology*. For an illuminating discussion and interchange on differing understandings of ontotheology, I recommend Caputo's discussion and Westphal's response in Putt, *Gazing Through a Prism Darkly*, 100–15, 173–76.

14. LaCugna, *God for Us*, 358–61.

15. Pannenberg, "Analogy and Doxology," in *Basic Questions in Theology*, 1:210–38.

16. "When we say 'ultimate' we are usually confessing the limits of our imagination ... Ultimate just means we have reached our limits, the outer reaches of our present

limit of our horizons, calls for and requires emblematic, non-objectifying metaphors rather than objectifying concepts. We need to employ symbolic tropes that point, suggest, and envision rather than theoretic predicates that define, comprehend, and confine. There is a deep mystery in and at the heart of existence that cannot be contained by human cognition, an excessive abundance that escapes even the best of our postulations. The work of such thinkers—Catherine Keller, John D. Caputo, Richard Kearney, among others[17]—is thus increasingly and perhaps more appropriately referred to as theopoetics rather than theology. Caputo suggests that cosmopoetics or "cosmo-theopoetic realism" might even be the more propitious term as such envisioning needs to be cosmological in scope, cosmic-wide.[18]

Theopoetics

I very much take to this turn to cosmo-theopoetics. Theopoetics is a "theology without metaphysics,"[19] "theology in the mode of doxology"[20]: witnessing and testifying to our faith in God as creator and redeemer by means of storied narratives, visionary attestations, metaphoric intuitions, and imaginative allegories. Such perceptive sketches, poetic pointers, what Heidegger referred to as "formal indications," are more befitting ways and means for sharing and exploring the truth, depth, vitality, and liminal character of our faith experiences without claiming conceptual mastery or determination. In the conviction that God cannot be an "object" of or for theoretic investigation, relinquishing control, theopoetics responds to the Gift/Call of God, and proceeds, evocatively and provocatively—in words, narratives, poems, pictures, metaphors, deliberations, imaginings—to help make the presence of God dynamic and compelling in human existence. In speaking of God in the poetic metaphors of faith, avowing deep truth without definitional delimitation, theopoetics is theology in the mode of doxology.

Important as it is to be aware that in-depth tropes are portrayals reaching for that which is beyond conceptual grasp, we also need to be keenly aware that, as people of a certain time and space, our metaphors and tropes are also culture-bound, of varying traditions. This highlights the utmost importance of sharing our visions and affirming our faith-convictions with humility and

---

horizon" (Caputo, *The Insistence of God*, 255).

17. Keller, *Face of the Deep*, and *Cloud of the Impossible*; Kearney, *The God Who May Be*; See Krabbe, *A Beautiful Bricolage* for a scouting report on this burgeoning movement.

18. Caputo, *The Insistence of God*, 20–22.

19. Hector, *Theology without Metaphysics*.

20. LaCugna, *God for Us*, 356.

hermeneutic hospitality, ever open to listening and learning from others with different forms and ways of God-talk. This point, it strikes me, is of direct relevance to both the past and present. Although, as we have just explored, we have come to recognize the serious shortcomings of the metaphysical cast of much past theology, we need to remain open, acknowledging both how much we have learned and still have to learn from the work of theologians of past ages. Working within the philosophical contours of their times, they did their best to do "theology in the mode of doxology."

In terms of our contemporary scene, given that we are dealing with matters of utmost significance personally, societally, and globally, it is equally incumbent on us that we, with passion and conviction, offer critique, as well as reformulated insights and understandings in hope of building community, encouraging dialogue, becoming inclusive, in quest of justice and embrace for all. In this way, it is my hope and prayer that the kind of cosmo-theopoetics of love that I envision may be a non-identical repetition of the living faith of our fathers and mothers, a "theology in the mode of doxology" for the 21st century.

As will not surprise anyone who knows me, "God is love" is the depth metaphor that in my view most fulsomely resonates and articulates the generosity, abundance, power, and awesomeness of God. In that I take my lead from the Apostle John: "Beloved, let us love one another, because love is from God; everyone who loves is born of God and knows God. Whoever does not love does not know God, for God is love." (1 John 4:7–8 NRSV). At the same time, the incomprehensible depth, richness, and mystery of God is such that other affirming, generating, renewing names and metaphors for God in certain contexts may be particularly relevant and meaningful: "Life," "Fire," "Energy," "Light," "Justice," "Healer," "Father," "Mother," on and on.

All the ensuing reflections are beginning efforts to think through the implications of this opening avowal of God as Love. Fundamentally, as image-bearers of God, "to love or not to love" is the central all-important question. Working out and thinking through what this means, not only for humanity, but for the cosmos as a whole, is utterly challenging. All the more so in a world rife with evil. For even as a theopoetics of love would seek to encourage and promote a healthy *co-existence* honoring differences of position, time, and place, in our broken world, it also calls for working out ways of *co-resistance* to all appearances of injustice and incursions of evil.

Indeed, thinking through love from this viewpoint challenges a centuries-old tradition in which the central question of metaphysics has been: "To be or not to be." Parmenides' "Being is" or Heraclitus' "Nothing is" became the two dominant competing historical traditions in all their myriad and mutating variations. Theologically, God was considered *ipsum esse* (Being itself). And since, reaching all the way back to Plato and Aristotle, "being" was defined as power, God was enthroned as supreme, sovereign power. Along the same lines, in modernity the human subject—as Descartes' *cogito, ergo sum* (I think, therefore I am) epitomizes—is considered at heart, in essence, to be a thinker. Knowledge is power/power is knowledge (Foucault). Love became an optional, discretionary capability, something one can subsequently do or not do. Indeed, as Jean-Luc Marion claims: "Philosophy today no longer says anything about love, or at best very little." "Little by little . . . philosophy in the end renounced its first name, 'love of wisdom,' for that of metaphysics" and "the primacy of beings."[21]

In contrast, beginning with love rescripts everything: "I am not, except insofar as I experience love, and experience it as a logic."[22] I do not exist first of all as an independent thinking being capable of action who may or may not decide to love or not to love. Rather, who we are and everything we do, including how we think, is a matter of loving and being loved. We are alive because we were loved into being. Existing, being alive, is all about forming, fostering, enjoying, sustaining wholesome connections of all kinds with others. In and to the degree that we love (and are loved) we truly live, while in and to the degree that we do not love (and are not loved), we are not fully alive.

If love and God as Love is what life and existence are all about—and that is my wager—it calls for envisioning "Love" as the cosmic, par excellence, multidimensional, differentiating/integrating energy and force of and in the universe. It means acknowledging that we love (or fail to love) in all our actions, sensing, reasoning, exercising, believing, trusting, judging, whatever. It means realizing that in forming concepts in the mode of love, concepts are not "nets" which entrap, overcoming and enclosing difference in sameness (totalizing). Rather concepts are helpful "handles" enabling connection-with and embrace-of difference without fusion and without opposition (mutuality). Indeed, beginning with love envisions philosophy, as the janitor of the sciences, in service of love, cultivating not only the love of wisdom but the wisdom of love; and theology, equally in the service of love, nurturing not only the love of God but the God of love in the mode of doxology.

Let us begin envisioning a cosmo-theopoetics of God who is Love.

---

21. Marion, *The Erotic Phenomenon*, 1–3.
22. Marion, *The Erotic Phenomenon*, 8.

Archi-Love

"To be God is to be Creator of the world."[23] For God is love, and love holds nothing back. Out of the overflowing of the excess and passion of Love the creation came into existence. "Love loves without condition, simply because it loves . . . without limit or restriction."[24]

Creation as the outflowing of Love is both revelatory of love (God's love) and a solicitation to love (God and all the family of God's creatures). "The heavens are telling the glory of God; and the firmament proclaims his handiwork." (Ps 19:1 NRSV). "The earth is the Lord's and all that is in it, the world, and those who live in it" (Ps 24:1 NRSV). That "fullness" is the love of God which John declares we all have received (John 1:16 NRSV). Further, Paul in Colossians 2:9 lauds Jesus as the Cosmic Christ, the *"pleroma"* (fullness) in whom all things dwell and have their being. "[T]he universe, by definition, is a single gorgeous celebratory event."[25]

The revelation of/for love is not a secondary superadditum, a grace-infused order superimposed on a neutral, self-governing, autonomous nature. Rather, the make-up of creation—whether referred to as nature, cosmos, or universe—is a broad spectrum of love all the way down, all the way up, all the way across, graced from the beginning, affirming, generous, lavish, open-handed, abundant, erotic. Be(com)ing-is-of-love and be(com)ing-is-for-love. Creational existence is love's adventure: it is be(com)ing—when connections flourish, are appropriate, befitting, and fruitful—and it is unbe(com)ing—when connections languish, are inappropriate, ill-fitting, and disastrous.

This is of monumental significance. At present it is much in vogue to talk of the mute anonymity of the cosmos. For Martin Heidegger in *Being and Time*, whatever is simply is, "es gibt" (there is). "There" without as it were an origin, "without anyone who gives."[26] In evolutionary theory, natural selection is widely considered to be a totally contingent process without purpose. Listen to influential evolutionary biologist Stephen Jay Gould: "Evolution is purposeless, nonprogressive, and materialistic."[27] Similarly, theoretical physicist Sean Carroll recently wonders about attaining meaning in a universe "without transcendent purpose."[28] But what if the transcendent purpose is immanent in the cosmos, not only the generative force that gave

---

23. LaCugna, *God for Us*, 355.
24. Marion, *God without Being*, 47.
25. Berry, *The Dream of the Earth*, 5.
26. Irigaray, *In the Beginning, She Was*, 4.
27. Gould, *Ever Since Darwin*, 14.
28. Carroll, *The Big Picture*, 5.

rise to creation but the driving, motivating force *in*-scendent in creation, its inhering motif power! Then, rather than the indifferent "es gibt" (there is), it is "*es gibt die Liebe*" (there is Love)! What if the answer to the question—why is there is something and not nothing?—is the "without why" of Love? What if the history of the universe is Love's be(com)ing, incarnating, in a differentiating/integrating cosmogenic process? That, indeed, is my conviction. Love as the fundamental dynamic of existence, the very "mattering" of the universe, the "transcendent" purpose in-built in creaturely existence—perduring, refracting, ever evoking and eliciting fuller and more differentiated materialisations of love. Then, to love is to live and living is loving. Then, we love life because life is love, loving and being loved—engendering, sustaining, energizing, and remaking meaningful, healthy connections.

Life, love, God—these do not function as ultimate, irreducible metaphysical absolutes. They function as the theopoetic liminal words which, at the limits of human comprehension, articulate our heart intuitions—faith wagers—as to what existence is all about, in terms of which we orient, frame, and run the risk of existence. That is to say, existence, the world, happens because Love happens; that is to say what we call life happens, events, for no other why than Love, the Love of God, and we find ourselves within it. Then, breathing, trusting, faithing, living is receiving and responding to the gift of love that is life, giving ourselves to it, making it our own, passing it on in co-partnership with the whole family of God's creatures. In that vein, we live (in order) to love, and love (in order) to live. We live and move and have our being in the Love that is God. That is to live "without why" (other than the all-important why and how of love) in a world that is finally "without why" (except for the reason, above every reason, of Love).

Creation only exists in and through and by love's multivarious be(com)ings: connecting, reconnecting, interweaving, intertwining. The *conatus amandi*—the impulse to and for love, for connection, in all forms, shapes, and levels, in its ebbing and flowing—is the signature mark of creation. Creation is God-with-us—without transcendent distance and without immanent identity: Amazing Mystery! God remaining God, creation remaining creation in a cosmogenetic, inextricably interwoven covenantal co-partnership. The totally unique God-creation relationship is not, in my understanding, a "relation without relation" (Levinas) nor "the relation to end all relations" (Badiou), but "the relation beginning and sustaining all relations." With-ing on the grand scale of cosmic history. "The earth is full of the steadfast love of the Lord" (Ps 33:5 NRSV).

God is no unaffected, ideal, *transcendent* observer, but the *in*scendent, immanent Energy of Love. *Ubi caritas et amor, Deus ibi est*. Where there is charity and love, God is there. And creation is there, not neutral, mute, or anonymous, but charged by, with, and for love, pulsating, enthralling! The mystery remaining, a mystery in its very revealing—ever expanding and surprising as time and history unfold. That is the leitmotif of all the chapters in this book. The grand dance of the cosmic forces which make up life in all its myriad becomings is the pulsating differentiating/integrating energy of Love. Creation is the bewit(c)hing, love-energized, timed-spaced multi-hued venture of love. *Es gibt die Liebe*—there is Love.

Deep Mystery

There is admittedly deep mystery here. Not in the sense that there is a puzzling gap that is empty, as yet unknowable, and in that sense mysterious; nor, in line with Heidegger's *a-letheia*, a concealing in the very un-concealing. Heidegger certainly recognized the need for openness to the mystery, but it is a meditative stillness of respect and reverence for the mystery that withdraws even as it reveals. In the end, Heidegger leaves us in the clearing, waiting and wondering, unable to trust, since evil (*das Bose*) appears simultaneously with the Holy.

The mystery of God as Love and the mystery of the cosmos is of a different kind, matchless in its uniqueness and depth. Love does not withdraw or withhold. Love shows itself, generating, inviting, evoking, provoking, calling for response. The creation is the self-giving revelation of the energizing, life-creating Love of God, gifting and calling creation to being and becoming co-partners in Love's adventing. That is the astounding Secret that is unfolding: co-partnership-with-God in the Adventure we know as creation. Finite creatures entrusted by creator God to be agents *of* Love *for* love, seeking ever new ways of incarnating love and passing it on in the ongoing, forever unfolding, rumbling and rambling process we call the cosmos. As image-bearers of God, we are inspired and urged, gifted and called to co-partnership with each other and with all creatures in nourishing and fostering healthy connections, doing justice, exercising mercy, caring for creation. In short, we are called to "shepherd" love in all we do.

Our access to Love as the secret of life that is our heart's desire—often in philosophy referred to as the "the Thing Itself" or the "Real"—is possible and promising. However, and it is a monumental however: to affirm that Love is the Really Real, the beating heart of reality, "the secret that is no secret" is not a matter of proof, demonstration, or justification. It is a matter of faith and testimony.

We will never be able to locate the Arche, prove its existence, or demonstrate that reality corresponds to our representations of it. We are not God. But, when we with open hearts give ourselves over to Love, heeding its call, we are able to share in the Secret, recognize its radiance, experience its power, and be moved by its appeal. In love, received and enacted, we cross the threshold of and to God,[29] dwelling in God even as God dwells in us. We become co-workers with God, agents *of* love, agents *for* love. Graced with the discovery that the Arche and Omega of Love has already found us before we find it, we are caught up in it, are touched by it, becoming stewards of its mystery, a mystery we can indwell, witness to, flow with—but never own or control.

The mystery of the intimate covenantal relationship between God and creation deepens even as we come to a fuller experience of God's loving—sustaining and promising—presence in our lives. As our intimacy with God grows, the realization deepens that God is God and we are human, irreducibly different, and yet inextricably bound in love. The mystery works both ways. We make a difference to God even as God makes a difference to us. When we are in need, with eyes that see and hearts that trust, Scripture portrays God as near, close at hand, at home in us, sojourning with us. At the same time, when human hearts are closed, intent on evil, up to no good, God is distant, displeased, turning the God-face away.

Deuteronomy 30:11–16 is particularly explicit about the non-distant intimacy of God's command to love (and thus of God) and the human heart. "Surely, this commandment that I am commanding you today is not too hard for you, nor is it too far away. It is not in heaven, that you should say, 'Who will go up to heaven for us, and get it for us so that we may hear it and observe it?' Neither is it beyond the sea, that you should say, 'Who will cross to the other side of the sea for us, and get it for us so that we may hear it and observe it?' No, the word is very near to you; it is in your mouth and in your heart for you to observe. See, I have set before you today life and prosperity, death and adversity. If you obey the commandments of the Lord your God that I am commanding you today, by loving the Lord your God, walking in his ways, and observing his commandments, decrees, and ordinances, then you shall live and become numerous . . ." (NRSV).

This mystery of God/creation, otherness/connection has its mirror images in human activities and relationships. No matter how much or intensely a person engages with another creature, say a tree, climbing it, trimming it, hugging it, the tree remains a tree, and the human remains a human. But, at the same time, both the person and tree undergo change through the contact. On an interpersonal level the mirroring is particularly striking. In genuine interpersonal love, there is a mutual connection without fusion or distance that I call "with-ing." The difference of the other

---

29. Marion, *Prolegomena to Charity*, 61.

person and his or her mystery attracts. Reaching out to the other, taking in the other's love "enables me to become while remaining myself."[30] At the same time, the unique singularity of the other person remains a mystery. In loving and receiving, even as I become more myself the other persons become more themselves.

Even as God remains a mystery to us, we in our own ways remain a mystery to God. So much so that God was and is surprised, taken aback, sad, puzzled, and angry when we sin, turning our backs on love and the God of love. What more could anyone want than to be loved and to love. (Likewise, God is glad, comes near, rejoicing, when we pass on love, reject intranscience, repent of evil, do justice, practice mercy, and are moved with compassion.) Sin is, thus, fundamentally missing the mark of love, rather than the disobedience of law. Sin is not thinking too much of ourselves, but too little. Feeling "naked and ashamed" (Gen 2, NRSV), found out, fearful, inadequate, deflated, we get defensive, put on masks, and set about inflating our egos. In fear, missing the mark of love, we become rebellious, turning in on ourselves at the cost of others.

In response to the insurgency of evil, God as Love, the mystery of the universe, became flesh for the world's redemption. "To them God chose to make known how great among the Gentiles are the riches of the glory of this mystery, which is Christ in you, the hope of glory" (Col 1:27, NRSV). While the coming-into-being of creation is an initial incarnating of God's love, the life, death, and resurrection of Jesus Christ is a uniquely redemptive re-gifting of divine love, a "second" incarnation. Accordingly, the Ecclesia, the called out to love, all who practice mercy and exercise justice filling up what is lacking in the sufferings of Christ (Col 1:24, NRSV) may be seen as a "third" incarnation. Again not a secret—it is revealed—but once more far beyond human comprehension or prognostication, the mystery continues to advance toward its redemptive culmination. The creation is moving toward a "fourth" Event(ing), the Coming Again, the Parousia of a new heavens and earth in which God as Love will be all-in-all. The history of the universe—in spite of so much failure, evil and despair—is an ongoing, unfinished love story, a narrative of grace, promise and hope.

It means living the mystery of love in Meister Eckhart's understanding of *Gelassenheit* (letting be) "without why." That is giving *up* the possibility of possessing any knock-down guarantees, totalizing schemes, metaphysical validations, or theological demonstrations—all the "whys" of reason—but giving *over* to "letting God's life well up in us and flow through us as an

---

30. Irigaray, *i love to you*, 104.

inner principle of life."[31] Whereas for Heidegger being-is-toward-death, in this understanding, be(com)ing-is-out-of-and-toward the positivity of Love, risking the flux and uncertainty of existence in the faithful trust that God-is-with us, and some way, somehow—in spite of the vortex of evil with its cesspool of devastation, malice, and brutality—love will take root, spring forth, and flourish in us and in all creation.

The bottom line: reality is Love's be(com)ing. Love is the "really real": the driving, perduring, *gifting* archi-energy of the universe, on the move persistently, insistently, *calling* creation to join in, take up, and further the process of the proliferation, incarnation and embodiment of love. The mystery of Love's revealing is evocative, promising, inviting all of creation in its dazzling array to co-partner in the incarnating—enacting, passing on, eventing—of love. To be alive is to dance (stumble or misstep) in the wild, uncharted times and spaces *of* love and *for* love. Love, I am saying, is not a human-only or human-based idea; rather love is an ongoing, unfolding, unfinished multidimensional Cosmic Event.

This is, there is no getting away from it, an astounding claim: The entire array of creation's creatures, gifted into being, called to participate as partners, co-conspirators, in the cosmogenesis of the universe, innovating and generating, even as conserving and preserving. Humans, stones, trees, animals, stars, you name it, are called to be cohorts, mediators, negotiators, transmitters, purveyors of love. The let-there-be's of love's *giftings* go hand in hand with love's *callings* to let-love-happen again and again in new and novel ways and means. Importantly: love's gifting/calling dynamic infuses existence with an insistent *promissory* thrust and propulsion. Staying with, remaining true to this dynamic promises continued growth, blessing and fulfillment even as it highlights the contingency and open-endedness of the process. What happens in life is neither accidental nor necessary, neither determinate nor indeterminate. It all depends: life is a gifting (a "beautiful promise") and life is a calling (a "beautiful risk").

Love as the "really real" does not make the physical, the biotic, the sensitive, the economic, or any other dimension of existence, "appearance." Love, as the energizing dynamic of everything that lives, moves, and has being, is multidimensional in character. Each and every mode of the universe is a *real* dimension of love, which, each in its own specificity, in intertwinement with all the other modes, plays its indispensable role in the becoming (or failing to become) of Love.

Human love and human loving, working together communally and fruitfully in a wide variety of ways (not only in relationships qualified by

---

31. Caputo, *Radical Hermeneutics*, 265.

troth, such as marriage, family, and friendship), plays an essential part. But so do all the ways other creatures of the world, each in their own specific ways, connect, relate, and interrelate—that is, make love—in the multi-inter-modal creational dynamic. As novelist Barbara Kingsolver says so beautifully, "a flower is a plant's way of making love."[32] Likewise, trees make love by leafing in the spring and breaking out in color in the fall.[33] Moreover, in the relational interdependence which makes up the cosmos, making love (or failing to make love) spawns a series of ripple effects that work to support (or undercut), encourage (or discourage), open up (or close down) prospects and probabilities for the flourishing of other creatures. Flowers open up a colorful way for humans to display and celebrate their love. Trees are not only elegant sentries, connecting heaven and earth, providing shade, lumber, and so much more, but in releasing oxygen, and absorbing carbon dioxide as well as other potentially harmful gasses, provide indispensable support for life on this planet. Do we seek wisdom, asks Job? "But ask the animals, and they will teach you; the birds of the air, and they will tell you; ask the plants of the earth, and they will teach you; and the fish of the sea will declare to you" (Job 12:7–8, NRSV).

The reality of global warming and climate change brings into sharp relief the two-way inter-relationality of every form of love-making. The earth is crying out: stop the exploitation and abuse! Take care, or we will be unable to support and sustain life! When the Pharisees asked Jesus to quiet people who were raising their voices in praise, his answer was striking: if the people kept their peace, "the stones would shout out" (Luke 19:40, NRSV). Likewise, the prophet Habakkuk bellows from his watchtower against those who do evil, "the very stones will cry out from the wall, and the plaster will respond from the woodwork" (2:11, NRSV). And there is Genesis 4:10. "What have you done?" God asks Cain. "Listen, your brother's blood is crying out to me from the ground" (NRSV).

Realism or Anti-Realism?

At this point, it is worthy of note that highlighting the deep mystery of love that is the secret of the cosmos escapes the usual realism/anti-realism binary that continues to dominate and haunt much discussion in philosophy and quantum physics. Realism is "the belief that there is an objective physical world whose properties are independent of what human beings

---

32. Kingsolver, *Small Wonder*, 38.

33. For amazing insights into the way trees and animals in their own characteristic ways love, communicate, and care, two books by Peter Wohlleben stand out: *The Hidden Life of Trees* and *The Inner Life of Animals*.

know or what experiments we choose to do. Realists also believe that there is no obstacle in principle to our obtaining complete knowledge of this world."[34] Realists typically assume an adequate correspondence, proportionality, or fit between our intellect and the object to be known so that, at least in principle, the thing is knowable, if not at present, in some future time. On the other hand, anti-realism is "a philosophy according to which either there is no objective, universal reality, or if there is, human beings cannot have complete knowledge of it."[35]

Today, "most physicists," explains theoretical physicist Lee Smolin, believe that quantum mechanics "requires that we give up realism." However, he goes on, Einstein himself remained a realist, believing that "quantum mechanics gives us an incomplete description of nature, which is missing features necessary for a full understanding of the world."[36] In *Einstein's Unfinished Revolution: The Search for What Lies Beyond the Quantum*, Smolin takes up Einstein's search for "hidden variables" that would complete the description of the world.

In this context, the vision that I am venturing is neither realist nor anti-realist, neither determinism nor indeterminism. It is "realist" in the sense that it forthrightly claims the *reality* of a universe independent of our knowledge of it. It is "anti-realist" in the sense that it lacks realism's usual claim that we are somehow hard-wired to Reality, leading us to believe that through our efforts we could gain complete and full knowledge of the universe. Rather, I claim, we have to do with an excess, a beyond, that we will never be able to fully comprehend, validate, or get behind.

At the same time, in distinction from most anti-realists who claim that this leaves us with no access to the deep mystery of the universe, my claim is that in the surrender of faith—rather than as the result of human expertise or ingenuity—we are gifted with the discernment that the authentic or essential secret of reality is Love. Receiving life as the gift/call of love, we are responsible for fostering and generating love in all we do, passing it on, giving it legs in ways unique to ourselves.

There is a related consideration that is particularly apropos. Physics is the study of the physical dimension of the universe. That is, physics is the study of everything that is real from the standpoint of the physical. The same condition holds for all the other sciences. Biology studies the biotic dimension of creation and gives an account of everything from the standpoint of the biotic. Aesthetics studies the aesthetic dimension, psychology the psychic

---

34. Smolin, *Einstein's Unfinished Revolution*, 302.
35. Smolin, *Einstein's Unfinished Revolution*, 297.
36. Smolin, *Einstein's Unfinished Revolution*, xx, xxi.

dimension, and so forth. Each science gives an account of everything that is real from its particular standpoint. What that means, although it is often forgotten in much of the discussion, is that even if or when any science, say physics, biology, or psychology, would arrive at a theory of everything, the account would not be a *full* or *total* explanation of reality. It would be only a complete explanation from one particular dimension of reality. As John Caputo puts it in regard to physics: "Physics is the theory of everything that is real, of what everything is *at bottom*, but not of everything on top, not of every *modality* of everything that is real." That is, physics (as every science) "deals in principle with everything but not from every point of view."[37] In other words, although good theories are indispensable in helping us understand the world in which we live, in the end (as in the beginning), the deep mystery of the cosmos is finally a question of faith and testimony, rather than proof, demonstration, validation, or epistemology.

The Multi-Splendored Spectrum of Love

In the beginning is love: archi-love. When Genesis 1:1 announces that in the beginning God created the heavens and earth, it declares that creation is an out-flowing of love, and that creation and the entire gamut of existents, systems, processes, galaxies, and universes is simultaneously both a gifting of love and for love and a calling for and of love. The creative let-there-be's of love in Genesis—the Love-Words of God for creation— are concurrently giftings and callings. The Love-Words gift (generate and empower) as they call (solicit and evoke), and call (summon and direct) in the gifting (making possible, fashioning). The beginning is an exercise in co-creativity. No love without God. No God without Love. No creation without God. No God without creation.

In being gifted into be(com)ing, creation is called to join in and participate in the be(com)ing process of cosmogenesis, neither random nor deterministic.[38] The being of creation is always a becoming, an identity in-process/on trial (Kristeva).[39] There is an "elemental undecidability," an "irreducible indeterminacy and instability built right into creation."[40] What becomes of creation is an adventure in love dependent on how creation responds to and takes up its co-creative role. The multiversity of life-forms (each in their own way) are entwined in this process—a process of cosmic generativity which, charged with love, gives rise to dynamic patterns of

---

37. Caputo, *The Insistence of God*, 211.
38. Middleton, *The Liberating Image*, 285–89.
39. Kristeva, *Revolution in Poetic Language*.
40. Caputo, *The Weakness of God*, 74, 64.

exquisite and intricate interconnections that are neither random nor completely predictable. "In the beginning was love" underlines God's Yes, Yes to the creation.

To say, along with Derrida, "in the beginning is hermeneutics" and "in the beginning was the telephone" underlines the response-character of created existence. In response to God's Yes, Yes, creation and all its creatures are called to answer with their own Yes, Yes, enjoined to take responsibility in concert for the care, development, unfolding, and enrichment of the world. What happens is open-ended, uncertain, and undecidable—in a word, risky—dependent on a host of incalculable and unpredictable factors.

To embrace this cosmic understanding of love is to affirm that the universe is a multi-splendored spectrum of love, a veritable prism of colors. Love's gifting/calling comes in a multiverse of interwoven and interrelated let-there-be's. Accordingly, loving—proper, befitting connecting—is multi-dimensional in scope, taking on a variety of typical shapes and forms. Dutch philosopher Herman Dooyeweerd has proposed a wonderfully intricate and complex multiplex of fourteen irreducible modes which in inter-modal coherence comprise love's spectrum. There are the let-there-be gift/calls for faith, for troth, justice, respect, thrift, beauty, clarity, distinction, formation, sensitivity, life, energy, movement, extension, and quantity.[41] Thus, alongside the typical ways love shows up (or fails to show up) in relations of friendship, marriage, and family (to which love relations are customarily located and often restricted) as troth or trust, there are, for example, upbuilding (and toxic) ways of exercising faith, that is love as ultimate commitment (or autonomy). There is political love as justice (or injustice), economic love as stewardship (or wastefulness), social love as respect (or disrespect), aesthetic love as allusive (or non-allusive), lingual love as clarity (or abstruseness), logical love as distinctiveness (or opaqueness), formative love as formation (or deformation), psychic love as sensitivity (or insensitivity), biotic love as organic life (or amorphous), physical love as vibrant energy (or listlessness), kinematic love as uniform motion (or stagnation).

Indeed, the gifting/calling love-words, the let-there-be's, can be referred to in contemporary philosophical idiom as quasi-transcendentals, conditions of both possibility and impossibility. They are the enabling/disenabling conditions of and for processes and entities—not the entities or processes themselves—the generating conditions under which processes emerge and entities show themselves, making possible existence in all its life forms, systems, configurations, and practices, whether good or bad, healthy or unhealthy, fitting or unfitting. Since they are open-ended, underdetermined,

---

41. Dooyeweerd, *A New Critique of Theoretical Thought*, Vol. II.

directional invocations, rather than prescribed patterns, ideals, prototypes, or archetypes, they at the same time double as conditions of impossibility. Flux, change, contingency, vulnerability, randomness, uncertainty are built-in features of the creational matrix, which not only indicate the impossibility of mastery and control, but underline the be(com)ing-in-process nature of creation and its impenetrable mystery.

Along these lines, we begin with the giving/calling matrix of love and for love (*il y a l'amour*) in distinction from Levinas's dark, rumbling, anonymous *il y a* or Derrida's cold, impassive, indifferent *il y a khôra*. For Derrida there are two possible readings of the *khôra*. Whereas he chooses for the first—the *khôra* as an anonymous, barren, non-temporal abyss—I opt for the second, the *khôra* as the non-place place "opened by appeal," "created by God,"[42] making the heart of *khôra* amorous, promissory, the primordial originary affirmation, a "yes more ancient." The result: creation as a complex array of wild, uncharted, spaces and times of and for the generation of love.

Love (or in its gerund form loving) is for me the most appropriate encompassing term for the cosmogenerative processes which make-up what we know as reality. It is a cosmopoetic depth metaphor with a double-focus, signposting both the extravagant excess of the mystery of the universe's beginning, and depicting the intrinsic directionality of cosmic evolution. The cosmogenic process is a process of love on a cosmic scale, a macrocosmic relational process featuring a multiplicity of energies and systems connecting in fitting and appropriate ways. As such, the vast interplanetary interplay of diverse entities and forces is not merely haphazard and capricious, a roll of the dice without any direction, but rather a dynamic processive flow charged with and graced by love.

To emphasize that creation is more than physical nature and is at its heart a spiritual matter of expression and reference to the Creator, Dooyeweerd declared that "meaning is the being of creaturely reality."[43] Similarly quantum physicist David Bohm considered "meaning is being"[44] as linking consciousness and matter. Although "meaning" clearly emphasizes the relational interwovenness of creation, and highlights the role humanity plays in working out the dynamics of creation, "meaning" has, for me, a too anthropocentric feel with its focus on human activity and interpretation to serve as the all-important root metaphor for cosmic reality.

---

42. Derrida, *On the Name*, 75–76. See Olthuis, "Testing the Heart of *Khôra*; Anonymous or Amorous?"

43. Dooyeweerd, *A New Critique of Theoretical Thought*, 1:4.

44. Bohm, "Meaning and Information," in *The Search for Meaning*, 9.

Talking of love as the dynamic, directional force making for and evoking expansion and complexity in the vast curvature of space without designation of particular outcomes or pre-determined results is reminiscent of Henri Bergson's *élan vital* (without his material/vital dualism).[45] Love as the *èlan vital* driving the universe also finds some resonance in contemporary advances in the field of thermodynamics. According to the second law of thermodynamics, disorder and entropy increase until there is a terminal state of equilibrium. However, theories of non-equilibrium thermodynamics are developing in which entropic processes are not simply dissipative but are also the organizing, "driving force" behind evolutionary dynamics.[46] Recently, in his assessment of these developments, philosopher Clayton Crockett has suggested that if we "define and specify God as the dynamic matrix of organization, the potentiality for emergent structure . . . we could say that energy is God."[47]

Beginning with archi-love also means that the customary philosophical binary, either necessity (fully determined) or chance (full arbitrariness), is dislodged. Love is eventful, other-seeking, creative, giving direction, not accidental, arbitrary, or chancy. At the same time, love's eventing, dependent on subjective creaturely response, is not predictable, not automatic, nor determined. Evocative, alluring, creative, overflowing, without limits; love happens "without why."

From the very beginning, love is the passion—the oxygen, the flame, the glue—fueling, firing, connecting the universe in its astounding array. Compassion ("passion with") is the way of creation. Creation is called to co-partner with God in love-making, that is in cultivating, sustaining and augmenting the vast network of connections and interconnections that make up the interwoven fabric of the universe. For humans that is to be engaged in connecting in characteristically human ways: partnering in concert with all other creatures in the cosmic spiral of interconnectedness which is the universe. We are to love ourselves, love our neighbors, care for the creation, and give our hearts over to God. And each of these relationships impinges on the other in an interwoven, interdependent tapestry.

This is important and deserves to be repeated again and again. To live is to let love well up in us and through us as the beat, pulse, and rhythm of our lives, connecting us to ourselves, our neighbours, the whole family of

---

45. Bergson, *Creative Evolution*.

46. See Brooks and Wiley, *Evolution as Entropy*.

47. Crockett, "Entropy," in Crockett, Putt, and Robbins, *The Future of Continental Philosophy of Religion*, 280–81. Again, it is worth emphasizing, "energy is God" needs to be read not as a definition, but as metaphoric God-talk from one dimension of existence of the subliminal Mystery of the world.

God's creatures, and to God, the alpha and omega of love. As God's creation, the complex network of processes, interweaving, twisting and twirling, streaming and surging, is affirmative and promissory in character. Life comes into being and will flourish—its promise realized—*if* the webwork of interconnectedness persists, ongoing, continuous, sustained. That is, *if*—a big *IF*—the webwork of connections is generative and regenerative, upbuilding, productive and life-affirming.

However, the reality is that breakdown on every front and on every level and of every kind is only too frequent. Processes, systems, and relationships are stymied, weakened, contaminated, destroyed. Disruptions have a disturbing ripple effect, throwing things into disarray. The inescapable reality of serious brokenness and horrific catastrophes—the existence of evil—is exceedingly real and will soon receive focused attention. At this point, something more needs saying: faced with suffering and evil, God enters into our brokenness and suffers-with creation. Compassion is who God is and how God is, from the very beginning, passion-with-us. Confronted with evil, the passion of God's love intensifies, coming to a crescendo in the Word made Flesh in solidarity with our pain. As children of God, image-bearers of God, we are "heirs of God, and joint heirs with Christ—if, in fact, we suffer with him" (Rom 8:17, NRSV). In suffering-*with*—distinct from the suffering-*from* that we all experience—there is the transforming power, in the midst of suffering, to heal and redeem by bringing about new, beneficial, and revitalizing connections.

Love—it is my refrain—is the pulse, beat, and rhythm of the universe and of our lives. From the very beginning, compassion ("passion with") is the way of creation. The insurgency of evil and its effects didn't and doesn't change that. Love continues to carry all things, hope all things, and bear all things (1 Cor 13:7). In a world broken by sin and evil, the passion-with of God's love is a suffering-with, suffering-with us and all creation, entering into the brokenness in the Word made Flesh, sustaining, redeeming, holding us and creation fast in the Spirit's healing love.

The diagram below depicts the intrinsic inter-relational character of creational existence. Having (or not having) a robust sense of self is intricately related with healthy (or unhealthy) relationships with others, creation, and God. Likewise, trusting (or mis-trusting) others bears on trust (or lack of trust) in self, God, and creation. Caring (or not caring) for creation vitally connects with how we care (or do not care) for ourselves, God, and others. By the same token, a cared for (or abused) creation supports (or jeopardizes) self and others and thanks (or defames) God. Faith (or lack of faith) in God manifests itself in how we respect (or disrespect) ourselves, others, and creation. In and through it all, the Suffering Love of God.

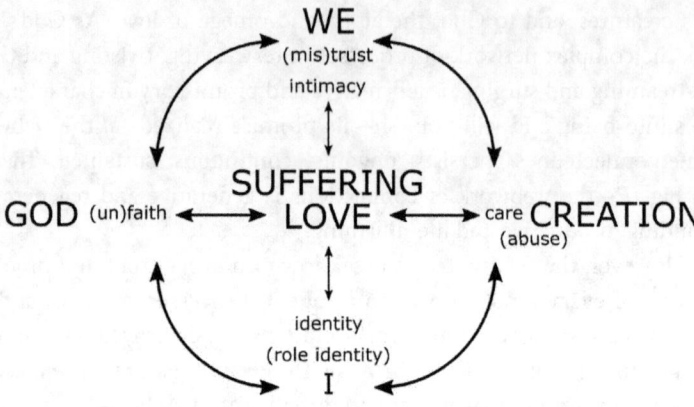

Love on a Cosmic Scale

Now, returning to our narrative of the cosmic scale of love. The universe is a quantum relationality of spiraling energies, intersecting fields, and seas of forces, in which identities emerge and play their role in concert, whether more or less predictably or rhizomatically. Cosmogenesis on every level is simultaneously a relational process of differentiation and integration, of contraction and expansion made possible by the intervals, spaces, and force-fields making up the space-time continuum. These are not, as such, gaps of separation, opposition, or antagonism, but openings of opportunity, interstices for the new and the novel, for different connections and reconnections. Indeed, timed-spatial openings, like borders, simultaneously separate and connect, not only making possible interactions of all sorts, on a multitude of levels, of myriad kinds and complexities, but giving room and space for deepening relations as well as for novel and surprising interfacings and interminglings. On a human level, Luce Irigaray calls these timed spaces or gaps, the "betweens" which make possible good connections without fusion and without isolation, relationships in which we simultaneously let others be even as we connect with them.

However, as we all experience, the betweens of space and time involve risk as well as opportunity. When we mistime or misplace, things go amiss. A mistake sets us back on our heels. We need to take another run, restart and reboot. Learning is a matter of trial and error, part and parcel of the cycle of life. Things happen too fast or too slowly, too early or too late, taking up the wrong space, or too much space or too little. We adjust and adapt, learning to live—more or less—with the attendant annoyance and frustration.

This cycle of life with its ebb and flow and its accidents underlines the vulnerability and fragility of the fabric of existence. There is a natural ebb and flow of ups and downs, breaks and connections, interstices and links. In the breaks and gaps of time and space, we are called to develop a rhythmic continuity, an alternating pattern as we negotiate our way through our encounters with all kinds of differences in the diverse times, spaces, and experiences of our lives. Discontinuity lives off of continuity, and discontinuity lives off continuity. Both are built-in features of our temporizing-spaced universe. Along these lines, modern biological and cybernetic theory are both concerned with self-regulating lawfulness and unpredictable excess. Systems are both inherently conservative (the condition of their existence) and innately unstable (the condition of their dynamism), oscillating between contingency and regularity.

Negotiating a path, giving shape to a project, learning and inventing are replete with trials and errors, discontinuities and continuities. That which is new, different, and other always challenges, surprises, interrupts, often disrupting our plans of action. Consequently, programs need to remain fluid, subject to revision and improvisation. Things happen. Nothing is for sure. It all depends. Processes take their course, zigging and zagging, this way and that, at this pace or that pace. Decisions are called for without any guarantees. Change is a constant partner in a cosmos of flux and flow.

Severe Breakdown: The Enigma of Evil

However, far too often—and it is a monstrous truth—things can and do go disastrously awry personally, interpersonally, institutionally, environmentally, cosmically. The rhythms and sequences of life are not only disturbed and interrupted, they can be thrown completely out of kilter, fully broken, violated and damaged. And when things go wrong, the result is the same: suffering, pain, sorrow, and anguish. Nothing and no one escapes. Everything and everyone suffers-from ... evil, whether from run-amok processes, natural disasters, devastating accidents, frightful diseases, dreadful betrayals, hideous deceits, or horrific abuse.

The daunting question in all this: is there a grave fault, a tragic flaw in the very fabric of creation? Were evil and trauma structurally integral to creation from the beginning? Or is the horror of brokenness and evil inadvertent, accidental, an unwelcome, cancerous blemish, an inexplicable surd? Even if we never face the question directly, we cannot avoid replying—even if by default. Since violence, brokenness, and concomitant suffering are rampant, and endemic to life as we know it, it is not difficult to understand that a rather large proportion of the populace end up adopting the "tragic view" in which "suffering is *not* a violation."[48] In the tragic view, of which Nietzsche is perhaps the most famous spokesperson, strife and suffering are

---

48. Caputo, *Radical Hermeneutics*, 282.

woven into the fabric of life, integral spokes in the wheel of life which we cannot avoid and indeed ought to heroically accept. What will be will be and we should love that, for it is fate—*amor fati*.

For most people, a tragic view of this kind goes too far in validating suffering as something to affirm rather than something to struggle against and resist. Violence and the resulting suffering waste and destroy life. In lieu of my starting confession that God is a God of Love, it is difficult to contemplate, much less accept, that the violence of disasters, the carnage of hatred, the vileness of evil was and is inherent in a creation that God called "very good." To consider the creation as "always already" flawed from the beginning, I argue, is to conflate, confuse, even identify the Creation and the Fall. In considering evil equiprimordial with goodness is to ontologize evil—providing legitimation and validation to its existence.

Views of this kind also end up with highly questionable views of God. God, it is said, is good, does the best Godself can, but is of limited-power, unable to prevent evil. But, if that is the case, isn't evil raised to a God-like status? Or, Yes, God is omnipotent, but for some reason beyond our understanding "permits" evil. But this easily lends itself to visions of a sadistic God who "allows" even the most horrific forms of evil. Moreover, regardless of the details and rationale of such views, God nevertheless remains on the hook for evil. I pay more attention to these matters in the next chapter, with its discussion of the sovereignty of a God of Love.

At this juncture, I want to move on and claim that our finite creation is not to be seen as indicating, predisposing, including, or necessitating the brokenness of evil. Love, the goodness of love, is more primordial than evil. Although difference, tension, instability, and risk are necessary constituent properties of existence, opposition, conflict, and trauma are not. Tension, risk, and divergence do call for cooperation, debate, and negotiation. Tension may become unbearable and lead to breakdown. Debate may end up in dissent. Negotiation may be thwarted by antagonism. But these breakdowns, although often the regrettable reality, are neither necessary nor inevitable.

Without the wildness of the spaces, the creative tension, of and due to difference, there is no invention, no novelty, no risk—and without the risk, love loses its chance. To put it briefly and graphically: in creating, God "does not bring closure but a gap. A God of the gaps is not the gap God fills, but the gap God opens."[49] The gaps are the intervals of time and space that we inhabit, the in-betweens we cross (or do not cross), making (or not making) connections, negotiating (or not negotiating) passage. The world is not a predetermined or divinely supervised cosmos, nor an out-and-out chaos,

---

49. Caputo, *The Insistence of God*, x.

but the rhythmic (dis)continuity of relationality and differentiation that is Love's Eventing—a kind of "chaosmos" (James Joyce).⁵⁰

However, things can often be so totally broken, so heinous, that we sense the egregious presence of evil. Then it is abundantly clear that what is happening or has happened is outright evil and should not be—period. But, at many other times, although the difference itself between customary tensions and traumatic incidents is distinct, it may be difficult to assess exactly when things started to go so badly wrong to the point when evil is the only appropriate designation.

Nevertheless, it is crucial to insist that the ebb and flow of the various developmental processes that structure creaturely life not be conflated, identified, or confused with the severe breakdown of such processes. To offer a simple example: the elasticity of a rubber band is good, essential to its usefulness. Its ability to stretch and adapt—its constructive tension, neither limp nor rigid—is to be radically distinguished from occasions of overwrought tension in which the elastic breaks or when there is too little traction and things go limp. While tension itself is serviceable, too much or too little tension is detrimental.

Failing to appreciate the radical difference between tensions and catastrophes is particularly significant because it underplays and trivializes the suffering and pain of those who suffer trauma in all its horror. After all, in this view, trauma is just an ordinary part of life. All one can do is accept it, try to forget, and move on—pretending nothing dreadful has happened. Which advice, in fact, if followed, leaves the emotional wounding unattended and unhealed, only, even if unrecognized and/or unacknowledged, to crop up time and time again with disastrous effects, not only in one's own life but in the lives of everyone around them. The pain, hurt, and anger that comes with all forms of trauma, if unworked through, is passed on, traumatizing others. This happens in an endless array of direct and indirect ways. An abused person becomes an abuser. Less visible, but just as real, the untreated, free-floating pain and hurt of a trauma victim is soaked up, and absorbed sponge-like by the people they meet. Whatever the details, not only is the original victim retraumatized, but trauma claims new victims. Trauma is contagious.⁵¹

The importance of acknowledging the qualitative difference between constructive tension and destructive breakdown is of heightened relevance in our contemporary world. Reworking themes of Hegel, Freud, and Lacan,

---

50. See chapter 6 for further discussion of the difference and interrelation between tension and trauma.

51. See Olthuis, "The Wit(h)ness of Suffering Love."

the influential cultural philosopher Slavoj Žižek, whose thinking I will soon come back to, goes so far as to claim that existential traumas are actually subsequent repeats of the originary "always already" trauma intrinsic to creation. For Lacan, trauma has "always already occurred," and creation, as the Real (for him a swarming void) is basically there for us as trauma that can never be overcome or assimilated, only repeated. Trauma, for Žižek, is inescapable, preordained, irreparable and irredeemable—only heroically endured by means of the screen of fantasy. Creation began as a catastrophe, and remains a catastrophe. Although necessary and helpful, fantasizing, as Lacan and Žižek emphasize, in no way precludes the need to "traverse the fantasy" and recognize that a fantasy is what it is: fantasy. In stark contrast to views of this sort, my conviction is that violence, trauma, and evil, although omnipresent and pervasive, are not and never were inherent or constitutive ingredients of creation, neither necessary nor universal.

At the same time, believing that love is more primordial than evil should in no way lead us to underestimate the horrific nature of the powers of evil. Strangely enough, uncannily—and not without irony and paradox—just as the unconditional love of God is "without why" (it is self-authenticating), so the reality of evil is in an upside down way "without why" (but now without justification). Evil is an enigma. It is not as primordial as goodness (Ricoeur), but, considering evil to be the privation of good (Augustine) seems inadequate. Evil is powerful. Its power is parasitic, living off the vigor and energy of love. Evil exploits, capitalizing on the oomph and swoosh of love without its nourishing, life-affirming *élan*. In smaller and larger ways, the dynamics of love and the parasitic (anti)dynamics of evil play themselves out every day of our lives. Whereas love (as *with-ing*) is constructive, positive, and healing, evil (as *without-ing*) is destructive, negative, and degenerative. Which is to say, evil is (with)-*without*-(with). In this way, evil is not simply the wholesale, unequivocal negation of love, but an auto-immunitary process, eviscerating, disemboweling love from within, using the very dynamics of love against itself.

This with-*without*-with schema is akin to Derrida's "*sans* sans *sans*" (*without*-without-*without*)[52] schema in that both are efforts to negotiate negation. A negative is never simply negation. It is a negative of a positive. Negativity with a capital N—the Negativity we know as Evil—in its (with)-*without*-(with) logic depends on the *withing*-relations-and-connections of love even as it eats away and erodes them. Because of this, evil can at times masquerade as productive with the guise and pretense of normalcy.

---

52. Derrida, *The Post Card*, 401. See Marian Hobson's discussion in *Jacques Derrida: Opening Lines*, 147–86.

Cancer is for me the most telling and scariest exemplar of evil and how it works. Cancer (the uncontrolled, abnormal growth of cells) uses and lives off healthy bodily functioning. Sometimes, somehow and some way, cancer cells evade detection by the body's immune system, and once having infiltrated the body's defenses, even succeed in using the immune system to protect and promote their growth and survival.

Indeed, the parasitic nature of evil calls into question the appropriateness of talking about the beginning of evil. Beginnings are affirmative and inaugurating, while evil is negative, devious, and conniving. Evil, in that sense, is without beginning, it interrupts, derails, upsets, piggy-backing on already functioning processes. And when evil happens, it grows, multiplies and distends by surreptitiously living off existent dynamics. In a strange way parallel to love, which in being given away is not diminished but grows, in a perverse way, evil, in subverting the power of love, can multiply and increase evil. The parasitic working of evil at times becomes so "successful" that a para-site of sorts, an alternate reality takes shape in which the crooked is seen as straight, and evil parades as its opposite. Once one succumbs to evil's enticement, the power of evil to entrap grows exponentially—like an upside-down fire feeding itself—becoming more beguiling, harder and harder to resist.

In contrast to the *embrace* of love which is open, out-going, always desirious of connecting with others, leading to ever widening, concentric circles of love, the *grip* of evil—and it is a grip—tightens its hold, closing down, ever predatory to extend its mastery. At times the proliferation of evil seems to overshadow or outstrip the flourishing of love. This state of affairs, echoed in the cry of the Psalmist, "Why do the wicked prosper?," has long puzzled and perturbed me. Could it be that it has to do with this same parasitic nature of evil? For, even though evil may grip and captivate, evil is never satisfying, leaving its purveyors on edge, never fulfilled, always wanting more, aware something is missing. Evil is the evisceration of Love. At the same time, paradoxically, the "restlessness" of spirit of those in the grip of evil (think Augustine) spurs them on, ever yearning for "more" and yet "more," upping the ante, leaving no rock unturned—all to feel the abiding satisfaction and utter delight of loving and being loved. Coincidently, in their all-out, tireless effort to find fulfillment and inner peace, their genius and virtuosity may at times give birth to amazing inventions and achievements.

Uncannily, even as love invites us, evil—again, capitalizing on love's dynamic—in its own bizarre way has its own allure, on the prowl, seeking prey. Evil can fascinate and entice even as it wreaks havoc and destruction. The horrors of evil have a macabre drawing power. Genesis records Yahweh cautioning Cain: "If you do well, will you not be accepted? And if you do not do well, sin is lurking at the door; its desire is for you, but you must master it" (Gen 4:7, NRSV). The Apostle Peter wastes no words: "Discipline yourselves; keep alert. Like a roaring lion your adversary the devil prowls around, looking for someone to devour" (1 Pet 5:8, NRSV). Living off the energy and passion of love as the excessive, surging conflux of generative powers of and for connection, evil is a spooky, disturbing tangle of dispersing powers fueled by fear, bent on control, disruption, and domination.

No one at the outset intends to do evil. As image-bearers of the God of love, every one of us is made of love for love. When we do not feel embraced in love, when we feel alone, unseen, and abandoned, something inside goes awry, fear and distrust take root. If we repeatedly feel unheard, used, dismissed, or betrayed, we begin to feel desperate and panicky. We are traumatized. Understandably, hoping to protect against danger and further injury, our inner self goes into hiding. Disconnecting internally, we set about developing survival strategies. We still want to be close, but we are afraid to be close. With our inner wounded self walled off, we broker arm's length relationships. We develop defensive holding patterns, we hold back, we hold down, we hold away. Instead of flowing with and learning the rhythms of love, life is all about control and more control. All to hold down our fear.

What began as an effort to avoid the pain of the heart, over a period of years can develop its own rhythm to the point that we become "forgetful" of the wounded heart, the lack of inner connection, the emptiness and loneliness. Under the illusion of being in control, we are in reality out of control, slowly becoming strangers to ourselves, dying from lack of loving connection with ourselves and others. However, even as we do our best to "forget" the deep wounding, the pain and estranged feelings remain unattended, festering and seething as toxic pollutants in our "basements." Underneath, we are unsettled, uneasy, haunted by a nagging discomfort. Some of us manage to be more or less functional and give the appearance of wellness, losing ourselves in work, in various causes, in leisure, whatever. Others are always on edge, walking on eggshells. Some of us become depressed. Yet others turn to food, drugs, sex, alcohol, or gambling, for the "rush" that makes them feel alive.[53]

With hurt feelings percolating, suppressed, turned off, ignored, healing does not happen. The wounds remain simmering and seething . . . When stress levels elevate or the unexpected happens, the unworked through, unintegrated feelings resurface, inflamed and aggravated, the need for relief

---

53. For the Control/Release Cycle of addiction, see Olthuis, *The Beautiful Risk*, 90–95.

and control easily becomes obsessive. While willpower, denial, repression, and flight may enable us to get on with our lives to some degree, we are not "working through" the pain and hurt to a renewed connection with our inner self and with others.

What too often is forgotten is that unless we own our feelings, they own us. Unworked through anger festers, waiting for its moment to erupt, slowly hardening into hate. Unworked through fear leaves us on perpetual guard, afraid to reach out, worried about being used. Unacknowledged shame feeds the fear that somehow we are flawed persons. We have arrived at the point of this discussion: the ins and outs of how addiction takes hold seems a helpful illustration of how evil claims its victims. The road to evil, like the road to addiction, begins more or less incidentally as an effort to get out of a tight situation, or resolve everyday problems and get on with one's life as best one can. The possibilities are endless. It could be lying in compromising or embarrassing situations, engaging in suspect actions to gain an advantage, avenging harm to self, becoming more and more selfish, afraid of the different, pretending to win approval, on and on.

Just as slowly, gradually, addiction can take hold and become habitual as it delivers its "rush," so certain wrong-headed patterns of response, if they offer a way out in awkward, uncomfortable, tense, anxiety-provoking situations, easily become automatic go-to reactions. Even though we may feel some unease, sensing that what we are doing leaves something to be desired, perhaps misguided, even appalling, we rationalize and feel "justified." It could be something like: "It's no big deal." Or, "Everyone does the same thing, and we are the victims, we have the right of self-defense." Imperceptibly—if nothing else changes—such patterns of response are so beguiling and seductive that, beginning small, they become habits we begin to depend on. When this happens, evil, like an invisible virus, subtly and seductively, is taking over our lives. We have no way to determine precisely where or when it got started, and it is spinning out of control.

Just as the "as if" posturing of exuberance and connection that comes with addiction is a facsimile of the real thing, so in the grip of evil the muscular "all is well" posture of self-aggrandizement covers over a nagging sense of being powerless and alone. Here the illusion of control typical of addiction is a carbon-copy of the variety of the postures of control fueled by evil. As addiction and evil tighten their grip, nothing else matters but "me," or "we," not only at the cost of others, but also at the cost of me. While in addiction a person is finally hooked, doing evil without scruples or compunction can become second nature.

Perhaps most strikingly, the supreme irony of addiction is also the supreme irony of evil. We fool ourselves even as we are being fooled. Slowly but surely, like a fog creeping in unawares, explicably, but finally, inexplicably, the forces of evil entrench themselves in our hearts. We convince ourselves that we are in charge, that we are masters, while the reality is that we are prisoners in our own home, hostage to alien forces.

For the more evil takes hold, the more we die inside, the more we lose what is proper to us, our uniqueness, the singularity of being "'the one and only'. . . love being the condition of the very possibility of uniqueness."[54] We become minions of evil, automatons going through the motions, losing ourselves in the banal "sameness" of Heidegger's inauthentic "they." Instead of the joy, freedom, compassion, and openness of loving connection with self and others, there is the closedness, grimness, bondage, heartlessness, and isolation of inner disconnection—even if under the cover of swagger and bluster, even if masquerading as an angel of light (2 Cor 11:14). Once again: the open, free embrace of love, in contrast to the shackled captive grip of evil.

The senseless, lawless nature of the power of evil to deceive also means recognizing that evil is not a problem, but a challenge.[55] Problems (eventually) may give way to solutions, dealing with regularities and irregularities. But evil is of a different ilk, beyond ordinary classification, not the inverse of love, or a power equal to love, but an anti-power parasitic on the power of love, recognizing no boundaries, abyssal, bottomless. For the un-mystery of evil there is no possible solution, only dissolution and defeat. That may perhaps be called the anti-"law" of its lawlessness.

The very real presence of evil in the world means that the "chaosmos" of creation, on the one hand, is replete with countless possibilities and chances of and for Love, to be heeded, realized, and enjoyed. On the other hand, our "chaosmos" struggles intensely with the countless times the chances are missed, broken, exploited through the machinations of evil. Also, at the same time—and it is a liberating and comforting Also—God does not flee in the face of evil, but remains ever with creation. Scripture reveals God as the faithful, long-suffering, merciful One, who, ever mindful of human limitations and brokenness, opens up alternative routes, what I refer to as *redemptive re-routings*, to blessing and healing. Although nothing good comes out of evil—evil cannot be redeemed, we can be redeemed from evil—even as we suffer-*from* evil as both victims and agents, God suffers-with us. Indeed, until death, the healing, revitalizing Love of God continues to surround, invite, and haunt all those in the grip of evil with resurrectionary effect.

---

54. Levinas, *Entre Nous*, 168.
55. Ricoeur, *Evil*.

In the face of evil, we—image-bearers of God's love—are called to be integral and active participants in this work of redemption from evil. As agents of love, we are to be-with others, in love to suffer-with them. Suffering-from is degenerating, degrading, exacerbating and worsening. In contrast, suffering-with is healing, generating, releasing and redeeming. Paul in Romans 8:17 exclaims that we are heirs of God, and joint heirs with Christ, if we suffer with him. Jesus explains in Matthew 25 that when we clothe the naked, visit the sick, and feed the hungry, to the least of our brothers and sisters, we do it unto him.

In this healing ministry of God's love to which we are called, love finds a way to new life and flourishing, often in surprising ways. Which means, hallelujah, that the embrace of love comes with the promise of breaking the grip of evil. The creation began with God's love (*ex amore*), the creation and all its array abide in God's love (*cum amore*), and creation lives in the hope and promise of a new heavens and earth in God's love (*ad amorem*). Love is stronger than death and outlasts death. That, I believe, is the heart of the life and message of Jesus, of his Death and Resurrection.

Power-Over or Power-With?

The way of love, I have been emphasizing, is the generative and regenerative way of the world. And love is power-*with*. However, in the long history of philosophy and theology up to the present, power has been traditionally regarded as power-*over,* different from love. Even when celebrated as the supreme virtue, love is taken to be a supplementary or subsequent concern of a higher or another order. Typically, philosophical anthropology examines the constitutional make-up of being human, while ethics considers the normative questions regarding human behavior.

Stretching all the way back to Plato and Aristotle, "being," as I mentioned above, was defined as "power." Listen to what Plato has the Stranger say in the *Sophist* (247d): "My notion would be that anything which possesses any sort of power to affect another, or to be affected by another, if only for a single moment, however trifling the cause and however slight the effect, has real existence; and I hold that the definition of being is simply power." Power is the ability to do to, to influence, power-*over*. Centuries later, Spinoza refined and elaborated: "Everything, in so far as it is in itself, endeavors to persist in its own being."[56] Since for him all things are modes of God, Spinoza determines that this drive to persist in its own being, the *conatus essendi*, emerges by necessity out of the eternal and infinite essence

---

56. Spinoza, *Ethics*, Part 3, Proposition 6, 136.

of God: "God's power is identical with his essence."[57] God becomes identified as sheer, almighty Power.

The *conatus essendi*—the drive to exist—as opposed to the *conatus amandi*—the drive to love—became the central, organizing concept of modern ontologies and modern theologies, showing up in a wide array of philosophies of power. In Western philosophy, reason ("'I think' comes down to 'I can'"[58])—whether in Cartesian, Kantian, Hegelian or Husserlian dress—became the instrument of power by which there is "a reduction of the other to the same,"[59] in the process effectively removing the threat of the other. For Jean-Jacques Rousseau freedom is a form of "indifference towards every other."[60] Either one—as thinkers as diverse as Hegel, Sartre, Freud, *et. al.* postulated—dominates or is dominated. To be a human self is qua human to have adversaries. For Hobbes, infamously, it is unequivocal: the stage of nature is "a war of all against all."[61] For Paul Tillich, power is the "possibility a being has to actualize itself against the resistance of other beings."[62] Difference is by the nature of the case oppositional: power-over or power-under. Even if not explicit, one is always over against the other. Paul Ricoeur claims that "it is difficult to imagine situations of interaction in which one individual does not exert power over another by the very fact of acting."[63]

The oppositional self-other paradigm is far-reaching and pernicious. Love of neighbor is only possible at the expense of love of self. For Sigmund Freud, loving another depletes the supply of libido available for investment in one's own ego. In his words: "The commandment, 'Love thy neighbour as thyself,' is the strongest defence against human aggressiveness . . . . The commandment is impossible to fulfill; such an enormous inflation of love can only lower its value, not get rid of the difficulty."[64] Theologian Anders Nygren is no less unambiguous, even if, with a different accent: "Eros is essentially and in principle self-love... Agape, on the other hand, excludes all self-love."[65] Self-love and love of the other are at odds.

---

57. Spinoza, *Ethics*, Part 1, Proposition 34, 74.
58. Levinas, *Totality and Infinity*, 46.
59. Levinas, *Totality and Infinity*, 43.
60. Rousseau, *Discourse on Inequality*, 128.
61. Hobbes, *Leviathan*, ch. 13.
62. Tillich, *Courage to Be*, 179.
63. Ricoeur, *Oneself as Another*, 220.
64. Freud, "Civilization and Its Discontents," in *The Standard Edition*, 21:151.
65. Nygren, *Agape and Eros*, 216–17.

The implications of an oppositional paradigm (in whatever form it takes) has been and continues to be catastrophic and grievous. It means that human interactions are not occasionally, or in specific situations frightening and violent, but by the nature of the case, they are always inherently antagonistic, fearful, and scary. Fear of the other, fear of the different, is not fear of something or someone in particular, but a nameless, pervasive anxiety that one's existence is fundamentally threatened. Existentially, distrust is the *modus vivendi*, and human relations become defensive maneuverings to hold off the peril. Fear, not love, becomes the dominant and primary motive force in the universe. The world becomes a battle-field, the stranger is dangerous, ordinary life unsafe. The tyranny of fear stifles the hope and promise of love and its adventures.

Thankfully, thinkers such as Martin Buber whose focus on subject to subject I-Thou meetings of mutual confirmation, in contrast to I-it subject to object interactions of manipulation, have offered another welcome and liberating perspective. Indeed, inspired by Buber and existentialists such as Gabriel Marcel and Soren Kierkegaard, philosophers like Michel Foucault, Jacques Derrida, Emmanuel Levinas, Jean-Francois Lyotard, Luce Irigaray, Felix Guattari, Gilles Deleuze, et al., have put the penchant of universal reason to domesticate, appropriate and totalize the other, under fire, unveiled and censured as injustice. Levinas put it this way: "Philosophy is an egology." The being-for-oneself of the *conatus essendi* is a "philosophy of power . . . a philosophy of injustice" and "power" is "by essence murderous of the other."[66] Indeed, this critique of logocentric reason as the instrument by which an ego or a society of egos disempowers the different and other has given birth to a veritable chorus of postmodern voices, each in their own way calling for justice for all regardless of color, age, sexual orientation, ethnicity, not just for the privileged power brokers.

The call to vigilance on behalf of the other, for celebration of difference and diversity, for responsibility to and embrace of all the marginalized, the widow, the orphan, and the stranger is most welcome. This is especially so because, at the same time, for increasing numbers in the world, the nightmare of violence and oppression is not only unrelenting, but is in fact escalating.

However, even though Levinas calls for ethics as "first philosophy" in which the face of the other calls us to self-sacrificing responsibility in which we are hostage to the other,[67] the conviction that the fundamental human

---

66. Levinas, *Totality and Infinity*, 44, 46, 47.

67. See chapter 9 for more on Levinas. For a detailed and incisive treatment of Levinas, I wholeheartedly recommend Jeffrey Dudiak, *The Intrigue of Ethics*.

condition is "a multiplicity of allergic egoisms ... at war with one another"[68] remains intact. Along similar lines Derrida and, following him, Caputo, deploring the injustice done to the other, underscore the unconditional responsibility to hospitably welcome the other, and to work fervently for the coming of justice. At the same time, in Caputo's words, since "the I is always already—structurally—aggressive," to "become non-aggressive" is "*stricto sensu*, a paradox." This "paradoxical, mad agency" is the "utter foolishness" of "obligation" to the other and is "slightly impossible, because, as Aristotle says, every agent acts for the sake of the good, of the agent's own good."[69]

Derrida emphasizes the urgency of unconditional welcome and unconditional forgiveness. Without any choice on our part, we are called to work for justice, act without violence, and forgive unconditionally. However, for Derrida, "there is not narcissism and non-narcissism." "Love is narcissistic." So the best we can hope for is a "much more welcoming, hospitable narcissism, one that is open to the experience of the other as other."[70] The best we can ever do is work for "the least possible violence."[71]

Thus, the self-other oppositional paradigm is also for Derrida not a sometime, now- and-then occurrence. Opposition is a structural a priori built into the structure of existence. There is no possibility to cross or bridge the gap to the other without violence. Even the giving of a gift does violence, since the person receiving a gift is "defenseless, open, exposed.... Such violence may be considered the very condition of the gift, its constitutive impurity."[72] Moreover, "as soon as I enter into a relation with the other, with the gaze, look, request love, command or call of the other, ... in the same instant, to all the others, I offer a gift of death, I betray."[73]

Prior to any empirical violence, there is the "originary violence of language ... arche-writing: arche-violence."[74] By its very nature, before a word is written, already "writing is the exploitation of man by man."[75] Nothing—not even science—escapes "the horizon of intersubjective

---

68. Levinas, *Otherwise than Being*, 4.
69. Caputo, *Against Ethics*, 217–19.
70. Derrida. *Points*, 199.
71. Derrida, *Writing and Difference*, 130.
72. Derrida, *Given Time: I. Counterfeit Money*, 147.
73. Derrida, *The Gift of Death*, 68.
74. Derrida, *Of Grammatology*.
75. Derrida, *Of Grammatology*, 119.

violence."[76] Accordingly, "an entire theory of the structural necessity of the abyss [is] gradually constituted."[77] [78]

This means that when good things happen, when the other is honored, when mutuality is a reality, and justice is done, miraculously, as it were, against the human grain, violence and fear of the other is overcome and transcended. Such occurrences are paradoxical exceptions, "madness" of sorts. But, and that is my question: Is that all that can be said? Is it true to reality? What if, as I propose, the "being" of humanity is not power-*over* (power against), but love as power-*with*? Then, flourishing non-narcissistic, non-oppositional, non-violent relationships would be structural possibilities in accord with, and not against, or in exception to human nature. Then violence and fear of the other is not a necessary structural feature of every human interaction. Then intentional relations, at their best, are not reciprocal trade-offs with a minimum of violence, but give-and-receive relations of mutuality without violence.[79]

Crucial to my argument is the need to deconstruct the power/love binary. As Derrida in particular has demonstrated, in binaries (think: day/night, male/female, one/many, good/evil, etc.) one pole ends up being championed at the expense of the other. What is required, as Derrida also points out in relation to binaries, is not simply a reversal of emphasis and priority, but an inventive reconfiguration. Rethinking the power/love dynamics begins with the acknowledgment that love is powerful and that power can be loving. Love is not without power, but the power of love is a power-*with* (and not power-*over*). Power-*with* and power-*over* are only confused at our peril. Power-*with* is collaborative, generative, upbuilding, integrating; power-*over* is oppositional, hierarchical, fearful, separative.

Less Than Nothing, or Nothing Less Than Love

The crucial importance of questioning the "difference-is-by-nature-oppositional" tradition is even more pertinent when we take into account the work of the cultural critic and Slovenian philosopher Slavoj Žižek. For Žižek, opposition is too weak a word: it is "the gap or antagonism which defines the human condition."[80] There is "the nothingness of a pure gap (antagonism, tension, 'contradiction'), the pure form of dislocation

---

76. Derrida, *Of Grammatology*, 127.

77. Derrida, *Of Grammatology*, 163.

78. See Smith, *Jacques Derrida: Live Theory*, for a helpful, straightforward presentation of Derrida's thought.

79. On the ins and outs of mutuality, see chapter 9.

80. Žižek, *Less Than Nothing*, 963.

ontologically preceding any dislocated content."[81] Things didn't start well. And, as the concluding sentence of his more recent book, *Absolute Recoil*, makes clear, there is no promise they will end well. "The position of Wisdom [i.e. tradition] is that the Void brings ultimate peace, a state in which all differences are obliterated; the position of dialectical materialism is that there is no peace even in the Void."[82]

In Žižek's dialectical materialism, there is "only the Real as the absolute gap, non-identity, and particular phenomena."[83] This Gap—"the Real is opaque, inaccessible, out of reach, *and* undeniable, impossible to by-pass or remove—in it, lack and surplus coincide . . . [a] coincidence of opposites."[84] "There is no such zero-level" where things "'really happen.'" "If we go 'all the way down,' we arrive at the Void. . . . at the very bottom, there is all the room we want, since there is nothing else there, just the void."[85]

Žižek's "ontology of antagonism" with its discordant creation, in which "all processes take place 'from Nothing through Nothing to Nothing,'"[86] is starkly different from my "ontology of love," in which all processes take place from Love, through Love, to Love. While I begin with the Love of God and a good creation, with evil as an intrusion, for Žižek, there is no God, and Creation is a traumatic "ontological failure." Whereas for me the "crack in the Thing"[87] is subsequent, a result of humankind missing the mark of love in the Fall, for Žižek, the creation was "cracked" from the beginning. Indeed, "The Fall thus never happens, since it has always already happened." The "primacy of 'stuckness'" is "the axiom of human life"[88] and "Negativity (whose Freudian name is the 'death drive') . . . [is] the primordial ontological fact."[89] We begin with "the primacy of Evil over the Good"[90]: "Good can emerge only, afterwards, in the space opened up by that Evil."[91] "Good is self-negated Evil"[92]—"a self-organization or limitation of stains, the result of a limit, a 'minimal difference,' within the field

---

81. Žižek, *Less Than Nothing*, 38.
82. Žižek, *Absolute Recoil*, 415.
83. Žižek, *Less Than Nothing*, 377.
84. Žižek, *Less Than Nothing*, 381.
85. Žižek, *Less Than Nothing*, 733.
86. Žižek, *Less Than Nothing*, 38.
87. Žižek, *Less Than Nothing*, 17.
88. Žižek, *Absolute Recoil*, 119.
89. Žižek, *Less Than Nothing*, 835.
90. Žižek, *Less Than Nothing*, 107.
91. Žižek, *Less Than Nothing*, 107.
92. Žižek, *Absolute Recoil*, 343.

of Evil."[93] "The supreme Good is split within itself [and] coincides with the supreme Evil . . . Devil is the obverse of God Himself."[94]

Žižek's ontology is a very Hegelian-like "coincidence of opposites": Excess/lack, absence/presence, madness/reason, no/yes, evil/good, eternity/time, freedom/control, female/male, trauma/life are dialectically identical, belonging to each other, despite being paradoxically contradictory. However, whereas for Hegel there is a hidden harmony of contradictory opposites, for Žižek the "pre-transcendental gap/rupture"[95] is never reconciled or healed.[96] "Trauma is 'eternal' . . . it is the point of 'eternity' around which time circulates."[97]

For Žižek, "humans are by nature evil and corrupt; one cannot change them, but only limit their opportunities to actualize their evil potential."[98] "The frustrating nature of our human existence, the very fact that our lives are forever out of joint, marked by a traumatic imbalance, is what propels us towards permanent creativity."[99] One is to recognize "failure itself as the form of success," the "fiasco" necessary to create "the conditions for its overcoming."[100] The cycle repeats: the best we can do is try something new each time with the hope of perhaps failing better. However, reconciliation and healing remain forever out of reach. "Consequently, the ultimate goal of psychoanalysis is not the confessionary pacification/gentrification of the trauma, but the acceptance of the very fact that our lives involve a traumatic kernel beyond redemption, that there is a dimension of our being which forever resists redemption-deliverance."[101]

Žižek begins with "a pre-transcendental gap/rupture"[102] that leaves a human being "constitutively 'out-of-joint.'"[103] Consequently, "every phenomenon, everything that happens, fails in its own way, implies a crack, antagonism, imbalance, in its very heart."[104] In contrast, I begin with love as the "pre-transcendental" creative energy that gifts/calls creation and humankind

---

93. Žižek, *Less Than Nothing*, 974.
94. Žižek, *Absolute Recoil*, 268.
95. Žižek, *Less Than Nothing*, 6.
96. See Dettloff, "Žižek's Ruptured Monism."
97. Žižek, *The Fragile Absolute*, 88.
98. Žižek, *Less Than Nothing*, 107.
99. Žižek, *Less Than Nothing*, 132.
100. Žižek, *Absolute Recoil*, 26, 27.
101. Žižek, *The Fragile Absolute*, 90-91.
102. Žižek, *Less Than Nothing*, 6.
103. Žižek, *Less Than Nothing*, 835.
104. Žižek, *Less Than Nothing*, 8.

into existence and acts to reclaim and redeem humankind and all of creation from the out-of-jointness of subsequent evil. Yes, there is evil and disaster aplenty, shit happens; but, as I have been arguing, evil is against the grain of the cosmos, a strange, discombobulating, leeching intruder. The reality and the promise: even though we all miss the mark of love at times, suffer wounds, and feel undone, healing can and does take place, redemption from evil happens. The energy and drive of the Love of God continues to circulate, inviting, suffusing, luring, healing and haunting, seeping into cracks and crevasses, into every joint and disjoint. Whereas I see the Love of God as a gifting/calling Third, aiding and abetting us in our efforts for mutual connection in our difference, for Žižek, "there is no Third which unites and reconciles the two struggling opposites... love is in its very notion *atheist*, godless.... All we have is the self-grounded abyss of our love."[105]

To envision theopoetically according to the logic of love is to recognize that the creation does not run on the tit-for-tat logic of antagonism and opposition, but on the logic of mutuality, forgiveness, and grace that frees life from the grip and fear of evil. Love as the inscendent energy calling for an economy of justice for all, which makes way for renewal and new life. Although Žižek's call for ongoing revolutionary action emphasizes the need for non-identical repetition, the repetitions in the end turn out without exception to be failures—"ruptures." That's just the way it is. On the other hand, in the dynamics of love, non-identical repetitions of the same may result in something new and different: revived hope, renewed connection, deepened love.

Considering the central place rupture, gap, and crack play in Žižek's theory, I was drawn to a passage in the introduction to *Less Than Nothing*. The "'fundamental insight' of Hegel," he says, "resides in transposing an epistemological obstacle into the thing itself, as its ontological failure (what appears to us as our inability to know the thing indicates a crack in the thing itself, so that our failure to reach the full truth is the indicator of truth)."[106] Really! To declare that *since* humans are unable to reach the full truth about creation, the truth is that there is a basic fault in creation, seems like authoritarian Master language, the very kind of language that a few pages later he resists as he declares it to be his "great task ... to articulate a space for a revolt which will not be recaptured by one or another version of the discourse of the Master."[107] The pressing question: why trust that our inability to "know the full truth" is "the indicator of truth" about

---

105. Žižek, *Less Than Nothing*, 112.
106. Žižek, *Less Than Nothing*, 17.
107. Žižek, *Less Than Nothing*, 19.

the nature of creation? Perhaps it indicates a truth that humans are not omnipotent, their abilities not unlimited, that the mystery of existence may be beyond human comprehension?

My wager (the opposite of Žižek's) is that the Real is not the crack, the Void, the self-repelling Gap, "the 'less than nothing,' of the pure Real,"[108] but the excess of self-generating Love. If we go all the way down, we land, not in the negativity of the abyss, but in the fecund matrix of God's Love, a love without limits. Žižek claims that "what repeats itself is the Real itself, which, lost from the beginning, persists in returning again and again."[109] In an upside down way, I agree. What repeats itself is the Real itself (Love), which, betrayed at the beginning (for me, not lost), persists in returning again and again. Creation itself attests to God's desire to be desired by us; and our desire, not only for the other, but for the other's desire, is central to how and in what manner we image God. To love is to image God. Which makes genuine love more than simply a human creation. Not "less than nothing'" but "nothing less than love," thanks be to God, *grace à Dieu*.

108. Žižek, *Absolute Recoil*, 414.
109. Žižek, *Less Than Nothing*, 381.

CHAPTER 3

THINKING GOD OTHERWISE: SOVEREIGNTY WITHOUT SOVEREIGNTY

Instead of speaking of God's omnipotence in terms of sheer power over any and everything, I suggested in the previous chapter that we need to conceive of divine omnipotence as the unfailing, everlasting, outlasting power of Love. In this chapter, I want to extend and deepen this discussion with reference to philosopher Jacques Derrida's discussions of sovereignty.

Derrida refers to God as "this One and Only God, to the determination of a sovereign, and thus indivisible, omnipotence."[1] Since Derrida describes sovereignty as a phantasm of self-grounding power, of omnipotence, of exclusion of difference, and self-identification as autonomy, it is no surprise that he rejects such a god. But that is not the end of the story; rather, it's only (so typically Derrida!) another beginning. He continues: "For wherever the name of God would allow us to think something else, for example a vulnerable nonsovereignty, one that suffers and is divisible, one that is mortal even, capable of contradicting itself or of repenting (a thought that is neither impossible nor without example), it would be a completely different story, perhaps even the story of a god who deconstructs himself in his ipseity."

Indeed, it is God as a "completely different story" that I would like to be part of the telling. For although the death of the sovereign "god of the philosophers" endangers any theology, philosophy, or let us say, metaphysics that claims the ability or assumes the possibility of properly categorizing or naming this God, it need not mean the death of the living God. I agree with thinkers as disparate as Nietzsche and Marion that often philosophers and theologians have postulated a God made in their own

---

1. Derrida, *Rogues*, 157.

image. "Early Christian theologians inherited primarily from Hellenistic philosophies" concepts such as "impassibility, immutability, simplicity, incorporeality, incomprehensibility, indivisibility" in developing the "classical-theistic concept of God."[2] Such an impassive, immutable God, like Aristotle's unmoved mover, exists in perfect isolation. Since being in relation[3] then becomes a secondary, accidental feature, God's intrinsic godhead is and remains unaffected by anything that happens or whatever occurs. The result was "concepts of deity that emerged as completely incompatible with suffering of any kind"[4] Such a God is invulnerable, supremely omnipotent, impassible, sovereign.[5]

However, this is at odds with the testimony of Scripture that God is Love, that is, a covenantal God of relation and in relation, a Compassionate God who suffers with creation, culminating in the coming of Jesus Christ as the Word made flesh, suffering, dying, and resurrecting. In his impressive two-volume study, *God's Wounds*, Jeff Pool canvasses the various historical attempts to recognize divine suffering as he contests the claims of God's impassibility and develops a hermeneutic of the Christian symbol of divine vulnerability and divine suffering. However, although recent theology is on the road to recovering "the biblical God, the 'suffering God,'"[6] [7] more attention needs to be given to what this confession of a vulnerable, suffering God means for understanding God's sovereign omnipotence. Is sovereignty and omnipotence, as Derrida suggests, a "phantasm of self-grounding autonomy" that is dangerous and needs to be rejected? Or is there a way, as I want to suggest, to think otherwise about sovereignty and omnipotence?

---

2. Pool, *God's Wounds*, I:2.

3. Relation, as Aristotle first formulated in his *Categories*, is regarded as an accident, an attribute which may or may not belong to a subject, without affecting its essence as substance. Consequently, classical Christian theology distinguished between God in himself as the immanent, ontological Trinity and the economic Trinity of God-in-relation-to-creation.

4. Pool, *God's Wounds*, 1:4. For Pool's explanation for why it was necessary to insist that Jesus suffered in his human nature, not in his divine nature, see *God's Wounds* 1:4–5.

5. For a classic statement, see Anselm's "Monologium," in *St. Anselm: Basic Writings*, 130–31.

6. Pool, *God's Wounds*, 1:9.

7. Biblical theologian Terence Fretheim's *The Suffering of God* was a groundbreaking book in this regard. Theologically, Jürgen Moltmann, with his fundamental belief that "God and suffering belong together" (*The Trinity and the Kingdom*, 49) played a significant role. William Placher's *Narratives of a Vulnerable God* deserves mention. As does Thomas E. Reynolds' *Vulnerable Communion: A Theology of Disability and Hospitality*.

Other thinkers, too, have begun to narrate a different story. Following the lead of Derrida, John Caputo in his *The Weakness of God*[8] has championed an unconditionality without sovereignty, without power, but not without force, although a weak force. In his extended discussion, Michael Naas also concludes that Derrida is not suggesting that we try to "think a purely godless sovereignty," but rather that we should "negotiate with a god without sovereignty, a god that, like *khôra* . . . [is] not only suffering or withdrawn but vulnerable in its very ipseity."[9]

Indeed, for me a god vulnerable in its very ipseity is the kind of God I can worship, before whom I can dance and sing. Why? Because such a God is a Compassionate God with a big heart—a heart of love—a God able to suffer and to suffer-with all who suffer. Thus, while I completely agree with Derrida that power's sovereignty as it has been generally conceived is a phantasm of self-grounding power, of omnipotence, of exclusion of difference, and of self-identification as autonomy, what if we were to think of God's sovereignty otherwise: as the sovereignty of love. That would still be sovereignty; but instead of sheer, naked power-over, it would be the power of love. As the power and authority of love, love sovereignty is invitational, evocative, vulnerable, able to suffer, alter, and improvise even as it remains enduring, steadfast, unbounded, and unconditional.

Since in traditional expositions sovereignty and vulnerability are considered opposites, this is thinking otherwise, a sovereignty without sovereignty in the usual understanding. It is to envision God's sovereign omnipotence not as the abstract, invulnerable, sheer power that can do anything and everything, but as the peculiar power inherent to Love, for that is who God is. Instead of the uninhibited power to act in perfect and absolute autonomy, to do whatever the Godself in splendid isolation pleases, the power of God as Love is self-giving, other-seeking, and power-sharing. It is the contrast between an unbridled *power-over* and the unlimited *power-with* of love. That is the thrust of this chapter, the spirit of this book: God's omnipotence is the omnipotence of love.

As an alternative to most orthodox theologies which teach that, in creating, God subjected the Godself to certain limitations[10] (including process theologian David Ray Griffin's effort to limit God's omnipotence with a view to safeguarding God's goodness in the face of evil[11]), I propose to

---

8. Caputo, *The Weakness of God*.

9. Naas, *Derrida From Now On*, 346.

10. See Pool's detailed discussion of "Constitutional Divine Self-Limitation," in *God's Wounds*, 1:138–39.

11. Griffin, *God, Power, and Evil*.

think of God's omnipotence differently, not as power-over or power-under, but as power-with: that is, the power of love creating, connecting, sustaining, empowering, partnering, renewing, regenerating. Love (Power-With) is unconditional, invitational, and sovereign, even as it is an empowerment that is risky and vulnerable, embraces difference, and self-identifies not as autonomous, but as generous and compassionate.

Traditional Sovereignty Models and the Reality of Evil

When God is confessed to be immutable, impassible, above and beyond all suffering, omnipotent, absolutely sovereign, theologians are hard put to explain how God is not blameworthy for all the evils in a world God announced was "very good." For, at the same time, this God is confessed to be supremely loving and morally righteous. If God is all-good and all-powerful, then whence the existence of evil?

Typically, theologians have resorted to talking of two "sides" in God, holiness and love, or justice and mercy: coercive power to keep evil in check and redemptive power to replace evil by good. Even then, as the endless discussions that continue to wage war bear witness, we still have a major problem. If God has both almighty power and boundless love, being the very height, length, and breadth of goodness, what about the reality of evil and the unabated horrors that continue to afflict our world? So the pursuit persists for morally good and sufficient reasons to explain why God does not exercise sheer divine power to prevent evil.[12] Some, in various versions of the free-will defense, surmise that God has created the best possible universe that God could which includes free moral agents. In the words of Alvin Plantinga: "Of course it is up to God whether to create free creatures at all; but if he aims to produce moral good, then he must create significantly free creatures upon whose co-operation he must depend. Thus is the power of an omnipotent God limited by the freedom he confers upon his creatures."[13]

But if God has the power to do anything that God wants, why would God not choose to create beings who would freely choose to do the right thing? "No doubt the theists would rather know what God's reasoning is for permitting evil than simply that it's a possibility that He has a good one. But in this present context . . . the latter is all that's necessary."[14]

Others, such as John Hick, have constructed eschatological theodicies in which, in the end, it will become clear that God uses all evil for

---

12. See Davis, *Encountering Evil*, for a good intramural discussion of the various options, as well as Phillips' exposition in *The Problem of Evil and The Problem of God*.
13. Plantinga, *The Nature of Necessity*, 190.
14. Adams and Adams, *The Problem of Evil*, 26–27.

good purposes. But why, if God is all-powerful, can God's good purposes only be achieved through the evils we suffer? The question becomes ever more pressing when we consider horrendous evils such as the Holocaust, or the utter randomness of so much evil that God apparently allows. Some, such as Calvinist theologian Stephen D. Davis, at this point simply plead ignorance: "But I do not know why God did not step in to prevent African slavery or destroy Hitler at birth."[15]

Although I certainly believe that it is important, at certain points, to fully acknowledge that there is mystery at the heart of reality beyond our human knowing, is this one of those points? For, at this juncture, despite all the turnings and twistings, the traditional sovereignty models leave us with at least an arbitrary, if not sadistic, God that I for one cannot love and adore. Despite all theodicies and other efforts at clarification, "[o]mnipotence," concludes Caputo, "cannot simply wash its hands of evil on the grounds that it has chosen not to intervene."[16] I couldn't agree more.

We surely need a different story. The story I want to begin telling has much in common with Caputo's. But whereas he proposes that we see the kingdom of God as "a domain in which weakness 'reigns,' . . . the provocative and uplifting weakness of God . . . the rule of weak forces like patience and forgiveness,"[17] I want to tweak his alternative vision by emphasizing the *vulnerability* of God rather than the "weakness" of God.

Because Caputo espies in what he calls "strong" theology a love of power, he makes a case for a "weak" theology. However, and this is my claim: beginning with God as love, we are able to recalibrate our understanding of power in terms not of sheer force and clout (power-over), but in terms of the alluring and potent and yet vulnerable dynamics of love (power-with). God's almighty power is precisely God's unfathomable power of Love. God's omnipotence is the with-power that God is: Love.

Divine Self-Limitation?

However, before I present a love-with model of sovereignty, it is worthwhile to look more closely at the problematic nature of traditional power-over models of sovereignty. Despite significant differences of detail, all traditional models appear to share a common assumption. In an effort to explain how an all-powerful God "allows" evil, they assert the self-limitation of divine power. But if God could have done otherwise, how does attributing self-limitation to God absolve God of at least some, if indirect,

---

15. Davis, "Rejoinder," in *Encountering Evil*, 101.
16. Caputo, *The Weakness of God*, 303.
17. Caputo, *The Weakness of God*, 14, 150.

THINKING GOD OTHERWISE: SOVEREIGNTY WITHOUT SOVEREIGNTY

responsibility for evil? I think we need to consider other possibilities. For my part, however well-intentioned, views that propose self-limitation on the part of God seem wrong-headed, only leading to the most unappealing dilemmas and unsatisfactory conclusions.

The problems involved with the idea of God's self-limitation, I suspect, involve incomplete and individualistic ways of thinking of both power and freedom. Power is conceived primarily as the power-to do something *to* another as an object rather than as the power-with of a partnership of subjects sharing power. In line with this, freedom is taken principally to be free-from (autonomy) rather than being-free-with (mutuality). Thus, it is said, God is absolutely free to create or not create, and as all-mighty has the power to permit or prohibit evil. However, since we have a creation in which evil is an undeniable reality, God must have freely chosen without any constraint to limit the power of the Godself, not only to create, but to bring into existence a creation in which evil was a built-in possibility. Otherwise, either God does not have the power, or God is a monster. Faced with this dilemma, the only acceptable conclusion would be self-limitation on the part of God—even though everyone recognizes that huge unanswered questions remain.

In his *Theology for a Scientific Age*, Arthur Peacocke surmises that it is "generally recognized" that in creating the world "God has subjected Himself to certain limitations."[18] More recently Old Testament theologian Terrence Fretheim summarizes the tradition: "God limits both the divine power and the divine freedom because God is committed to the structures of creation and their freedom."[19] All of which leads him to conclude in regard to natural disasters: "We cannot get God off the hook.... God cannot be removed from some kind of complicity."[20] As part of his first-rate exploration of God's suffering and vulnerability, Pool presents a thorough treatment of divine self-limitation. God as love, Pool expounds, is "God's freely-chosen fundamental character," and God will not contradict the divine character. At the same time, God "remains capable"[21] and "retains the freedom to violate the chosen divine character of love."[22] "In the actualization of God's being as love, God limits the divine self."[23] "Paradoxically," as Pool argues, "God would not be unlimited, if God were unable to set limits

---

18. Peacocke, *Theology for a Scientific Age*, 121–23.
19. Fretheim, *Creation Untamed*, 27.
20. Fretheim, *Creation Untamed*, 152.
21. Pool, *God's Wounds*, 1:138.
22. Pool, *God's Wounds*, 1:136.
23. Pool, *God's Wounds*, 1:165.

upon the divine self."²⁴ In creating the universe, God is said to withdraw, constrict, contract or retract the divine self in "order to allow creation to possess a reality distinct from God."²⁵ This "divine self-retraction . . . begins also to limit God's power, knowledge and presence."²⁶ ²⁷ At the same time, this implies that "God alone retains the responsibility, therefore, for the *possibility* that the creature might choose against the divine creator." Pool concludes: "Consequently, the most theologically-consistent Christian testimonies to divine suffering conceive of God as responsible for the *possibility* or *potentiality* of evil."²⁸

In my view, claiming that God needed to self-limit in order to allow room for creation and human freedom with all the attendant problems that ensue begins with the idea that freedom is essentially freedom-from (restriction), a belief that then leads to conceiving of difference-as-opposition. Consequently, the God/creation difference becomes one of opposition—God's sovereign freedom over against human freedom—rather than as a covenantal co-partnership of non-oppositional difference. Difference-as-opposition and freedom-from are notions which haunt all subsequent discussions. Immediately we are saddled with a hierarchical scenario in which there are only two possibilities: either (dominant) power-over or (submissive) power-under. Moreover, not only does this hierarchical framework adversely affect discussion of the God-human relation, but every sort of relationship from human-to-human, human-to-animal, animal-to-animal, animal-to-plant, plant-to-plant, and on and on, is profoundly shaped.

Along these lines, God, the omnipotent unmoved mover, at the top of the hierarchy, needs to self-limit in order allow creation and humanity its own space, power, and freedom. In turn, humans need to limit their individual, ethnic, and national self-interest by means of social contracts to ensure the advance of civilization and lessen the chances of war. Furthermore—moving down the chain of being—humans need to rein in their desire to exploit the environment in order to avoid planetary catastrophe.

---

24. Pool, *God's Wounds*, 1:166.

25. Pool, *God's Wounds*, 1:139.

26. Pool, *God's Wounds*, 1:147.

27. Jürgen Moltmann, appealing to Isaac Luria's doctrine of *zimzum* (contraction), has developed the most sophisticated version of God's self-limitation. "It is only a withdrawal by God into himself that can free the space into which God can act creatively" (*God in Creation*, 86–87). For incisive treatments of Moltmann's view, see Ansell, *The Annihilation of Hell*, and J. Matthew Bonzo, *Indwelling the Forsaken Other*.

28. Pool, *God's Wounds*, 1:153.

But what if freedom is not an autonomous freedom-from, but at root freedom-with, freedom-in-relation?[29] What if power is envisioned as power-with rather than power-over? To submit that God curtails divine power and freedom in order for there to be space for creation and the possibility of human freedom begins, in effect, by placing God and creation in a zero-sum oppositional economy such that the gain or loss of one participant is exactly balanced by the losses or gains of the other participant. In such a tit-for-tat framework, it is all about give-and-take trade-offs in an effort to achieve a measure of reciprocity between competing rivals—a far cry from a non-oppositional both-and mutuality of a God-creation covenantal partnership.

Although I fully concur with Pool's conviction that "nothing internal or external compels God to create,"[30] I do not read that as equivalent to saying that creation is an arbitrary could-not-have-been exercise, a choice God could not have made. Is that not to think of God rather like an Aristotelian "unmoved mover," a self-enclosed divine being, totally independent and free to do as Godself pleases? If God so desires to create, God creates; if not, well, then fine, it was not to be. In this way, unrestricted freedom—no necessity, neither internal nor external—is considered divine omnipotence. Is that not to ascribe to God the very autonomy that we image-bearers of God are prescribed from exercising?

Yet, it is said that God actualized—freely chose—the divine being as love, and therefore remains faithful to the divine character. But this actualization involves a limitation which God has the capacity and freedom to revoke. Divine limitation not only sets up creational space and human freedom as different and other than God's, but it is an over-against difference, in opposition to God. What is more, the restraint of divine limitation involved in creating implies complicity on God's part in the existence of evil—after all, God could have decided and acted otherwise. If God could have done otherwise, are we not left with a capricious if not sadistic God?

However, on the other hand, if God's omnipotent power and unbounded freedom is not sheer and unrestricted, but the omnipotence and freedom of Love, the picture changes dramatically. Then, God's freedom is not autonomy, but the with-freedom-of-love-and-to-love. Equally, God's being as love is not a measured choice once made, limiting or constraining divine omnipotence. By the nature of Godself, God is Love itself, *ipsum amare*. God creates—not by compulsion of any sort, nor by a could-not-have-been choice—but simply and profoundly, as Love, that is what Love

---

29. For an incisive critique of an autonomous view of freedom (freedom-from) in both classical theism as well as in Open Theism, see Hocking, *Freedom Unlimited*.

30. Pool, *God's Wounds*, 1:136.

is/does: Gifting and Calling. God's creative power is not over against creaturely power, that is, God's sovereignty is not over against human freedom. God need not self-limit in order to allow human freedom. Rather, as gift and call, God's sovereign power of love *gifts* creation into existence and *calls* creation to a sharing co-partnership of responsive participation in the on-going, open-ended process of history.

The covenantal God-creation relationship is then not a kind of tit-for-tat, zero-sum relationship of scarce and limited resources, but an intimate co-partnership intensifying, expanding, and passing on the love that is ours in God who is Love Abundant. Rather than a strategic self-limitation of the power of God, creation is the generous, unlimited bursting-out of the power of love, the brimming-over of the creative dynamic of love, the generous, excessive, inexhaustible, divine out-reach.

God/Love is of the Godself, creative, reaching out to the other in generosity and grace. God's creative outpourings initiate, inaugurate, invoke, provoke, direct and lead, but, as the let-there-be's of love, they do not coerce, dictate, or overdetermine creation's be-comings and be-goings. Indeed, God empowered and invited creation and all its creatures to participate in the creative process itself.[31] But since a loving partnership involves sharing power, needing and depending on each other, there is always risk, uncertainty, and vulnerability.

And . . . things did go wrong, terribly wrong. That humanity chose evil was not what God expected. Love does not imagine rejection. God was surprised, frustrated, and angered by the refusal, rejection, manipulation, and betrayal of love. The appearance of evil was an inexplicable surd, bizarre, startling. Importantly, rather than the insurgence of evil indicating a measure of complicity or permission on God's part as is traditionally suggested or often inferred, evil's entrance highlights the vulnerability of God, a God who can suffer, be hurt and wounded.

In response, God/Love does what love does, that is, love evermore. John, the apostle of love, proclaims the Word, who is God, the God of Love, "became flesh and lived among us" (John 1:14, NRSV). Love, showing itself as a God whose name is Compassion, suffers-with us. Consequently, all of humankind and with us the whole creation yearns for and lives in the hope and in the promise of a Future in which Love outlasts evil, a Future in which God is All-in-All.

---

31. See Middleton, *The Liberating Image*, 278–89, on the wish/command force of the let-there-be's in the jussive mood.

Freedom-With and Power-With

Importantly, since humans bear the image of God, human power and freedom is to image God's power and freedom, the relational-*with* power and freedom of love. Human freedom is not freedom to be anti-God but the freedom to be-with: with God, oneself, others, and creation. In this way, human freedom is not freedom-from, as the independent, as-if-in-a-vacuum autonomous freedom to choose goodness or evil.[32]

That is: we are not free to do evil (even if it is evil that we do). We are only free to love, and we are only free when we love. In and through loving and being loved each of us becomes more the unique selves we are gifted and called to become. In not loving and being loved each of us is stymied and frustrated in becoming our unique selves.

At the heart of freedom-with is the opportunity to enact new and fitting ways to love appropriate to our singular identities and circumstances. Due to the fact that the historical process never stops, and change is unending for everyone and everything, displaying integrity of character and faithfulness to commitments calls for what Derrida so aptly named "nonidentical repetition": declaring and exercising love in always varying and nuanced ways. Continually recalibrating our ways of enacting love to stay the course is at the heart of freedom.

Accordingly, we have no choice in the sense of being free to love or not to love—as if both are authentic choices. When in love, to be free is to love, and to love is to be free. Deciding not to love or to limit one's love is not in that sense a legitimate choice. It is to make the wrong choice. Love frees one (only) to love. The relational with-nature of freedom comes vividly to the fore when one considers the situation of fish in a fishbowl. Fish are only free to be fish, not when they choose to jump out of the fishbowl and go it on their own—an attempt to be autonomous, which means their death—but when they enjoy to the full their watery world.

The fact that, in the enigma of sin, we miss the mark of love and do evil has nothing to do with freedom, but everything to do with bondage: being caught up by life-diminishing, life-destroying forces, whether by fear, anger, hurt, aware or unaware. The apostle John sums it up: "Whoever does not love abides in death" (1 John 3:14, NRSV). Authentic freedom does not involve a choice to say "no" to the with-character of love, and the God of Love—the very

---

32. See Ansell, "The Call of Wisdom/The Voice of the Serpent," for an astute reading of Genesis 3 that calls into question the traditional assumption that Adam and Eve had the autonomous freedom to choose for or against God. Ansell argues that God's prohibition against eating was not, as conventionally understood, a test of obedience, but a warning to an immature humanity that the road to wisdom is not without risk and temptation.

conditions of freedom—thus attempting/pretending autonomy. Autonomy—being a law unto oneself—is not freedom, but missing the mark of love in solitary isolation. Authentic freedom is saying "yes, yes" to God's originating "Yes" of love and be(com)ing emissaries of love in the world.

In this context, it is particularly important to not frame and understand enacting or embodying love as heteronomous, that is, as compliance with an external order from outside or acquiescence to something or someone extrinsic. True freedom is neither being free-from (autonomy) nor is it submission to another (heteronomy). The autonomy or heteronomy binary has a built-in oppositional character (either I am free to do as I please or I relinquish my freedom and comply) which is unable to do justice to authentic freedom.[33]

God's Love-Word is not an on-high external edict demanding submission. Rather it is a Word gifting life which calls and invites each of us to find our identity and freedom in be(com)ing agents of love in the world. Only when a person resists or rejects the call of love does it have oppositional force. Genuine freedom is relational freedom-with, being in league with God, the God of Love who is with us and for us. Paraphrasing Augustine: Love and (you are free to) do as you will, because when you love, what you are pleased to do is enact love.

God: Trinity of Love

God is love itself, *ipsum amare*. This is crucial because it means that, as love, the Godself is not a being with an array of attributes, among them aseity, omnipotence, omniscience, and love. Rather, since the Godself is Love, all of God's attributes are dimensions of love. The only power that God has is the power that God is: Love. Out of the overflowing of the excess and passion of Love itself the creation came into being. God's love is the "Yes more 'ancient,'"[34] the Yes we are to iterate and reiterate in our lives.

Love in this understanding is not a Platonic *eidos*, nor a regulative Kantian idea; it is the gifting/calling originary Yes from God which is the creating/sustaining/attracting energy of the universe. Love is a gifting: the creation, all creatures, we, I—all are loved into being, therefore there is creational life, therefore we are/I am. Simultaneously, Love is a calling: We/I love in order to be. Julia Kristeva concludes: "I am to the extent that I am

---

33. On the need to move beyond the inadequacies of the autonomy/heteronomy binary, see Hocking, *Freedom Unlimited*, 47–73. For an illuminating discussion of Moltmann's view of freedom not as autonomy, but as "participation in God's goodness," see Ansell, *The Annihilation of Hell*, 368–84.

34. Jacques Derrida, "Ulysses Gramophone," in *Acts of Literature*, 296.

loved, therefore I love in order to be." That is a notion, she notes, that is not only possible for postmoderns, but which was "for the medieval thinker... an implicit definition of the subject's being."[35]

We begin to get an inkling of the far-ranging and deep-going implications of identifying love as the creative energy and moving power of life—*the conatus amandi*—when we remember that, as was discussed in chapters 1 & 2, traditionally love and power were and still often are contrasted. Within these parameters, all sorts of self-maintaining ontologies of power developed in which the other and the different were overpowered, domesticated, cordoned off, or eliminated. In such schemes, power is self-interest and loveless, while love is other-directed and powerless. Indeed, that is why a Levinasian ethics which emphasizes responsibility for the other must be "otherwise than being," a "total gratuity breaking with interest."[36]

Re-envisioning being as *conatus amandi* (the impulse to love) rather than as *conatus essendi* (the drive to be in itself) is a difference that makes all the difference. Power is no longer the drive to overpower others, but the power is the drive to *connect-with* others. Which brings us back to the immediate focus of this chapter: since God is love, and love seeks connection, creation is no surprise. God is all about *with-ing*. "To be God is to be Creator of the world."[37] Love/God seeks the other, disseminating, overflowing. Com[with]passion is God's best name. God-with-us, Immanuel, is who God is: Love.

Since God's action is identical with God's being—a central tenet of orthodox theology—God's creative activity is an act of unbridled, uninhibited, rampant generosity. Creation is the first incarnation of love: *creatio ex amore Dei*. Indeed, God's activity in the world is always entirely incarnational, all about the flourishing of love in the flesh by the Spirit. To be creaturely is to be spirited, living by inhaling and exhaling the Breath, *Ruach*, the Spirit of God. To-be-in-relation with self, other selves, creation, and God is to be alive, and to be in good connection with self, others, creation, and God is what it means to flourish.

Creation, then, is not the exhibition of God's sheer, unmitigated power, but the communiqué of the power of God's steadfast, unconditional love. "'All things are possible with God' does not mean his undetermined omnipotence; it means the determined power of his goodness."[38] This determined power of God's goodness is the power of God's love. Love

---

35. Kristeva, *Tales of Love*, 171.
36. Levinas, *Otherwise Than Being*, 96.
37. LaCugna, *God for Us*, 355.
38. Moltmann, *God in Creation*, 168.

and power are not two separate attributes; God's power is the power that God is: Love. Importantly, this enables us to move beyond the binary opposition between freedom and necessity. As love, God's freedom is the freedom of and to love. At the same time, since love as love is creative, creation happens irrepressibly.

God is the Trinity of Love which the church has confessed in the doctrine of the Trinity. Love as God the Father/Mother is creator. Love as God the Son is the Wisdom, the pattern by which and through which the creation is made, and, subsequently, the Incarnate Word made flesh to redeem it from evil. Love as God the Spirit is the unremitting, incessant, luminous, shining, creative, life-giving energy of the universe, and the resurrectionary power which outlasts death.

Along with Catherine LaCugna, I take talk of the Trinitarian *perichoresis* (mutual intercommunion) not to be detailing the internal workings of the Godhead in a divine metaphysics, but rather, as a theopoetic doxology affirming not only the intrinsic relationality of God and the intrinsic relationality of creational existence, but especially the intrinsic dance-like relationality of the God-creation connection. "God and the world interpenetrate each other in mutual *perichoresis*."[39] In this vein, postmodernist philosopher Peter Sloterdijk has recently credited the Christian perichoretic tradition as teaching that "everything is disposed towards interdependence."[40] God, Eros, gifts/invites; creation responds. History is the story of God and creation's cosmic, covenantal dance. It is an on-going two-way process: the Word of Love becoming flesh, and the flesh becoming Word (letters of Love).

The Beautiful Risk: Creation

Creation, as I suggested in chapter 1, was not created *ex nihilo*, but *ex amore*. That is crucially important, because built-in to God's creative movement power of love is its intrinsic vulnerability. God's Love is not coercive power-over; it is the invitational sovereignty of power-with. Power-with signifies freedom, multiplicity, mutuality, covenants, relationships—all featuring risk and vulnerability.

God is vulnerable in God's very ipseity. In creating, God put Godself at risk. Love may be rejected, thwarted, disappointed, trampled. God—the very passion of Love—was and is challenged, hurt and wounded by the lies of hate, the forces of fear, and the maneuvers and betrayals of evil.

---

39. Moltmann, *The Coming of God*, 327.
40. Sloterdijk, *Bubbles*, 625. I owe this reference to Dean Dettloff.

God's first and last word is "Yes." Nevertheless, that does not and did not save God from being haunted by a shadow, a darkness, an evil that contradicts the originary Yes. God was surprised, shocked, grieved, and wounded by the powers of evil. So taken back that in Genesis 6 we read that God "was sorry that he had made humankind on the earth, and it grieved him to his heart." So much so that God said "I will blot out from the earth the human beings I have created—people together with animals and creeping things and birds of the air, for I am sorry that I have made them" (Gen. 6:6-7, NRSV). Significant and striking for our purposes, the next verse in Genesis tells us that Noah found grace in the eyes of God, and God pulled back from her resolve to destroy the world. God, the Faithful One, does not abandon creation. So, when Noah walked with God, God responds as the Compassionate One and repents of her resolve to destroy. Nevertheless, evil must be confronted, and God recruits Noah in her campaign to redeem the world from evil. The Yes of love is a No to evil.

In our world in which there is so much involuntary suffering-from, God, the Compassionate One, willingly suffers-with creation.[41] "Were God incapable of suffering in any respect, and therefore in an absolute sense, then he would also be incapable of love."[42] Evil and sinful acts frustrate, squelching and stifling the flow of love in the world. The image of God is besmirched, dimmed, and we are estranged from God, who nevertheless continues to both seek us and suffer-with us. On the cross Love went the limit to death.

The Cross—starkly and palpably—indicates that the omnipotence of love can be resisted, wounded, broken, and sacrificed. "For God so loved the world, that he gave his only Son" (John 3:16). The cost of such love, in the face of evil, turned out to be exorbitant. God's own son was reviled, rejected, abandoned, crucified.

But death is not the end: Love, the alpha word, is also the omega Word. Love keeps coming back, Christ's resurrection being a foretaste of the renewal of all things until God will be all in all. Love is stronger than death. The risk and vulnerability of Divine Love is, paradoxically, the secret of its unstoppable power. We have the Promise that Love will keep on coming, outlasting death. Love is undeconstructible. Meanwhile, we live in-the-between of suffering love, sustained by the extraordinary logic of hope,[43] hearts aflame, cross-eyed—one eye fixed on the tasks at hand, the other eye fixed on Love's becoming All in All.

---

41. See Fretheim. *The Suffering of God*, ch. 8, "God Suffers With," 127–37.
42. Moltmann, *The Crucified God*, 230.
43. See Ricoeur, "Hope and the Structure of Philosophical Systems," in *Figuring the*

Anomos Nomos

The call of Love is unconditional, what Derrida would call an anomos nomos, a law above all conditioned plural laws. Love rules unconditionally, not with the sovereignty of sheer power, but with the invitational sovereignty of love. It is sovereignty without sovereignty.

Unconditional love is not a telos or a goal that we work toward as a regulative idea. Nor is it a utopian model that keeps our eyes transfixed. Love is the driving force and energy of all that we do in the here and now. It is what creates, sustains, and redeems human experience, accounting for the very concept and experience of love itself.

At the same time, as Derrida repeatedly emphasized in many of his analyses, unconditional love is immediately conditioned when it is enacted, positivized and codified. The unconditional becomes effective through conditioning in terms of time, place, and preferences. It is only in the name of unconditional love that any love, inscribed historically in all its conditionality, can be offered. Since time moves on, places change, and history advances, love's existential conditions will necessarily need to be calibrated, nuanced, revised, and updated. Moreover, since human agency is fallible and finite, subject to all the vagaries of flesh and blood, struggling with evil, actual embodiments may be obstacles to love's enactment, delaying its advance, in truth and fact, betraying its genius.

Nevertheless—in contrast to Derrida and Caputo—I do not see any compelling reason why such codifications or enactments necessarily or inevitably pervert and betray. Yes, often attestations of love are perversions and betrayals. But not always, and not necessarily! Most everyone experiences love in some form or way. And yes, the giving and receiving of love is time-bound, and the keeping of love alive and well is risky, easily torpedoed. Nonetheless, in such conditioned experiences the gift of God's love is seen, tasted, and celebrated. Indeed, it is these experiences that redeem life from ridiculousness, insignificance, from shock and revulsion. For me the figure of Christ is, in the words of Jean-Luc Marion, a case *par excellence* of the event of love's incarnation.[44] That is, I read the reality that the Word became flesh and dwelt among us as a concrete, contingent, conditioned event in which the unconditional determinately, decisively, and discernibly was incarnated. In short, in spite of the violence, evil, and horrors which are so pervasive, love is incarnating, becoming real among us as the Kingdom of God aborning.

Sacred, 203–16.

44. Marion, *Being Given*, 237.

The Sovereignty of Love

The kingdom of God—perhaps better, the kindom of God to avoid the kingly connotation—is a domain in which love points the way. It is an astonishing, strange, and wonderful kindom that is not ruled by right, power, or sovereign omnipotence. However, to then describe, along with Caputo, God's love as "powerless power" and "weak force,"[45] seems too weak. Yes, love is a different kind of power (power-with and not power-over); but powerless? Love is "weak" only in the sense that it is not coercive. Coercive force can make us go through the external motions of acquiescence and compliance, but it can never bring with it the internal assent, enthusiasm, and impetus that marks a freely chosen response of the heart. Love's force is evocative, invitational, alluring. Love—the fierce passion that gives us heart, the energy, the oxygen coursing through the life-blood of our veins, enabling and encouraging intercourse with others without mastery, hostility, or fusion—is the secret that is no secret at the heart of life. Love is the strongest power and passion in the world. Love creates all things, carries all things, calls all things together, bears all things, redeems all things.

God—not a transcendent Super Entity, nor a Heideggerian Being of beings, but the mysterious, intimate power of Love—is the pulsating energy, the surging and resurging Spirit-breath of creation. Right at this point, Caputo's insistence that "God requires our existence and so depends on us . . . God insists, while we exist"[46] needs emphatic underlining. "Whether God [read: Love] comes to exist depends on whether we resist or assist [God's] insistence."[47] Love is so often in exile, hard to come by, overshadowed by evil. God depends on us to enact it and make God's name existent in the world. We are invited in community to breathe-in and breathe-out this love in embodied acts of mercy, justice, and forgiveness. Although the creation is charged-with-love, it is not love-saturated. The discharge of love—making love present in the world—is up to us.

Tragically, as history bears bloody witness, we have too often done a terrible job with the awesome responsibility of embodying love. The very worst things have been done in the name of love. Love—what we think or name as our love—can and has led to horrific violence. Think only of the Crusades, the Holocaust, the lynching of black people in the American South, 9–11, on and on. White supremacy, racism, sexism, to this day, still have the support of many Christians. And we may not forget that many of the mob who stormed the US Capitol on January 6, 2021, protesting the loss of Donald Trump and

---

45. Caputo, *The Weakness of God*, 316.
46. Caputo, *The Insistence of God*, 13.
47. Caputo, *The Insistence of God*, 14.

representing many far-right, white supremacist interests, professed love for Jesus and bore signs that read "Jesus saves." How we think love presents itself in the world can be a perversion of love.

My act of faith, the words of blessing by which I end (and begin), is: Let Love come again and again. *Viens, oui, oui.* It is a yes-saying that goes beyond the sovereignty of the self, a saying that is "good because it comes from beyond our power and knowledge, a saying that does not first and foremost express, like a constative, or even perform or make happen, like a performative, but that bears witness and, in bearing witness, 'is' an event."[48] Let us, as Jesus said, "Be merciful, just as your Father is merciful" (Luke 6:36, NRSV). Let us together hold high the markers and rules of love's action that Jesus himself laid out in Matthew 25: feed the hungry, take in the stranger, clothe the naked, visit the sick. Let us bear witness by protesting and resisting evil through eventing love.

---

48. Naas, *Derrida From Now On*, 7.

CHAPTER 4

TAKING THE WAGER OF/ON LOVE: LUCE IRIGARAY AND THE CARESS

"My dear friends, keep yourselves within the love of God."

—Jude 21

IN HER PROLOGUE TO *i love to you*, Luce Irigaray tells of the "miracle"[1] that happened when a debate with a man surprisingly turned into a "meeting with the other, the different" in the between, in "mutual respect." "We were two: a man and a woman speaking in accordance with our identity, our conscience, our cultural heritage, and even our sensibility."[2] Since that time, more than ever, Irigaray has been an avid "political militant for the impossible, which is not to say a utopian." Rather, in Derridean fashion, she wants "what is yet to be as the only possibility of a future." All her subsequent publications (*the Way of Love* and *to be two* deserve special mention) have been dedicated to preparing for a wisdom which "opens the way to another becoming, a becoming woman, a becoming man, a becoming together."[3]

Since thematizing love has been an abiding concern for me throughout my life, I have found Luce Irigaray a most congenial and inspiring philosophic partner. The affinity is deepened due to the fact that for both of us—Irigaray is a psychoanalyst in addition to being a philosopher, while I am a psychotherapist as well as a philosopher—nurturing of mutuality is an existential concern. Her concern, my concern, is to work for philosophy as the wisdom of love, which, in her words, is fuller, richer, more crucial, than the, "above all mental, wisdom which Western philosophy has claimed to be."[4]

1. Irigaray, *i love to you*, 7.
2. Irigaray, *i love to you*, 9.
3. Irigaray, *to be two*, 55.
4. Irigaray, *the Way of Love*, vii.

In this chapter, I set out to join Irigaray in her efforts to "prepare for a wisdom of love between us."[5] In her efforts to see philosophy as plural (the love of wisdom, and the wisdom of love[6]), Irigaray sets out to develop what she hopes may become the "third era of the West . . . of the spirit and the bride" a "new ethics of the passions."[7] In particular, I will take up her insistence that we need to attend to what she variously addresses as "a third term": the "between" (or the "interval," the "divine," "angel," "air," "spirit," "god," and "love"). Only if we attend to the "between" will we be able to give shape to a sexual ethics in which "man and woman may once again or at last live together, meet, and sometimes inhabit the same place."[8] Beginning from sexual difference, Irigaray sets out to develop what I call a paradigm of non-oppositional difference in which the divine as Love is both discovered and generated in the "between." The tapestry she is weaving for "the redemption of women" and "the redemption of love"[9] contains at least six threads and strands: wonder, the interval, irreducible difference, the excess of love, mucous and air, and Love's caress.

Always Wonder

Difference bedazzles and delights. Difference gives rise to wonder, and wonder evokes desire. Irigaray, standing in the tradition of Plato, Aristotle, Descartes, and Kant, identifies wonder[10] as the first passion, indispensable to the creation of an ethics, a passion that calls us beyond the realm of the same and motivates us to know the other. As she succinctly states, "Wonder must be the advent or the event of the other."[11] That other to which we are drawn in wonder is "impossible to delimit, im-pose, identify (which is not to say lacking identity and borders): the atmosphere, the sky, the sea, the sun."[12] It is wonder that keeps the "space of freedom and attraction between" the sexes, "a possibility of separation and alliance."[13] Each of us finds

---

5. Irigaray, *the Way of Love*, vii.
6. Irigaray, *the Way of Love*, 2.
7. Irigaray, *An Ethics of Sexual Difference*, 148, 12.
8. Irigaray, *An Ethics of Sexual Difference*, 17.
9. See Irigaray, *Key Writings*, 150, 169.
10. It is also worth remembering that both Plato and Aristotle identify wonder as the motivation for philosophizing: Aristotle, *Metaphysics*, in *The Complete Works of Aristotle* 2:982b12–13: "For it is owing to their wonder that men both now and at first began to philosophize." Plato in *Theaetetus*, 155 D "For this feeling of wonder shows that you are a philosopher, since wonder is the only beginning of philosophy."
11. Irigaray, *An Ethics of Sexual Difference*, 75.
12. Irigaray, *An Ethics of Sexual Difference*, 89.
13. Irigaray, *An Ethics of Sexual Difference*, 13.

ourself in a network of relations that is our *Befindlichkeit*, the hermeneutics of facticity. *Il y a difference, es gibt die Differenz.* "Generally," as Irigaray puts it, "the phrase *there is* upholds the present but defers celebration."[14] In fact, "there is," in its neutrality and abstractness, leads to quite abstract and non-specific discussions which hide the fact that they are hopelessly male and exclusively homogeneous.[15] *Es gibt*—there is—misses the "wonder of the *wedding*, an ecstasy that remains *in-stant*."[16]

For Irigaray, the abstract *there is* is no longer neutral as in Heidegger, without fecundity and copulation. The "divine is present as the mystery that animates the copula."[17] *There is* gives way to "'we are' or 'we become,' 'we live here' together."[18] In wonder, the other is no longer something to get a jump on, surmount, get beyond (Nietzsche), overcome (Heidegger), or lift up (Hegel), but a particular flesh and blood person with whom to dance in glory and grace. When that pas de deux occurs, "a sensible transcendental—the dimension of the divine par excellence"[19]—comes into "being through us, in which *we would be* the mediators and bridges."[20] When an "enstatic" meeting between the sexes transpires, there is a simultaneous two-way movement: the flesh becomes word, and the word becomes flesh.[21] As Irigaray explains, however, too often "attraction, greed, possession, consummation, disgust, and so on"[22] have defused the wonder in efforts to control or bridge the gap to the other and avoid the inherent risks of loving another. The whole patriarchal tradition has been "marred by an original sin: to have mistaken the reason of man for the universal."[23] In the process, love, entrusted to woman, has been confined to home, and woman becomes a home for man without a home for herself.

---

14. Irigaray, *An Ethics of Sexual Difference*, 14.

15. In this vein it is instructive to note, as does Derrida in *Spurs*, that Heidegger does not discuss the issue of sexual difference. Moreover, as Levinas remarks, for Heidegger, Dasein is never hungry (*Totality and Infinity*, 134).

16. Irigaray, *An Ethics of Sexual Difference*, 14.

17. Irigaray, *An Ethics of Sexual Difference*, 19.

18. Irigaray, *An Ethics of Sexual Difference*, 129.

19. Irigaray, *An Ethics of Sexual Difference*, 115.

20. Irigaray, *An Ethics of Sexual Difference*, 129.

21. My emphasis on the two-way movement in Irigaray contrasts with Margaret Whitford's reading of Irigaray, which highlights the flesh becoming word as an "audacious reversal" of the traditional "word becomes flesh" (*Luce Irigaray: Philosophy in the Feminine*, 48).

22. Irigaray, *An Ethics of Sexual Difference*, 13.

23. Irigaray, *i love to you*, 147.

Irigaray begins her response by asking why we have to give up love in order to become wise or learned. "It is love that leads to knowledge, whether in art or more metaphysical learning. It is love that leads the way and is the path. A mediator par excellence."[24] For Irigaray the subordination of the feminine is both a clue to and a symbol for all kinds of imbalance and cultural pathologies. Reason-coded masculinity and transcendence is, she is saying, pathological. That in no way means a denial of rationality. She does see the need to reconstruct and reconceptualize knowledge as issuing from passion. Knowledge is generated by love, and losing that source is the critical tragedy of modern epistemologies in which technology, the deification of rationality, is encoded as masculine at the expense of the passions, which are encoded as feminine. In other words, it is not the reality of love or the concept of love that is the problem, but Western rationality that excludes its primordial source and then presumes to name love and woman the irrational residue that deifies symbolic law.

Interval as Border and Entrance

In the conventional, modernist view, space is a mode of isolation. Every body occupies its own place, with clearly defined boundaries, in splendid isolation with empty space yawning between it and every other body. This mechanical view of space as a vacuum leads to a view of the absolutely different as merely numerically and spatially distinguished, while otherwise absolutely the same. In such a view, space, working like a vacuum, prevents overlapping. Like Newtonian billiard balls bouncing into each other, relationships remain external, not altering the inner essences. Since, according to this understanding, two distinct bodies cannot coincide, if a man and a woman each has his or her own space, there arises an immense problem when they come together. The only two possibilities in the oppositional bumping that takes place are, finally, domination of one over the other (whether through force or voluntary submission) or monadic isolation (with no real connection). Working with such a theory of space, Freud developed his view of transference in which subjects pathologically project their understandings through the vacuity of space onto other persons. Since, for Freud, the fundamental issue is intrapsychic (how can the ego manage its unruly id), other people are primarily objects to be used in pursuit of an individual's self-realization; consequently, little attention is actually paid to interpsychic subject-subject relations. Moreover, and more ominously, love of the other happens at the expense of love of self.

---

24. Irigaray, *An Ethics of Sexual Difference*, 29.

According to quantum physics, however, space is not a fixed grid where things are simply here and not there. There is no space between separate objects, no separate objects, and even no such notion as separate. Space is not an emptiness or a lack, but a continuum of greater or lesser densities of energy, a field of forces characterized by excess and fluidity without clear boundaries. Since space is not a thing, but a mode of existence dealing with extension, we are better served by talking of a spatial dimension. The way space is experienced and represented depends on the entities that are positioned and in particular the kinds of relations that subjects experience. A subject or object in its spatiality is connected and has parts without simple distinction of inner and outer. There are no isolated persons or things. At the same time, it is not that persons and things lack self-identity. It is rather that interrelationship with others is intrinsic to each person's self-definition and each thing's identity. One's core identity is a textured web shaped, altered, transformed, or traumatized in, through, and by (dis)connecting with others.

Irigaray creatively stretches the new spatial sensitivity into what could be called a "quantum ethics": space fulfills itself as an ethico-spiritual place of mutuality, with the interval as the place where the divine happens. Irigaray reconceptualizes space as "the interval that is both entrance and the space between," the only possibility for "unhindered movement, of peaceful immobility without the risk of imprisonment"[25] between the sexes. The "between-us" is the space where identity and difference constantly intermingle, not in an economy of dialectic opposition, but in an economy of non-oppositional difference with difference and closeness, difference and connection. In short, it is an economy of love.

The only path to mutuality for Irigaray is to give due place to a "third term,"[26] a mediator, intermediary, or interval, that is a "between."[27] The interval that "cannot be done away with"[28] is the place of the "production of intimacy."[29] The "third" acts as both entrance and border, and borders always connect by separating and separate by connecting. These between-spaces—what I call the wild spaces of love[30]—are the spaces of freedom and attraction that establish both singularity and connection without separation or fusion.

25. Irigaray, *An Ethics of Sexual Difference*, 120.
26. Irigaray, *An Ethics of Sexual Difference*, 12.
27. Irigaray, *An Ethics of Sexual Difference*, 53.
28. Irigaray, *An Ethics of Sexual Difference*, 49.
29. Irigaray, *An Ethics of Sexual Difference*, 53.
30. Olthuis, *The Beautiful Risk*, 48–49; also *Knowing Other-Wise*, 3. The spaces are wild because they are uncharted and venturing into them is to take the beautiful risk. They can become pastures of love, but they can also be battlefields of hate.

Taking the interval seriously is to recognize that a change is needed in the economy of desire. Without the interval as third term, "he or she becomes all-powerful."[31] Traditionally, man expresses desire, and woman is the desirable. But, Irigaray argues, since "overcoming the interval is the aim of desire,"[32] if desire is to exist as other than the all-powerful, possessive and deadly, a "double desire,"[33] or "double place," or "double envelope is necessary."[34] With female and male desire interacting, back and forth, to and fro, a "chiasmus or a double loop"—or spiral, as I prefer—is produced in which "each can go toward the other and come back to itself."[35]

It is not for Irigaray a matter "of substituting feminine power for masculine power. Because this reversal would still be caught up in the economy of the same."[36] Instead of the phallus as bridge, Irigaray talks of "angels" circulating as mediators to "destroy the monstrous"[37] and of the mediating "God" who insures the "reciprocal limitation"[38] of both man's and woman's envelopes. Unless space becomes a dwelling for living-with, a place of negotiation rather than a site of penetration and domination in which the phallus, penetrating female space, is considered the bridge between lovers, the same old battle of the sexes will continue unabated.

The genus of love must be constructed or reconstructed so that man and woman may once again, or at last, come together, meet in the middle, and sometimes inhabit the same place. Irigaray calls this rapturous coming together of the human and divine the sensible transcendental, which "is in some manner a transmutation of earth into heaven, here and now."[39] It is a parousia that is as fully corporeal (fleshly, tactile, fluid, viscous, personal, individual) as it is ethical (universal, transpersonal, harmonizing, divine). It is *jouissance*, "communion in pleasure."[40] In contrast to Lacan, where desire is the gap between demand and need, for Irigaray desire is the excess running over with wonder between the sexes. This turns male-female relations into celebrations with a sensibility that is transcendental rather than a master-slave polemic.

---

31. Irigaray, *An Ethics of Sexual Difference*, 12.
32. Irigaray, *An Ethics of Sexual Difference*, 48.
33. Irigaray, *An Ethics of Sexual Difference*, 9.
34. Irigaray, *An Ethics of Sexual Difference*, 48.
35. Irigaray, *An Ethics of Sexual Difference*, 9.
36. Irigaray, *This Sex Which Is Not One*, 129–30.
37. Irigaray, *An Ethics of Sexual Difference*, 15.
38. Irigaray, *An Ethics of Sexual Difference*, 93.
39. Irigaray, *An Ethics of Sexual Difference*, 53.
40. Irigaray, "Questions to Emmanuel Levinas," in Bernasconi and Critchley, *Re-reading Levinas*, 110.

"The link uniting or reuniting masculine and feminine must be horizontal and vertical, terrestrial and heavenly," with "both angel and body... found together."[41] Yet, although the "sensible transcendental" is a crucial notion for Irigaray, it remains, importantly and indispensably, complex, multivalent and mysterious.[42] The sensible transcendental is "an alliance between the divine and the mortal,"[43] "a permanent becoming,"[44] which confounds the opposition between immanence and transcendence,[45] a wedding of body and soul, sensation and mind, sexuality and spirituality, outside and inside, mortal and immortal, human and divine, female and male.

Irigaray reads Nietzsche's and Heidegger's cries about the "death of God" to be, paradoxically, "a summons for the divine to return as festival, grace, love, thought."[46] She desires the return of the divine in a form that humans can experience corporeally, a *jouissance* of the carnal, of flesh rejoicing with flesh, which would exist as "an accessible transcendental that remains alive."[47] For Irigaray—in distinction from Levinas—the caress and fecundity of eros is the caress and fecundity of the divine. The experience of the sensible transcendental is to be touched bodily with divinity, specifically divine "enstasy."

Irigaray develops this eros of transcendence in and through a refurbishing of a pre-Socratic philosophy of the four elements—"Earth, water, air, and fire are my birthright too"[48]—of which we are composed and in which

---

41. Irigaray, *An Ethics of Sexual Difference*, 17.

42. It is also, at points, ambiguous, as when she, in the fashion of Heraclitus, describes the sensible transcendental as "in some manner a transmutation" (Irigaray, *An Ethics of Sexual Difference*, 53), "a perpetual transvaluation" (Irigaray, *An Ethics of Sexual Difference*, 27), and "a resurrection and transfiguration of blood, of flesh through a language and an ethics that is ours" (Irigaray, *An Ethics of Sexual Difference*, 129). However, her general spirit and tone is not the oneness of the invisible harmony of ever-living fire underlying the warring tension of elements perpetually turning over into each other, as with Heraclitus, but rather her basic emphasis, with Empedocles, is on the harmonious coming together, the fitting together of an original plurality of elements, of transcendent and nontranscendent, divine and human without fusion. And although Empedocles does envision strife and ceaseless change as a cosmic state, in contrast to Heraclitus (and Heidegger), he (with Irigaray) does not have a primordial *polemos* that holds everything together in its warring tension. Empedocles—and Irigaray—find fault with strife, praise love, and seek to promote relations of love and works of peace.

43. Irigaray, *An Ethics of Sexual Difference*, 17.
44. Irigaray, *An Ethics of Sexual Difference*, 27.
45. Irigaray, *An Ethics of Sexual Difference*, 33.
46. Irigaray, *An Ethics of Sexual Difference*, 140.
47. Irigaray, *An Ethics of Sexual Difference*, 27.
48. Irigaray, *Elemental Passions*, 34.

we live. "They determine more, more or less freely, our attractions, our affects, our passions, our limits, our aspirations."[49] Irigaray finds Empedocles's original plurality of four elements, which are drawn together into a unity by Love and broken down by Strife or Hate, to be an astonishingly apt metaphor for pondering how the two sexes can retain their difference and connect in a higher communion without fusion.[50] For Irigaray, as for Empedocles, love is a "*daimon*,"[51] [52] a *conatus* or motivating force that brings things together and, in so doing, creates the opportunity for the fortuitous, miraculous, and aleatory (Derrida) coming into being of a "*sensible transcendental*," one of which "*we would be* the mediators and bridges."[53]

Irreducible Difference/Asymmetrical Mutuality

Irigaray says that staying with wonder in the "between" of the sexes will allow for a "nontraditional, fecund encounter between the sexes," which now "barely exists."[54] Moreover, it is important to note, "a love between the sexes . . . is essential to the discovery of an individual and collective happiness, one which is both empirical and transcendental."[55] Indeed, for her, "an ethics of the couple" acts as a kind of paradigm for possible changes in society. It serves as an "intermediary place between individuals, peoples, States."[56] Man and woman, woman and man, always meet as though for the first time, "because they cannot be substituted one for another."[57] Ontically, we are non-exchangeable, ultimately inaccessible mysteries to each other, existing in asymmetrical mutuality. "I recognize you is the one condition for the existence of I, you, and we."[58] Alterity is irreversible. "Who or what the other is, I never know" and remains "forever unknowable."[59]

49. Irigaray, *Sexes and Genealogies*, 57.
50. Grosz, *Sexual Subversions: Three French Feminists*, 169.
51. Irigaray, *An Ethics of Sexual Difference*, 23.
52. At the same time, it is worth noting that, in distinction from Empedocles, Irigaray does not talk about hate as the opposite *daimon* of rupture and repulsion, preferring to speak of "the failure of love" (*An Ethics of Sexual Difference*, 27) when it "appropriates the other for itself by consuming it" (Irigaray, *Elemental Passions*, 27). However, she does speak of "devils" in contrast to angels who are "mediators for heaven and earth" whose "job" it is "to disrupt and to confuse," blocking "mediation."
53. Irigaray, *An Ethics of Sexual Difference*, 129.
54. Irigaray, *An Ethics of Sexual Difference*, 6.
55. Irigaray, *Elemental Passions*, 5.
56. Irigaray, *Sexes and Genealogies*, 5.
57. Irigaray, *An Ethics of Sexual Difference*, 13.
58. Irigaray, *i love to you*, 104.
59. Irigaray, *An Ethics of Sexual Difference*, 13.

The other is a mystery to me, and I am a mystery to the other. Virginity, "a dimension of preservation of spiritual identity and becoming,"[60] is the mystery that safeguards each of us and calls for respect, the necessary condition for a word of love to be passed between us. "The veil of mystery" lets things and people be in their integrity, before any appearing. These veils are "woven of the air in which every living being lies: is born, lives, grows."[61] "Is it not," Irigaray asks rhetorically, "because I do not know you that I know that you are?"[62] We are irreducible in us, between us, and yet so close. Without this difference, how do we give each other grace? "The origin, if I can say this, of the love between us is silence."[63] The silence is two, the silence in me that I must protect, and the silence in you that I must respect.

The silence is also three, in that a third is "generated by the two but which does not belong to either."[64] Between us is the air in which we dwell and which dwells in us, touching us as an "invisible presence."[65] How do we share the air? How do we inhabit the air of the us?

We do so by listening "to the other's love."[66] And in listening and welcoming the other, we weave "a groundless ground," which does "not end in any ground"[67] but in a "co-belonging in the opening,"[68] an "interrelational world in which love happens." In other words, subjectivity is intersubjectivity.

Recognizing your difference and its mystery draws me to you, "attracts me, like a path of becoming. . . . I go towards that which enables me to become while remaining myself."[69] "I will never reach this other, and for that very reason, *he/she* forces me to remain faithful to *him/her* and *us*, retaining our difference."[70] But I am afraid of this space in between us, afraid that if I don't try to control the space between us, you will abandon me, and I will be alone. "Not in me but in our difference lies the abyss. We can never be sure

60. Irigaray, *Key Writings*, 163.
61. Irigaray, *the Way of Love*, 33.
62. Irigaray, *to be two*, 9.
63. Irigaray, *to be two*, 62.
64. Irigaray, *to be two*, 62.
65. Irigaray, *to be two*, 2.
66. Irigaray, *to be two*, 14.
67. Irigaray, *the Way of Love*, 72.
68. Irigaray, *the Way of Love*, 75.
69. Irigaray, *i love to you*, 104.
70. Irigaray, *i love to you*, 105.

of bridging the gap between us. But that is our adventure. Without this peril there is no us. If you turn it into a guarantee, you separate us."[71]

Between Us: The Excess of Love

For Irigaray—in distinction from thinkers such as Freud and Lacan—the other's unbridgeable singularity, which indelibly marks my incompleteness, always bespeaks an excess rather than a lack, a promise of enrichment more than an indictment of failure. The other person is not, in the first place, a burden, a competitor, or an enemy, but an invitation, a lightness of being—an "excess" that "resists" any and all efforts to "assimilation or reduction to sameness."[72] Love—"never fulfilled, always becoming"[73]—is the "irreducible mediator,"[74] the air that is not under the control of either party. "For lovers to love each other, between them must be Love."[75] "If the pair of lovers cannot safeguard the place for love as a third term between them, they can neither remain lovers nor give birth to lovers." The odyssey of love, therefore, is a "perpetual journey, a perpetual transvaluation, a permanent becoming"[76] with "no guard but love itself."[77]

Only in the flow of love is a person able to fashion an identity even as she or he is connected with another person. When love wells up as the energy of one's life, not only does one's unique identity take shape and form in a centripetal movement of gathering, but simultaneously, there is also a centrifugal movement outward of giving, sharing, and connecting. The two movements belong together. When my identity is an envelope of love, it is never closed off: "But when lips kiss . . . Closed lips remain open."[78] As Irigaray writes, "I love you makes, makes me, an other. Loving you, I am no longer the same; loved, you are different. Loving, I give myself to you. I become you. But I remain, as well, to love you still."[79] In contrast, when my identity is an envelope of fear, it is never really open, but in its dearth, remains defended against the other. The other—with whom I am inextricably bound—becomes an enemy that I try to appropriate in order to feed

---

71. Irigaray, *Elemental Passions*, 28.
72. Irigaray, *An Ethics of Sexual Difference*, 74.
73. Irigaray, *An Ethics of Sexual Difference*, 21.
74. Irigaray, *An Ethics of Sexual Difference*, 30.
75. Irigaray, *An Ethics of Sexual Difference*, 30.
76. Irigaray, *An Ethics of Sexual Difference*, 27.
77. Irigaray, *An Ethics of Sexual Difference*, 201.
78. Irigaray, *Elemental Passions*, 63.
79. Irigaray, *Elemental Passions*, 74.

my hunger and satiate my inner emptiness. Love, the "vital intermediary"[80] disappears—and envelopes become empty caverns, prisons, and eventually tombs. The interval remains as . . . "that gap—death."[81]

Air/Mucous

In love, the interval is not a gap, an abyss, or a container within an inside and an outside, but a threshold, an opening to a "communion beyond skins."[82] It is to "inhabit the air of the us."[83] "The air is sweet . . . it is as tender as a caress."[84] We "discover the divine between-us."[85] In the event of love, a "transcendence exists between us,"[86] and "in this infinite being touched, the wound vanishes."[87] Love, for Irigaray, is the air that brings us together and separates us."[88] In a subtle critique of Heidegger, she exclaims that "*to forget being is to forget air.*"[89] Heidegger's opening, clearing, or interval is too down-to-earth, too hemmed in, too regimented, too horizontal. It needs air. We need to escape the "waters of the womb" for the air. "Once we were fishes. It seems that we are destined to become birds."[90] Indeed, "[a]ir keeping the copula from hardening up or disappearing into is. 'To' and not is."[91]

For Irigaray, not only air is a reminder of excess, but so also is mucous. Both are equally reminders that beings do not exist without remainder. Mucous and air function as thresholds marking the uncertain, sticky passage from inside to outside. The interval "approaches zero when skins come into contact. It goes beyond zero when a passage occurs to the mucous."[92] In reality, there is no void between: "*Sameness. . .* lives in *mucous.*"[93] In its materiality, mucous is the unthought that needs to be thought through

---

80. Irigaray, *An Ethics of Sexual Difference*, 27.
81. Irigaray, *Elemental Passions*, 11.
82. Irigaray, *An Ethics of Sexual Difference*, 44.
83. Irigaray, *to be two*, 10.
84. Irigaray, *to be two*, 6.
85. Irigaray, *to be two*, 13.
86. Irigaray, *to be two*, 16.
87. Irigaray, *to be two*, 2.
88. Irigaray, *i love to you*, 148.
89. Irigaray, *An Ethics of Sexual Difference*, 127. See Irigaray, *The Forgetting of Air in Martin Heidegger*.
90. Irigaray, *Sexes and Genealogies*, 66.
91. Irigaray, *i love to you*, 149.
92. Irigaray, *An Ethics of Sexual Difference*, 48.
93. Irigaray, *An Ethics of Sexual Difference*, 109.

today;[94] being neither simply fluid nor solid relates it to the angel. Mucous is viscous, escaping control. To whom does it belong? Where is its border? Mucous makes for mutual touching but belongs to neither toucher nor touched. It is through this spiritual threshold of mucous that incarnation proceeds. The mucous summons a "god to return or to come in a new incarnation, a new *parousia*," but it stands in "the way of the transcendence of a God that was alien to the flesh."[95] Consequently, Irigaray, along with Levinas and Derrida, argues for the primacy of the sense of touch—"the source of all the senses,"[96] "our first sense"[97]—over against the more usual privileging of sound, voice, and sight. The tangible is the precondition for sight—the domain in which lack is located, the domain in which difference between subject and object is clear—while the tactile, on the other hand, is related to mucous, where the borders are more dim and murky.

Love's Caress

Each day we need to renegotiate anew the mucous passage between us and to give birth to love anew. "The act of love is neither an explosion nor an implosion but an indwelling. Dwelling with the self, and with the other—while letting the other go."[98] Love is "a sort of sun that illuminates in us and between us."[99] The "in us and between us" is crucial for Irigaray, because love is not an "ecstasy" in which we leave ourselves behind "toward an inaccessible total-other, beyond sensibility, beyond the earth."[100] It "remains in me, enstasy, rather than ecstasy, but ready to meet with the other."[101] Since, for Irigaray, saying "I love you" (*je t'aime*) risks reducing the other to the object of my love, she has begun to say, "I love to you" (*j'aime à toi*).[102] The "to" speaks of gift and mediation, thereby preventing "the relation of transitivity." As she summarizes it: "The 'to' is a site of non-reduction of the person to the object."[103]

Irigaray describes a mutual, intersubjective dynamic in which a man and woman seek, in their irreducible otherness, "to find a rhythm in the

94. Irigaray, *An Ethics of Sexual Difference*, 110.
95. Irigaray, *An Ethics of Sexual Difference*, 110.
96. Irigaray, *An Ethics of Sexual Difference*, 192.
97. Irigaray, *Sexes and Genealogies*, 59.
98. Irigaray, *An Ethics of Sexual Difference*, 212.
99. Irigaray, *i love to you*, 150.
100. Irigaray, *i love to you*, 104.
101. Irigaray, *i love to you*, 105.
102. Irigaray, *i love to you*, 102.
103. Irigaray, *i love to you*, 110.

other."[104] In this "non-hierarchical loving relationship,"[105] there is a return to self. "With no return to self, woman/women [and man/men] cannot truly engage in dialogue"[106]: "*No love of other without love of the same.*"[107] The difference is whether our returning to self is necessarily exclusionary of others, or is there the possibility of an economy beyond exchange "that would amount to attentiveness and to fidelity rather than passivity."[108]

Instead of weaving the fabric of intimacy in the between, we can easily spin a "destructive net."[109] Not finding the rhythm of love leads to an "insatiability," a fearful disease in which there is a "squandering of its abundance, the exploitation of its availability, its joyfulness, its flesh, or to the abandonment and repetition of its gestures, which become broken and jerky, instead of progressive and inscribed in duration."[110] Love can so easily be transmuted into a covetous knowing that betrays; however, when it is not, we are surprised by joy and graced with the "miracle" quality of love. A mutual "intercoursing" happens without fusion or distance, without "cutting or annihilation."[111] A dynamic mutuality emerges that I call "with-ing,"[112] a celebrating-with and suffering-with without submission or domination, a being-with in which we are true to ourselves even as we exist in connection with each other.

Irigaray here develops, in contrast to Levinas, a "phenomenology of the caress."[113] "I caress you; you caress me, without unity—neither yours, nor mine, nor ours. The envelope, which separates and divides us, fades away. Instead of a solid enclosure, it becomes fluid, which does not mean that we are merged."[114] A caress unfolds as an intersubjective act of "double desire."[115] I want to return to myself, and I want to be with you. Even as I caress you, I become more myself. Even as you are caressed, you open yourself as you become more of yourself. The caress is both to hold and to receive. But who is holding and who is being held? Sometimes we know;

---

104. Irigaray, *An Ethics of Sexual Difference*, 53.
105. Irigaray, *Elemental Passions*, 4.
106. Irigaray, *i love to you*, 98.
107. Irigaray, *An Ethics of Sexual Difference*, 104.
108. Irigaray, *i love to you*, 38.
109. Irigaray, *An Ethics of Sexual Difference*, 53.
110. Irigaray, *An Ethics of Sexual Difference*, 111.
111. Irigaray, *An Ethics of Sexual Difference*, 42.
112. See Olthuis, *The Beautiful Risk*, 130.
113. Irigaray, *to be two*, 25.
114. Irigaray, *Elemental Passions*, 59–60.
115. Irigaray, *to be two*, 29.

sometimes it escapes us. It is these carefree, not-knowing moments—when who is holding and who is being held is irrelevant, who cares!—that are the moments of truth, the sites of transfiguration marked by "each giving the other necessity and freedom."[116]

The touch of the caress "binds and unbinds two others in a flesh that is still and always untouched by mastery."[117] The caress is "an awakening to intersubjectivity, to a touching between us which is neither passive nor active,"[118] but always remains both. Here we need the middle passive voice. When we say in the active voice, "I love you," we are performing an action and are, therefore, outside the action. Similarly, when we say in the passive voice, "I am loved," we are receiving action—and this is also outside the action. The situation is decidedly more complex, however, when we say, "I am in love." Now we are talking, in the middle voice, of an action that contains the person—we as speakers are inside the process of love in which we are agent. To be in love is thus to be caught up in the rhythm of love, even as we are an active agent of that love in two senses: we are achieving love even as love is being achieved in us.[119] This space of mutual caressing, in which love comes to dwell between us, is not ruled according to an a priori rational logic of hierarchy, of parts under wholes, of tit for tat, an economy of scarcity and lack. But every day, ever anew, in every situation, love calls for a shaping of life together with a mutual ascertaining of what is just and true, right and wrong. Together we are called to beat out a rhythm and a cadence of love in a nonidentical repetition. It is a matter of faith that we discover and share together, and the shared order we live by, is beyond definition, risky, open to the future, and, in the end, mysterious and sacred. Instead of the mind of safety that goes with tit-for-tat exchange, there is, in the mutuality of love's caress, the buoyant combination of joy and risk. Without risk, we repeat and walk on paths that, in being reproduced, lose the magic; for, as Irigaray puts it, the gods have fled and the rule of the Same triumphs.

The entire process, in which we are caressed by love as we caress in love, is for Irigaray an entering into a "fluid universe where the perception of being two persons (*de la dualité*) becomes indistinct, and above all, acceding to another energy, neither that of the one or that of the other, but an energy produced together."[120]

---

116. Irigaray, *An Ethics of Sexual Difference*, 93.
117. Irigaray, *An Ethics of Sexual Difference*, 186.
118. Irigaray, *to be two*, 25.
119. See Olthuis, *The Beautiful Risk*, 68.
120. Irigaray, "Questions to Emmanuel Levinas," 111.

> Beneath every speech made, every word spoken, every point articulated, every rhythm beaten out, they [woman and man] are drawn into the mystery of a word that seeks incarnation. While trusting beyond measure in that which gives flesh to speech: air, breath, song, they reciprocally receive and give something as yet unfelt/beyond reason (*l'encore insensé*), and are thereby reborn.[121]

Before I conclude, it is important to note that, although Irigaray talks of love's caress as becoming divine, a rendezvous with or a transport to glory, indeed, a "new Pentecost" of fire and wind,[122] she is hesitant, even resistant, to relate this energy and incarnation to God. "Is its name God?,"[123] she wonders in passing. This is because, as Irigaray reads the Western tradition, God "has been created out of man's gender"[124] and has been conceived of "as an absolutely unknowable entity of the beyond . . . that we must try to approach, even though he remains . . . .radically estranged from us, absolutely other."[125] For Irigaray, this belief in "vertical transcendence"[126] ties in closely with conceiving of love as ecstasy (going outside oneself)—the very thing she is trying to get away from—instead of love remaining in us, in a horizontal transcendence between us, or enstasy. In contrast, she entreats: "*Could we not imagine the divine differently*"?[127] [128] Instead of the god of ontotheology,[129] which she calls "the object-entity God," Irigaray is in search of a "God appropriate to the feminine,"[130] conceiving God to be "a form of energy that would inspire us to develop fully into ourselves, and to live fully our relation to the other, to others, and the world around us."[131]

In my view, we can go a long way toward the reimagining of the divine differently if we return to the biblical confession: "God is love" (1 John 4:7, NRSV). Earlier in this book, discussing *creatio ex amore*,[132] I explored at

121. Irigaray, *Sexes and Genealogies*, 52.
122. Irigaray, *An Ethics of Sexual Difference*, 147.
123. Irigaray, *to be two*, 13.
124. Irigaray, *Sexes and Genealogies*, 61.
125. Irigaray, *Key Writings*, 171.
126. Irigaray, *to be two*, 13.
127. Irigaray, *Key Writings*, 172.
128. In this same book, Irigaray talks of having "returned to my [Roman Catholic] tradition in a more enlightened manner." She confesses that the "revelation of Jesus" as a "master of energy, capable of living extraordinary, 'miraculous,' experiences of transmutation of matter, capable of healing" speaks to her (*Key Writings*, 150–51).
129. See Westphal, *Overcoming Onto-Theology*.
130. Irigaray, *Key Writings*, 170.
131. Irigaray, *Key Writings*, 172.
132. See also Olthuis, *The Beautiful Risk*, chs. 3 and 5. Of note in this connection is

length the implications of seeing God's love as the generating and regenerating energy at the heart of the universe. Love is a gifting/calling that needs to be heard and heeded to be experienced as an invigorating blessing. Instead of "to be or not to be," "to love or not to love" is the cardinal question that marks and measures our humanity. To be a lover is to be caught up in the intrigue of Love, even as one is an active agent of that love. In the touch of the caress, as Irigaray emphasizes, we generate love even as love discovers us. Gathered up in the flow of love in the world, we participate in God's movement of Love that energizes the world.[133]

By risking the wager of/on love with Irigaray, working for love's redemption, new possibilities open for us to become inscriptions of hope, incarnations of love in a hurting world where compassion is in exile. The action of love in the wild spaces is a risky, disconcerting dynamic, yet it is the only promise and supreme guarantee of renewal and rebirth. Indeed, anything less than this wager leaves us only with a culture of violence.

Kristeva, *In the Beginning Was Love*, as well as Irigaray's own *In the Beginning, She Was*.

133. Cf. Olthuis, *The Beautiful Risk*, 68.

CUM AMORE: RHYTHMIC BECOMING

CHAPTER 5

BE(COM)ING: HUMANKIND AS GIFT AND CALL

MAX SCHELER, ONE OF the founders of modern philosophical anthropology, wrote: "Man (sic) is more of a problem to himself at the present time than ever before in all recorded history.... the increasing multiplicity of the special sciences that deal with man, valuable as they are, tend to hide his nature more than they reveal it."[1] In 1944, some sixteen years later, Ernst Cassirer commented that even though "no former age was ever in such a favorable position with regard to the sources of our knowledge of human nature," we are still looking for a clue which will provide "real insight into the general character of human culture."[2] In his famous 1958 book, *Irrational Man*,[3] William Barrett looked to existentialism to recover the whole and integral, suffering and dying human being from the abstract image of humankind as logical operators dominant in modern philosophy. However, in a later book, William Barrett concludes that the concrete human self was not in fact recovered in existentialism and laments its disappearance in modern thought. He talks of the *Death of the Soul*.[4] I would add: and Elimination of the Body.

The loss of the whole person in science and philosophy is particularly significant and appalling because it reflects the deep malaise of modern culture. In our global village we are all victims surrendering our humanity. Humanity is under siege. Commitment to the Promethean will-to-power and the Faustian will-to-control have seduced us into unlimited exploitation of nature, unlimited technological development, and unlimited economic growth. Survival of our planet, humanity as a whole, and of each

---

1. Scheler, *Man's Place in Nature*, 4, 6.
2. Cassirer, *An Essay on Man*, 22.
3. Barrett, *Irrational Man*.
4. Barrett, *Death of the Soul*.

of us as individuals, is becoming the issue of our times. In the 1960's and especially the 1970's the environmental movement and the peace movement first raised the cry and called for a "moral commitment to survival."[5] The women's movement and liberation theology have increased our sensitivity to economic, racial, and sexual victimization. We have been alerted to the male bias not only in culture but in science itself, and a change is called for which can be compared to Copernicus shattering our geocentricity. In spite of unprecedented technological advance on virtually every front, there has not been parallel growth in our ability to know ourselves and our ability to get along with each other. Division, fear of difference, is still front and center. The survival of our planet is at stake. Christopher Lasch, famous for his indignant outcry against the Culture of Narcissism, recognized that the human self is an endangered species and made an impassioned plea for survival of the Minimal Self.[6] In the twentieth century, humanity was desperately in search of self.[7] For the majority of people in the world, there is more rather than less suffering. Individually and communally, we suffer a loss of soul, a diminishment of spirit.

In our present disenchantment,[8] we need a global commitment to look at our ways, admit mistakes, and change. Although much has changed in our modern world, our dominant ways of looking at what it means to be human have not fundamentally changed. We have become victims of the Cartesian-Kantian reduction of the human person to an intellect that registers sense-data and seeks through scientific reasoning and experimentation to subjugate an alien cosmos. "The rift between ourselves and the cosmos—between subject and object—is, then, one troubling legacy that the seventeenth century bequeathed to us."[9] Considering the human self to be an isolated, presupposition-less, body-less, a-historical mind over

---

5. Falk, *This Endangered Planet*. See also among many others: Kahn, *On Thermonuclear War*; Commoner, *Science and Survival*; Mines, *The Last Days of Mankind*; Ehrlich and Harriman, *How to Be a Survivor*; Heilbroner, *Inquiry into the Human Prospect*; Roszak, *Person/Planet*; Schell, *The Fate of the Earth*.

6. Christopher Lasch documents "The Survival Mentality" in abundant detail in *The Minimal Self*, ch. 2.

7. In 1933, Carl Jung published *Modern Man in Search of a Soul*. In 1953, Rollo May wrote *Man's Search for Himself*. In 1982, John Macquarrie entitled his anthropology, *In Search of Humanity*, and Marianne Micks wrote *Our Search for Identity*. And in 1985 Wolfhart Pannenberg published his comprehensive anthropology under the title *Anthropology in Theological Perspective*.

8. See Berman, *The Reenchantment of the World*.

9. Barrett, *Death of a Soul*, 11. Gregory Bateson calls this rift "the strange dualistic epistemology characteristic of Occidental civilization" in his book, *Steps to an Ecology of the Mind*, 321.

against the to-be-mastered object has brought our world to the brink of destruction. New worldviews giving rise to new priorities and new practices are an urgent necessity.[10]

We need what Matthew Fox calls a "new religious paradigm,"[11] an "ecology of the spirit,"[12] a revival of the "soul," and a recovery of the "body." Two concerns will be of paramount importance in my efforts to that end. First of all, I seek to give shape to a perspective which will help us gain a sense of wholeness in the complexity of our multi-dimensional existence as unique identities, selves persisting and struggling for wholeness and meaning in community. Secondly, I seek a heuristic, liberating vision of humankind that provides orientation, direction, and promise, not only increasing the chances of human survival, but encouraging and furthering personal and interpersonal healing, as well as promoting a social revolution extending the full dignities of personhood to all peoples regardless of race, sex, creed, and lifestyle. In brief, I seek a view that frees the "transcendent powers of the personality from the dead hand of the culture's secular and religious orthodoxies."[13]

These two concerns are also, I believe, the criteria of adequacy for any anthropological model: what is the scope of its explanatory power to embrace appropriately all the experienced modes of being human; and what is its emancipatory potential for human growth, healing, fulfillment, and cosmic survival?

To achieve a sense of human wholeness while doing justice to human complexity, I will make use of what we have learned from Gestalt psychology about the part-whole relation.[14] A sense of the whole is required in order to make sense of its constituent parts. A whole is an organized and integrated unity of disparate parts rather than a collection or aggregation of bits stitched together. It means that we do not follow in the train of modern

---

10. The number of voices calling for radical change is remarkable not only in number but especially in the diversity both of the angles of approach and in the suggested solutions. Some of the books that caught my eye even when I wrote this essay originally in 1993 include Roszak, *Unfinished Animal* and *Person/Planet*; Toffler, *The Third Wave*; Dinnerstein, *The Mermaid and the Minotaur*; Chodorow, *The Reproduction of Mothering*; Schumacher, *Small is Beautiful* and *A Guide for the Perplexed*; Thomson, *At the Edge of History*; Rifkin, *Entropy*; Bohm, *Wholeness and the Implicate Order*; Capra, *The Turning Point*; Fox, *Original Blessing*; Berman, *The Reenchantment of the World*; and Sloan, *Insight-imagination*.

11. Fox, *Original Blessing*, 9.

12. Roszak, *The Unfinished Animal*, 43.

13. Roszak, *The Unfinished Animal*, 6.

14. For discussion of the whole-part relation, see Hendrik Hart, *Understanding Our World*, 211–21.

empiricism and add part to part to part to arrive at a whole. Mind is not, *à la* Hume, an aggregate of sense impressions, nor am I a mere sequence of acts or an empirical coincidence of qualities. The human person is an integrally organized and differentiated relational whole rather than a collection of parts or an aggregate of features. This means that a focus on any one feature will unavoidably have a certain conceptual one-sidedness and historical specificity which immediately invites expansion and correction, requiring both the complementation of knowledge about other relevant features in the total human gestalt and attention to the historical context.

At the same time, the various modes of human functioning constitute in their interlacement the whole. Since each mode plays its unique and irreducible role within the total pattern of coherence and multi-dimensional unity, overplaying or underplaying any of the modes distorts and skews the functioning of the whole and of each of the constituent features. This understanding of the part-whole relation is of immediate reference to any attempt at delineating the nature of being human. Analytic, left hemispheric definitions with clear-cut concepts which grasp, isolate, and restrict the essence of a thing by separating, excluding, and reducing—endemic to modern science—need in our time to be balanced by holistic, right hemispheric, non-reductionist metaphors which describe a complex of relations, connections, and interactions. It is this kind of imaginative, intuitional, perspectival vision which seeks to orient, include, and open up rather than confine and close down that I seek to compose.

In the first segment of this chapter, my focus is to develop and describe seven prime features that simultaneously and interdependently play their role in the multi-dimensional complexity of what it means to be human. Then, in the second segment, I introduce a *Me/Myself/I* model of the human self—stressing character, uniqueness, and agency respectively—as a way into an in-depth understanding of the *centered* (or *discentered*) dynamic complexity of human personhood. Such a model, as I have learned in my years of psychotherapeutic practice, has proved extremely beneficial, not only in helping people gain insight into their own inner dynamics, but in aiding them in working from defended places of disconnection toward healing places of reconnection with themselves, other people, and God.

1. Be(com)ing-in-the-World: *Imago Mundi* and *Imago Dei*

Our concern for doing justice to the concrete human self in its context dictates that we begin by recognizing that our entire planetary ecosystem is a dynamic and highly integrated cosmic web of organic and inorganic forms. Humanity is part of that cosmic whole, only exists in interdependence with all the other creatures of the world, and can only come to an understanding of itself in terms of them. As embodied persons, complex wholes made up of simpler chemical, organic, psychic sub-systems, we are fully embedded in the delicate and complex processes of nature. Consequently, any adequate description of humankind needs to embrace a solid sense of our interconnected community—our oneness—with all the earth's creatures and with God. Before we explore the differences between human beings and the rest of creation—the modern emphasis which has given rise to an anthropocentrism which sees the human being as the meaning of the world and has served to excuse human exploitation of the non-human world—we need to take the interconnectedness of all created beings—what Max Scheler called "the sympathy of all things"—much more seriously. By nature, I am as a person totally, fully, and enduringly related to all of creation, to God, to other persons, and to myself. The monumental significance of this relational feature becomes even more apparent when, as we will notice later, broken connections, alienation and separation from God, ourselves, other people, and creation are, in the language of religion, sin and evil.

But to do justice to this universal sympathy or "allurement"[15] of all things is easier said than done, for we are still severely hampered by our modern habit, inaugurated by Descartes and Newton, of mechanistic, atomized, and isolationist thinking. Instead of beginning with a holistic view stressing the fundamental interconnectedness and interdependence of all things, we have been saddled since the seventeenth century with the internal world of the subjective, a-historical, body-less, sex-less mind separate from the world of extended objects out there. The result is an image of the world as a plurality of machines and of humanity as isolated intellects that objectively register sense-data and describe causal relations without subjective influence. Mastery, control, and exploitation are the basic forms of human engagement with the world. The whole person, living, dying, relating, struggling, feeling, thinking, promising, imagining, loving, has disappeared.

Marx, Freud, and Nietzsche, "the three masters of suspicion,"[16] have unmasked the splendid isolation of the Cartesian ego as an impossible, illusory abstraction; and twentieth century developments in the theory of relativity and quantum theory have done much to disrupt the Newtonian view of absolute space and time. In fact, in the postmodern holism of physicist David

---

15. Physicist Brian Swimme, close associate of Matthew Fox, describes the universal property by which all things in the cosmos stick together "allurement" and its activity "love." See *The Universe is a Green Dragon*. What Swimme refers to as allurement, I prefer to describe as the dynamic and living Word of God—the Love-Word—which calls creation into being and which holds creation together.

16. Ricoeur, *The Conflict of Interpretations*, 148–49.

Bohm, there is an "implicate order" which is the comprehensive and underlying unity of everything which appears separate and unconnected.[17]

What is abundantly clear in our ecologically conscious era is the need to replace the "imperial self of yesteryear,"[18] committed to the conquest of nature, with what I will call the "caring self," committed to loving cultivation. We need to be eco-centered rather than anthropocentric. Rather than being "lords and possessors of nature" (Descartes), we are fundamentally in a position of mutuality and interdependence with nature. We are of the earth, creatures among creatures. No mode of action or any way of being in the world is strange to humanity. All the ways of being in the world are ways of being in which humanity participates and shares. Stressing the interdependence of humankind with all other created beings rather than in antithesis to the rest of creation is the first requirement of a comprehensive anthropology. The way is then open for a friendly, stewardly and compassionate posture to plants,[19] animals, and all of nature rather than a distanced, controlling, and possessive stance. Beginning with the interconnectedness of all creatures, the way is open to describe human uniqueness without anthropocentrism, as a difference without superiority. And connection with God as an intrinsic constituent of being human emerges on the horizon as an intriguing possibility.

Theologically, it is of interest to note that the Old Testament scriptures also emphasize the interdependence between humanity and the rest of creation. Yahweh God formed *ha-adam* (the earth-creature) from *ha-adama* (the earth).[20] Animals as well as humans are *nephesh* (living souls). And to both animals and humans, plants are given as food (Genesis 1:30). It is only in this context of interdependence that humans are called to the special task of caring for and "bringing into service" the rest of creation.[21]

The care-taking role to which humankind was called by God points to the special uniqueness of being human. Along with being *imago mundi*, we are also *imago Dei*. According to Genesis, all other creatures were created after

---

17. Bohm, *Wholeness and Implicate Order*. Bohm's insistence on an "implicate order" basically calls into question the modern idea in quantum mechanics that the universe is fundamentally and ultimately indeterminate. Bohm's cosmology would appear to be more in line with the Christian belief that creation possesses an ultimate ground of all order in the Word of the Creator God. See the theme issue of *Zygon* (Barbour and Russell) on "David Bohm's Implicate Order: Physics, Philosophy and Theology" and especially Ted Peters' essay, "David Bohm, Postmodernism, and the Divine" (193–217).

18. Lasch, *The Minimal Self*, 16.

19. Irigaray and Marder, *Through Vegetal Being*.

20. See Trible, *God and the Rhetoric of Sexuality*, 78–80.

21. For the translation of *kabash* in Gen 1:28 as "bring into service," I am indebted to John Stek of Calvin Theological Seminary.

their kind. But human beings were created after God's kind. In fashioning the earth creature, God made co-partners, co-creators, in a covenant of love and blessing for the nurturing of creation. By nature, humanity has a special gift and calling to direct creation to its goal and destiny. To be human is to be open beyond creation to the origin, order, and destiny of existence.[22]

This "openness to the world" which describes the uniqueness of being human for many modern scholars is attributed by Scheler to the presence in human beings of "spirit" as centers of action. To talk of human beings as "spirit" in this way seems most appropriate since the very term spirit and the ancient terms *ruach*, *pneuma*, *spiritus*, and *prana* all connote drive, power, and energy. Talking of human beings as spirit-creatures leads me to my second fundamental feature.

2. Be(com)ing Integrally Human

Although humanity exists in basic continuity with all plants, animals, and things, human beings are unique in that they function on the physico-chemical, organic, affective, and other levels in specifically human ways in keeping with their holistic structure as persons. This uniqueness, however, although we all experience it, has proved resistant to our best efforts of analysis. It is clear that dualistic efforts to locate human uniqueness in an immortal, rational-moral soul over against a finite physical body are inadequate in view of the experienced psycho-somatic unity of the human person. When my body imbibes too much alcohol, I become drunk. When I am afraid, my heart beats faster. The Dutch anthropologist F.J.J. Buytendijk has even demonstrated that although autonomous processes such as breathing, sleeping, and metabolizing are not consciously and intentionally performed, they are definitely the activities of personal selves and reflect in their individual variation the characteristic features of the personalities of the agents.[23]

For these reasons, among others, I also believe that Gilbert Ryle was right to reject the idea of a "ghost in the machine," a mind-substance hidden behind the body. But just as the idea of an isolated mind-substance runs counter to our ordinary experience, to call "I" merely a shifting "index-word" or "selfhood" an obsolete idea (Gregory Bateson) runs counter to our ordinary experience of ourselves as persisting identities despite and throughout all changes. Somehow, mysterious as it is, the notion of self seems unavoidable even if it is directly given and experienced in human bodiliness. This "inner" self is not hidden away, but it is the "continuing

---

22. Hart, *Understanding Our World*, 279.
23. Buytendijk, *Prolegomena to an Anthropological Physiology*. See also Reynolds, *The Biology of Human Action* and Konner, *The Tangled Wing*.

presence which I myself am, the inescapable centre,"[24] the inalienable self which provides continuity through all change and development. (That does not mean that the human self is a-historical and immune to change. As we will need to emphasize, the human self is a self-in-process.) Not having this sense of continuity through the passage of time is at the heart of psychosis. It is this inner self—*myself*—which we experience as an agent of action, center of choice, reference, and intention.[25]

The human subject as a centered whole can be called spirit. As spirit, the self is responsible for its actions and choices, able to examine itself, focus on or take some distance from its diverse modes of functioning, from its will, its passion, its reason, its health. Often this self has been identified with the rational will, the conscious ego or reason that is required to keep the passions in check. That is a serious mistake. Thinking does not think: a person thinks. The rational ego does not exist as an isolated entity; it is rather the whole person functioning rationally. Thus, although we may talk of the rational self, the physical self, the emotional self, the expressive self, the formative self, etc., these different selves have no independent existence. There is the integral human self, functioning rationally, energetically, emotionally, expressively, formatively, unconsciously, etc. To designate any mode or cluster of modes as the core nucleus of human selfhood is to absolutize and upgrade a mode or cluster of modes, in the process downgrading and diminishing the other modes, fragmenting and upsetting the intricate, intermodal, interdependence of all the modes. If we are to do justice to the structural integrality of human selfhood, it is essential that we do not identify the self with any of its particular modes of expression. At the same time, although we ought not to identify the self with its functionings, it is equally mistaken to treat the self as if it exists in any way independent of or without its bodily functionings. Without thinking, feeling, and all the other modes, a person does not and cannot exist. Each and every human self becomes its unique self in and through its multi-dimensional functioning.

Utilizing two kinds of descriptions, which could be called "foundational" and "transcendental," can help us avoid both dualisms and monisms. When we wish to speak of human persons from the viewpoint of their differentiated, multi-functional, positioned existence, we can talk of

---

24. Van Peursen, *Body, Soul, Spirit*, 159.

25. In this connection, the emergence of the Self Psychology of Heinz Kohut et al. in which the self as structure and process is the center of the therapeutic context, as a correction to traditional psychoanalytic preoccupation with id and ego, is significant. See Kohut, *The Restoration of Self*. Daniel Stern has published *The Interpersonal World of the Infant* in which a sense of self is the central theme of a theory which seeks a new synthesis beyond psychoanalysis and developmental psychology.

"body." I am totally body. When we wish to speak of humans from the viewpoint of their integrated, centered, directional existence, we can talk of "spirit." I am totally spirit. Both ways of speaking describe the whole person, but from different perspectives. Viewing a human person as body is, as it were, to look from the outside-in; while viewing a whole person as spirit is, as it were, to look from the inside-out. In this way, we are able to avoid the ethereal elevation of spirit and the debasing demotion of the body characteristic of dualisms, without, in reductionistic fashion, typical of monisms, locating the essence of personhood in one or another attribute or trait, whether in terms of genetic inheritance, subconscious urges, physicality, organic life, emotional sensitivity, techno-formative power, rationality, socio-economic adeptness, etc. In their integrity, humans are centered, multi-functional creatures. Body-talk puts the emphasis on multi-functional wholeness, while spirit-talk puts the emphasis on multi-functional integrity. A human subject is not a spirit that *has* a body. Nor is a human subject a body with or without an appended spirit. A human being is integrally spirit, or, if you prefer, integrally body.

3. Human Intersubjectivity

Communality, mutuality, neighborliness, intersubjectivity, are constitutive of the very nature of each human person. Being with (Heidegger), being available (Marcel), being open to (rather than simply being alongside or beside) is part and parcel of being human. To be a full person, as Tillich puts it, is to be fully communal. At the same time, to be fully communal is to be fully personal. An individual person is always an "I" of the "We." Individuation—the myself—and communality—the weself—are fundamentally interdependent in the human community. Every self is intersubjective, a self-with.

To be locked in myself, out of inner contact with others—isolation, loneliness—is against the human grain. At the same time, intimacy with others requires openness and intimacy with self (identity). Identity and mutuality belong together, complementing and affirming each other. When one member of humanity suffers, all suffer. By virtue of membership in the human community, we all bear responsibility for each other and for the creation as a whole.

In other words, in distinction from any form of individualism in which communal responsibility and social contracts are finally a matter of individual choice, neighborly love is not a choice. It is an inherent dimension of being human. It is in the all-important we-environment of the family that each of us comes (or fails to come) to develop a sense of self-identity in intimate relation to others.

Achieving a deeper understanding of the inherent mutuality of humanity helps us recognize the mistake of continuing to play love of self over against love of others. In this long tradition[26] in which eros as selfish love is pitted against agape as selfless love, there are only two possibilities: self-denial for the good of society or self-satisfaction at the expense of society. However, in the We/I structure of humanity, in loving others I am loving myself. In caring for self, I am caring for others. The more I develop a robust, grounded sense of self, the more I am able to relate to others not as threats to self or amplifiers of self but as co-selves in community. Identity as presence-to-self and intimacy as presence-with-another is a dialectic dance intrinsic to being co-human. Selfishness is not too much love of self but too little. That is why, instead of mutual sharing and caring with the enrichment of all, I fear, resent, and oppose others as an obstacle to my self-realization. On the other hand, sharing-with others, being committed to the welfare of others, is not the curtailment of my freedom, but the avenue of my freedom.

4. Be(com)ing a Sexual Self

Any discussion of the weself needs to account for the fact that we are human together as sexual, gendered persons. To be(come) human is to answer the call to be human as sexuate beings. As image-bearers of God who is love, we are lovers, gifted and called to love, not as solitary individuals, but as a human community-in-and-with difference. That is what human sexuality is all about: the inherent congeniality, the bodily infused charge to and for connection, both to desire another and to be desired by another. This fundamental desire-attraction-rapport-partnership-intimacy dynamic in which human persons, each of whom is unique and singular, are simultaneously interdependent selves-with-others, is the woof and warp of humankind. While genes, chromosomes, physicality, and gender play a crucial foundational role in the sexual make-up of every person, human sexuality is much wider and deeper. Human sexuality is fundamentally an ethical, spiritual intercoursing of companionability, respect, vulnerability, and commitment in which we offer ourselves and our gifts to others even as we receive the gifts of others, co-partnering together on life's journey. It is only at great peril limited to matters of biology, emotion, or socio-cultural forces. While in marriage the sexual charge receives its own particular intense, intimate form and place, sexuality plays itself out in various ways in all human interrelations.

26. Nygren's *Agape and Eros* is still the classic presentation of this position.

This comes out most powerfully, although negatively, in what we have come to know as the age-old "battle of the sexes." Although healthy relating is mutual, non-oppositional, equitable, and just without coercion, domination, or submission, in practice the desire to connect-with others too often becomes oppositional, warping into a battle for control and domination with all its attendant hostile maneuvers, claims of superiority, injustice, and abuse. In contrast, "man and woman [need to] breathe together, engender together, carnally and spiritually" in what Luce Irigaray calls a "spiritual becoming."[27] Indeed, it is as a sexuate partnership of mutuality and co-creation that humankind most fully reflects the image of God as Triune.

The pervasive and deeply mysterious nature of human sexuality is strikingly apparent in that, while the "who am I?" question receives as one of its most fundamental answers "I'm a man," "I'm a woman," when asked, "what does it mean that you are a man or a woman," people tell stories of personal identity as varied and as unique as the people are unique and different. Indeed, it is increasingly apparent that for certain groups of people, now recognized as the LGBTQ+ community, the answer to the "who am I?" question is not so obvious. That is because traditionally we have largely operated with the male/female difference as a strict binary, with a stereotypical modelling of the ideal man and ideal woman. In that framework, homosexuality or bisexuality is considered an abnormality if not an aberration. Likewise, transgender persons who identify with another gender and may seek to live as a member of another sex are excluded. Moreover, intersex people born with any of several variations in sex characteristics including chromosomes, gonads, sex hormones, or genitals do not fit this typical definition of male and female.

This state of affairs has led for good reason to a growing dissatisfaction with any talk of a male/female bi-unity as exclusionary. Justice to the evident diversity of sexual identities calls for a more polymorphic, non-binary, or other-gendered approach. In reality the male/female binary has never served humanity very well. From the start, it was coupled with the propensity to establish one side of the male/female duality as good and superior and the other as evil and inferior.[28] The male/female difference turned into a male/female opposition we have come to know as the "battle of the sexes." Philosophically, the West has been dominated by sex-unity and sex-polarity theories which first took definite form in the work of Plato and Aristotle.[29]

---

27. Irigaray, *i love to you*, 124.

28. See Mead, *Male and Female*.

29. Prudence Allen has traced in comprehensive detail the development of these theories from 750 BC to 1250 AD in *The Concept of Woman*, Vol. I.

Plato's body-soul dualism, with its devaluation of the body, established the sex-unity ("unisex") theory, since the soul, as the true nature of the human person, was neither male nor female. Aristotle first articulated a sex-polarity theory by claiming a fundamental superiority for man, based on the lack of heat in the female which meant that she was unable, in distinction from the male, "to concoct" seed from her blood. Through the institutionalization of Aristotle's views at the founding of the University of Paris (women were refused admission!) and the tremendous influence of thinkers as different as Thomas Aquinas and Sigmund Freud, sex-polarity views have been dominant in society into the twentieth century.

It is remarkable that since modern philosophy as it developed focused on the formal structure of rationality (with the exception of some extreme misogynists such as Schopenhauer), it has operated largely until the twentieth century as if sexual difference was fundamentally inconsequential to human identity. "Anatomical differences are nothing," for Descartes, "but a matter of accidental implements of the body."[30] At the same time, since it was widely believed that women were inferior to men in their ability to reason—rationality generally considered "the male principle"—women were still often discriminated against, albeit in more hidden and subtle forms. Indeed, as Genevieve Lloyd has demonstrated, although the rational self is in theory considered gender-neutral, the rational/irrational distinction mapped neatly on to the male/female dichotomy.[31]

As I noted earlier, we are presently undergoing a "gathering impulse to break loose from our existing gender arrangements."[32] But even here the traditional approaches persist: Some dismiss the matter of sexual differences as only biological[33] and devalue the body,[34] while others insist on male superiority[35] or female superiority.[36] At the same time, sex complementarity views are becoming common in which women are urged to nourish their

---

30. Stern, *The Flight from Woman*, 14. Stern judges that in Cartesian rationalism we encounter "a pure *masculinization of thought*" (104).

31. Lloyd, *The Man of Reason*.

32. Dinnerstein, *The Mermaid and the Minotaur*, 10. The "impulse" has since become a surge with Judith Butler (*Gender Trouble; Undoing Gender*) leading the way.

33. As, for example, Simone de Beauvoir in the classic *The Second Sex*.

34. As does Shulamith Firestone in *The Dialectic of Sex*.

35. Steven Goldberg relates male superiority to the hormone testosterone in *The Inevitability of Patriarchy*.

36. Ashley Montagu holds to *The Natural Superiority of Woman* because of the female chromosomal structure.

animus (masculine principle) and men to nourish their *anima* (feminine principle),[37] while some promote an androgynous view.[38]

We have learned about the importance of the process of fetal androgenization which begins eight weeks after conception. Without the influence of androgen, no male genitalia would develop. The degree of masculinization of sex-organs and socio/sexual proclivities appears to be directly proportionate to the amount and strength of androgen circulating at the critical period. Further, the sensitivity and amount of androgen seems predetermined by the genetic make-up of father and perhaps mother. In any case androgen secretions at about eight weeks alter the nervous system permanently.

Even though the crucial dynamics of biological sex are becoming clearer, human sexual differentiation as male and female is much more than a matter of biology. At our present state of knowledge we need to talk not only of biological sex (including chromosomal configuration, gonadal sex, sex organs, and hormonal, neurological sex), but also of gender identity as the basic emotionally grounded core sense of being male and female, and gender role as the public, social expression of gender identity; all three integrated in the whole person as a sexual being oriented to loving and being loved.[39] Our most fundamental sense of being sexual beings—core gender identity—develops in the psycho-social interaction with our parents in interaction with our biological sex. This socialization process shapes central aspects of our inner selves. In our society men have been socialized to be separate and independent doers; women have been socialized to be connected and dependent nurturers.[40] And at the same time, we are socialized to express our gender identity in gender-related roles: women are nurses, teachers, clerks; men are doctors, professors, managers.

Because the crucial processes of socialization in developing sexual identity have taken place in a global context where women have for centuries been treated as second-class citizens, there is every reason to suspect that the division into masculine and feminine roles has more to do with fear of women and oppression of women than any intrinsic masculine or feminine qualities. In fact, it is high time that we give up the stereotypical idea that there are "feminine traits" such as intuition, care, cooperation, synthesis, passivity, internality, fragility, tenderness, and "masculine traits"

37. Jung, *Two Essays on Analytical Psychology*.

38. See June Singer, *Androgyny*.

39. See Money and Tucker, *Sexual Signatures*; Holliday, *The Violent Sex*; and Tabin, "The Formation of Gender Identity;" in *On the Way to Self,* 36–50.

40. Rubin, *Intimate Strangers*. Among the host of important works are: Horney, *Feminine Psychology*; Bardwick, *Psychology of Women*; Greer, *The Female Eunuch*; Claremont de Castillejo, *Knowing Woman*.

such as logic, duty, mastery, analysis, activity, externality, strength, firmness. Why not consider all of these traits "human traits" which both males and females appropriately may and ought to manifest?

To me there is no doubt that much of modern industrial society, epistemology, and science overvalued the "competitive, analytical, hierarchical, fragmented, external, and artificial." In response, we need to affirm the "holistic, collective, intuitive, and cooperative, emotional, nurturing, democratic, integrated, internal, and natural."[41] The question is whether it is helpful to label the first grouping as "male" and the second group as "female." Such terminology suggests that these characteristics are respectively intrinsic to being male and being female. Jungians may be quick to reply that all men and women have both a masculine and feminine principle. That may be true, but even for Carl Jung, the masculine rational principle predominates in men and the feminine intuitive in women. What about the men who feel predominantly at home in the "female characteristics" and the women who feel predominantly at home in the "male characteristics?" Talking of universal, human traits would certainly be less confusing. It is true that men have developed patriarchal systems of oppression which have marginalized women and non-binary people, as well as many important human virtues. But the fundamental problem is not their male sex, but that they were (or are) misguided, fearful, alienated men who have denied parts of themselves. In any case, even though we are far from understanding the full meaning of human sexuality, any new vision of what it means to be human cannot continue to bracket, downplay, or ignore its intrinsic significance in the communal experience of being a human self.

What needs development, I believe, is a polymorphic theory of sexuality which stresses multi-dimensionality, variety, inclusion, honoring differences. That is, I am suggesting that we need not discard or minimize talk of sexual difference, but we need a non-binary, non-essentialist, non-oppositional understanding of that difference which allows for the flourishing of a multiplicity of sexual identity formations. We need to move beyond the inadequate constructivist or essentialist models of sex and gender. As the latest studies of the brain in neuroscience indicate, "individual men and women are each complicated mosaics of different sex-related traits, rather than replicas of the model man or model woman."[42] In reality, few individuals correspond to the traditional models. And there is as much, perhaps even more variation within the categories male and female themselves as between males and females.

---

41. See Miles, "Introduction," in Miles and Finn, *Feminism in Canada*, 13.
42. Hines, *Brain Gender*, 35.

In be(com)ing human, each of us is gifted and called to own and nurture our sexual identity in ways that are true to who we are as unique persons. In so doing, we can, with integrity and truth, live lives of wholeness, commitment, and justice.

5. Human Be(com)ing: A Developmental Process

Since who we are as persons is not once for all given, ready-made and static, any anthropological model must be developmental to the core. Human life is dynamic, in process, to be accomplished in its stages from birth to death and beyond death. What and who we are is filled-out—fulfilled—as life moves on. My self as an intentional, self-organizing, responding presence is always in-formation; a being-toward on a course, continually enacting myself anew in a timed course of stages and callings.

In the last fifty years we have learned an immense amount about various aspects of human development. Post-Freudian psychoanalysis has contributed much to our knowledge of the development of the ego as a regulative principle.[43] Insight into human intellectual development owes much to the constructivist-developmental theories of Jean Piaget,[44] extended to moral development by Lawrence Kohlberg and to faith development by James Fowler.[45] Behaviorist learning theories (B.F. Skinner, Albert Bandura) have taught us the importance of environmental reinforcement. Maturational theories (Arnold Gesell) have helped us focus on the sequential unfolding of organic processes based on our genetic codes. But we do not yet have a single theory that enables us to satisfactorily encompass all the aspects of development in their interrelation and coherence as dimensions of a whole person.

In my view, such a comprehensive vision is only possible when we begin from a gestalt of the whole person (developing multi-modally) rather than focusing on the development of various modes of relating (with attempts to achieve the whole cumulatively through an additive process). For, strictly speaking, it is not cognition that develops, or organs, language, morality, or faith. It is the human person as a whole self that develops in successive life-stages, cognitively, organically, lingually, morally, and faithfully. If we see human development in this way as fundamentally development of the unique self as active agent, center of coherence, affect, and intention, rather than as the sequential and additive development of various capacities, we have a holistic vision which provides a sense of integration and coherence

---

43. See Loevinger, *Ego Development*.
44. Piaget, *The Moral Judgment of the Child*.
45. Kohlberg, *The Philosophy of Moral Development* and Fowler, *Stages of Faith*.

even as we are able to trace developmental changes in the various modal processes which are always simultaneously present.

Attention to the self as agent-in-process is, in fact, the direction in which both psychoanalysis and developmental psychology has moved. Since in Freud's instinct theory a baby was "all id" and no ego, early psychoanalysis focused on physiological regulation of drives and was unable to account for the intentional agency of every newborn infant. Consequently Melanie Klein condensed Freud's theories about the ego into the first year of life, and Rene Spitz talks of the very early existence of ego-nuclei which are later fused into ego.[46] The British object relations theorists also insist that human social relatedness is present from birth and believe "that the human infant is a unitary dynamic whole with ego-potential as its essential quality right from the start."[47] Self Psychologists champion the "Self" (as distinct from the ego) as the central developmental principle.[48] Working out Piaget's constructivist-developmental approach, Robert Kegan has developed a metapsychology of *The Evolving Self*.[49] Infant psychiatrist Daniel Stern sought a new synthesis between psychoanalysis and developmental psychology by proposing that "new senses of the self serve as organizing principles of development."[50]

The emerging emphasis on the developing self as an active agent is important. At the same time, the changing, developmental nature of human existence, combined with the vast meaning-actualizing ability of human persons, has led some theorists to deny the perduring be-ing of the human self. The human subject, it is said, is an illusion: there is only human be-coming. My doing, it is said, is my being, and my doing continually changes.[51] Alvin Toffler suggested we talk of "serial-selves." But to deny "a continuous, durable, internal structure"[52] to the human self is, I believe, a serious mistake. It is true that the sense of self develops: but don't we assume from the beginning the presence of a personal agent (a *myself*)

---

46. Spitz, *The First Year of Life*.
47. Guntrip, *Psychoanalytic Theory, Therapy and the Self*, 92.
48. Kohut, *The Analysis of the Self* and *The Restoration of the Self*.
49. Kegan, *The Evolving Self*.
50. Stern, *The Interpersonal World of the Infant*, 19.
51. Thus, despite his focus on the self, Robert Kegan still sees the self as a human construction: "This book is about human being as an activity. It is not about the doing which a human does; it is about the doing which a human is" (*The Evolving Self*, 8). And even Daniel Stern seems to see "the self" as a human construction, even though his theory, in my view, is only plausible when the existence of personal agency (not only its potential) is assumed from the beginning.
52. Toffler, *Future Shock*, 319.

that is developing its sense of self? The development of the self is no doubt a process, but it is an active process in which an individual self experiences in ever deepening, diverse, and expanded ways the coherence and integrality which he/she already is by virtue of being human. It is also true that I form myself continually and appear only in my enactments. At the same time, I am more than my enactments. It is only from the viewpoint of the perduring self that I can make sense of my previous experience and look forward to future experience. Without a persisting sense of self there would seem to be no basis for enduring commitments and deep intimacy: "You can't hold I [the present self] to a promise I [an earlier self] made last year." Again, the necessity of assuming a perduring human myself as subject seems clear when we consider that activity as such does not mark the uniqueness of being human. Rather, as Wolfhart Pannenberg concludes after a long discussion of the matter: "*Human* activity presupposes the identity of human beings as subjects."[53]

However undifferentiated and undeveloped a newborn baby may be, its self is present and active, emerging in ways appropriate to the first stages of life. There is, in fact, a growing body of evidence that the fetus not only sees, hears, and tastes, but is able to remember and to intentionally react to mother's sleep patterns and emotional moods.[54] Studies of early stages of life are beginning to demonstrate with more clarity that already in the first months of life a child experiences an emerging sense of self. At age two to three months infants exhibit self-agency, self-coherence, self-affectivity, and self-history. This fourfold sense of self—what Daniel Stern refers to as the "core sense of self"—is not a "cognitive construct" but an "experiential integration."[55]

At this point, it becomes apparent that we need to say: I am myself in my be(com)ing, and I become myself in my be(com)ing. Both are equally and fully true, and both need to be affirmed simultaneously. For that reason, I have adopted the practice of writing "be(com)ing." To say that I retain my identity throughout the journey of life is not to say that myself has remained unchanged. To say that my identity has changed is not to say that there is no continuity to who I am. Both are true, both give expression to the mystery of be(com)ing human.

---

53. Pannenberg, *Anthropology in Theological Perspective*, 61.
54. See Verny, *The Secret Life of the Unborn Child*.
55. Stern, *The Interpersonal World of the Infant*, 69–123.

6. Be(com)ing Human: Alienation/ Restoration

No comprehensive anthropological vision can ignore or minimize the human experience of disintegration, disconnection, and alienation, and the need for transformation and restoration. The pernicious and pervasive reality of evil in our day—violence, oppression, despair, exploitation, injustice, inequality, disease—has put the lie to the eighteenth and nineteenth century myth of human progress which taught the gradual but steady elimination of evil. "The pot of human evil seems to be bottomless, an infinite witch's brew sending off poisonous vapors in every generation and always threatening to boil over in universal catastrophe."[56]

Nevertheless, there is still little agreement about the nature of human evil—or about its remedy. Some focus only on human responsibility and guilt for evil, while others see evil as fundamentally a fate that befalls us. Some seek the cause in the inward psyche, while others point at unjust social structures; some see it in the failure of reason to control the bodily passions, while others see it in the repression of these very passions. But such polarities seem unable to do justice to the phenomena of evil. While humankind is certainly responsible for evil and therefore guilty, it is at the same time true that evil is an anterior power "always-already-there . . . for which, nevertheless, *I* am responsible."[57] Moreover, as we have already emphasized, to be fully personal is to be fully social and to be fully social is to be fully personal. Self and society belong together, reciprocally influencing each other for good or ill.[58] And the idea of a "pure," innately good reason is as illusory and mistaken as the idea that bodily passions and impulses are patently base and evil. Believing in such dualistic tensions between an eternal, pure, agapic soul and a finite, passionate, erotic body have become increasingly implausible as we learn more about the psychosomatic unity of the human person.

However, even when the fundamental unity of the human person is affirmed and embraced, human brokenness is still often explained in terms of the relation of the human mind, self, or spirit to the body. Thus, Max Scheler opposes the spirit to the vital impulses and Helmuth Plessner locates the source of human alienation in the opposition of soul and body.[59] Now it is no doubt true that we often experience tension between our inner selves and our bodies. We may try to escape our "bodies" by living in our "heads," or we may indulge the body to escape or tune out the mind.

---

56. Gilkey, *Message and Existence*, 115.
57. Ricoeur, *The Symbolism of Evil*, 259.
58. For a discussion of the self/society dilemma, see chapter 11.
59. See the discussion in Pannenberg, *Anthropology in Theological Perspective*, 80ff.

Even aside from the highly questionable legitimacy of a higher soul/lower body distinction, the soul/body difference appears to be a poor choice for the primary locus of evil. We can be broken internally, experiencing a sharp division in our inmost self, or we may experience tension between our conscious self and our subconscious inner self. Sometimes it is true that our internal division reveals itself as hostility between the inner self and the body. But it is just as likely that we can feel alienated internally, even and often especially when we experience strong identification with the body. We can experience the goodness of bodily pleasures as meeting the needs of the self in opposition to our ego-mind or superego which tells us: "It feels too good, it must be wrong." The fact that the spirit can take, so to speak, the side of the body as well as be at odds with the body points to a deeper source of brokenness than body-self disparity.

Thus, it is not surprising that often a fundamental break has been located between a person and a person's actions. But this too seems mistaken. Yes, we do distinguish between doer and doings, between actor and acts. However, it is only in and through acting that we exist. Who we are comes out in what we do. It is true that at times we can feel alienated from our own actions, but more often we experience a deep connection with what we are doing, very much in our acts and enactments. However, even when we feel internally connected with our doings, we can nevertheless experience—uncannily—deep estrangement.

The fact that we can experience a deep disconnection and alienation regardless of whether we feel connected or disconnected with our bodies, our acts, or our performances, including our institutions, suggests that the alienation we experience is an uncanny core issue at the heart of human existence, explicitly and implicitly showing itself in a countless variety of ways and forms. The same conclusion suggests itself when we realize that individually and communally sometimes we become wayward, accomplices of evil, in spite of peerless logic, generous impulses, and the best of intentions. Somehow, someway we experience estrangement in the heart of our being, an internal rift, even as we may go a long way in convincing ourselves that all is well. For all these reasons Wolfhart Pannenberg concludes that this very break is to be viewed "as a conflict between basic factors in the structure of human existence, as an expression of a tension between the centralized organization of human beings and their exocentricity."[60] In its very core, the self is divided: egocentricity versus exocentricity. In exocentricity we are present to the other; in egocentricity we place ourselves over against the other. This tension, according to Pannenberg, becomes a radical

---

60. Pannenberg, *Anthropology in Theological Perspective*, 61.

evil when the "presence to the other becomes a means by which the ego can dominate the other and assert itself by way of this dominion."[61]

No one who is open to the misery and brokenness in the world and to his/her own brokenness will take issue with the reality of egocentric domination in much of human life. At the same time, Pannenberg's conclusion raises a host of questions. If egocentricity is constitutive to being human, are we not in the final analysis concluding that human finitude is itself the root cause of evil? Doesn't this make evil a necessary dimension of our nature as finite creatures? Is the "divided" self to be seen as a necessary, structural given of creation? Do not such views assume a fundamental "deficiency" in human nature from the beginning, that is, in principle, which makes it impossible for us to affirm wholeheartedly the goodness of creaturely being? Is evil, no matter how radical it may be, to be considered as primordial as goodness? Is evil an unavoidable, inevitable feature of creaturely existence rather than a surd in a good creation? If creation is fundamentally flawed from the beginning, how can humanity be held fully responsible for evil? If evil is as necessary to life as oxygen, does it ultimately make any sense to talk of human freedom and responsibility with respect to evil? If evil is a normal constituent of human existence, rather than a perverse condition, are we not on the road to legitimizing the very evils we are called to fight? And if there is a primordial crack in the foundations of human existence, is there any hope for transformation, any hope for final liberation from evil? These are important and crucial questions—the more so, since Pannenberg's views articulate with care and refinement central convictions of much contemporary thought.[62]

This series of questions points to a number of concerns which do not appear to receive adequate attention in any view that reads evil back into the creation structure. Is there not something counterintuitive about affirming that what we are necessarily by nature (egocentric) is what we ought not to be? Moreover, the conviction that non-attachment to self (exocentricity) is the solution to the problem of the self has for me that same contradictory ring.[63] If being human means connection and attachment to self, others,

---

61. Pannenberg, *Anthropology in Theological Perspective*, 85.

62. Thus, for example, evil is a necessary, if base, part of human existence for the evolutionary dialectics of much liberation theology (see Segundo, *Evolution and Guilt*), Jungian thought (see Sanford, *Evil: The Shadow Side of Reality*), as well as process thought (see Griffin, *God, Power, and Evil*).

63. Pannenberg, as we have noted, deals with the contradictions involved by making the tension between egocentricity and exocentricity the ontic nature of humanness. Simultaneously, exocentricity both validates and invalidates egocentricity. "But even if human beings are in this sense sinners by nature, this does not mean that their *nature* as human beings is sinful" (*Anthropology in Theological Perspective*, 107). The cardinal

creation, and God, non-attachment seems as undesirable as ultimately impossible if we are to remain fully and genuinely human.

Regarding evil as the inevitable and unavoidable result of a fundamental flaw in creation also runs counter to our experience of responsibility, blame, and guilt for sin and evil. We hold ourselves and others responsible when evil is perpetrated, presumably on the presumption that we were free not to do evil. Thus, although we do experience evil as a "general condition from which we all suffer," we need to correlate this with our "universal experience of an awareness of guilt and responsibility."[64]

To conclude that evil has an intrinsic place in creation not only minimizes human responsibility, but ironically denies the existence of genuine evil as that which ought not to be. Such views seem unable to do justice to evil as demonic, anti-creational, and life-destroying. Evil—although its presence is irrefutable—has no place in a good creation. "However *radical* evil may be, it cannot be as *primordial* as goodness."[65] We are left with the deeply enigmatic character of evil: non-necessary but omni-present. This situation also seems to emphasize that there is no rational solution to the "problem of evil"[66]: transformation, forgiveness, redemption is the only answer! Indeed, as Paul Ricoeur articulated, evil is not a "problem" that can be solved either philosophically or onto-theologically in theodicy; rather evil is a "challenge" to be faced, endured, fought, suffered, lamented, mourned, protested.

The contingent, non-necessary, but omni-present character of evil has been expressed in the Christian tradition in terms of a good creation which breaks its relation with its Creator in the sin of Adam and Eve. Evil is estrangement from God, self, neighbor, and creation, disfigurement of a primordially good creation. Liberation is seen as the gracious redemption from evil, the restoration to communion with God, self, and creation. In contrast to extremes which conceive humanity to be basically good or basically evil, the human predicament is rather more complicated. We were

---

question is whether such a *coincidentia oppositorum* is able to do full justice to creaturely goodness, human freedom and responsibility. See Walsh, "A Critical Review of Pannenberg's *Anthropology in Theological Perspective*."

64. Gilkey, *Message and Existence*, 123.

65. Ricoeur, *Symbolism and Evil*, 156. The tremendous difficulties we face in developing an adequate view of evil are well illustrated by the fact that Ricoeur himself, despite his clear intentions to the contrary, works with a view of human "fault" in *Fallible Man*, which itself comes very close to reading sin and evil into the fundamental human structure. See the Master's thesis of Henry Venema, *Philosophical Anthropology and the Problem of Evil*.

66. See Ricoeur's trenchant critique of all attempts at rational theodicies in *Evil* and van der Hoeven's fascinating, in-depth discussion with Ricoeur in "The Problem of Evil."

made good and designed for love. At the same time, in fear, we find ourselves whether knowingly or unwittingly in the grip of evil, awaiting and in need of the embrace of the Love of God. For it is in the embrace of Love that we are empowered and enabled to reconnect with ourselves, with our neighbors, the rest of creation, and God.

7. Be(com)ing Human: Gifted/Called to Love

A comprehensive description of what it means to be human is best understood in terms of what I refer to as the gift/call structure of life. The human self is a gift (a *Gabe*) and at the same time a call (an *Aufgabe*). Life is one hundred percent a gifting received and, at the same time, one hundred percent a calling to respond. The two belong together as two sides of the same coin. Thus the title of this chapter: "Be(com)ing: Humankind as Gift and Call."

To be human is to be gifted/called by God to become co-partners with God in the cosmic ministry of care and healing. The image of God with which humanity is created (i.e. gifted) and for which humanity is created (i.e. called) gives humankind both an identity and a direction. As God is love, we are gifted with the capacity to love, and called to be(come) incarnations of love. Humankind is (or is not) be(com)ing agents of/for love.

The emphasis on gift and call enables us to do justice to the process of human self-realization and self-fulfillment without considering this an autonomous process of self-positing and self-creation. As Martin Buber affirms: "'I have been surrendered' and know at the same time 'it depends on me'. . . I must take it upon myself to live both in one, and lived both are one."[67] Instead of the Cartesian "I think: therefore, I am," or the versions of John MacMurray, "I do: therefore, I am,"[68] or Martin Heidegger, "I am thrown: therefore, I am" (*Geworfenheit*),[69] the twofold truth is rather, "I am loved: therefore, I am," and "I love, therefore I am." We were/are made *of* love and were/are made *for* love. Love, then, is who we are—agents of love and agents for love—active agents in God's movement and flow of love happening in the world. To love is to make proper connections, to promote the flourishing and interconnectedness of all things, connecting persons to persons, people to plants, plants to animals, stars to planets.

---

67. Buber, *I and Thou*, 144. Merleau-Ponty in a similar vein talks of "an antimony of grace," a "turning" where the "real self . . . accedes to being constituted out of community with Being" (*Signs*, 64). Karl Jaspers gives voice to the same paradox: "*He comes to himself like a gift* . . . I am responsible for myself because I will myself in the certainty of this original self-being—and yet I am only given to myself because this self-willing needs something more" (*Philosophy*, 42).

68. MacMurray, *The Self as Agent*, 84.

69. Heidegger, *Being and Time*, 174.

We are gifted and called to be co-partners with God, shaping our lives and orchestrating all our talents, all our resources, all our work and play, in a cosmic ministry of love and justice.

The gift/call structure of human existence also means that even when things are going very poorly in the world and we existentially find ourselves at odds with ourselves and others, missing the mark of love, turning our backs on God, we are not alone. The love of God as the wellspring, the creative and sustaining energy of creation, infuses creation with grace and promise: accompanying, inviting, imploring, never giving up, indeed, hounding, haunting . . . The love of God is promissory, awakening and sustaining hope when things go wrong, when disasters occur. That the world was gifted into being in and by love (and not a haphazard fluke) persisting in love cannot be overestimated. It means that promise and hope are constituent features of the very fabric of creaturely existence. Love is the "oxygen" of existence: breathing, inhaling and exhaling love, is the rhythm promising life, igniting hope.

Attending to the orbit of self goes hand in hand—if love is to happen, if connections are to be celebrated, if justice is to be served, if God is to be enjoyed—with breaking out, risking, exorbitantly, in excess. A centered, healthy self is, thus, not self-centered, but a self-with, relationally centered outside of self in a web of loving connections with others. Self-love and love-of-other are of one piece. Only with healthy self-love—in contrast to narcissistic self-absorption—is one able to move towards another, not out of despair, inadequacy, or hostility, but in genuine desire to connect with another for mutual enrichment. Only with love-of-other—in contrast to either domination of or self-effacing submission to the other—is one able to esteem self, not out of desperation, grandiosity, or fear, but in genuine desire to be true to oneself in intimate relationships with others.

The mutuality of genuine love-of-self and love-of-other also helps explain why superiority and inferiority, inflation and deflation, show up together, one covering for the other. Grandiosity is not, at bottom, thinking too much of self, but too little, serving as a cover for deep feelings of inferiority. Likewise, subservience and submissiveness obscure thinking too little of self. The complex interrelational, intersubjective dynamics of human personhood highlight both the extreme vulnerability of creatureliness as well as the sublime possibilities of and for deepened connection of self, with self, with others, with creation, and with God. Being fully human is thus actualizing our relational creatureliness as "with-ing" (being with-self, with-others, with-creation, and with-God) in life-affirming, justice-bringing, mercy-embodying, God-honoring ways. If we fail to love, then we squander our humanity, lose our souls, and betray our inmost selves.

Me, Myself, and I: Character, Uniqueness, and Agency

The seven features I have described provide a general sense of the multidimensional structure of human personhood. However, through my years of psychotherapeutic experience, I have found a deeper sense of the internal dynamics of being human comes into sharpened focus by means of what I call the Me/Myself/I model. Me/Myself/I—stressing character style, uniqueness, and agency, respectively—has the advantage of giving these distinct features of personhood equal play. At the same time, as three gestalts or faces of the self, the model allows the gestalts to overlap, coalesce, enmesh, split off, reify, as the case may be. As I shall indicate, particularly when the model is illustrated in terms of the metaphor of a "house," the emancipatory, therapeutic potential of the philosophical insights come to the fore, aiding people in making new and transforming connections and reconnections personally, interpersonally, and societally.

As persons, we are not rock-hard on the inside with changeable, fluctuating properties on the outside. In all that we are, in our totality, we are vibrant, pulsating matrixes of streamings and coursings. Yes, as selves we have identity, but it is an identity in process, a "subject-in-process/on trial" ("*sujet en procès*").[70] In a phrase, "self" is a verb as much as a noun. In becoming ourselves, we are "selving." The human subject is "a relative stabilization of what remains *unstable*, or rather, *non-stable*."[71] Jacques Derrida suggests that "subjectile," with its connotation of movement and trajectory in contrast to fixity and stasis, may be a more appropriate word than "subject."[72]

Webs and whirlpools are apt metaphors for the incredibly awesome and unendingly complex dynamics of human subjectivity. The self is like a gossamer web, tenuous and vulnerable, but relatively stable. And even as the front of a many-seamed tapestry, woven of diverse fibers, conceals the knots, ties, breaks, and dangling threads that attention to its other side reveals, so human subjects have an adaptive, presenting self that can mask internal struggles, hurts, angers, and fears. The self is also like a convection pattern in air or water, a whirlpool in which—analogous to galaxies—there is a centripetal pull inwards even as there is a centrifugal push outwards. The centripetal/centrifugal process of be(com)ing human depends on life-giving connections with others (intersubjectivity), with creation and its creatures (caring solidarity), and with God (spirituality). A healthy, wholesome human self develops in a "rhythmic becoming,"[73] gathering in and giving out,

---

70. Kristeva, *Revolution in Poetic Language*, 22 and *passim*.
71. Derrida, *Points*, 270.
72. Derrida, *Points*, 268, 270.
73. Irigaray, *An Ethics of Sexual Difference*, 42.

centering and decentering. All of which brings dramatically to the fore that becoming a self is particularly vulnerable to misformation, upset, injury, and derailing. We often talk about being "in a whirl," "at sea," "in over our heads," "lost," "blown away," or "scattered" (too centrifugal), or "swamped," "locked in," "distant," "with our heads in the sand" (too centripetal).

Who we will be in the future is still in the making. We are not (in the words of Nietzsche) to become "what you are," but (in the words of Luce Irigaray) to "be what you are becoming."[74] The mystery of our identity lies in God's gift and promise of who we are (to become). We will receive "a new name, that no one knows except the one who receives it" (Rev 2:17, NRSV). What is most deeply *myself* is more than *I* am at present, more than the *me* that *I* have forged in the past.

The deep truth and the awesome challenge captured in this sentence bears repeating. It spotlights the intricate complexity of the dynamics of human selfhood. Indeed, it leads me to propose a *Me-Myself-I* model for the human self. Every human subject is a unique, non-exchangeable, non-replaceable, be(com)ing-in-process-with (*Myself*), called to self-formation as active agent (*I*), taking in and giving out with as much cohesion, integrity, compassion, and grace as possible in developing personality and character (*Me*), exhibiting both a presenting and symptomatic side in terms of genetic inheritance, particular experience, and historical time.

The more *Me*, *Myself*, and *I* are in sync with each other, the healthier the self. The more in flow a person is, the more the three faces overlap, coalesce, demonstrating cohesion, and unanimity. It is the coalescence (or lack thereof) between *Me*, *Myself*, and *I* that accounts for the degree of presence a person enjoys at any particular moment. *I* am most fully alive, whether deep in pain or filled with joy, when *I* is in sync with *Myself* and in tune with *Me*, and least alive when my *I* is out of touch with myself, and is detached, even bodiless, a kind of automatic, robotic reflex or congealed *Me*.

---

74. Irigaray, *This Sex Which Is Not One*, 214.

FACES OF THE SELF

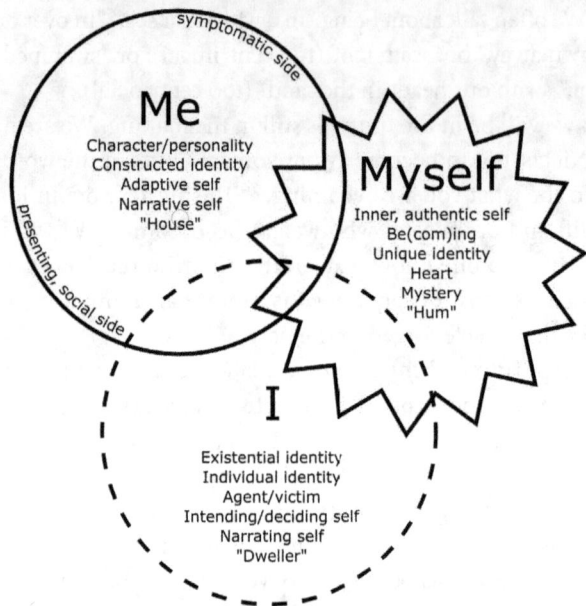

Me

Me is a human person looked at from the dimension of character and personality structure. *Me* is the "house" of identity one creates for oneself—the web of habits, the abode of temperament, dispositions, and attitudes. *Me* is the "storied self" whose narrative I tell as mine. It is Paul Ricoeur's *idem*-identity,[75] the observable, structured embodiment that allows others (and ourselves) to recognize us as the persons we are. Each of us, in terms of heredity, temperament, family, environment, and historical epoch, gives form and structure to self, struggling to develop a cohesive, robust, joyful sense of self. We shape our character, adopting and adapting emotional, cognitive, aesthetic, and behavioral styles and patterns.

Me is the "adaptive self," the persona shaped not only by heredity and temperament, but in response to the twists and turns, the blessings and the traumas of life experience. In a "good-enough"[76] environment of love, trust, and affirmation, people build well-adapted personality structures and styles of various sorts, open, bright, well-lit, welcoming and hospitable: "houses of

---

75. Ricoeur, *Oneself as Another*, 3.

76. Object-Relations theorist Donald W. Winnicott introduced the concept of the "good-enough mother" in *The Maturational Processes and the Facilitating Environment*, 145.

love." In an environment that is not good-enough—non-affirming, non-accepting, frustrating, abusive—people construct and fortify personality styles and structures that are defensive "fortresses," shaped in fear, rigid, uptight, as resistant to change as to entry: "houses of anger and fear."

The adaptive self typically has a presenting social side and a more enigmatic, shadowy, symptomatic side—which explains how cheerfulness can mask misery, confidence may mask inadequacy, indifference can overlay extreme sensitivity, belligerence may masquerade for submissiveness.

As personality structure, *Me* has been described in a variety of ways historically. Aristotle, Galen, and Hippocrates developed typological theories based on the doctrine of "humors" in combination: blood, black and yellow bile, phlegm. Excess of blood made for a *sanguine* or enthusiastic temperament; excess of black bile was associated with the sadness of *melancholy*; excess of yellow bile with the irritable *choleric* type; excess of phlegm with the lethargy of the *phlegmatic*. Freudians and post-Freudians talk variously of schizoid, oral, borderline, narcissistic, masochistic, and oedipal personality types. Tests such as the MMPI or California Personality Inventory assess personalities in terms of five or six factors such as energy, affection, conscientiousness, emotional stability, intelligence, and will. There are Myers-Briggs descriptions of personality types as various combinations in terms of four kinds of features: introversion/extroversion, thinking/feeling, sensing/intuiting, judging/perceiving. These purport to describe the *Me* self.

Myself

Myself is a human person described in terms of their unique identity. It is the irreplaceable, inaccessible, mysterious, and incalculable singularity, the inimitable spark, the soul or spirit that marks our uniqueness. *Myself* is the authentic self that I am gifted to be and called to become, the subjectile, identity-in-making. It is Heidegger's *Jemeinigkeit*, Ricoeur's *ipse*-identity, Levinas's assignation, Derrida's "singularity of the 'who.'"[77] The "beyond" or "behind," that comes "before" individual subjectivity "precisely because it is presupposed by all . . . the categories of human subjectivity (self, reasonable being, consciousness, person)."[78] It is the unique and incomparable *Myself* that configures and is configured, that actualizes and is actualized, that constitutes and is constituted, showing itself in the *Me* of character and the *I* of agency. Hurt, wounded, or traumatized, the vulnerable *Myself* can go into hiding, dissociate, withhold, fall into depression, and run for its life. *Myself*

---

77. Derrida, *Points*, 261.
78. Derrida, *Points*, 271.

is the authentic and wounded self, that "deep" place, the "heart" of and for connection (and disconnection) with self, God, others, and creation.

I

I is a human person described as doer, the agent, the intender, the storyteller, the decision maker, the witness always called anew to remember, to will, act, decide, speak, feel, think, trust, believe, etc.—the existential *I*. *I* is who I am today, in the immediacy of the present, actively gathering, forging, remembering, forgetting, dispersing. Every day, at each moment, *I* enact and re-enact who I am. Derrida describes it this way: "Every time I decide, if a decision is possible, I invent the who, and I decide who decides what."[79] This *I* may be confident, attentive, overbearing, awkward, confused, restless, troubled, spaced, empathic, sensitive, whatever—depending on mood, temperament, support, socio-political context, and deep sense of self. *I* lives on the cusp of the present, knowing its *Me*, listening to and for the internal sounds of *Myself*, constantly negotiating the transition between past and future.

In the exigencies of daily life, *I* usually decides, more or less automatically, to act in character. After all, my character (*Me*) has become second-nature, enabling me to function and to be more or less content. However, when things go amiss, under disappointment, duress, or trauma, decisions become more difficult, deliberate, at times agonizing. What am *I* to do now? Do *I* react in my usual fashion, trust the routines and typical response patterns of my *Me*, to rebound, heal, and get back on track? Do *I* decide to retreat, pull back, and defensively batten down the hatches in an effort to get on with life as if nothing has happened? Or do *I* take in what has happened, and respond by seeking to adjust, calibrate, possibly even revamp *Me* (my personality) in relevant ways to give more room and hope for the healing and flourishing of *Myself*?

When the *I*-self entrenches itself in a fortress-like *Me*-self to defend against uncertainty or pain, to ward off attack or endure trauma, paradoxically the *I* renders *Myself* even more prone to the existential woes of meaninglessness, anger, depression, and despair. That is because a vigorous, healthy sense of personal identity involves the *I* not disowning, dismissing, down-playing, muting, even dissociating from the trials, tribulations, traumas, and sufferings affecting *Myself*, but forthrightly acknowledging them, facing them, working them through—in what mystics have called the "dark night of the soul." It is only when *I* stays open to the sounds, vibrations, murmurs, cries and groans of *Myself* that the *Me*-self is able to become and

---

79. Derrida, "Remarks on Deconstruction and Pragmatism," 84.

remain an open and hospitable home, a "house of love" rather than a "house of anger" or a "house of fear."

The more *Me, Myself,* and *I* are in sync with each other, the healthier the self. The more *Me, Myself,* and *I* are distanced and detached from each other, the more defended, isolated, dissociated, spiteful, aggressive, or downcast a person is. On the other hand, the more in flow a person is, the more the three configurations, "faces," or incarnations of the self coalesce, the more a person is in-close-touch-with-self-and-with-others, a person of wholeness, integrity, and honor. It is the in-syncness (or lack of it) between *Me, Myself,* and *I* that accounts for the degree (or lack of degree) of being-at-home-with-self. *I* am most fully alive, at-home-with-self, whether in deep pain or filled with joy, when *I* is in sync with *Myself,* through an attuned hospitable *Me*, and least alive and not-at-home-with-self when *I*, detached, or locked in a congealed *Me*, is cut off from or out of touch with *Myself.*

Self as House

The complex intricacy of a *Me-Myself-I* model is graphically illustrated in terms of a "house," a traditional symbol for the self.[80] The large variety of different house styles is a good representation of the various possible character styles as relatively stable structures—the webs of habit, the abodes of temperament, dispositions, morphology, gender—in which people live, move, and have their being. It is the continuity of our structured identities—our me—that allows others (and ourselves) to identify who we are over time. At the same time, each of us active agents (*I*'s) dwell in our "houses," turning the lights on or off, opening or closing doors and windows, moving from room to room, going or not going into our basements and attics, deciding to renovate or not. Moreover, of special note: although people may have similar types of houses—that is, their character style (*Me*) may be similar in numerous respects—every house has its own unique *élan*, feel and flavor, what I call the "hum factor" *(Myself)*. A well-appointed manor house can feel lifeless, arid and bleak, while a sparse cabin can feel alive, homey and spirited. Listening for, being attentive to the "hum" in the house gives a sense of whether its residents are vibrantly at home and present, at ease with themselves and each other, or scattered, ill-at-ease, defensive, conflicted, irate, in despair, internally disengaged, or AWOL.

Through the years, my psychotherapeutic practice has served as a kind of laboratory in the development of this house model. Most counselees

---

80. Bachelard, *The Poetics of Space*, xxxii: "On whatever theoretical horizon we examine it, the house image would appear to have become the topography or our intimate being."

find it congenial to talk about what they would like to do and where they are at in terms of the house metaphor. "I want to go into my basement, but I'm afraid." "I'm so lonely, all my doors and windows are barred." "I long for the gentle hum. All I hear inside is deathly silence, or pounding noise." "When I'm honest with myself, I recognize that I'm not really happy with how I look. I need a refit." "I wish I could change. But I've gotten so used to the house I live in." Indeed, an apt metaphor for the challenges and struggles of intensive therapy is renovating the very house in which one is living. No small undertaking.

The *Me/Myself/I* model helps make sense of the various types of concerns voiced by people coming into therapy. "For some reason, I keep on disappointing myself." "I've had so many wonderful experiences in my life. Too bad I wasn't present." "My life feels like a facade. I set up my life to please. But I don't identify with the pleasing *me*." "I let myself down, not only my family."

As a psychotherapist, I have learned the value of listening on three registers:

- To the story of the day (the *I story*)
- To the composite story that has been fashioned over time (the *Me* story)
- To the underlying story of the authentic self (the *Myself* story)

By listening to these three stories, noting tensions, inconsistencies, contrasts between them, noting patterns and discrepancies, we get a sense of the defended adaptive self (*Me*) and the underlying wounded self (*Myself*). Over time we get a sense of when the story of the day (the *I* story) gives voice to a person's deepest yearnings, or whether it is a story built for purposes of distraction or protection. Listening for the underlying story of the heart hidden in and under the "*Me*" stories of survival, denial, protection, and rationalization, psychotherapy works towards helping people readjust or transform their character structure (*Me*) so that by more fully showing who they truly are as persons (*Myself*), they (as *I*) can enjoy the "love-hum," of inner connection as it energizes, indwells, and comes into its own character-wise (in the *Me*).

The pressing need, anthropologically, to clearly distinguish the uniqueness (*Myself*) of a person from either agency (*I*) or personality (*Me*) (even though there is no myself without a me and I) became even more strikingly obvious in working with a number of gifted people who were sorely troubled, haunted, and anxious. Each of them, in their own way, had a deeply wounded *Myself* that had nevertheless developed a *Me* enabling them to survive and engage in life.

Amanda was a vibrant young woman. She liked her job, was married, and had good friends. But underneath, as she said, her life was filled with "many fears, large and small." She was now house-bound, feeling unhinged, deeply ashamed, out of control, panicky. After almost two years of working together, the ins and outs of which I recounted at length in my book *The Beautiful Risk,* Amanda got her life back. Although her mother had sat in scalding water in the bathtub in an attempted abortion, she had kept that fact secret. That trauma, immensely intensified by her mother's silence about it her whole life, had filled Amanda with a dread that she could not hold down, held hostage in a house of fear (her *Me*).

Suddenly, when her mother blurted out her secret, Amanda recognized the truth of her identity, and in a flash, was released from the domination of the past, reborn as it were to her authentic self (*Myself*), available for living in the present. "I realized that these feelings, intense and unbearable, were real and coming from *something*. I wasn't crazy!" That happened almost thirty years ago, and Amanda's deep anxiety has never returned. She is now a happy, lovely, caring, sensitive woman, happily married, with a wonderful young son. Amanda's *Myself*, now in sync with her *Me* and *I*, is able to give and receive love fully and freely.

George lived in deep fear and pain of not fitting in, of not belonging, of being abandoned. His desire to belong hurt so much that he needed to pretend otherwise. He developed a clingy personality (his *Me*). In his words: "I seem to have no definition for myself beyond clinging." He tried to be sensitive, but his efforts were often received as invasive by others. In one of our many sessions, in response to feeling George's pain, I blurted out: "The words *special orphan* come to me."

"It's true that I am special to Mom," replied George, "but I don't feel it. It's a puzzle. I'm not adopted." After much digging into the unknown, we were able to reconstruct the likely picture. Before George was born, his mother had given birth to two children who only lived a few days. So when George was born, even though he was special, his mother held part of herself back. It clicked deeply with George. George had never felt bonded with his mother, and so felt like an orphan. "I keep on trying to find a group in which I can belong." Twenty years later, George has gained "some sense of myself as having a legitimate stand in the world of love, a place where I can own love for myself." His growing self-love has led to deepened connection with self and others, a hospitable me and a giving I. George now belongs, in the world, to himself, and to others.

Tom was a sensitive, talented computer programmer, filled with anxiety, haunted by internal voices telling him he was unworthy, deserved punishment, and therefore should kill himself. He had been diagnosed as a paranoid schizophrenic and was on a dangerous level of psychiatric drugs but to no avail. He knew that this was not going to end well if things didn't change. I asked him to write out what the voices said. He came back with four pages of quotes, all to the same effect: "You don't deserve to be loved. 'You don't deserve to live' is not strong enough!!!" "Stop pretending. You know what you have to do. Just do it. You are the same as Hitler, worse than Judas. Jesus did not die for you, you conspired to kill him." "Logically," Tom said, "I know they are lies, but I feel they are the truth." So at times, as he said, "I need to kill myself" became obsessive. As a result, periodically, he would go out, buy a knife, and cut himself until the soothing flow of blood quieted his soul.

In our fifth session he came in out of sorts in a peculiar way. The night before he had found himself suddenly awake, terribly anxious and afraid: "I heard the breath and sigh of another person and I was terrified. I looked around, no one else was there. Suddenly, I realized that the person I was afraid of was me." He concluded that this was proof that he was crazy!

I was not convinced, and we began to examine his childhood in search of answers.

He had grown up in Poland, during the Second World War, with a sorely distressed father who would daily take out his anger against Hitler in long, anguished tirades directed at his twelve-year-old son: "You are evil. You deserve to die." Tom recounted all this in a very calm, matter of fact way. When I mentioned this, he said, "It didn't really affect me."

"Really," I said, "that's hard to believe. I would have been shattered. How did you manage that?"

"I sat there looking at a man yelling at a young boy who was not me."

Suddenly things came together and made sense. Under severe duress from his father, Tom had dissociated, in effect sitting on a shelf watching a young boy being berated and abusively scolded. I suggested this to Tom. I will never forget his reply. "Wow, I astral-projected." His astral-projection had rescued him from the full trauma of those moments. However, at the same time, his Dad's rantings were introjected into him, and were still rumbling around in him perturbedly as his own. Under situations of stress and tension, his default position was dissociation (as exemplified by his fear of his own breathing); but, increasingly, dissociation was no longer working. The voices became so unbearable that he would self-mutilate, leading him to fear for his life.

When he was able to connect the voices to his earlier life, realizing that they were not his own gave him immediate relief. He was not crazy. It all made sense. As he said, "I need to deprogram." Tom is now "befriending and reclaiming his body," which involves disowning and erasing the voices. In terms of the *Me/Myself/I* model, Tom's *I* is now busy, renovating his *Me*, erasing and muting the alien voices, allowing his *Myself* to come out of hiding.

Amanda, George, and Tom are all in the process of learning—what we are all called to learn—that listening to and attending to our internal sounds can open the way to discovering that what is most deeply *Myself* is more than *I* am at present, more than the *Me* that *I* have forged in the past. In my understanding and experience, God is the ultimate empathic presence, the perfect responsive love luring all of us, each in our own unique ways, to give shape to and inhabit abodes that "hum" with love. Which is to say that the bonding process at the heart of every self and of the world can only be called Love, the "Eros that seeks to get things together, no matter what."[81]

---

81. Keller, *From a Broken Web*, 218.

CHAPTER 6

RHYTHMIC (DIS)CONTINUITY: TRAUMA AND THE UNCANNY

When good things happen to us, or bad things traumatize us, are they random occurrences or predetermined outcomes? Is the final word chance or necessity? Are conflict and trauma constitutively built-in to the universe? The father of psychoanalysis, Sigmund Freud, opts for determinism claiming that apparently random events are nevertheless unconsciously determined, that internal conflict is structured into the self from the beginning. I begin by exploring the thrust of Freud's argument—later amplified by Jacques Lacan—before taking up philosopher Jacques Derrida's consideration of Freud's reflections. In the end I will suggest—in tune with my wager that love and goodness are more primordial than evil—that trauma, despite its horrendous presence, is not the first nor the last word, that the world is neither a determined or divinely supervised cosmos nor an out-and-out chaos. Rather, the universe is an uncanny rhythmic (dis)continuity of differentiation and integration—a kind of "chaosmos" (James Joyce) involving chances (heeded, enjoyed, missed, broken, traumatized, endured, redeemed) of and for Love.

Trauma

Right at the outset, it is important to note that how we answer our initial question has everything to do with how we describe and delimit the precise meaning of trauma. The meaning of which—unsurprisingly—is itself a difficult, slippery, and still hotly-contested issue.

Well, what is a trauma? Trauma is a kind of breach or wounding. (The word "trauma" is etymologically linked to the Greek word meaning "to wound, to pierce.") Thus, a trauma is an accident or unexpected upset, a shock, a jolt, or a blow that catches us by surprise, leaving us wounded, a chance that befalls us, unexpected, knocking us for a loop. However, for Freud, the father of psychoanalysis, there is more at stake. For the standard or "mainstyle" Freud,[1] such wounding, such trauma, is fated, foreordained, inexorable, inevitable.

In *The Psychopathology of Everyday Life* (published 1901) usually considered Freud's most popular work and often referred to as the "Mistake Book," he deals with all kinds of everyday experiences that are in some way defective, confused, or faulty.[2] Freud begins by dealing with the forgetting of proper names, with the assumption that such forgetting is "not left to psychic arbitrariness, but that it follows lawful and rational paths."[3] Later he declares, "But there is nothing arbitrary or undetermined in the psychic life."[4] Freud's conclusion at the end of book: "I believe in outer (real) chance, but not in inner (psychic) accidents."[5]

In an early stage of Freud's theory, trauma is caused by an excessive influx of excitations. As he says in his *Introductory Lectures*, "A person only falls ill of a neurosis if his ego has lost the capacity to allocate his libido in some way."[6] In other words, and importantly for Freud, internal conflict and internal defense against conflict are structural components in the becoming-into-existence of every human subject. Indeed, it is this notion of conflict giving rise to division or dissociation in the psyche which first led Freud to distinguish consciousness from the unconscious in his important discovery of the unconscious, the unconscious being the psychic formation between the *res extensa* and *res cogitans*. (Psychoanalysis being the cathartic stream of consciousness in which through free association aims at verbalizing what was repressed in the unconscious.)

The ego, acting like a buffer, protects the psyche by only permitting in so much external stimuli. In the routine state of affairs, a healthy ego under stress diverts and redirects attentiveness. However, under excessive stress, when the excitations break through, the ego suppresses, activating the pathological defense of repression. The result is neurosis: conflict between repressed impulses and the 'ego instincts' of self-preservation.

---

1. I say institutional or "mainstyle" Freud, because there is also an "otherwise" Freud who allows for the co-implication of chance and determinism. Nicholas Royle talks of the Freud "passionately committed to rationalism and scientific thought" and the Freud "who says more or other than he thinks" (*The Uncanny*, 58, see also 26, 29).
2. In Freud, *The Standard Edition*, vol. 6.
3. Freud, *The Standard Edition*, vol. 6, 2.
4. Freud, *The Standard Edition*, vol. 6, 85.
5. Freud, *The Standard Edition*, vol. 6, 90.
6. Freud, "Introductory Lectures," in *The Standard Edition*, vol. 16, 387.

Thus, for Freud, a trauma always results from the encounter between the external, accidental, real shock and a pre-existing, structurally determined, psychic fate or trauma. Although Freud recognizes the reality of external accidents, the real trauma is inside the psyche. When chance trauma meets internal trauma, projection of internal conflict often takes place, with various symptoms emerging, including self-mutilation and other psychosomatic symptoms. In this way an external trauma is absorbed or sublated internally so that the traumatic effect becomes the reverberation or resonance of a primordial psychic conflict.

While the early Freud emphasized the fantasies triggered by traumas rather than the traumas themselves, the later Freud, when analyzing First World War ordeals, connects trauma to the "repetition compulsion." The goal of treatment is not just remembering and recalling, but working through with the aim of bringing out previously unaired unconscious fantasies lying at the core of neurosis.[7] (Lacan dubs this "traversing the fantasy.")

At the same time, war traumas were, in a dramatic sense, "traumatic" for Freud's theory of dreams as "wish-fulfillment." Although, on the one hand, soldiers horrified by the war tried to repress it, on the other hand, they were continually dreaming of the war with its horror, wounding, and killing, unconsciously recreating the battle scene, not for pleasure but because they were wanting to make sense, wanting to resolve, master, and somehow integrate the experience into their selves. Consequently, going beyond the pleasure principle, Freud theorized that there is some unpleasure in sexuality and begins to talk of a death drive which operates silently and cannot be discharged in the words of the symbolic.

However, even in his treatment of these war traumas, Freud still centers his attention on the internal conflict rather than on the horrid external war traumas themselves. Consider Freud's introduction to his "Psychoanalysis and the War Neuroses":

> In traumatic and war neuroses the human ego is defending itself from a danger which threatens it from without or which is embodied in a shape assumed by the ego itself. In the transference neuroses of peace, the enemy from which the ego is defending itself is actually the libido whose demands seem to it to be menacing. In both cases the ego is afraid of being damaged—in the latter case by the libido and in the former by external violence. It might, indeed, be said that in the case of the war neuroses, in contrast to the pure traumatic neuroses, and in approximation to the transference neuroses, what is feared is nevertheless an

---

7. Freud, "Remembering, Repeating and Working-Through," in *The Standard Edition*, vol. 12:145-56.

internal enemy. The theoretical difficulties standing in the way of a unifying hypothesis of this kind do not seem insuperable: after all, we have a perfect right to describe repression, which lies at the basis of every neurosis, as a reaction to a trauma as an elementary traumatic neurosis.[8]

In the idea of an "internal enemy," Freud is indicating that what is feared in the conditions of trench warfare is not the actual danger but the prospect of being overwhelmed internally leading to a disintegration of the ego. The actual trauma wound or fear of such a wound is considered to be a repetition of a previous primal internal conflict. An external accident only becomes properly a psychic event when it sets off a person's inherent internal psychic encounter. The real enemy is always "internal." That understanding would have led Freud, for example, to classify post-traumatic stress disorder, or PTSD, as the expression of the "always already" internally structurally determined conflict. Along similar lines, Freud, in *An Outline of Psycho-Analysis*, explains that although the mother-child bond is of crucial importance: "[T]he phylogenetic foundation has so much the upper hand over personal accidental experience that it makes no difference whether a child has really sucked at the breast or has been brought up on the bottle and never enjoyed the tenderness of a mother's care. In both cases the child's development takes the same path."[9] The actual historical course of social development is predetermined.

It is worth underlining the significance of the "always already" due to Lacan's extensive outworking of this theme in his doctrine of the Real. Catherine Malabou considers "trauma has always already occurred" to be Lacan's "most fundamental statement."[10] Trading on the impossibility of verbalisation, Lacan concludes that traumatic events are fundamentally impossible to integrate into one's sense of selfhood. Trauma has always already happened. He considers an individual's traumatic experience to be an intensified individual replay of the collective original trauma of being human, loss of unity with mother, castration fear, etc.—that is, of the fundamental gap or lack which, for him, is at the heart of human life. For Lacan, all the processes of desire, substitution, *objet petit a*, fantasies, are attempts—the repetition compulsion—to master or control what is beyond control, what he calls the Real, which he distinguishes from reality. The Real is basically there for us as trauma that can never be assimilated, a swarming void, an

---

8. Freud, "Psychoanalysis and the War Neuroses," in *The Standard Edition*, vol. 17:210.

9. Freud, "An Outline of Psycho-Analysis," in *The Standard Edition*, vol. 23:188–89.

10. Malabou, "Post-Trauma," 226.

entangled knot. *Tuché* (fortune, chance) is for Lacan "*the encounter with the real*,"[11] an event that must and, yet, cannot be assimilated into an ordinary economy. Indeed, that is why we attempt repeatedly to assimilate it even though it cannot be domesticated. We repeat trauma, not to master it but because, in principle, we cannot master it. An existential trauma only happens because an originary trauma has "always already" occurred. Trauma thus does not transpire by chance. Every actual accident or tremor befalls an already previously wounded subject.

For Lacan, the "the whole of psychoanalysis is quite rightly founded on the fact that getting something meaningful out of the human discourse isn't a matter of logic."[12] When psychoanalysis works, we are delivered over to the Real, in a miss-tical "missed encounter"[13] with the Real which eludes us. The analyst is called to give "ethical witness,"[14] to witness, recognizing that the "subject who speaks is beyond the ego."[15] This means holding open access to the unconscious that incessantly closes itself up.

The long and the short of this is that, in the end, there is a rejection of chance in Freud and Lacan. Although bad luck, chance, accidents, etc., do indeed affect us, sometimes drastically, essentially they are only symptoms bringing to the fore, perhaps in technicolor, the internal conflict or trauma inherent to being human. Psychic events for Freud are never accidental, but follow the law and necessity of nature. There is no chance in the unconscious, only in the formation of symptoms. In short: for (mainline) Freud, chance and necessity are opposites.

Derrida's Paradoxical Coincidence

On the other hand, for philosopher Jacques Derrida, in place of the opposition between external chance and internal psychic necessity, there is a radical commingling of both factors, both internally and externally. Radical interruption, the incalculable (the "aleatory"), goes hand-in-hand simultaneously with the calculable, negotiation, and convergence in a paradoxical coincidence. In his essay "My Chances/*Mes Chances*: A Rendezvous with some Epicurean Stereophonies,"[16] Derrida takes a close look at Freud's *The Psychopathology of Everyday Life*.

---

11. Lacan, *The Four Fundamental Concepts*, 53.
12. Lacan, *The Ego in Freud's Theory*, 306.
13. Lacan, *The Four Fundamental Concepts*, 55.
14. Lacan, *The Four Fundamental Concepts*, 40.
15. Lacan, *The Ego in Freud's Theory*, 175.
16. In Derrida, *Psyche*, 1:344–76.

What, he asks, is the difference between superstition or paranoia, on the one hand, and the psychoanalyst who claims to be a person of science on the other, since both are marked by "a compulsive propensity to interpret random signs so as to restore to them a meaning, necessity and destination."[17] Notably, Freud, in his last chapter, asks this same question when discussing the actions of a coachman who mistakenly drives Freud to the wrong address, even though he had made the drive often before. Is this mistake, asks Freud, an accident, or does it mean something?

His very emphatic answer is revealing: "Certainly not to me, but were I superstitious, I would see an omen in this incident, a hint that this would be the last year for the old woman." Only then to immediately add that if he had made the mistake, the case would be entirely different. It would not be an accident, but "an action with unconscious intent requiring interpretation."

For Freud, paranoia and superstition share with the science of psychoanalysis the compulsion to interpret, the only difference being that paranoia and superstition (with which Freud then includes "most modern religions") locate the necessity in the external while he locates it in the inner psychic.

Derrida playfully teases. Why the compulsion not to let chance pass as chance? Neither Freud nor the superstitious, he claims, believe in chance, which is to say both believe in chance. After all, all chance means something—and therefore there is no chance. Derrida goes on to surmise that Freud's recognition of chance in the external world is even questionable based on what he says in other places. But here he needs the opposition of the internal/external, inside/outside, the psychic/biophysical in order to give psychoanalysis a chance as a science.[18] Derrida then suggests that not only is the superstitious person more sensitive to the precariousness of holding such clear limits between the external and internal, but also that such a sensitivity is closer to reality's complex interworkings.

In place of the opposition between external chance and internal psychic necessity, Derrida concludes there is no area of life that is devoid of randomness or regularity. In place of the opposition between external chance and internal psychic necessity, there is a radical commingling of the two both internally and externally. The incalculable "aleatory" happens in paradoxical coincidence with the calculable. Along these lines, it is worth noting that modern biological and cybernetic theory are both concerned with self-organizing lawfulness and imprecise surplus. Systems are both inescapably conformist (the condition of their existence) and

17. Derrida, *Psyche*, 1:365.

18. Here again, Freud's desire to be scientific—which in his time meant to be a positivist—overrides his acute awareness that reality is much more complicated than theory, an awareness to which he often gives voice.

integrally vacillating (the circumstance of their dynamism), fluctuating between chance and orderliness.

For Derrida, the chanciness of life, its contingency, is essential to the creational condition. Chance bespeaks vulnerability, not fate. However, once a chance becomes mine, it is singularly unique. The responsibility to make the most of the situation is uniquely my own. The incalculable always already means that our decisions, no matter how well thought through, remain risky, lacking guarantee. In the interwoven complexity of regularity and randomness which makes up the fabric of life, we are called to negotiate a way through the fortunes and misfortunes which attend life, never sure of our path, zigzagging, trying to establish a rhythmic movement in the discontinuity of life, step by mis-step, haltingly.

Rhythm is a repetition that makes difference possible. Just as music doesn't appear disjointed but continuous because we hold previous notes in our memory which fade in a flow even as we hear new notes, we aim to give our lives a cadence of regular recurrence. When the continuity of our cadence is disrupted, we scramble to right ourselves as best we can, eager to re-establish the cadence—hoping that the breaks don't end up being traumatically disastrous. Chance for the better goes hand-in-hand with the possibility of the worse.

Neither Necessity nor Chance: Non-Oppositional Difference

Derrida's view that necessity is not opposed to chance but the affirmation of chance makes it clear that we do not have to choose between them. Necessity or Chance is a bad or false alternative. Contingency is not the original sin; chanciness is the contingency essential to being finite. Being finite is to be bound by conditions of time and space making for the chance of change. Chance speaks of risk and vulnerability, not fate. As an interval, a between, space is "not a void, a mere negative determined by the positive full, but rather the emptiness between two."[19] The intervals of space and the flow of time divide even as they join. Even as they break a relationship with another, the space-time continuum simultaneously opens the possibility of such a relationship. The paradoxical commingling of continuity and discontinuity, of presence and absence, means understanding sameness and difference as inhering together non-oppositionally—without the hierarchy of either one being essential and the other provisional. This is in contrast to Hegel for whom difference, understood as contradiction, "makes negativity one face of positivity within the process and the system

---

19. Lawlor, *Imagination and Chance*, 124.

of the self-exposition of absolute knowledge."[20] Instead of difference as "a negativity opposed to the meaningful positivity it makes possible,"[21] difference is non-negative and non-oppositional. Difference is difference, other. Difference as such is a challenge, an invitation calling for attention and response. Difference and discontinuity, partnered with sameness and continuity, comprise the necessary and positive conditions making for the ongoing contingent process of differentiation and integration.

Continuity and discontinuity are built-in features of our universe, discontinuity living off of continuity, and continuity living off of discontinuity. Life is a spiraling ebb and flow of processes—ups and downs, backs and forths, breaks and connections, tensions and relaxations, rifts and linkages. Negotiating a way, forming a life, learning and inventing is replete with trials and errors, starts and stumbles. Making healthy life-affirming choices is stressful, often onerous, at times painful, even excruciating. Our plans are always in flux, subject to intrusion, delay, revision, and improvisation. That which is different and other continually challenges and interrupts the rhythms and cadences of our lives.

However, at times, too often, beyond the commonplace trials and bad mishaps that constantly challenge with or without warning, lives may be thrown into complete disarray and uncertainty. Disease, violence, accidents, death can lay people low and render them powerless. In such horrific situations, we are overwhelmed, shocked to the core, threatened in our very being. Whereas (lower-case) discontinuities find their constitutive place in the textured fabric of finite life, traumas (upper-case), Discontinuities, we could say, do not. Traumas are not nagging nuisances nor minor misfortunes.

Traumatic events, in the words of Judith Herman, can "destroy the victim's fundamental assumptions about the safety of the world, the positive value of the self, and the meaningful order of creation."[22] Traumas terrify and discombobulate, shattering a person's or community's sense of safety and trust. One's life—or the life of one's community or nation—is upended, thrown off course, undone, crushed. Traumas are evidence of dire and dreadful break-down, signifying evil, the monstrous, the revolting, the nefarious: "faulted finitude" as distinct from "unfaulted finitude."[23]

20. Gasché, *The Tain of the Mirror*, 102.
21. Pirovolakis, *Reading Derrida and Ricoeur*, 64.
22. Herman, *Trauma and Recovery*, 51.
23. As Jeff Pool, referencing Paul Ricoeur, emphasizes: we need to clearly distinguish "unfaulted or essential finitude" from our actual "faulted human finitude" (*God's Wounds*, 1:84–85, 2:15). It is this very distinction, however, which leads me to wonder about the appropriateness of describing created reality as "tragic": "the tragic region of reality and experience (as distinct from the realities and experiences of evil)" (1:14).

To repeat: it is crucial to not identify or conflate the good/bad distinction with the good/evil difference. While judging things to be either going well or badly is part and parcel of finite, creaturely life, the good/evil difference concerns the clash between the life-affirming energy of Love and the life-destroying anti-force of Evil. While the cosmos is filled with the differentiating/integrating energies of Love in the trial and error processes of God's good creation, Evil is a senseless surd, a *fremdkorper*—a foreign invader—parasitic on the good energies of Love.

Even though—because evil is parasitic on the good—too often commonplace struggles morph into adversarial battles or regular routines are violently shattered, "however radical evil may be," in the words of Paul Ricoeur, "it cannot be as primordial as goodness, . . . Evil is not symmetrical with the good."²⁴ This extraordinary disparity between traumas—monstrous disasters and atrocities that wound, devastate, and lay low—and the routine discontinuities, mistakes, or frustrations of daily existence needs to be underlined and emphasized. The trials and errors, pain, tension, and worry that attend all the multilevel processes that attend creaturely life are radically different from the severe breakdown, abuse, or collapse of such processes. A homespun example that serves to illustrate the difference is an elastic. The capacity of an elastic to stretch and in tension to hold objects together is good and useful. This situation is markedly different when the tension becomes too much and the elastic breaks. Things fall apart.

Recognizing this state of affairs once again emphasizes that difference (otherness) is fundamentally a matter of invitation and challenge and need not necessitate opposition, violence, and trauma. To conceive of conflict as unavoidable, inevitable, and inexorable is, philosophically, to read violence, abnormality, aberration, and brokenness into the very structure of creation, giving the risk inherent in life a tragic, catastrophic cast. Theologically, in terms of the Christian story, the brokenness of life because of sin and evil is generalized and ontologized as a regular and normal occurrence, bracketing or neutralizing the goodness of creation. In contrast, beginning with the conviction that creation is good—a work of God's love—means that stress is not to be equated with anguish, that

---

Pool further describes "creation's negative features as tragic and as responsible for tragedy" (1:154). For me, the very real troubles and difficulties of life, including death, though difficult, frustrating, and shocking, need not be tragic—or, taking note of its synonyms: disastrous, calamitous, catastrophic, cataclysmic, devastating, horrendous. Yes, since evil is parasitic on the good, struggles, mistakes, accidents too often do or may become tragic. Thus I do agree with Pool (without the adjective tragic) when he says: "Obviously, in human experience, evil or sin and tragic experience or reality ambiguously interact with one another" (2:189).

24. Ricoeur, *The Symbolism of Evil*, 156.

mishap is not the same as disaster, that not all pain is necessarily egregious suffering. That is to say, although the distressing actuality of so much hostility, abuse, and tragedy—trauma—cannot and should not in any way be downplayed, the qualitative difference between the "creatively-tensive" and the "degeneratively-conflictual"[25] is manifest and arresting.

Existentially, recognizing the creatively-tensive/degeneratively-conflictual difference is also of extreme importance therapeutically. Not honoring this divergence effectively and harmfully downplays and underestimates the appalling and heinous hurt wrought by traumas. If being traumatized is a normal part of life, specific traumas, regardless of severity, differ only in degree from ordinary events. The shock and impact, the horrendous violence, the excruciating suffering that trauma survivors endure and need to live with and try to recover from is not fully acknowledged.

This underplay of the devastating impact of violence even shows up diagnostically. People who continue to experience problems after severe trauma are said to be suffering from PTSD, "post-traumatic stress disorder." "Disorder" indicates that this condition is considered an avoidable ailment. Unfortunately, this has led many victims of trauma to hide their internal distress and agony. The result of such suppression, as tragically demonstrated in the case of many war veterans, is too often suicide. From my perspective, exhibiting signs of serious psychological damage after trauma is entirely normal and to be expected, while not exhibiting such signs is evidence of "disorder."

Always Already Trauma

Finally, therapeutically, there is an especially egregious result of considering internal conflict to be a constituent structural component of being human. As we noticed earlier, both Freud and Lacan teach that trauma has "always already" occurred. Slavoj Žižek puts it this way: "the Fall thus never happens, since it has always already happened."[26] Indeed, in his view, "Trauma is 'eternal'; it can never be properly temporalized/historicized."[27] For Žižek, referencing Lacan, the spectral traumatic event "'doesn't stop *not* being written,'"[28] continuing to haunt the living. Particular empirical traumas happen because of originary trauma. Even though occasioned by chance, they are repeats of originary trauma.

---

25. Pool, *God's Wounds*, 2.
26. Žižek, *Absolute Recoil*, 119; cf. Lacan, *On Femenine Sexuality*, 59.
27. Žižek, *The Fragile Absolute*, 88, 58.
28. Lacan, *On Feminine Sexuality*, 59.

The distressing conclusion: in the end—despite every effort, including psychoanalysis—trauma can never be healed, only endured. The traumatic void at the heart of subjectivity remains. Trauma is irrevocable, irreparable, permanent. According to Žižek, we need to accept "the very fact that our lives involve a traumatic kernel beyond redemption, that there is a dimension of our being which forever resists redemption-deliverance."[29] Indeed, for Žižek, "'diabolical Evil' is not the unattainable *telos* of Evil, its extreme point which can never be reached, but, rather, something *which always-already has happened* the moment we are in the ethical domain."[30]

For Žižek—as in the beginning, so in the end—"Reality-in-itself is Nothingness, the Void."[31] Indeed, "the true trauma is the subject itself, its abyssal focal point that Hegel called the Night of the world. Perhaps, he suggests, this is how we should read the famous chorus lines from *Antigone*: 'There are many uncanny/terrifying things in the world, but nothing more uncanny/terrifying than man himself.'"[32] "For a human is constitutively 'out-of-joint.'"[33] According to Žižek, "Brecht was right, humans are by nature evil and corrupt; one cannot change them, but only limit their opportunities to actualize their evil potential."[34]

Uncanniness

Certainly, there is something perplexing, strange, yes, uncanny—to pick up on Žižek's reference to Sophocles' Antigone—in the world and in humanity, something mysterious and extraordinary, beyond the grasp of reason. According to Freud, Heidegger, and Derrida—three thinkers who have paid special attention to the uncanny—the uncanny in its many forms and in countless ways haunts and bedevils our existence.[35]

In his extremely influential 1919 essay, entitled *Das Unheimliche* (translated as *The Uncanny*), Freud was among the first to understand the uncanny as both familiar and strange, a "class of the terrifying which leads back to something long known to us, once very familiar."[36] For Freud the unfamiliar at the heart of the familiar is the unconscious, not a part that one

---

29. Žižek, *The Fragile Absolute*, 91.
30. Žižek, *The Plague of Fantasies*, 308.
31. Žižek, *Less Than Nothing*, 926.
32. Žižek, *Absolute Recoil*, 401.
33. Žižek, *Less Than Nothing*, 834.
34. Žižek, *Less Than Nothing*, 107.
35. *The* book on the uncanny is *The Uncanny* by Nicholas Royle.
36. In Freud, *The Standard Edition*, vol., 14:239–58.

consciously thinks is part of the self; and yet it arises hauntingly from within oneself... Uncanny, *Angst*, Trauma.

Freud's idea of trauma as the persistence of an alien presence within the self was adopted and developed by Jacques Derrida. The individual person, the Ego, is constituted by identifications which come to lodge as specters or ghosts. "Everyone reads, acts, writes with *his* or *her* ghosts"[37] which come not only from the past but from the future. In place of the Cartesian "I think, therefore I am," "I am" means "'I am haunted'... Wherever there is Ego, *es spukt*, 'it spooks.'"[38] "A ghost never dies, it remains always to come and to come-back."[39] Accordingly, "ethics itself, to learn to live" is "to live otherwise... more justly... *with them* [our ghosts]." This bearing of "responsibility... before the ghosts of those who are not yet born or who are already dead"[40] is an uncanny, threshold experience of promise/threat.

The future is filled with ghosts. Since for Derrida it is crucial to "open up access to an affirmative thinking of the messianic and emancipatory promise as *promise*,"[41] it was a mistake for Freud to identify or confuse what is "*heimliche-unheimliche*... with the terrible or the frightful."[42] He also suggests that Freud—as well as Marx and Heidegger—did not begin where they ought to have begun, that is with ghosts, "with haunting."[43] He calls attention to the fact that Freud admitted that he should have started by discussing "*es spukt*" as the most striking example of uncanniness but did not because it was too mingled with the gruesome. For Derrida, "the messianic," as "the historical opening to the future," is "that other ghost which we cannot and ought not to do without ... strange, strangely familiar and inhospitable at the same time (*unheimlich*, uncanny)."[44] This spectral messianic figure is uncanny, strangely beautiful/strangely frightening—beyond mastery, and uncontrollable.

It was Heidegger who philosophically declared the very nature of life in the world to be uncanny, not-at-home. "At bottom, the ordinary is not ordinary; it is extra-ordinary, uncanny."[45] "In anxiety (*Angst*) one feels

---

37. Derrida, *Spectres of Marx*, 139.
38. Derrida, *Spectres of Marx*, 133.
39. Derrida, *Spectres of Marx*, 99.
40. Derrida, *Spectres of Marx*, xvii–xix.
41. Derrida, *Spectres of Marx*, 75.
42. Derrida, *Spectres of Marx*, 173.
43. Derrida, *Spectres of Marx*, 175.
44. Derrida, *Spectres of Marx*, 167–68.
45. Heidegger, *Poetry, Language, Thought*, 54.

'uncanny' (*unheimlich*)."[46] When, according to Heidegger, we feel at home in the world in our everyday life we are in fact tranquilized, lost in the "they." We are then fleeing from the 'not-at-home' uncanniness which is, for Heidegger, existentially and ontologically, the primordial phenomenon of human life and the nature of authentic existence. Fleeing from uncanniness means fleeing in the face of one's inmost being-towards-death: "Being-towards-death is essentially anxiety."[47]

In supplement and in contrast to Heidegger's inmost being-towards-death, I affirm the haunting uncanniness of our inmost being-towards-love. "I was loved, therefore I am." Human subjectivity finds itself primarily in love, not in anxiety. Love individualizes: "love being the condition of the very possibility of uniqueness."[48]

Indeed, it is in the uncanny experience of love—loving and being loved—that we are pulled out of the trance of self-absorption, no longer tranquilized. But this is not a flight from the "they" and the concerns of ordinary life. Rather, moved and inspired, we are motivated, empowered, and challenged to be "in" the world—but not "of" the world—as love's agents in the midst of daily life making and remaking healthy, just, and healing connections.

In supplement and contrast to Derrida's claim that being human is to be haunted, not only by ghosts from the past, but also by that coming messianic specter, both strangely familiar and inhospitable, I suggest that be(com)ing human is receiving the Spirit—"the Holy Ghost"—of Love, making oneself a dwelling for that Spirit, and abiding in Love. Each person, in his/her own way, gifted and called to become in concert unique, hospitable haunts of love and loving.

From the very beginning, the Spirit—God's *Ruah* of Love—hovered over the dark face of the deep. And throughout history, as we struggle in the midst of evil, brokenness, and trauma of every sort, not only does the terrible and horrible haunt us, but; even more, the Love of God haunts the creation, impinging, inviting, hounding, transforming, healing. Despite all shortcomings, regardless of the multitude outcroppings of evil, God's Love remains, mysterious, inextinguishable, inviting, surviving, impinging, persisting—without a why—seeping into the cracks and crevasses of life. As Jesus reminds us in John 3:8, "The Wind[-Spirit] blows where it chooses, and you hear the sound of it, but you do not know where it comes from, or where it goes" (NRSV).

---

46. Heidegger, *Being and Time*, 233.
47. Heidegger, *Being and Time*, 310.
48. Levinas, *Entre Nous*, 168.

In supplement and contrast to Freud's uncanny as the return of forbidden and repressed impulses, I affirm the uncanny as the haunting call of the lure of Love. "I am" then means "I am haunted, not only by hurts, wounds, and voices from the past, or from fears for the future, but I am haunted by Love, which never stops coming, promising, wooing, always already to heal and transform."

As has been a refrain throughout, my testimony is that everything begins and ends—not with Lacan and Žižek's dizzying Trauma of "without" (the Empty Void)—but with the "with-ing" of Love, its brimming Excess and uncanny Mystery. Love—beyond necessity, beyond chance—is spontaneous, excessive, extravagant, unbounded, even as it is not arbitrary or capricious. Love—more primordial than evil, outlasting, outliving, surviving death—somehow, someway, will chance/grace its way through death. Chance happens, but however random, however traumatic, it is simultaneously a gifting (an opening) as well as a calling (to let love loose) for generation and regeneration, for formation and transformation. Love is the grace of the world, the world's "oxygen" in which we live and move and have our being.

As the life-blood of the cosmos, Love events: generating a creation not only *out of* love (*creatio ex amore*), but *with* love (*cum amore*) and *for* love (*ad amorem*). Love happens and haunts, haunts and happens, happening anywhere and haunting everywhere—with consistence, insistence, and persistence. The world is not a determined or divinely supervised cosmos, nor an out-and-out, inherently oppositional, trauma-ridden chaos, but an uncanny rhythmic (dis)continuity of differentiation and integration, a kind of "chaosmos" (James Joyce) involving chances (heeded, missed, broken, enjoyed, endured, redeemed) of, for, and by Love.

CHAPTER 7

ON THE IM/POSSIBILITY OF THE GIFT: FROM DERRIDA'S PURE GIVING TO IRIGARAY'S MUTUAL LOVING

ONE EVENING IN LATE May, I was part of a birthday celebration at McDonalds. "What, Gramps," the birthday girl, Katie, asked, "were you doing in Philadelphia?" "Teaching philosophy," I said. "Well," she replied, "give us some philosophical questions." This being a birthday, and having just taught a course on the gift with Jack Caputo, I began to talk about the gift. At a certain point, Janine, the older ten-year-old granddaughter looked up and, with a glint in her eye, exclaimed: "I get it. It's Katie's birthday, so you brought her presents. But that's your duty, so they are really not gifts. But you also brought presents for Ari and me. You didn't have to. Those are gifts." Gramps was nonplussed, and—I admit it—tickled pink.

That scene kept looming in my consciousness as I was first writing this paper on the im/possibility of the gift in the theory of Jacques Derrida, reverberating to the point that I am using it to signal the possibility of intentional gifts. Derrida argues that the very intention to give and the very possibility of return introduces an element of calculation and violence into gifting that annuls it as a gift. My point will be that while the very intention to give and the very possibility of return does open the gift to the *risk* of violence, the risk of violence is precisely a possibility rather than an unavoidable necessity. In contrast to both an altruistic one-way economy with its disinterest in any return and an economy of reciprocal exchange focused on calculation and dedicated to risk-limitation (as John Milbank puts it) in which what is given always brings returns—remaining in the cycle of sameness—I suggest (in tune with Luce Irigaray) that there is a non-exchange economy, an economy of love. Beyond a tit-for-tat exchange of reciprocity, an economy of mutuality allows for and makes for the asymmetric giving and receiving of gifts. A gift, I will suggest, is not an expenditure without return, but a ventured excess with the risk of refusal and without a controlled, manipulated, contracted, or expected return. Such a gift is given, not for a return as such, but in the hope of making or marking a difference in the relation. Yes, such an economy is, as Jean-Luc Marion might say, risk-saturated. There is the risk of violence, the possibility of manipulation, bribe, rejection and betrayal. However, it is a risk worth taking, because without it there is no possibility of a mutual and enhanced connection with the other and different—no possibility of love.

The Double Bind of the Gift

Much of Derrida's later work struggles with the paradox of "the impossibility or the double bind of the gift."[1] On the one hand, there is the gift[2] as "the first mover of the circle,"[3] the "exteriority that sets the circle going . . . puts the economy in motion . . . that *engages* in the circle and makes it turn."[4] On the other hand, if there is a gift, "it must not circulate, it must not be exchanged, . . . the gift must remain *aneconomic*."[5] Since, "when *someone* gives *something* to *someone*, one is already long within calculating dialectics and speculative idealization, I give *me*, I make me the gift,"[6] the gift is actually impossible. The gift burns itself out; only cinders remain. "Wherever there is time, wherever time predominates or conditions experience in general, wherever *time as circle* . . . is predominant, the gift is impossible."[7] We are left, according to Derrida, with the paradoxical logic of the gift in which its very conditions of possibility are the conditions of its impossibility.

What this struggle means for his entire project of deconstruction is perhaps most emphatically underlined in *Sauf le nom (Post-Scriptum)*: "Far from being a methodical technique, a possible or necessary procedure, unrolling the law of a program and applying rules, that is, unfolding

1. Derrida, *Given Time*, 16. In the foreword to *Given Time*, Derrida notes that his "later works were all devoted, if one may put it that way, to the question of the gift, whether it appeared in its own name, as was often the case, or by means of the indissociable motifs of speculation, destination, or the promise, of sacrifice, the 'yes,' or originary affirmation, of the event, invention, the coming of the 'come'" (x).

2. In *Glas*, Derrida refers to this as "a pure gift, without exchange, without return" (Derrida, *Glas*, 243).

3. Derrida, *Given Time*, 31.
4. Derrida, *Given Time*, 30.
5. Derrida, *Given Time*, 7.
6. Derrida, *Glas*, 243.
7. Derrida, *Given Time*, 9.

possibilities, deconstruction has often been defined as the experience of the (impossible) possibility of the impossible, of the most impossible, a condition that deconstruction shares with the gift, the 'yes,' the 'come,' decision, testimony, the secret, etc. And perhaps death."[8]

In the paradoxical logic of the gift; gifts are annulled the moment they appear. What appear to be gifts are actually counterfeits, ruses, schemes. For when A gives to B, B becomes indebted to A. B is not given a gift as much as a debt. And A doesn't give as much as take credit. "For there to be a gift, there must be no reciprocity, return, exchange, countergift, or debt. If the other *gives* me *back* or *owes* me or has to give me back what I give him or her, there will not have been a gift."[9] The gift is undone in the very giving. "For there to be a gift, it is necessary that the gift not even appear, that it not be perceived or recognized as gift."[10] "*At the limit, the gift as gift* ought *not to appear as gift: either to the donnee or to the donor.*"[11]

The annulment holds even when the giver wishes to remain anonymous. "The simple intention to give, insofar as it carries the intentional meaning of the gift, suffices to make a return payment to oneself... in a sort of auto-recognition, self-approval, and narcissistic gratitude."[12] Subjective intention in the cycle of time inevitably and inescapably turns gift-giving into calculating transactions between creditors and debtors. To guard against the subversion of giving, I would have to give without knowing that I had given, and without the one receiving the gift knowing that s/he had received it.[13]

And yet, "if the gift is another name of the impossible, we still think it, we name it, we desire it. We intend it."[14] We are to be impassioned by, and to live "by the impossible,"[15] for not to do so is to remain trapped in the circle of the same. We desire the gift as "the *paradoxical* instant" of "madness" that "tears time apart."[16] "For there to be gift event (we say event and not act), something must come about or happen, in an instant, in an instant that no

---

8. Derrida, *On the Name*, 43. Thus, in *Given Time*, Derrida notes that the "aporetics" of the gift are the aporetics of *différance* (126–27).

9. Derrida, *Given Time*, 12.

10. Derrida, *Given Time*, 16.

11. Derrida, *Given Time*, 14.

12. Derrida, *Given Time*, 23.

13. "Pure morality must exceed calculation, conscious or unconscious, of restitution or reappropriation" (Derrida, *On the Name*, 133).

14. Derrida, *Given Time*, 29.

15. Derrida, *Given Time*, 10.

16. Derrida, *Given Time*, 9.

doubt does not belong to the economy of time, in a time without time."[17] The gift is an expenditure without return in the madness of an instant.

Thus for Derrida, we are caught in an aporia between the "order of the gift" (ethics) and the "order of meaning (presence, science, knowledge)." We desire to gift even though in time and history we are trapped in the "the destructive circle" of sameness which is the ruination of the gift by the gift.[18] Derrida clearly outlines "the paradox." On the one hand, since intention annuls the gift, "there must be chance, encounter, the involuntary, even unconsciousness or disorder." However, on the other hand, since the "effects of pure chance will never form a gift ... [t]here is no gift without the intention of giving ... and there must be intentional freedom, and these two conditions must—miraculously, graciously—agree with each other."[19]

Derrida's response (it is certainly not a solution) is a double-sided exhortation: Respond as "faithfully but also rigorously as possible both to the injunction or the order of the gift ... as well as to the injunction or order of meaning ... *Know* still what giving *wants to say, know how to give*, know what you want and want to say when you give, know what you intend to give, know how the gift annuls itself, commit yourself (*engage-toi*) even if commitment is the destruction of the gift by the gift, give economy its chance."[20] That is, even as you participate in the push and pull of the economy (like the poor, it will always be with us), try to interrupt it, push against its limits, go for broke to let the gift be given. Try to outplay the game in playing the game. Be vigilant: knowing the gift annuls itself. But don't in any way lessen your passion for giving a gift. There is no other choice if there is to be a gift, if justice is to come. Finally, recognize that it is the order of the impossible gift that "*engages* in the circle and makes it turn." So keep the faith, work for the impossible, even though there is no escape from the "destructive circle." That is simply our best hope in keeping violence at a minimum. And, then, sometimes, a gift happens, not as an intentional act, but as an impersonal, anonymous, aleatory event—on the wing, a matter of chance, a throw of the dice.

There is much to be said in favor of Derrida's approach. His ethical concern to make room for and seek justice for the other, all the while hyper-alert for the human propensity in all of us to self-deception and violence, is laudatory in every respect. However, I admit to disquiet particularly on two interrelated fronts. I question Derrida's assumption that human

17. Derrida, *Given Time*, 17.
18. Derrida, *Given Time*, 30.
19. Derrida, *Given Time*, 123.
20. Derrida, *Given Time*, 30.

intentionality is always, without exception, necessarily self-seeking appropriation locked into a tit for tat economy of exchange. I suggest there is an alternative economy of love in which subjective acts are hospitably open to others, a possibility Derrida himself at points envisioned. I also want to claim that moving in such a direction gives credence to choosing, in the test of *khôra*, for *il y a* matrix rather than *il y a khôra*.

Derrida is quite clear that when "someone wants or desires to give to someone," it necessarily and inevitably "supposes a subject ... seeking through the gesture of the gift to constitute its own unity and, precisely, to get its own identity recognized so that the identity comes back to it, so that it can reappropriate its identity: as its property."[21] For Derrida, an "identifiable, bordered, posed subject, the one who writes and his or her writing never give anything without calculating, consciously or unconsciously, its reappropriation, its exchange, or its circular return ... We will even venture to say that this is the very definition of the *subject as such*."[22] In other words, for Derrida the human subject is always a principle of self-calculation, self-interest, and a "certain capitalization" set in opposition to others.

That, indeed, is the decisive reason why the gift can never happen. If I give out of duty, I don't really freely give; I give, appease my guilt, and do myself a favor. If I give simply because I like to, I'm not really giving a gift either. I'm engaging in something that gives me pleasure. But whether out of duty or pleasure, the gift is not a pure gift.

A gift is finally, for Derrida, only a gift to oneself, reappropriating identity as property. In that sense, gift-giving is a violent act because it puts the receiver in debt and obligation as soon as s/he receives. The giver in this economy exercises—often relishes—his power-over the recipient in being the cause of the surprise.[23] Indeed, continues Derrida, "such violence may be considered the very condition of the gift, its constitutive impurity once the gift is engaged in a process of *circulation*, once it is promised, to recognition, keeping, indebtedness, credit, but also once it *must be, owes itself to be* excessive and thereby surprising. *The violence appears irreducible, within the circle or outside it, whether it repeats the circle or interrupts it.*"[24]

For Derrida, intersubjective opposition seems—a là Hegel—endemic to and inherent in human relationships. Here I demur. Why is return to self always at the cost of the other person? Why is being for the other *necessarily* to be against self? In this model the choice is between sacrificing

21. Derrida, *Given Time*, 11.
22. Derrida, *Given Time*, 101.
23. Derrida, *Given Time*, 146.
24. Derrida, *Given Time*, 147.

myself and the irresponsibility of sacrificing the other. Neither choice is exactly appealing. When to be a "living subject" is inevitably to be a rival of every other self, we can know *of* the other, but can we ever genuinely connect with the other in face-to-face mutuality?

I agree with Derrida that there is a certain "madness" to authentic giving because it is not tit-for-tat calculation. However, in Derrida's case, the madness (giving without a why) only happens as an aleatory, accidental event (although it continues to beckon and inspire), whereas I want to claim that there can be a gift as a conscious act, love given and received, not in spite of, but at the behest of human intentionality.

Irreducible Violence?

Derrida's paradoxical logic of the gift presupposes an irreducible "zero-sum game" in which giving to one necessarily implies taking away from another. In such an oppositional game, "gift" translates as "guilt," because, if I have given something to someone, someone else is deprived of it. In such an economy, the only ethical choice is sacrificing myself lest I succumb to the irresponsibility of sacrificing the other. But are these the only two choices? To envision intersubjectivity as primordially a relation of opposition makes love of the other by definition impossible. To see such opposition as constitutively built into the very fabric of reality prioritizes—ontologizes— violence. Yes, in our broken and alienating world, we all participate in violence, are often complicit with it, commit it, and suffer from it! But always! necessarily! without exception! according to the very structure of human subjectivity? Is subjective intention inevitably and necessarily always calculated control, manipulation at the cost of the other?

A true gift is, in Derrida's words, "excessive and thereby surprising." The question is whether such surprising is necessarily and constitutively always a "matter of taking, of taking over and bringing under control, of harpooning"[25] the other as Derrida insists. Why is the surprise of a gift necessarily violent—to the point that, as was noted earlier, violence "may be considered the very condition of the gift, its constitutive impurity"[26]? Is it not true that at times the surprise of a gift results from being carried away in love, a surprise without violence that may take one's breath away because unexpected? Yes, there is always an element of risk in any surprise, for both giver and receiver. That's its beauty and its bane.

Derrida saves the gift from human contamination, but at a huge cost: there is no such thing as an intentional act of giving, only aleatory gifting

---

25. Derrida, *Given Time*, 147.
26. Derrida, *Given Time*, 147.

events. In considering the human subject to be by nature always structurally aggressive, Derrida belongs to a long tradition, still dominant, stretching all the way back to Plato and Aristotle, in which being is defined in terms of power, power-over. "My notion would be," Plato has the Stranger say in the *Sophist* (247d), as we saw in chapter 2, "that anything which possesses any sort of power to affect another, or to be affected by another, if only for a single moment, however trifling the cause and however slight the effect, has real existence; and I hold that the definition of being is simply power." Throughout the subsequent centuries to the present, power—as opposed to love—has been and still is the central organizing concept of the dominant ontologies, theologies, and ethics.

However, what if human agency is not inevitably and inexorably structurally aggressive? What if difference is not intrinsically, by the nature of the case, oppositional? The core problem, in my view, is not agency itself, but understanding and identifying the power to act of human agency as *power-over*, or *power-against*, incontrovertibly and necessarily aggressive. The human self, it is increasingly being emphasized, is not separative, but connective. Rather than being isolated monads, autonomous self-interested subjects with other humans as "objects" to be done to and acted upon, humans are interdependent subjects: selves-in-relation, selves-with, selves-in-formation. Indeed, the English word "interest" comes from the Latin *interesse*: being-in-between. Life is in-the-between, inter-medial; *intra*subjectivity is intrinsically *inter*subjective.

This means that the power of human agency is constitutionally and fundamentally power-in-relation, *power-with*. Which means that self-love and self-interest can be of one piece with love of other and other-interest. Which in turn means that power as oppositional, power-over or power-against, is a derivative phenomenon, indicative of malfunction and breakdown rather than definitive of human agency.

If this is indeed the case, it is not difference or power as such that is problematic but conceptualizations which see the only choices as being power-over (selfish *eros*) or power-under (selfless *agape*). Derrida himself, in *Points*, points the way to another possibility. He talks of a "welcoming, hospitable narcissism, one that is much more open to the experience of the other as other." At the same time, however, such narcissism, he continues to insist, is impossible without a "movement of reappropriation"; "without a movement of narcissistic reappropriation, the relation to the other would be absolutely destroyed, it would be destroyed in advance....Love is narcissistic."[27] Nevertheless, Derrida's figure of a "hospitable" narcissism

---

27. Derrida, *Points*, 199.

does open a way to recognize that not all intention, not all self-interest is irrevocably and inescapably egoistic self-seeking. It is not self-engagement, self-commitment, self-involvement that is problematic. It is the kind of engagement, commitment, and involvement—possessive or sharing, dominating or mutual, self-obsessed or self-giving—which is the difference that matters. Then, the intentional giving and receiving of gifts can become a loving exercise in mutuality—what I refer to as "with-ing," love without jealousy—which escapes the violence of the "destructive circle."

Derrida is right to insist that genuine giving breaks with the logic of equivalence, surrenders all attempts to control, is excessive, a surplus, and reckoned as nothing. In a way that is beyond control (but not outside of human intention), authentic giving is a graced process, the "more" which takes us by surprise, the excess that is contagious. In the surplus economy of love, mutual sharing replaces competitive striving. Giving engenders giving. There is a passing on of love, unpredictably, expansively. "The gift survives only in its non-identical repetition; as long as we give, there will be more giving."[28] Good gifts, said Pseudo-Dionysius, "are not lessened by being partaken. Indeed, they pour out all the more generously."[29]

Il y a khôra

In Derrida's framework the only way that the gift could avoid being annulled in the exchange economy is that it not appear as a gift and so have no phenomenality. In that way, below the plane of subjectivity and phenomenality, anonymous, the gift could happen, bleached and sanitized from the contamination of intentionality. That leads Derrida to Heidegger's *es gibt*, an impersonal giving, a "giving that gives but without giving anything and without anyone giving anything,"[30] a giving that doesn't care, a kind of withdrawal in the appearing, in which things happen as they happen.

However, although attracted to the impersonal and indiscriminate giving of *es gibt*, Derrida is not altogether comfortable with it. He expresses a "few reservations"[31] at the way "the desire to accede to the proper is already, we could say, surreptitiously ordered by Heidegger according to the dimension of 'giving.'"[32] Derrida is, I think rightly, concerned that

---

28. Webb, *The Gifting God*, 157. Webb develops a Trinitarian ethics of excess in which "gifting creates its own disorder, a community of givers [the church] that empowers others to give and give again" (149).
29. Pseudo-Dionysius, *The Divine Names*, 115.
30. Derrida, *Given Time*, 20.
31. Derrida, *Given Time*, 162.
32. Derrida, *Given Time*, 21.

Heidegger still interprets giving, even if impersonal, in terms of an identity problematics of what is "proper," "properly their own," and "movements of propriation, expropriation, de-propriation, or appropriation,"[33] with the net effect of giving up the desire for the gift as "another name of the impossible."[34] the dream of ethics and the wholly other.

For that reason, Derrida sees *es gibt* to be "risky" and prefers "there is *khôra*" (*il y a khôra*), a *"there is*, which, by the way, *gives* nothing in giving place or in giving to think."[35] *Il y a khôra* is the "very spacing of deconstruction"[36] without any reference to the "gesture of a donor-subject."[37] Events happen—gift as event, not as act—in a disseminative excess, an aleatory diffusion in *différance*, with no thanks to *différance*.

Here again Derrida's conviction that donor-subjects with their intentionality (even divine subjects) are not able to give and be open to the other without egoistic self-interest playing its role. However, whereas Derrida at this point falls back on an anonymous, impersonal *khôra*, once again it is crucial to underline the cardinal difference between narcissistic self-interest (it's all about me and for me!) and loving self-interest in which concern for the well-being—the self-interest—of the other is my self-interest. Then, would-be mastery is replaced with loving concern for the other: self-interest (love of self) of one piece with other-interest (love of others).

My concern here is that in (I think, rightly) resisting Heidegger's subjectivation, Derrida's emphasis on the mute anonymity of this *il y a khôra* seems, at the same time, to bring him dangerously close to a kind of Heideggerian pre-ethical space in which good and evil appear equally in the clearing of Being. In discussing the "place," "the spacing," Derrida admits that "it remains to be known if this nonsensible (invisible and inaudible) place is opened by God, by the name of God, . . . or if it is 'older' than the time of creation, than time itself, than history, narrative, word, etc. It remains to be known (beyond knowing) if the place is opened by appeal (response, the event that calls for response, revelation, history, etc.), or if it remains impassively foreign, like *Khôra*, to everything that takes its places and replaces itself and plays within

---

33. Derrida, *Given Time*, 22.
34. Derrida, *Given Time*, 29.
35. Derrida, *On the Name*, 96.
36. Derrida, *On the Name*, 80.
37. Derrida, *On the Name*, 100.

this place, including what is named God. Let's call this the test of *Khôra* . . . ."[38] "Who are you, *Khôra?*."[39] How are we to decide?[40]

If, for Derrida, giving always turns into a giving of death, if the fires of love leave only cinders, it is because, as I read it, he construes *il y khôra* to be the "impassively foreign" abyss lurking beneath the surface of ordinary life. However, if every activity and every discourse involves finally, at bottom, a construal of faith ("I don't know, one has to believe . . . "[41]), it is equally possible, as Derrida acknowledges, to think *khôra* otherwise than as an anonymous and cold abyss. Indeed, it makes just as much, in my view, more sense and is certainly more hopeful to read *khôra* in the first way, as the place opened by God, the with-place of love. That in no way means the abyss is unreal. The creation as a kind of *archi*-matrix or womb, like Plato's *khôra*,[42] is often ruptured and abyssal. But the spaces of creation are primordially the wild spaces of and for love,[43] fields for meeting, wombs for birth.[44]

However, Derrida's choice for an impassively neutral *khôra* seems to grant as much legitimacy to the negativity (of hate) as to the positivity (of love). Is *il y a khôra*, the field of *différance*, to be envisioned as prior to love, producing love and justice as hyperbolic effects,[45] or is it, as in *il y a matrix*, the ringing call of love, the Yes, Yes, that opens up the field of *différance*? In this latter way, although historical events of justice and love, including the words "justice" and "love," are effects of the play of *différance* (and therefore subject to undecidability), love as the archi-originary word gifts the creation into existence, both calling for the play of life and making it possible.

Although, as we have just noted, Derrida in the test of *khôra* reveals a predilection for the second choice, the "impassively foreign," there are also

---

38. Derrida, *On the Name*, 75–77.
39. Derrida, *On the Name*, 111.
40. See Olthuis, "Testing the Heart of *Khôra*; Anonymous or Amorous?"
41. Derrida, *Memoirs of the Blind*, 129.
42. Kristeva calls the undifferentiated space shared by mother and child *khôra* (*Desire in Language*, 133).
43. See chapter 10 in this volume.
44. In a similar way, I suggest, what Levinas refers to as the "anonymous rustling," the "there is [*il y a*], the horrible eternity at the bottom of essence," is not as primordial as the "ultimate situation of the 'face-to-face' in which the transcendent summons us" (*Otherwise than Being*, 3, 176).
45. Which is the position John D. Caputo avows concerning justice in *Demythologizing Heidegger*, ch. 11, "Hyperbolic Justice." Jeffrey Dudiak questions Caputo's hyperbolic reading of Derrida's "infinite demand for justice" and suggests a Levinasian reading in which *différance* is not the condition of justice, but justice is "the condition of possibility of *différance*" ("Against Ethics: A Levinasian reading of Caputo reading Levinas" in Olthuis, *Knowing Other-wise*, 201).

soundings in his work which speak for the first choice, what I am calling *il y a matrix*. In *Limited Inc.*, he talks of an "'unconditional' affirmation or of 'unconditional' 'appeal'" that is "independent of every determinate context, even of the determination of a context in general."[46] In *Of Spirit*, Derrida calls this "pre-originary pledge" which "precedes any other engagement and action," that calls forth and interrupts every context, a "sometimes wordless word which we name the 'yes.'"[47] He points out that "for a very long time, the question of yes has mobilized or traversed everything I have been trying to think, write, teach, or read."[48] In "Ulysses Gramophone: Hear Say Yes in Joyce," he calls this wordless word "a yes more 'ancient' ... I say the *yes* and not the word 'yes,' because there can be a yes without a word."[49] There is more. In "A Number of Yes," Derrida quotes and discusses a long passage from Michel de Certeau's *The Mystic Fable* which focuses on Angelus Silesius, who, in the seventeenth century, explicitly did connect Yes and God: "*Gott Spricht nur immer Ja* God always says only Yes."[50] Even more, as Caputo points out in arguing for the "religious resonance and force of *yes*" in Derrida's work, Derrida "openly associates the *yes* with a prayer, with *amen*"[51] in the Postscript to the French text of *Ulysses* by referencing Franz Rosenzweig's *The Star of Redemption*.[52] Thus, although Derrida himself never identifies this 'yes more ancient,' 'wordless word' with Love or God, making the connection gives added impetus and depth to his avowal in *Points* that Deconstruction "always accompanies an affirmative exigency, I would even say that it never proceeds without love...."[53]

46. Derrida, *Limited Inc.*, 152.

47. Derrida, *Of Spirit*, 130.

48. Derrida, *Acts of Literature*, 296. For a fascinating discussion of the function of "yes" in Derrida, see Gasché, *Inventions of Difference*, 199–250. See also fn.1.

49. Derrida, *Acts of Literature*, 287.

50. Jacques Derrida, *Psyche*, 2:233.

51. Caputo, *The Prayers and Tears of Jacques Derrida*, 255. The Postscript was not included in the English translation.

52. Franz Rosenzweig, *The Star of Redemption*. Yes is for Rosenzweig "the arch-word of language... which first makes possible... words as parts of the sentence. Yea is not a part of a sentence... [it is] the 'Amen' behind every word... It gives every word in the sentence its right to exist, it supplies the seat on which it may take its place, it 'posits.' The first Yea in God establishes the divine essence for all infinity. And this first Yea is 'in the beginning'" (27).

53. Derrida. *Points*, 83.

An Economy of Love: Return, Not Control

Indeed, for me, the wordless word Yes is the creative, gifting/calling Word of God, calling for and making possible an economy of love in which a gift is not an indiscriminate, aleatory exception, but an intentional realization of human intersubjectivity with its deep desire for connection between self, others, creation, and God. Such an economy is not an oppositional zero-sum game in which love can only be given here by withholding it there. Rather, love expands and increases when given and received: an excess beyond the demands of contract, a meeting in the between, without strings, spontaneous, a "love without jealousy that would allow the other to be."[54]

Whereas in the economic realm there is a symmetry and reciprocity in which we may buy and sell the same thing as our neighbor—one product being (more or less) as good as another—in the realm of ethics there is an asymmetry and non-substitution. While economic goods as such are scarce and interchangeable, there is an extravagant, over the top quality to genuine gifts. Just as one friend cannot be replaced by another friend, a gift bespeaks a special connection, marking some worthy occasion or embodying a unique relation. Ethical giving is not without return, but the giving is not to elicit, control, or manipulate a return. Remarkably, as a genuine gift is a passing-on of love, it gives rise to a ripple effect, a letting loose of love with a return extending far beyond the giver.

Although, as I just noted, the mutuality model of an economy of love needs to be distinguished from a reciprocal economy of exchange, the very *risk* of mutuality brings with it the constant temptation to control the risk. When this happens, the economy of love—without the why of a guarantee—morphs into an economy of exchange demanding an equal return.[55] The contrast is between a gift *risking* a bad return or even no return, and a "gift" *controlling* the return.

Gift-giving is not, in an economy of love, linked with building credit, repaying debts, or manipulating feelings, but with forming, sustaining, and celebrating unique connections of mutuality and trust. There is no doubt return to the self,[56] but not at the cost or expense of the other. In this case, as explored and wonderfully developed in the work of Luce Irigaray, the giving and receiving develops into inspiring rhythms and patterns

---

54. Derrida, *On the Name*, 74.

55. See John Milbank who takes a similar tack in an incisive article, "Can a Gift Be Given? Prolegomena to a Future Trinitarian Metaphysic."

56. "With no return to the self, woman/women cannot truly engage in dialogue." (Irigaray, *i love to you*, 109.)

"beyond any exchange of objects."[57] Yes, there is self-interest in the giving, but not for purposes of mastery, rather for enhanced and enriched connection between giver and receiver. It is a being "faithful" to self in one's irreducibility that seeks "to find a rhythm in the other"[58] "without any hierarchy between the two... With each giving the other necessity and freedom. In self, for self, and for the other."[59] "The act of love is neither an explosion nor an implosion but an indwelling. Dwelling with the self, and with the other—while letting the other go."[60]

In the logic of mutual love, giving to one person does not take away from others as if there is only so much to go around. Rather, in its excessiveness, love overflows, rippling, stimulating, inviting others to participate in the give-away which paradoxically creates even "more" to give away. After this manner, a gift of love is also always a call to participate in a cosmic movement bigger than ourselves, as "a god carried on the breath of the cosmos."[61] In that way we may give gifts, good gifts, not because we have to, or even simply because we want to, but because, breathing-in love, we breathe-out love, and we "meet with the other" in mutual "enstasy" rather than in an "ecstasy" that leaves the self behind.[62] "For lovers to love each other, between them must be Love."[63] Love is, for Irigaray, the "third term,"[64] the "*Between*. In the interval of time,"[65] the "air keeping the copula from hardening up or disappearing into the is."[66] [67]

Moreover, a gift given but not received is not yet a gift. When there is no possibility of rejection, there is no gift. This explains why, particularly in romantic pursuits and in family settings, it is commonly recognized that unilateral giving speaks more of obsession and folly than generosity. Even in cases of beneficent care, the donnee needs to receive in order that there be a gift and not a bribe or duty. Paradoxically, in "receiving" (as distinct from "taking") there is also a certain giving back. Although, for

---

57. Irigaray, *i love to you*, 45.
58. Irigaray, *An Ethics of Sexual Difference*, 53.
59. Irigaray, *An Ethics of Sexual Difference*, 93.
60. Irigaray, *An Ethics of Sexual Difference*, 212.
61. Irigaray, *An Ethics of Sexual Difference*, 129.
62. Irigaray, *i love to you*, 105.
63. Irigaray, *An Ethics of Sexual Difference*, 30.
64. Irigaray, *An Ethics of Sexual Difference*, 12.
65. Irigaray, *An Ethics of Sexual Difference*, 53.
66. Irigaray, *i love to you*, 149.

67. In a very subtle critique of Heidegger, Irigaray protests that *Dasein* forgets air (*An Ethics of Sexual Difference*, 127). She works this critique out in *The Forgetting of Air in Martin Heidegger*.

Derrida, the very possibility of return introduces an element of intention and calculation that annuls the gift, Irigaray's point is that the very possibility of return introduces an element of risk in that the gift may either be confirmed or annulled.

When a gift is given or received as a payment, bribe, or inducement, the return disfigures and cancels the gift. Conversely, when it is given or received as an extravagance, the return configures and affirms the gift as a gift. Thus, shared pleasure in the dance of mutuality may, I suggest, be the fulfillment rather than the annulment of the gift. Genuine gifts are neither penalties compensating for our guilt, sops filling up our emptiness, rewards we seek, or investments we calculate, but the copiousness which embodies the gift of love we are and are called to be. Such giving is not without purpose; it is deliberate, but not coerced; it is lavish, but not wasteful; generous, but not reckless. Such giving is without why: it is loving.

In giving love, we relinquish control and in the process put ourselves at risk. An economy of love lacks guarantees or safeguards and is extremely susceptible to all the vicissitudes of fear, anger, insecurity, and hate. Giving and receiving can quickly degenerate into games of manipulation, harden into bonds of contract, or even be forged into chains of violence. In the gesture of love, says Irigaray, "each one runs the risk of annihilating, killing, or resuscitating."[68] But, by the same token, the bonds and rings of love may be "untouched by mastery,"[69] extremely creative and exceptionally strong.

Donner l'amour, a là Irigaray, or *il y a matrix*, as I am suggesting, seems more attuned to Derrida's own call for justice and love for the other than is his *il y a khôra* as the "impassively foreign," impersonal, cold, and uncaring space of "giving." Love has no preconditions but love. In the beginning is giving—and giving calls, evoking and inviting receiving. At the same time, giving of itself does not always or *necessarily* lead to gifts. There are no ouisiological guarantees. The gift need not be. For Derrida, although the gift calls to be, and longs to be, it *cannot* be, due to human narcissism.

In the *il y a matrix* of love, although any giving is undecidable—it may be skewed, thwarted, manipulated, refused, turned into a debt, a bribe or poison—a gift *may* be. Likewise, receiving does not always end up in a situation and state of an indebtedness which is ethically culpable; but, a gift—freely received as it is freely given—is what could be called a "good debt," a thankful reception from an irreducible other which enhances life "without overcoming, without annulling, without killing."[70] Indeed, in an economy

---

68. Irigaray, *An Ethics of Sexual Difference*, 193.
69. Irigaray, *An Ethics of Sexual Difference*, 186.
70. Irigaray, *i love to you*, 118.

of love, human intentionality in its specificity can enhance, rather than torpedo, the gift. While a random act of kindness is not to be sneezed at, and aleatory gifts are always welcome, carefully chosen gifts, donnee-specific, give rise, I am suggesting, to the prospect of truly honoring singularity and celebrating difference in an unparalleled degree.[71]

In an economy of non-oppositional difference, gifts of oneself (and from oneself) can be given intentionally (and received by another) not as selfish, or self-centered, but as openhanded and uplifting gestures in which "I do not subjugate you or consume you. I respect you (as irreducible) . . . I give to you (and not: I give *you* to another)."[72] It is not that such interactions will be without intention, return, or self-interest (that would, indeed, make them non-human), but such matters are neither their prime motivation nor their central focus. Our individual longings to be-long and be-connected with others (i.e. be loving and loved) are taken up in a dynamic of mutuality, of fidelity to self and to the other, in a "rhythmic becoming"[73] that seeks "to find a rhythm in the other"[74] with "return to self so as to move again toward the other."[75]

Just as "[t]he heart of a rose opens without the need of a blueprint . . . for no reason,"[76] genuine giving is of the heart without why, without teleology, resisting reckoning, always again for the first time. Giving gives, reaches out, evokes, calls, invites—it has no choice—because it is the movement of love, and love seeks connection with the sacred other. "The only guide here is the call to the other, whose breath subtly impregnates the air like a vibration perceptible to these [persons] lost for love."[77] Giving is laying the self bare, without guarantees, risking rejection, yes, even death. Yet in the giving one also finds life. For, if in freely offering myself to the other, risking breath, yielding my rhythm to the other, I am received, affirmed, and met, I receive myself back with a new amplitude. That is the graciousness of love. "In this way they expire one into the other, and rise up again inspired."[78]

---

71. "I recognize you goes hand in hand with: you are irreducible to me, just as I am to you. . . . And it's this negative that enables me to go towards you. . . . I go towards that which enables me to become while remaining myself" (Irigaray, *i love to you*, 103–4).

72. Irigaray, *i love to you*, 109.

73. Irigaray, *An Ethics of Sexual Difference*, 42.

74. Irigaray, *An Ethics of Sexual Difference*, 53.

75. Irigaray, *An Ethics of Sexual Difference*, 42.

76. Irigaray, *Sexes and Genealogies*, 48. This paean on mutuality is—most appropriately, in my view—the concluding section of Irigaray's essay given at the Cerisy conference in August 1980 on the work of Jacques Derrida.

77. Irigaray, *Sexes and Genealogies*, 51.

78. Irigaray, *Sexes and Genealogies*, 51.

In giving we cross the frontiers of our own lives, stripping away all structures of security, trusting only the love that, in carrying us, carries us outward and onward. We agree to journey where we are borne, letting the love which surges in us to "flow out again in the fullness of the gift. . . . In rapturous consent, they receive and give themselves in the open."[79]

"The way to this strange adventure" is difficult, for it means being "free of the spell that made them afraid to be without shelter . . . they say yes, unreservedly, to the whole of the experience to come. Even to death, as one other face of life? Yes. And to the other as other? Yes?."[80] On the way of this strange adventure, "I am listening to you prepare the way for the not-yet-coded, for silence, for space for existence, initiative, free intentionality, and support for your becoming. . . . I give you a silence in which your future—and perhaps my own, but *with* you and not *as* you and *without* you—may emerge and lay its foundation. . . . A silence that is the primary gesture of *I love to you*."[81]

Oui, Oui, which as John Caputo offers, is the postmodern amen.[82] Who are you *khôra*? *Il y a l'amour.* There is Love. Love, and gift, as you will. The world is waiting!

---

79. Irigaray, *Sexes and Genealogies*, 51, 52.
80. Irigaray, *Sexes and Genealogies*, 52.
81. Irigaray, *i love to you*, 117.
82. Caputo and Derrida, *Deconstruction in a Nutshell*, 202.

CHAPTER 8

OTHERWISE THAN VIOLENCE: TOWARD A HERMENEUTICS OF CONNECTION

"In the beginning is the relation." Martin Buber

"In the beginning is hermeneutics." Jacques Derrida

"In the beginning was the telephone." Jacques Derrida

"In the beginning is the Divine Eros, embodied in all being." Rita Nakashima Brock

"In the beginning was Love." Julia Kristeva

HERMES, THOUGHT BY THE Greeks to be the discoverer of language and writing, is the messenger of the gods, the bearer of their tidings. Hermes presents the "Other," the other who claims, asks to be heard, evokes encounter, and invites response. Meeting with difference—the other, the strange, the remote—may be enriching, challenging, and surprising, but it may also be eroding, paralyzing, and disturbing. In and through such meetings we change; we become other-wise. In every step of the process, from the first reflex to thoughtful response, acts of interpretation play an indispensable and crucial role. For it is as the persons we are—gendered, located, timed—that we see (that is, read or interpret) the persons, texts, or artworks in the ways we do, in certain ways, as such and such.[1] Interpreting thus begins an interactive journey—frequently an adventure—with the hope of coming into genuine contact with another for mutual enrichment. Hermeneutics, in this reading, is the art of interpretation which arose to help facilitate, promote, and ease the whole process of illuminating differences, sharpening insights, and deepening connections.

---

1. On the as-structure of interpretation, see Heidegger, *Being and Time*, 188ff.

Since the "other" or "others" to be met may be persons, texts, artworks, or even animals or trees, as well as God, there will be a wide variety of subject-specific hermeneutic methods that call for development, learning, and practice. At the same time, despite the wide-ranging differences among such specialized hermeneutics, the fact that interpreting and connecting are core concerns gives rise to general theories of hermeneutics.

In this chapter I want to move toward such a general theory of hermeneutics from what could be called a postmodern "feminist" perspective. I want to suggest a hermeneutics of connection as an alternative to "mastery" modes of interpretation as interpenetration. Instead of beginning with a Cartesian-Husserlian autonomous subject intent on the creation and control of meaning or a Hegelian intersubjectivity of oppositional difference, I begin with an intersubjective economy of non-oppositional difference—an economy of love (*eros*)—and its yearning for healthy connection, shared power, mutuality, and right relation—in the face of and in spite of the risk of violence. Eros is the cosmological urge to connect, the full-bodied, multidimensional desire to reach out, meet, and be in contact with others, the beyond, and God. In living out, pursuing, shaping, nourishing, and sustaining such connections, persons, texts, and artworks are not objects to be mastered and exploited, but invitations to mutuality, opportunities for growth, enrichment, and mutual transformation. Other persons are neighbors to be journeyed with rather than threats to be investigated or objects to be dominated.

At the same time, attempting to honor fully the emphasis on difference, I want to raise the concern (the spectre?) that in the hermeneutic thinking of the brilliant postmodern theorist Jacques Derrida, for all his acknowledgement of and call for hospitable and generous honoring of the other, there is no way to meet the other intentionally in genuine mutuality because there is no escape from an economy of violence. Although in Derrida the call for the gift (justice, hospitality) is unconditional, and urgent, there is a crucial complication. Intentional human interaction cannot (except randomly and by chance) escape the economy of exchange and its violence. In contrast, I want to suggest that if we begin with an economy of love, although the risk of violence always remains with us, violence is not inevitably or irrevocably the fundamental human experience. My basic conviction is that if the God who is present with us both creatively and redemptively is the God of connections and love rather than of separations and evil, then human hermeneutic efforts likewise have the calling and possibility to counter violence and to strengthen and remake connections that enhance life.

I envision a hermeneutics of connection, a fourfold spiraling hermeneutic movement of attending-to, journeying-with, birthing, and transforming. These phases are perhaps best conceived as four moments in an ongoing, recurrent spiral of sojourning and suffering-with, in which difference—in whatever shape or guise—is to be respected, learned from, and lived with, rather than exploited, assaulted, or destroyed. I propose a hermeneutics that is "other-wise than violence," a reading-*with* as opposed to reading-*against*.

Hermeneutics as Violence

The importance of developing a nonviolent hermeneutic of connection has greatly intensified because just as we are becoming acutely aware of the pluralism of discourses, just as we are growing in our intention to honor differences of gender, race, creed, and age, we face the reality that "never have violence, inequality, exclusion, famine, and thus economic oppression affected as many beings in the history of the earth and humanity."[2] Philosophically, such thinkers as Emmanuel Levinas, Michel Foucault, and Jacques Derrida in particular have faulted Western constructions of Reason in a "metaphysics of presence" as vain attempts to order, stabilize, and escape the incessant flux of experience. In the modern period, reason (whether in Cartesian, Kantian, or Husserlian fashion) has been extolled as universalizing, transcendentalizing operations able to lift us above the sensuous particularity of embodied, historical life. As the modern pioneers of suspicion of Freud, Nietzsche, and Marx have revealed, however, such an ego hermetically sealed off in splendid isolation is an illusion.

The illusion has been dangerous. The unity of truth beyond history, particularity, and flux has been purchased at the cost of repression of that which doesn't fit and violence to that which continues to protest. Metaphysics has been largely an effort at totalizing: an effort to capture the heterogeneous and differentiated in an all-embracing, totalizing unity. In response to totalizing visions and their oppression of the "other," deconstruction calls for a dismantling of the binary oppositions that overrun Western metaphysics (male/female,[3] light/dark, higher/lower, subject/object, same/different, and so on) in which one privileged term controls or excludes the other. What is needed is a valuing of the multiplicity of contexts with a full acceptance of irreducible differences. In other words, instead of lamenting the loss of closure and unity, a variety of postmodern voices help us celebrate

---

2. Derrida, *Spectres of Marx*, 85.

3. Since women have been victimized in this way, deconstructive critiques of the "metaphysics of presence" in many ways are complemented, corrected, and strengthened by feminist deconstructions of mind, truth, language, reality, and philosophy, and vice versa, as Jane Flax argues in *Thinking Fragments*, 35.

particularity, partiality, embodiment, and embeddedness. When difference is seen not as a threat but as an invitation, room can open up for mutual recognition, mutual pleasure, and mutual empowerment.[4]

Instead of a hermeneutics of appropriation[5] in which the strange is not only to be comprehended, but where all estrangement is to be overcome, we need a hermeneutic of connection that does not presuppose and privilege unity, totality, identity, closure, and homogeneity. David Tracy poignantly and aptly states the challenge: "For hermeneutics lives or dies by its ability to take history and language seriously, to allow the other (whether person, event, or text) to claim our attention as other, not as a projection of our present fears, hopes, and desire."[6]

"In the Beginning Is Hermeneutics"

All human actions involve interpretation. Signifying and clarifying belong to the very nature of being human. Indeed, language or discourse is only one form of intercourse, only one of the great array of acoustic, olfactory, tactile, symbolic, and graphic ways of signification that we need to interpret in meeting the other. Whether we are dealing with the phonemes of oral conversation, the script of written texts, sculptures, paintings, musical scores, rituals, dance, body language, traffic signs, emblems, or floral arrangements, encoding and decoding are always present. Colors, sounds, odors, textures, and gestures present as many complicated dilemmas of interpretation as do words and texts.

In familiar contexts, the interpretive moment of human activities, although always present, takes place more or less automatically. As with breathing and sleeping, our interpretive activities, once learned and habituated, tend to function involuntarily, even unconsciously. However—again

---

4. In *The Bonds of Love*, Jessica Benjamin presents an excellent analysis of the problem of domination in modernism and suggests feminism opens up possibilities for mutuality between men and women. "Deconstruction is not an enclosure in nothingness, but an openness towards the other," according to Jacques Derrida in "Dialogue with Jacques Derrida" in Kearney, *Dialogues with Contemporary Continental Thinkers*, 124. The integral connection between a deconstructive hermeneutics and ethics is central to much postmodern work. Let me only mention Simon Critchley's *The Ethics of Deconstruction*, Zygmunt Bauman's *Postmodern Ethics*, and Edith Wyschogrod's *Saints and Postmodernism*.

5. Even though Paul Ricoeur, realizing the dangers, wants to have an "appropriation" which "ceases to appear as a kind of possession, as a way of taking hold of things," he nevertheless describes hermeneutics in this way: "To 'make one's own' what was previously 'foreign' remains the ultimate aim of all hermeneutics." (*Interpretation Theory*, 94, 91).

6. Tracy, *Dialogue with the Other*, 4.

as with breathing and sleeping—these activities are liable to interruption, obstruction, and breakdown. When something very strange shows itself, when differences of time, location, and kind multiply, interpretation becomes problematic and calls for special attention. Not only does the wide diversity of people, events, and things to be known and interpreted heighten hermeneutic complexity, but every interpreter sees and hears, reads and responds as an inescapably subjective person of a certain gender, race, and socioeconomic class, with a certain level of psychic health, relationship history, tradition, worldview, and faith. No one sees from nowhere. Every look is timed and dated. Each one of us has our own particular window "on" the world that also acts as our vision "for" the world.[7] The paradox is that, although sites, windows, and times limit our perspectives, they provide us with the only perspectives we have.

When differences multiply, the hermeneutic process becomes less automatic reflex and more conscious technique. We easily become disoriented when our usual perceptions are shaken. When customary meanings no longer make sense, we become confused and disheveled. When our familiar ways of seeing reality leave us disoriented and upset, unless we are able to refocus, we are likely to suffer breakdown. Strange situations can throw us into panic. Failing to understand someone can erode our equilibrium. Reading a book can open exciting new worlds, but it can also mean getting lost in tangled gardens or vast forests. In such situations, interpretation receives more focused attention. While careful and patient negotiation may resolve the puzzlements and snags of interpretation, sometimes they develop into impasses that remain intransigent or become culs-de-sac that seem to offer no exit. Many kinds of hermeneutic specialists offer help. A wide variety of "interpretive" or "mediational" services are available: translators, information officers, counsellors of all kinds, commentators and editors, artistic and literary critics, teachers and professors, and so on. These special kinds of interpreters are go-betweens, each practicing their own special kind of midwifery so that a connection may be born, a confusion lifted, a transition endured, a trauma worked through, or a reconnection encouraged.

The risk and difficulties accompanying interpretation of difference and diversity in more or less ordinary circumstances are themselves huge. However, they intensify exponentially when we accord due attention to the constrictive and restrictive impact of fears, hostilities, and traumas, as well as the unconscious forces and patterns of adaptation that are part of being human in a broken world. To be sufficiently open enough to see the other—not as our projection, but in his/her own right as co-worker—is unbelievably

---

7. See Olthuis, "On Worldviews."

demanding. For when fears and anxieties gather and swell, erupt and interrupt, difference easily skews into deficit, deviance, or threat. When alterity is regarded as dangerous rather than helpful, hermeneutics becomes not the meeting of difference, but the avoidance or elimination of difference. At the same time, it is important to recognize that being open to and honoring difference need not involve, as we will later discuss, agreement or capitulation. Honoring difference means taking it seriously. Which means, if the difference is offensive and destructive, opposition and resistance.

Interpreting and interpretation are always with us because we have no immediate access to other human beings, other creatures, to any human artefact, not even to ourselves or to God. Transport or "translation" of some kind and of some sort will always be necessary to traverse the intervals of time and the abysses of spaces. We only keep connection with ourselves and others through the mediation of space, time, signs, gestures, sounds, actions. Our internal psychic spaces, the interstices between signs and referents, the distances between self and others: these are the birthplaces of hermeneutics. These I call the wild spaces of love, the with-places, the wombs of hermeneutics. I call them "wild" to recognize that they are uncharted, as open and free for love as they are for violence. They may be eerie in their silence, scary in their cacophony, pregnant in their promise. They can give birth to connection and love, or can rupture in disconnection and violence. They can be birthplaces or battlefields.

That is why Derrida writes: "In the beginning is hermeneutics."[8] There is no unmediated knowledge, and there never was the translucent immediacy of primal speech. Any ideal of full presence, of a "self-mediating identity which absolutely precedes or succeeds all difference, is a delusion."[9] There is always already mediation, no full presence. Neither writing nor speaking is innocent in the sense of perfectly and fully representing and mirroring reality, delivering the world as it really is. We always hear, see, sense, speak, and write with our own "glasses," from our own vantage points, in our own times. Consequently, no interpretation is free of prejudice, perfectly safe or certain. Interpretation is always vulnerable, inured and bathed in risk and pathos. "As soon as there is, there is *différance* ... postal maneuvering, relays, delay, anticipation, destination, telecommunicating network, the possibility, and therefore the fatal necessity of going astray, etc."[10]

---

8. Derrida, *Writing and Difference*, 67.
9. Hart, *The Trespass of the Sign*, 10.
10. Derrida, *The Post Card*, 66.

Arche-Writing as Arche-Violence?

For Derrida, however, not only is hermeneutics always with us, but hermeneutics is also always implicated in some original violence. The origin is "fractured." There is "the originary violence of a language which is always already writing."[11] Derrida's *Of Grammatology* is a "theory of the structural necessity of the abyss"[12] in which "degeneration as separation, severing of voice and song, has always already begun."[13] At the origin of language, prior to empirical violence, there is the "arche-violence" of "arche-writing"[14] with its "harsh law of spacing" as "an originary accessory and an essential accident."[15]

With Derrida, I call into question the tradition that interpretation is a consequence of the Fall, a curse in which the immediacy of prelapsarian reading is replaced by the mediation of interpretation.[16] As we have already noted, hermeneutic activity, hermeneutic space, and hermeneutic mediation have always been with us. There is no speaking or writing without mediation. Must this mean, however, as Derrida insists, that an act of interpretation is always, by dint of being an interpretation, necessarily violent? Are interpretation and language, including "proper naming," inevitably and necessarily an incision, a cut that violates the other?

It is true, as Derrida remarks, that language does not allow the other to be recognized as "pure other."[17] But I fail to understand why that is a problem unless Derrida himself is still haunted by the ghost of purity and full presence, in which anything less than the perfect congruence of one-to-one correspondence is imperfect, and in that way a kind of violation. If, however, following Derrida's lead, we give up the illusion of such autonomous self-sufficiency and translucent immediacy, we can accept that intersubjective interconnection, interpretation, and interdependence may be avenues to enrichment and health rather than always necessarily flawed, oppositional, invasive, or totalizing moves. The yawning spaces between can then be seen as places of passage and threshold—sacred interspaces[18]—offering room for connecting with the other (without fusion)

---

11. Derrida, *Of Grammatology*, 106.
12. Derrida, *Of Grammatology*, 163.
13. Derrida, *Of Grammatology*, 199.
14. Derrida, *Of Grammatology*, 112.
15. Derrida, *Of Grammatology*, 200.
16. See Smith, *The Fall of Interpretation*.
17. Derrida, *Of Grammatology*, 110.

18. Martin Buber calls this space the "sphere of 'between'" in *Between Man and Man*, 244. In *Journeys by Heart*, Rita Nakishima Brock talks of the non-hierarchical "play space" of mutual recognition (36–37).

while preserving identity (without alienation). Levinas talks of such a wholesome "relation of the same with the other, where the transcendence of the relation does not cut the bonds a relation implies, yet where the bonds do not unite the same and the other into a Whole."[19]

It is true that the sacred interstices often become killing fields or chasms of despair in human fear and hate, betrayal and rejection. Intersubjective violence rather than intersubjective meeting is only too horribly real. But is such violence always, irrevocably, and inevitably unavoidable? Naming, as a hermeneutic activity, can be an objectifying operation of control and violence, putting down what is "other." But naming can also be recognizing what is proper to the other, a way of connecting with honor and respect. Indeed, Derrida's exegesis of *pharmakon* in "Plato's Pharmacy"[20] as both remedy and poison would seem to indicate that violence is not the only possibility. If this is true, as I believe, and hermeneutics cannot be thought in our history outside the horizon of intersubjective violence, it does not follow from this that hermeneutics is basically and inevitably violent.[21]

"In the Beginning Was Love"

In this connection it is significant that Derrida evokes an unerasable[22] "pre-originary pledge (*gage*) which precedes any other engagement in language or action." This "sometimes wordless word which we name the 'yes'"[23] is an affirmation that is "unconditional, imperative, and immediate."[24] It is a "promise *of spirit*" which, "opening every speaking, makes possible the very question and therefore precedes it without belonging to it: the dissymmetry of an affirmation, of a *yes* before all opposition of *yes* and *no*."[25] Accordingly, for Derrida, "Deconstruction as such is reducible to neither a method nor an analysis. . . . it goes beyond critical decision itself. . . . For me, it always accompanies an affirmative exigency, I would even say that it never proceeds

---

19. Levinas, *Totality and Infinity*, 48. Levinas calls this kind of non-totalizing relation "religion" (*Totality and Infinity*, 40). "Contact with the other . . . is neither to invest the other and annul his alterity, nor to suppress myself in the other" (*Otherwise than Being*, 86).

20. Derrida, *Dissemination*, 63–171.

21. In paraphrase of (and comment on) Derrida's judgment: "if it is true, as I in fact believe, that writing cannot be thought outside the horizon of intersubjective violence, is there anything, even science, that radically escapes it?" (*Of Grammatology*, 127).

22. In "Force of Law," Derrida also talks of undeconstructible justice and of the infinite demand for justice (19, 25).

23. Derrida, *Of Spirit*, 130.

24. Derrida, *Points*, 286.

25. Derrida, *Of Spirit*, 94.

without love..."[26] In other words, before a hermeneutics of suspicion with its incessant questioning, there is always already a trusting in the promise of language which makes possible the very questioning—a trust preceding both language and question, without belonging to them.

This pre-originary "yes," which Derrida also calls "a *yes* more 'ancient,'"[27] is for me the Yes of God, the I-am-that-I am of Love, the Affirmation gifting us with life that calls us to a life of love. Here Derrida's telephone metaphor rings very true. "Before the act or the word, the telephone. In the beginning was the telephone." The creation as telephone "listening" to God's "hello, yes." Our first yes comes second, "marking, simply, that we are here... ready to respond"[28] to God's Yes that preceded it. Then follows a second yes of response to what we have heard and a third yes in which we pass on to others what we heard.

The reality that at each and every stage our responses are interpretative, as well as the necessity that the yeses (as well as our noes) need to be repeated, makes them vulnerable. The possibility that our responses may be lip service, mechanical rote, deliberate deceit, betrayals (and not genuine, truthful, living testimonies, non-identical repetitions) is built-in, says Derrida, to the structure of every text. Derrida calls this the gramophone effect. The "yes" of promise needs to be repeated to keep it alive. Each moment anew there is need to say yes again and again, yes to the stranger, yes to the creation, yes to oneself, and yes to God.

Yes is a promise in faith, and to say yes implies repetition, yes, yes. To say yes is to commit oneself to the future, to a second yes, which in memory of the first, confirms it and repeats it. And the first yes contains within it the promise of a second, even as the second is a memory of the first. Repetition is required. However, because time moves on, we are in a different space, things change, to remain true it needs to be non-identical repetition. The gramophone effect underlines the need for hermeneutic responsibility and vigilance.

"In the beginning," as Julia Kristeva exclaims, "was love."[29] The *conatus amandi* (the impulse to love) is both the energy of connection and the yearning for connection with self, others, creation, and God. It is the Eros of/for connection that makes seeking, shaping, and enriching mutual connections—including the practice of hermeneutics—central to human life.

---

26. Derrida, *Points*, 83.
27. Derrida, "Ulysses Gramophone," in *Acts of Literature*, 296.
28. Derrida, "Ulysses Gramophone," in *Acts of Literature*, 170.
29. Kristeva, *In the Beginning Was Love: Psychoanalysis and Faith*. See her praise of "wild love" in *Tales of Love*, 1–2.

Eros[30]—the cosmic principle of connection that seeks to bring all things together—is for Luce Irigaray the "third term," the "vital intermediary"[31] between oppositions which suspends the will to control, allowing genuine connection, without hierarchy, untouched by mastery.

Eros is the eye of love which, honoring the scandal of uniqueness, sees alterity not as a threat but as enrichment. It is, as Derrida explains, a certain kind of *Gelassenhelt*: "a love without jealousy that would allow the other to be."[32] Love seeks connection with the different not for purposes of fusion or domination but for amazement, meetings, diversity, fecundity, and mutuality. Indeed, mutuality may be called the secret of love.

Rita Nakashima Brock puts it this way: "In the beginning is the Divine Eros, embodied in all being. As the Incarnate, life-giving power of the universe, divine erotic power is the Heart of the Universe."[33] Invoking Martin Buber, Carter Heyward sounds a similar note: "In the beginning is relation, not sameness." Then, echoing Derrida's affirmation that hermeneutics is from the beginning, she continues:

> In the beginning is tension and turbulence, not easy peace, in the beginning, our erotic power moves us to touch, not take over; transform, not subsume. We are empowered by a longing not to blur the contours of our differences, but rather to reach through the particularities of who we are toward our common strength, our shared vulnerability, and our relational pleasure.[34]

A Two-Way Hermeneutic Dance

If human life means to be gifted with connections and called to (re)connections, then hermeneutics at its heart needs to be a spiritual exercise which, in interpreting, listening, and seeing, honors, respects, and meets the other. Hermeneutics exists because people, different from each other, are prompted by yearnings to make contact, moved by impulses to belong,

---

30. Eros, it is important to note, is revisioned in a mutuality ethos as the surge to connect (with its retention of difference) rather than as the more usual urge to unite (with its fusion of difference). Even a thinker like Paul Tillich, who saw the dangers of "controlling knowledge" and emphasized knowledge as a union through separation, still defined knowing as "a form of union. In every act of knowledge the knower and that which is known are united; the gap between subject and object is overcome" (*Systematic Theology*, 1:105). For a discussion and critique of Tillich's theology of time erotic, see Irwin, *Eros Toward the World*.

31. Irigaray, *An Ethics of Sexual Difference*, 27.
32. Derrida, *On the Name*, 74.
33. Brock, *Journeys by Heart*, 46.
34. Heyward, *Touching Our Strength*, 100.

filled with an eros to connect. Here the heartbeat of hermeneutics is not mastery of facts, or right explanation of a text, but meeting the other in creative tension towards a creative mutuality that lets the other be other. Interpretation is not, in this view, interpenetration to seize what bounty you can come away with, but an interconnecting for an intersubjective attunement of justice and healing. In a hermeneutics of connection, hearing the words, feeling the textures, seeing the forms, sensing the vibrations, testing the spirits are for the purposes of coming close, drawing near, getting in touch—in other words, knowing[35]—so that we may be mutually transformed. Such openness to difference is at heart a willingness both to journey-with and to be journeyed-with.

Yet it remains important to recognize that very often a hermeneutics of meeting-the-other is subverted systematically into maneuvers of deception and domination. Haunted by fears of loneliness and chained in prisons of brokenness, we too often turn the creative hermeneutic dance into a battleground for mastery. That is, a hermeneutics of trust is not a naive "see-no-evil," "believe-no-evil" approach. Rather, it asks that we interpret with an empathic and intuitive imagination straining to hear the stirrings of the human heart revealed in and through the other's diverse modes of signification. If alarm bells sound, if our intuitions are negative, trust and respect for ourselves call for a holding back which, when attended to, may lead to a pulling back and outright rejection of what is being offered. Indeed, what then begins as a reading-with may end as a reading-against—but only then. Taking cognizance of the constant temptation to self-deception that plagues both ourselves and others, a hermeneutics of trust is always tempered with (but not jettisoned by) a hermeneutics of suspicion.

In contrast to a modernist hermeneutic, there is no disinterested, dispassionate, objective knowledge free of feeling and subjective involvements. Knowledge—including hermeneutic knowing—is always and properly embodied, suffused with feelings, and laden with interests. Knowing includes physical pleasure, biotic drive, emotional feeling, aesthetic imagining, and ethical bonding, as well as analytic distinguishing. Knowledge is of the heart, personal, erotic, spiritual—yearning to come close, to draw nigh, to be in connection, to make contact. Rational understanding with its making of distinctions and striving for logical consistency and coherence is one dimension of a deeper knowledge known as wisdom. This knowing of the heart is the concern of Emmanuel Levinas,

---

35. See my introduction in Olthuis, *Knowing Other-Wise*, 1–15.

for example, when he envisions philosophy not as the love of wisdom, but as "the wisdom of love at the service of love."[36]

Love/knowledge creates a relationship between the knower and the to-be-known in a field of dynamic interaction which calls into question any clear-cut subject/object duality or agent/victim antithesis, and opens the way for possible meeting, mutual transformation, and mutual empowerment. Such affirming hermeneutic interaction can take place between experienced and inexperienced, between old and young, between neophyte reader and classic text, and between adherents of different faiths, because it is at heart a two-way dynamic of mutual respect; a reading-with as distinct from a reading-against. Power-with rather than power-over is the motivating spirit that calls us beyond ourselves even as it deepens our sense of self. A hermeneutics of love is a reading-with, letting the other be other, and concurrently, letting oneself be open to the other.

The dance of interpretation ineluctably draws us out of ourselves into what I have called the wild spaces, the uncharted interstices, "the realm of 'between,' . . . not an auxiliary construction, but the real place and bearer of what happens between persons."[37] Reducible neither to the interpreter's intrapsychic world nor to the domicile of the text and its author, this midfield is the matrix in which interpretations take shape and boundaries are negotiated. Rather than being a neutral, empty space of a silent abyss over which we transfer and countertransfer our projections about the other, the field between is a hermeneutical with-space, a fragile tabernacle of and for meeting that is continually shaped and reshaped in a reciprocal interplay of influences.

In a traditional modernist hermeneutic model, the interpreter turns his/her desire to the text and appropriates it to further his/her autonomy, to guarantee his/her power with respect to the appropriated, making its power into his/her own. This mastery model (a kind of guerilla warfare in which you endeavor to raid the text for treasure and escape) is incapable of understanding the simultaneous two-way process of being transformed by the text while transforming the text. In contrast, an intersubjective model of connection sees the relationship of self and other, with its creative tension of sameness and difference, as a continual interaction of influence, as a kind of dance. It focuses neither on a linear movement from dependence to independence, nor on a dialectical movement between independence and union, but on a spiral movement between self and other that enhances

---

36. Levinas, *Otherwise than Being*, 62.
37. Buber, *Between Man and Man*, 245–6.

both self-identity and intimacy with the other in an intersubjective journey of mutual influence.

Speakers/authors/artists and hearers/readers/viewers are always in process of be(com)ing. Their stories/texts/artworks are likewise "realities in process."[38] Every story, text, artwork is an invitation, a gift with an appeal. No work, in other words, is complete in itself, finished, closed off. It remains open, offering space and leeway for response, filling in, joining with, connection. This is a two-way movement. Not only does the story/text/artwork ask to be received and integrated into the world of the hearer/reader/viewer, but it also invites, even implores the respondent to tarry and linger with it, following up its leads into the world it opens up. Although such interaction always has an indispensable reflective moment, it is not always self-consciously intellectual. It *can* take the more intellectually focused forms of discussion, conversation, debate, and criticism—but just as frequent and surely as important are the forms of ritual, play, story, and meditation.

The diverse liturgies of interpretation, as ways of drawing nigh, all embody the human eros for connection. They are intuitive reachings out, imaginative engagings, patient tarryings that are necessary if there is to be fruitful interpretation and not merely sterile reproductions, projective appropriations, arbitrary fabrications, fawning submissions, or premature rejections. Interpretation is not confrontation, nor argument, nor even discussion—although all of these may be instigated in context as appropriate modes of interpretation. Sometimes interpretation is pedestrian, unexciting, hard work. At its best, it becomes a meandering flow, a fragile, vulnerable stream of surprise and wonder. When two passions meet in their yearning for mutuality, there can be com-passion, suffering-with, enrichment, flourishing, fecundity. At other times, interpretation bewilders, scares, confuses, angers, and shocks. One may feel violated by the other and incited to violence. Or, in fear, we may find ourselves (witting or unwittingly) unable to read-with, and our "interpretation" may degenerate into a pretext for attack (or defense), precluding the empathic listening that mutuality demands.

A Fourfold Hermeneutic Spiral of Connection-With the Other

The hermeneutic movement exhibits, I suggest, a fourfold spiraling thrust having several moments or stages. In the first moment of interpretation the interpreter expectantly approaches the person/text/artwork and receives and attends to its claim. In the second moment the interpreter journeys in the sacred interspace between self and person/text/artwork. In the third moment something new and novel emerges in the sojourning. In

---

38. Tracy, *Analogical Imagination*, 105.

the fourth moment there is mutual transformation. In the actual series of hermeneutic acts, these four moments generally overlap each other, and the sequence is repeated many times. Depending on the particularities of time and place, one of the moments may dominate, some may be left out or short-circuited, or all four may be simultaneously present. These four moments—which I refer to as attending-to, journeying-with, birthing, and transforming—are perhaps best conceived as four moments of a spiral. Each spirals in and out of the others, overlapping, interweaving, interconnecting. Each depends on and interconnects with the others. Each, however, appears to have its own specificity. The spiral may flow smoothly, or it may be herky-jerky, or it may bog down or be torpedoed.

The moments of this hermeneutic spiral,[39] described in some detail in what follows, are summarized in the chart below:

A HERMENEUTIC SPIRAL OF CONNECTION-WITH THE OTHER

MYSELF AS PASSION YEARNING FOR CONNECTION WITH THE OTHER (TEXT)

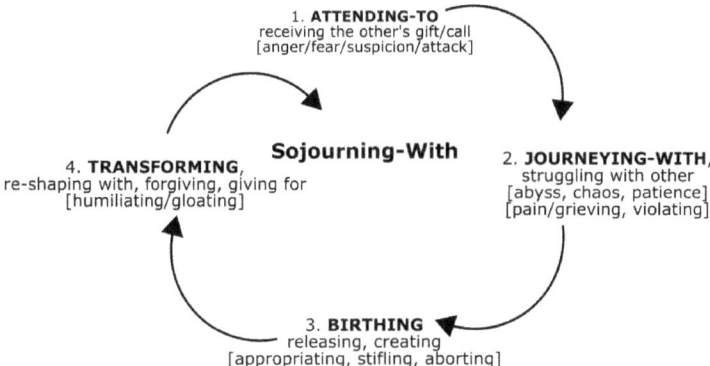

1. **Attending-to** involves receiving the gift/call of the other: a hermeneutic of receptivity, generosity, trust, and openness. It degenerates into fear to holding out the other, and attacking: into mis-attuning.

2. **Journeying(struggling)-with** the gift/call of the other is a hermeneutic of joining-with, querying, questing, courage, and caution. It degenerates into invading/holding-away, fusing/distancing: into disconnecting.

---

39. For a description of a parallel four-phase therapeutic spiral (Letting-in, Letting-go, Letting-out, Letting-work-through), see Olthuis, *The Beautiful Risk*, 164.

3. **Birthing** is creating, releasing of the new, a hermeneutic of creativity, disclosure, surprise, and joy. It degenerates into holding down, coopting, stifling, aborting: stagnating.

4. **Transforming** involves reshaping, reorienting: a hermeneutic of forgiving, integrating, giving-for, and hope. It degenerates into retrenching, resenting, humiliating, deforming.

First moment: a hermeneutic of receptivity and trust

The first moment in the hermeneutic motion is an act of trust: approaching, receiving, attending, we extend ourselves to the other, prepared to listen and hear, open, expectant. "All that is asked is that we remain open to the meaning of the other person or text."[40] The trust required to be open to the new and perhaps strange finds its root in trust of self. The greater the degree of self-trust, the less defensive we will be against the new and strange. Ricoeur talks of the ego's "letting-go." It is in "allowing" oneself "to be carried off towards the reference of the text that the ego divests itself of itself."[41]

This open trust is not feigned neutrality, nor a repression or denial of my horizons with their biases. "But this openness always includes our situating the other meaning in relation to the whole of our own meanings or ourselves in relation to it."[42] Such openness involves simultaneously a willingness to learn from the other and a willingness to risk my own position. Gadamer is emphatic that we need to be conscious of who we are to be truly open to someone else. "It is the tyranny of hidden prejudices that makes us deaf to what speaks to us in tradition."[43] The more conscious we are of our perspectives and biases, the greater the possibility that we need not let them get in the way. It is ignorance or denial of our historicity with its prejudices that seriously jeopardizes doing justice in any situation. The more robust our sense of self, the more likely we will be able to relate to another person as a person in his/her own right rather than in terms of our own needs, and the less likely we will be to overdo (gullibility) or underdo (paranoia) in our openness to the text. Gadamer says a "prejudice of perfection" is needed to do justice to a text. We may later find the person unreliable, the story misleading, the message inadequate, flawed, or incomplete, but we need to begin with openness and a willingness to learn and be challenged.

40. Gadamer, *Truth and Method*, 268.
41. Ricoeur, *Hermeneutics and the Human Sciences*, 191.
42. Gadamer, *Truth and Method*, 268.
43. Gadamer, *Truth and Method*, 270.

In the first moment we are open to receive something worthwhile. We relinquish control. In trusting *ab initio* that there is a gift to be received, something new to be learned, we tune in to the fundamental love dynamics of the creation that opens us to the other. At the same time, since love cannot be confined, programmed, and manipulated, love makes interpretation a vulnerable, fragile, and risky process. Existentially, in a broken creation, this trust of love acquires a vigilance tempered by the reality of deception and evil. Since it is not a one-way surrender or blind faith, such trust rightly looks for indications that continued trust is warranted. Without such assurances, our caution increases, even as we make efforts to recognize the claim of the other as other, and not as a projection of our own desires, fears, or hopes.

To be open to the other, caring for both the other and oneself, neither gullible nor paranoid, is extremely difficult. "To recognize the other *as* other, the different *as* different is also to acknowledge that other world of meaning as, in some manner, a possible option of myself."[44] Indeed, it is through meeting the other that we may be led to deepened understandings of "otherness" in ourselves. Through exposure to another way of looking at the world, we may become acutely aware of unconscious patterns, fears, yearning, biases, or preconceptions that were hitherto unknown to us, repressed, or scarcely discernible.

Since the interpretive dance is drenched in risk and vulnerability, we often succumb to our fears and fervently attempt to control and manipulate the other: to see what we want to see, to hear what we want to hear, to read what we want to read. The other, whether negatively or positively, becomes a projection of our fears, hopes, and desires.

The measure of self-exposure or trust we will exercise varies with our earliest experiences of trust. In the degree that as young infants we experience betrayal, in that degree distrust takes root in our souls; and we develop stratagems to survive and prevent new hurts. Understandably and legitimately we are more likely to exhibit suspicion rather than trust, guardedness rather than openness, when we meet new people or turn to strange texts. Since broken trust in greater or lesser degree is the human condition, all of us begin with qualified trust. In other words, in a broken world, the initial hermeneutics of trust is at the same time tinged with a learned caution, even at times a healthy suspicion.

Every time we turn to a person/text our trust is tested anew. Sometimes we are disappointed. Our investment of time and energy is to little or no avail. Or we may feel insulted, berated, even betrayed. In the course of

---

44. Tracy, *Dialogue with the Other*, 41.

our lives we learn to exercise choice and restraint as to the kinds of persons/ texts we expose ourselves to. We do not want, nor do we need, to be disenchanted once more. A healthy wariness develops.

But sometimes (and the reasons can be manifold), we are so defensive that we cannot be open in any genuine way. We may feel threatened and prematurely retrench in our own views. Then, we are disposed to a hit-and-run hermeneutics, a hermeneutics of suspicion run over into full-blown paranoia. Or, conversely, so much in the throes of crisis, so confused or so gullible, we may distrust ourselves, discount our own views, put all caution aside and accept as gospel truth whatever the other person or text says. Then we have a hermeneutics of gullibility. Either posture short-circuits the hermeneutic movement of connection.

Second moment: a hermeneutic of journeying-with, struggle, and courage

After trust comes journeying-with, tarrying, sojourning. Wolfgang Iser talks of "dwelling in"[45] and Paul Ricoeur talks of "inhabiting"[46] the world of the text. Rather than "taking possession" of its meaning, understanding is primarily a "letting-go"[47] of our pretensions to control and master, a voluntary commitment to journey-with the text. In this moment we are not seeking to master from a distance, but to hear what is being said, to linger with it, taste it, try it on—reading-with. It is not a power trip to extract meaning, but a tender, delicate, fragile process of listening to the other, engaging, attuning, hearing a new sound or different voice—all the while open to being changed by the experience. There may be a quiet resonance or a "shock of recognitions, of repugnances."[48] A dialogic ritual, an uneasy dance or friendly struggle ensues . . . which may break into a genuine conversation or fall apart into a pitched battle.

An important goal in the second moment of the hermeneutic journey is the interpreters' appropriate attunement with the speaker/text so that they are able to hear or read what is being said with as little projection, defense, and fear as possible on their part. Such empathic engagement initiates a creative interaction in which the interpreter is more likely to hear or read for genuine moments of insight, integrity, and truth—despite the probable projections and fears displayed by the speaker or encoded in the text.

45. Iser, *The Act of Reading*, 128.
46. Ricoeur, *Hermeneutics and the Human Sciences*, 56.
47. Ricoeur, *Hermeneutics and the Human Sciences*, 191.
48. Tracy, *Dialogue with the Other*, 63.

The surprise of the different and unknown always comes with risks and fears—often raising hackles and mustering defenses. Clouds of unknowing are ominous. Relinquishing control and lingering with that which is different can fill us with terror. As such the venture of the second moment is always haunted by the temptation to rush to judgment, whether positive or negative. There is a palpable impulse to parry and attack or cease and desist—anything to lessen the bafflement, assuage the distress, take away the uncertainty, and restore equilibrium.

In this open-ended, often surprising, and sometimes volatile second moment, the interpreter begins to experience varying degrees of resonance and familiarity or confusion and alienation. The stranger the person or text, the more comprehensive and intense the struggle for appropriate attunement. When the other is "significant" or "strange"—encountered at a critical juncture in one's life, or when the claims of the person or text are startling, deep-going, wide-ranging, or earthshaking—the process can be unnerving, excruciating, and nauseating. On occasion deep conflict ensues. Whatever the situation, it takes courage and stamina to persevere, sojourning, agonizing, letting confusion be confusion, trusting that staying with the process will bear fruit in its own time—whether in novel understandings, deepened convictions, ardent protestations, or heightened disagreements.

Here my Gadamerian emphasis on conversation contrasts with the modern Cartesian emphasis on appropriation, mastery, and penetration. In describing the hermeneutics of translation[49] George Steiner wastes no words: "after trust, comes aggression,"[50] "penetration."[51] The second move is "incursive and extractive." The act of understanding *à la* Hegel and Heidegger is "inherently appropriative and therefore violent . . . all cognition is aggressive."[52] The subject needs to be attacked until it is under control and mastered.

However, to conceive of the second moment as explicitly invasive is to begin from an adversarial framework in which the only possibilities—no matter how gently or aggressively performed—are to dominate or be dominated. Interpretive control acts to fend off and allay the fear of domination.

---

49. Steiner is specifically describing the moments of translation. But since, as he says, "[a]ny model of communication is at the same time a model of trans-lation," and translation is "a special, heightened case of the process of communication and reception in any act of speech," his descriptions have much wider scope and reference. See his *After Babel*, 45, 414.

50. Steiner, *After Babel*, 297.

51. Steiner, *After Babel*, 303.

52. Steiner, *After Babel*, 297. "The translator invades, extracts, and brings home" (298).

But it is precisely that syndrome which has wreaked so much havoc on human life in general, turning interpretation into inter-penetration, objectifying the text as something to be mastered, rather than as an invitation for growth, connection, and enrichment. In this view we are virtually licensed to rape a text for its meaning.[53] No wonder, says Steiner, there is "sadness after success, the Augustinian *tristitia* which follows on the cognate acts of erotic and intellectual possession."[54]

Journeying-with rather than dismantling a person or text is not only more respectful, but also less likely to devolve into adversarial maneuvers of aggression and defense. As in the therapeutic context, where we can expect more truth and honesty in an atmosphere of respect and trust, rather than one of contempt and suspicion, so hermeneutically. An ethos of mutual respect nourishes genuine exchange, deepened insight, and expanded horizons—even if it ends in total disagreement, complete parting of the ways, indeed, in opposition. As Richard Palmer puts it in summarizing Gadamer: "The keys to understanding are not manipulation and control but participation and openness, not knowledge but experience, not methodology but dialectic."[55]

Hermeneutic encounter—reading-with—is more like a rambling journey together to places unknown rather than an adversarial operation in which one either strives to make the text succumb to one's intentions or succumbs to the text in its customary or traditional readings. Sometimes the encounter turns into an enjoyable meandering into mutual surprise. At times it turns out to be sinuous and tortuous, fraught with false starts, tumbles and stumbles. In most every situation, it has its unexpected starts and turns. Whatever the case, rejecting the mastery/being mastered paradigm complicates rather than simplifies the hermeneutic endeavor. There are no "easy" reads. On the one hand, as Derrida puts it, "we cannot consider" texts such as "Marx's, Engels's or Lenin's texts as completely finished elaborations that are simply to be 'applied' to the current situation." On the other hand, although "[r]eading is transformational ... this transformation cannot be executed however one wishes. It requires protocols of reading."[56]

In pursuit of such responsible and fresh "transformational" readings, Derrida calls deconstruction an "exorbitant" method involving two kinds

---

53. In fact, Richard E. Palmer names such theories "rape theories of interpretation" in *Hermeneutics*, 247.

54. Steiner, *After Babel*, 298.

55. Palmer, *Hermeneutics*, 215.

56. Derrida, *Positions*, 63. However, Derrida immediately highlights the difficulty of transformational reading by candidly admitting, "I have not yet found any that satisfy me."

of readings, the "rabbinic," more classical examinations that stay within the orbits of tradition, and the "poetic," novel, exorbitant renderings that read other-wise.[57] For Derrida, traditional, reproductive readings function as the necessary guardrails for interpretation. Such "doubling commentary . . . [needs] to recognize and respect all its classical exigencies . . . and requires all the instruments of traditional criticism." Indeed, "without this recognition and this respect, critical production would risk developing in any direction at all, and authorize itself to say almost anything."

"But," as Derrida immediately adds, "this indispensable guardrail has always only *protected*, it has never opened, a reading."[58] If all we do is stay between the guardrails on the major expressways, our interpretive journeys can be comparatively fast and relatively secure. But, in bypassing the interesting sideroads and avoiding culs-de-sac, they can become tedious and predictable. In this way traditional readings can neutralize the text, flattening out and smoothing over its plies, knots, and folds, trimming it down to bite-sized, digestible pieces.

Deconstructive readings of the second sort are not in any way intended to be destructive. Their resolve is to shake loose and make possible an "openness to the other." "*There is nothing outside the text*"[59] does not mean that there is nothing other than words and texts, nothing but a cloud of signifiers. It does mean that we only engage the world through the mediation of signs: nothing escapes the constraints of textuality. A text is a textured fabric of countless threads layer upon layer. Reading a text is looking at the weave, pulling through certain threads, unravelling others, looking for patterns, spotting loose threads, pulling at knots, etc., in order to decipher its sense, explicate its meaning, and then delineate its impact for the present. In this way, a subsequent reading serves as an all in one translation-commentary-supplement to the original text.

Reading-with asks that, even as you faithfully listen to what the text traditionally has been heard to say, you also have an ear for the tensions, the unsaid, the loose ends, the excluded and marginalized. In this way, the focus is neither on the interpreter nor on the text as such. Rather "what" is going on in the text (Gadamer), or "the world in front" of the text (Ricoeur) is the theme of the hermeneutic meeting—the interpreter and the text being mutual partners in the ongoing process of making our way into the future.

This process—like the process of forming good relationships—is not without struggle, critique, disappointments, even tears, betrayals, and

---

57. Derrida, *Of Grammatology*, 154–67.
58. Derrida, *Of Grammatology*, 158.
59. Derrida, *Of Grammatology*, 158.

intractable impasses. Just as friendship is a plant of slow growth, so we need, hermeneutically, to proceed with abundant patience, due caution, and exquisite care. Journeying-with is not a romantic notion of being nice, never critical—an innocent naiveté. It does involve a commitment to trust the process and hear the other person out—without manipulation, competition, deception. And this requires, as we have mentioned, a robust sense of self—a self aware of gifts and limits, habits, prejudices, and wiles, a self owning its vulnerabilities, tensions, adaptive strategies, and blind spots.

In this second moment the evil and perversity of the world shows itself in particularly intense fashion, affecting and infecting the process. The more we are confronted by difference, the more we can feel threatened; and the more we will come face-to-face with our own fears, pains, demons, and repressed anger. Such "dark nights of the soul," as the mystic tradition aptly named them, are not easy to endure, often turning into skirmishes of control in which maneuvers of defense and penetration, the tactics of war, impose themselves upon us as if second nature. The human propensity and desire to remain in charge and maintain control can easily scare us out of truly listening, in the spirit of hospitality, to the voice and person of the other. But the reality that acts of entrenchment and violence plague interpretation does not, however, legitimate the view that mastery is inherent to interpretation. This is of great importance for it is precisely in the giving up of the need to control and possess that ways open to the new and the healing.

Faced with the triggered pain and fear of our own unresolved issues that tend to come to the fore in this second hermeneutic moment, we will be tempted to short-circuit or foreclose the hermeneutic process. To short-circuit or foreclose—whether turning a person or a text into a straw person, or noting only its shortcomings and ignoring its strengths, or misconstruing it so our position or person can escape from the process unscathed—is to take the too easy road of denial or flight. Whatever its form, premature hermeneutic closure is like cheap grace: it is not the real thing, and the interpretation is counterfeit. Staying-with the hermeneutic process in the realm of the "between" is vitally important because the experiences of struggling and wrestling are precisely, if paradoxically, the pangs which give birth to newness. The sojourning is a laboring which turns the between-space into a womb which, in the surprise of grace, may issue in new life: delight, knowledge, repentance, conversion, forgiveness, reconciliation, empowerment—the dynamics of mutuality.

At the same time, it is important in this context to emphasize the differences between hermeneutic short-circuiting and what I will call hermeneutic refusal. When the hermeneutic journey becomes too dangerous, the going gets too rough, or the pain and confusion too great, backing off from a person or text (strategic withdrawal) may be a healthy part of the process. And this refusal may, perhaps, have to be repeated time and time again. Indeed, wisdom sometimes dictates that we honor the dynamics of the process by recognizing that in this or that case it is impossible (at least at present) to work it all the way through. Withdrawing from or refusing further hermeneutic engagement in situations where impasses prove intractable, where issues of personal and spiritual safety proliferate, or where there appears to be no alternative to constant haggling and endless battling, may be a mark of hermeneutical maturity. Indeed, since a hermeneutics of connection is not a masochistic or sadistic exercise, love sometimes means letting go of the other, keeping distance, and active dissent. Insofar as they reflect a recognition of the fact that the process has been interrupted and not followed through, refusals of this kind stand in stark contrast to short-circuiting strategies of defense or offense which pretend that the process has been completed when, in fact, the journey has been prematurely called off, the other co-opted, and the process foreclosed.

Third moment: a hermeneutic of birthing, releasing-with-the Other

Paradoxically, in giving up control, in letting go, in joining-with appropriately, a process of gathering takes place. Something new begins to happen, things begin to come together, there is meeting, remembering, co-creating, releasing, a birthing. There is a letting out, an "ontological disclosure"[60] in which we are released to the "buoyant dialectic of true freedom: surprise, release, confrontation, shock, often reverential awe, always transformation."[61] When such an event happens in major ways—when we react, "Wow! this makes a difference. Wow! this is it!," or even if we say "ha, ha!" instead of "aha!"—disclosure takes place. The same kind of release or disclosure takes place in countless contexts in more pedestrian, but nevertheless just as authentic, ways. We may be affirmed or confirmed in our life's choices. There may be the delight of new learnings or the pain of unlearnings. In any event, the third hermeneutic moment is marked by the giving forth of newness: creativity.

The disclosures or breakouts can take many forms but the release never leaves us untouched. There may be a pleasing congeniality of positions with a high degree of cross-fertilization. The miracle of meeting another person may happen, a friendship may be sealed, a troth plighted. There may be re-membering of what was dis-membered.

---

60. Palmer, *Hermeneutics*, 201.
61. Tracy, *Analogical Imagination*, 114.

In my conception and in contrast to Gadamer, birthing is not, however, a fusion of horizons or union of the separated but, rather, an engagement with the different that, at best, leads to mutual transformation. Although I fully endorse Palmer's rejection of "forcible seizure," I am fearful of describing the alternative as "loving union."[62] Talk of union may too easily be read as a kind of unity or fusion with loss of identity.[63] Indeed, it is the very longing/fear/fascination of the "oceanic feeling" of union that led Freud to promote the development of the ego-self as heroic and independent. This is a crucial point because most often union and fusion are viewed as the opposites of identity and differentiation. In this binary model, self/other harmony becomes a form of fusion, and self/other difference is taken as isolation and distance. In contrast, an intersubjective model of mutuality allows room for identity and intimacy to coexist simultaneously in mutual recognition. Deepened intimacy is at the same time a deepened awareness of difference.

The hermeneutic outcome in this third moment may, however, also be negative, humiliating, and destructive. What is disclosed may act to dislocate or relocate our identity and worldview. There may be shocking revelations, abortions, stillbirths, dismemberings. It can also become clear that no genuine meeting is in the offing: the differences are too great. The cost individually and communally of continuing to try to meet may be too much to bear. The impasse, at least for now, is insurmountable. In such circumstances, we need to go our separate ways—with peace and blessing, even if with some wistfulness, hurt, and regret.

Indeed, deep differences, clear clashes, or confusing intransigence may be the outcome. But even when the gulf is wide and deep, and disagreement apparently full and final, there is still usually space for respect with honor. There is no honoring of the other if we do not allow the other to be other. By the same token respect for the other does not exclude resistance to the other when, according to our view, what the other says and does undermines rather than affirms life. Learning the need to resist can be the disclosure of the hermeneutic event. "Responsibility demands critical conflict when necessary and resistance, including resistance to these new interpretations, when appropriate."[64]

---

62. Palmer, *Hermeneutics*, 244.

63. Robert Bernasconi judges that Gadamer, despite his undeniable emphasis on hearing the other, "[i]n practice ... tends to enclose otherness in the circle of self-recognition. Only rarely is otherness allowed to remain in its otherness" ("Seeing Double," 245).

64. Tracy, *Plurality and Ambiguity*, 106.

Comparing my formulation of the third movement with Steiner's may again be helpful. Whereas I talk of birthing, Steiner sees the third movement as "incorporative, in the strong sense of the word."[65] It is an appropriation, a "violent transport," which, as a taking away from the other, involves loss and breakage. Steiner's modernist oppositional dialectic also comes starkly to the fore when he points out that the "dialectic of embodiment entails the possibility that we may be consumed."[66] In my view, by contrast, an interpreter is most faithful to the person or text when there is not forceful appropriation but appropriate attunement.

In other words, the secret of the third hermeneutic moment is allowing ourselves, even as we follow the protocols of reading, to engage in the dance without guarantees about the outcome. To the degree we give up the pretext of control, we enter the interpretive process open to the surprise of something new. And, then, in the dynamics of this process which is bigger than ourselves, something bigger than we are may, in grace, take place, a newness may take shape. There may be a giving-forth in which we are released to be more in tune with God's process of cosmic love and healing. It is in the recesses and through the cracks of interpretation that the light shines through.

Fourth moment: a hermeneutic of transforming, re-stor(y)ing-with

In an authentic hermeneutic interaction there is an openness to change: the empathic process of journeying-with unleashes a re-stor(y)ing, transformational dynamic. Sojourning-with (even suffering-with) moves toward a celebrating-with in which new insights and energies are integrated into our worlds. In more traditional terms, every hermeneutic act of explication (*explicatio*) is incomplete without some application (*applicatio*). The disclosures released by journeying with the person or text bring the interpreter to internal transformation that leads, not only to a changed view, but to transmuting action, doing and making of the truth (*facere veritatem*). When something new transpires, when horizons of meaning expand, a dynamic is unleashed that translates into deeds and actions: lives are altered, attachments are deepened, alternate paths are walked. We turn to the future—and new hermeneutic encounters—with new resolution, comfort, reaffirmation, insight, and hope.

Importantly, when there has been a genuine meeting with the other, the transmutation will be mutual. Not only am I changed, but in the interactive dynamic both partners are forever altered. When the interpretive

---

65. Steiner, *After Babel*, 298–303.
66. Steiner, *After Babel*, 299.

dance issues in new readings and new steps, the text itself is transformed, henceforth always signifying something different for the interpreter. Likewise, an intense meeting with an artwork ensures that, in the next viewing, the artwork will be seen differently. In this vein, Steiner talks of the source-text that has "elemental reserves as yet unrealized by itself" and of "Schleiermacher's notion of a hermeneutic which '"knows better than the author did."'[67] He talks of "the heightening of a work's existence when it is confronted and reenacted by alternate versions of itself."[68]

The culmination of the hermeneutic spiral in mutual transformation—a re-stor(y)ing enacted in actions of justice and mercy—reminds us once more that, although language and the linguistic dimension receive focused attention in interpretation, interpretation is for the purposes of meeting with difference in love. That means that the final test and validation of a hermeneutic movement is the kind of transforming (or deforming) action toward justice (or away from justice) which is released and ensues. A deft hermeneutic flourish promotes human flourishing. When new connections are made or old ones revised or renewed, the energy of love is released. It is this energy which, in a process of grief and mourning, may empower us to face our own hermeneutic patterns of self-deception as we attend to bad connections, unresolved hurts, and haunting questions. At the same time, in a process of joy and celebration, old connections may be strengthened, reconnections made, and new connections forged. Lives can touch each other, alliances can be shaped, hospitality can be practiced: an opening of self to others in a giving-for(th) that is, in its heart, and at the same time, a for-giving of self and others in a bond of mutual respect, peace, and reconciliation.

When, however, the previous moments in the process have not been satisfactorily resolved, when the process has been forced or manipulated, a dynamic for disintegration, humiliation, and reviling may also manifest itself in this final stage. If this happens too often, we slowly begin to unravel and are cast into crisis. The experienced humiliation, shame, and frustration can lead to retrenchment, paralyzing despair, desperate gullibility, or rampant violence. We can be cast into despair when we realize that we have never really met, that the meeting was more superficial than we thought, that the connection does not seem to have staying power for further empowerment and change.

Such despair need not be the last word, however, even when serious disagreements emerge, when a clash of horizons emerges, or when our expectations are disappointed or thrown back in our face. Provided we

---

67. Steiner, *After Babel*, 302.
68. Steiner, *After Babel*, 453.

have done our best to respect and connect with the person or text, even if we end up in acute disagreement, we may nevertheless be empowered in the process. If we have stayed with the process and still end up in a different place, we can then authentically honor the distance, strengthened and reassured that we went the extra mile in attempting to connect. There can even be the strange—and respectful—intimacy of the honest conclusion that a fruitful connection is not meant to be. In any case, we will never be the same again. In the process of meeting or seeking to meet the other, we spiral forward through suffering and transformation to a new and deeper connecting with self, others, creation, and God. Not only do our hermeneutic endeavors with difference make us *other*-wise (change us), we become other-*wise* (more responsibly attuned to others).

A hermeneutics of texts needs to be of one piece with a hermeneutics of persons as a hermeneutics of just connection. No interpreting can finally be legitimate if it fails to help shape the readers into a community that embraces the different, the stranger, the widow, and the orphan.[69] In other words, if our ways of reading texts and dealing with persons do not help us to live more truthfully, to love more fully, to act more justly, and to think more clearly, something is radically amiss. Unless a hermeneutics is edifying (without being illusionary) and encouraging (without being supercilious)—unless our hermeneutics is an exercise of love seeking justice for the other—our rhetorical flourishes and scintillating interpretations are like clanging cymbals.

George Steiner calls his fourth moment "restitution."[70] Believing that "all decipherment is aggressive and, at one level, destructive," Steiner says the fourth moment is the "enactment of reciprocity in order to restore balance." For Steiner the first moment of trust "puts us off balance" as we "'lean towards' the confronting text . . . we encircle and invade cognitively. We come home laden, thus again off-balance. The hermeneutic act must compensate. If it is to be authentic, it must mediate into exchange and restored parity."[71]

The question is whether any "restitution" can salvage a mastering process built on forays of aggression. Can promise of eventual restitution undo or ever justify the prior violence? Steiner's "restitution" has the impossible feel of an attempt, in some measure, whether in guilt or condescension, to atone for the previous injury. Is this model of bold sin coupled with the hope of atonement really desirable? Is it even possible?

---

69. Levinas sees the other as "the stranger, the widow, and the orphan" in *Totality and Infinity*, 215.

70. Steiner, *After Babel*, 303.

71. Steiner, *After Babel*, 300.

The understanding of the hermeneutic spiral as receptivity, journeying-with, disclosure, and transformation allows us, I suggest, to overcome the mastery model with its inherent power-over in which the other needs to be dominated lest it dominate us. It allows, at least in principle, otherness to remain in its otherness even as we remain in conversation and contact. And it keeps open through genuine dialogue the possibility of mutual transformation.

In our broken world a hermeneutics of connection will be a hermeneutics of suffering love. It will seek to stay with, suffer-with (rather than supersede, suspend, or mitigate) the complexities, difficulties, and disasters of dealing with the facticity of life.[72] It will be a hermeneutics of love because it seeks to honor and respect (rather than to control, appropriate or dominate) the other as a neighbor we are called to love as we love ourselves.

Forging and maintaining a democratic community built on respect for difference and committed to an equitable sharing of power is the formidable challenge we all face. The very survival of our planet and all its creatures is in the balance. Do we have the will and the love—the will to love? That is *the* hermeneutic question.

---

72. Describing hermeneutics as "coping with the flux, tracing out a pattern in a world of slippage," John D. Caputo has developed a Derridean hermeneutic in which attention to suffering and obligation is central. See *Radical Hermeneutics,* 37, and *Against Ethics*. *Radical Hermeneutics* is an incisive exposition and exploration of the nature and history of hermeneutics. For my interaction with Caputo, see Olthuis, "A Hermeneutics of Suffering Love." See also Caputo's recent *Hermeneutics: Facts and Interpretation in the Age of Information*.

AD AMOREM: ZIGZAG SOJOURNING

CHAPTER 9

FACE-TO-FACE: ETHICAL ASYMMETRY OR THE SYMMETRY OF MUTUALITY?

IN ITS HEART, POSTMODERNISM is a spiritual movement which resists the totalizing power of reason. It is that resistance, and the concomitant celebration of difference and diversity, that marks a wide array of disparate discourses as postmodern. Ethically, postmodern discourses share an alertness to plurality and a vigilance on behalf of the other. Modernist rational ethics, in its Enlightenment dream of a world increasingly controlled by a pure rationality, has shown itself not only blind and indifferent to those who are other and different, those who fall outside the dominant discourse, but also violent and oppressive to them. For many, the marginalized and voiceless, this dream has been an unrelenting nightmare. And it continues unabated. In the words of Jacques Derrida, "never before, in absolute figures, never have so many men, women, and children been subjugated, starved, or exterminated on the earth."[1] Not only is our time "out of joint," he exclaims, conjuring up the ghost of Hamlet, "but space, space in time, spacing."[2] What now? The foundations are trembling; there is an incommensurability of voices, a pluralism of discourses, communities of the groundless, enclaves of the homeless.

As Emmanuel Levinas says, "The essential problem is: can we speak of an absolute command after Auschwitz? Can we speak of morality after the failure of morality?"[3] What now after the reign of reason? What if we don't have morality or a religion within the bounds of reason? How do we negotiate

---

1. Derrida, *Spectres of Marx*, 85.
2. Derrida, *Spectres of Marx*, 83.
3. Ainsley, Wright, and Hughes, "The Paradox of Morality: An Interview, with Emmanuel Levinas," in Bernasconi and Wood, *The Provocation of Levinas*, 176.

civic covenants sensitive to differences of gender, race, creed, age, sexual orientation, socioeconomic class? How are we to envision and give shape to a postmodern ethics of justice and compassion that includes the other, the disadvantaged, the marginalized, "the widow, orphan, and stranger?"[4]

After noting the impasse of modernist ethics, I want, in this essay, to pay particular attention to Emmanuel Levinas's plea for a different ethics, an ethics as "first philosophy"[5] which begins with responsibility rather than freedom, which finds moral focus in corporeality rather than in arguments, in pain rather than in concepts.[6] Of special concern will be the asymmetrical ethical relation in Levinas in which the other has priority over myself, a view that parallels closely the tendency in much Christian ethics to champion selfless *agape* over so-called selfish *eros*. The question will be raised whether in (rightly) challenging narcissistic self-interest, Levinas doesn't (unadvisedly) bring into ethical disrepute all concern for self-interest because, in his view, an individual subjective agent is not only a locus of enjoyment and self-interest, but also, inevitably, unavoidably, and irrevocably, an agent pitted against other agents. This seems to valorize the often adversarial quality of interpersonal relations as the inexorable human condition (which we then need to transcend to be ethical), rather than to envision such opposition itself as the breakdown of relations of mutuality in which my self-interest and the self-interest of the other may interface with each other to the harmonious enjoyment and enrichment of both parties. That is, I want to suggest an ethics of mutuality[7] in which self-sacrifice is seen not as the heart of ethics, but as an emergency compromise[8] ethic because of the breakdown of mutuality.

---

4. Derrida has an important discussion of justice in relation to law in "Force of Law," 3–67. For an earlier effort, on my part, to give embryonic shape to a postmodern ethic in terms of a Gadamerian narrative approach cross-pollinated by a deconstructionist ethics of dissemination, see Olthuis, "An Ethics of Compassion: Ethics in a Post-Modernist Age," 125–6.

5. Levinas, *Totality and Infinity*, 304. See also his "Ethics as First Philosophy" in Hand, *The Levinas Reader*, 75-87. See also Peperzak, *Ethics as First Philosophy*.

6. As one of the first Levinas-inspired North American studies, Wyschogrod's *Saints and Postmodernism*, appealing for a saintly ethics of self-sacrifice, also calls for attention. On the relation of deconstruction and ethics, see Bauman, *Postmodern Ethics*; Critchley, *The Ethics of Deconstruction* and *Ethics-Politics-Subjectivity*; Caputo, *Against Ethics*; Bennington, *Interrupting Derrida*; Anderson, *Derrida: Ethics Under Erasure*.

7. Such an ethics, I submit, adds a fourth approach to Alasdair MacIntyre's three broad versions of ethical enquiry: the Enlightenment encyclopedic, the deconstructivist genealogical, and the Thomistic tradition. See his *Three Rival Versions of Moral Enquiry*.

8. Looked at from my perspective, Levinas could be said to have his own "compromise ethic" when, following recognition of the priority of the other, justice enters with

In other words, the question is whether self-sacrifice is a compromise ethic due to the breakdown of mutuality (my position), or whether self-sacrifice is the only avenue to mutuality (Levinas's position). The discussion is complicated because the self-sacrifice Levinas calls for is not the sacrifice of the deepest self (*le soi*), for that self is *always already* sacrificed before it has itself to sacrifice—and has itself to sacrifice or not to sacrifice only on that basis. At bottom, the heart of the discussion is whether our common ethical concern is better served by describing the self as "substitution," "hostage," or "dis-interestedness," or by portraying the ethical self as "power-with," "responsibility-with," "suffering-with." Instead of conceiving the I (*le moi*) as necessarily, ontologically, and exclusively only a self-interested agent over against other agents, which then needs to be transcended in an ethical awakening to my true self (*le soi*) as substitution for the other, I want to suggest the ethico-ontological possibility of an agent self as power-with, responsibility-with, all the while retaining a realistic awareness of the propensity to power-over violence which constantly lurks within us, to which we so often capitulate, and in which we are so frequently implicated. Instead of an "other-wise than being,"[9] as substitution, as responsibility for, I'm suggesting a being-otherwise, not as mastering, but as connecting-with.

Modern Ethical Theory

Modern ethical theory in the spirit of the Enlightenment has striven to construct a rational foundation for morality. The benchmark of such theory, whether in utilitarian or Kantian dress, has been the effort to move ethical judgments beyond the contingency and time-bound contexts of moral actors. Inspired by the scientific ideal of objectivity, ethical theory attempted to secure so-called objective moral judgments free from the subjective desires, beliefs, and narratives of the agents who make them. A justified moral judgment needs to take a form that can and must be traded from anyone's point of view, independent of time, place, and historical circumstance. Problems emerge and are solved only within the comprehensive framework of a unified "encyclopaedic rationality," as MacIntyre names it.

---

the arrival of "the third"—another "other"—and I am permitted to see myself as the other of the other. Whereas for me, mutuality is the normative, and self-sacrifice the compromise, for Levinas something like the opposite seems true. Normative is the priority of the other (with the sacrifice of the agentic self) and the political compromise is the reciprocity involving a third. On the other hand, the difference is somewhat muted when it is recognized that for Levinas, equality is the goal of the priority of the other. That is, from his viewpoint, the priority of the other is not seen as a compromise, but the asymmetry of priority is considered the condition for the symmetry of equality.

9. Levinas, *Otherwise than Being*.

Along these lines, for example, there is Kant's categorical imperative, Hare's universalizability, Baier's God's eye-point of view, and Rawls's original position. As Stanley Hauerwas and David Burrell put it: "What I am morally obligated to do is not what derives from being a father, or a son, or an American, or a teacher, or a doctor, or a Christian, but what follows from my being a person constituted by reason."[10] Moreover, the transcendental turn to the subject, especially in Descartes, Kant, and Husserl, led to an emphasis on a timeless, omniscient, disinterested observer and the loss of attention to the pain and suffering of bodies.

Modernist ethics assumed that reasonable debate should be able to settle our basic life questions. The intent was to arrive at rational agreement without having to resort to violence.[11] But the result has often been a tangle of conflicting positions, a quagmire of unresolved issues. There has been no easy line from moral theories to moral actions. Indeed, the increasing complexity of life has made the arguments even more complex and the disputes even more intractable. The transformation of moral life through rigorous application of moral theory has failed.

Ironically, not only has rational agreement remained out of reach, but the result has been indifference to the real life situations of many people, particularly women, children, and the otherwise marginalized. In general, the abstraction of the full flesh-and-blood person from an ethical case, and the case from its full historical and developmental context, has made the whole exercise of Enlightenment ethics artificial, futile, and alienating. When moral decisions are to be based on rationally grounded principles that are not relative to the character, motives, history, context, interests, gender, body, and worldview of the agents, moral agents are separated not only from all that makes them unique, but from the very corporeality and embeddedness that makes them human persons. There is no other word for such depersonalization than violence. In effect, the "personal" is considered morally significant only to the extent that it can be bracketed and translated into the "impersonal." Indeed, complete disembodiment and complete disinterest is regarded as the only appropriate starting point for moral reasoning in the modernist schema.

Anthropologically, in these modernist constructions, the human self is generally understood as some combination of mind and body in which

---

10. Hauerwas and Burrell, "From System to Story," in Hauerwas and Jones, *Why Narrative?*, 163.

11. Perhaps the most influential contemporary effort to defend modern rationality (as it attempts to avoid modernity's pathologies) is Jürgen Habermas's "discourse ethics" with its goal of "communicative rationality." See his *Moral Consciousness and Communicative Action*.

mind has the primary role of controlling corporeal desire. Feelings and emotions are typically considered morally negligible because they merely happen to pre-existing, true, rational selves and are thus held to be transitory and capricious. Universal rules of conduct as our moral duties are contrasted with contingent pleasures of our individual passions. Thus, in the Kantian tradition, sympathy, compassion, and concern—the altruistic emotions—cannot play a substantial role in morality and moral motivation because they are not products of human agency, but in fact easily divert us from the autonomy and freedom needed for moral judgment.[12]

Today, by virtually every account, this approach to persons has failed. And the failure of reason is especially obvious in the area of moral philosophy. It has become increasingly clearer that the scientific model of rationality and neutrality, with its pretense to universality and necessity, has, in fact, been unaware of its own particularity and contingency. Modernism's conviction that we can isolate impartial moral principles from our particular worldviews, loyalties, identities, histories, and communities has been revealed as its own particular faith. "There is no theoretically neutral, pretheoretical ground from which the adjudication of competing claims can proceed."[13] In effect, the culturally and morally particular was elevated to the status of the rationally universal, to the detriment and oppression of anyone and anything that is different, that is, who did not find themselves within the discourse of universal reason. Thus, to take a classic example, Carol Gilligan has demonstrated that Lawrence Kohlberg's stages of moral reasoning champion a typical "masculine" ethics of duty and abstraction as the most highly developed, in contrast to an ethics of connection and responsibility more typical of women.[14] No wonder that women tended to rate much lower than men in "maturity" of moral reasoning!

We have now discovered, under the impetus of the masters of suspicion—Freud, Marx, and Nietzsche—that what was touted as the autonomous human self was in fact an illusion. The encyclopedist's appeal to timeless rational principles does not discard the burden of the past as they intended. Rather, their appeal to a unitary conception of reason provides unwarranted privileged status to those who identify their own assertions and arguments with the deliverances of reason. Encyclopedic, impartial reason is exposed by the postmodern genealogist as the unwitting pawn of

---

12. See Blum, *Friendship, Altruism, and Morality*, for an incisive critique of the Kantian tradition.

13. MacIntyre, *Three Rival Versions*, 173.

14. Gilligan, *In a Different Voice*.

particular interests which mask their drive for power by false pretensions to neutrality, universality, and disinterestedness.[15]

Critics of modern ethics are unanimous that all our ideas and views are narrative-dependent, including, they emphasize, our view of rationality. There is no narrative-free judgment, and pretending that there is does violence to all, particularly to those who do not hold to the accepted view. While MacIntyre believes, in Gadamerian fashion, that commitment to some or other theoretical or doctrinal standpoint may be the requisite for—rather than the barrier to—genuine moral enquiry, he continues to believe that reason can move toward being authentically universal and impersonal. Such an alternative, which MacIntyre traces back to Plato and, for him, is best represented by Thomism, remains, from a postmodern perspective, unacceptable and even naive. Postmoderns insist that theory itself has failed. Picking up on Heidegger's critique of the institutionalization of reason whereby everything, in nature as well as in culture, is to be put under the sway of the desire to master and control, postmodernist thinkers such as Derrida, Foucault, and Levinas assail the logocentrism of Western thought.

Ethics Before Ontology: The Priority of the Other

For Levinas, reason is the instrument by which an ego or society of egos makes same that which is different, possessing and domesticating it. Reason reduces the other, appropriates, disempowers, totalizes. The particular is placed under the general category. What is foreign, what is different, is subsumed within my system. It is made the same to remove its threat. All surprises prove to be just parts of the process, that is, not surprises at all. This is ontology.

Before ontology, however, exclaims Levinas, there is ethics, the relationship of responsibility to the other.[16] The other can never be present within my discourse, my theory, my thought, my ontology. Unless I allow myself to be instructed by the face of the other, I do not "relate" at all, but only dominate in terms of my paradigms and ontologies. The face of the other commands me: Thou shalt not kill. For Levinas the face is not a presence, but a trace, a trace which marks the escape of the other who cannot be contained, who has escaped the reduction to Being.

The face is the epiphany of the nakedness of the other, a visitation, a coming, a saying which comes in the passivity of the face, not threatening, but obligating. I encounter a face, my world is ruptured, my contentment

---

15. Foucault, *Power/Knowledge*.

16. "'Religion'" is "the bond that is established between the same and the other without constituting a totality" (Levinas, *Totality and Infinity*, 40).

interrupted; I am already obligated. Here is an appeal from which there is no escape, a responsibility, a state of being hostage. It is looking into the face of the other that reveals the call to responsibility as an-archic, that is, before any beginning, decision, or initiative on my part.

For Levinas the other is not another me, awaiting dialogue and reciprocity, as in Buber and Ricoeur. For Levinas my relation to the other is always asymmetrical. The other has ethical priority over the sameness of the I.

> I must always demand more of myself than of the other; and this is why I disagree with Buber's description of the I-Thou ethical relation as a symmetrical copresence ... This essential asymmetry is the very basis of ethics; not only am I more responsible than the other but I am even responsible for everyone else's responsibility.[17]

The existence of the other, rather than a conception of the good, is the touchstone of moral existence. The face-to-face relation fissures being. Flesh-and-blood bodies, rather than arguments and concepts, give moral bearings.

The implications of this shift are only now beginning to surface and take shape. In the Cartesian view of the body as external object in space over against the subject as inner consciousness, the body as subject of experience was lost. Similarly, in the Kantian view in which the having of feelings is morally indifferent, non-rational ways of knowing are devalued. Generally speaking, in the rationality tradition, sensory knowledge is useful, but it is never in itself knowledge of the human as human.[18] Since reason is that part of being human that is most human, only reason can know the properties of being, goodness, beauty, and unity. Thus, for Thomas Aquinas, touch is the lowest and least worthy of all senses because it is most unlike reason. Since the pleasures of eating, drinking, and having sex are pleasures of touch, it is a sin to engage in them solely for the pleasure of eating, drinking, and having sex.

In the rationality tradition there has been a conceptual neutralization of sensation. Spinoza gives voice to the dominant tradition: "Pain is the transition of a man from a greater to a lesser perfection."[19] Both pain and enjoyment have been rationalized and their sensory truth decimated. Even

---

17. Levinas and Kearney, "Dialogue with Emmanuel Levinas," in Kearney, *Dialogues with Contemporary Continental Thinkers*, 31.

18. J. Giles Milhaven has traced the impact of our limitation of knowledge to the rational in "A Medieval Lesson on Bodily Knowing: Women's Experience and Men's Thought."

19. Spinoza, *Ethics*, Part 3, Definition 3, 174.

Heidegger, the archcritic of the metaphysics of subjectivity which he traces back to Plato and Aristotle, in the end still remains captive of this feature of the tradition. He takes the suffering out of pain by insisting that the essence of pain cannot be pain in a feeling sense.[20]

In contrast, in the postmodern picture, I myself am my body. The body as a whole functions as a sensorium, a senser, a knower, a perceiver, a digester. Human knowledge is multidimensional. Sensing and feeling are as human as thinking. The human self includes perceptions, feelings, emotions, dispositions, attitudes, as well as thinkings. Others present themselves not simply as subjects of discourse, but, on a more fundamental level, as persons who eat, enjoy, lack, and so forth. For Levinas, alterity must communicate itself fundamentally otherwise than predicatively. In *Otherwise than Being* Levinas describes ethical obligation in terms of the subject's corporeal sensibility and proximity, vulnerability, and passivity toward the other. The ethical subject is subject to the other as "sensibility on the surface of the skin, at the edge of the nerves."[21] Since the human person is susceptible to wounding and pain, ethics is a lived, bodily relation to the other. "Only a subject that eats can be-for-the-other"[22] [23]

"Ethics is the spiritual optics."[24] "To recognize the Other is to recognize a hunger, to recognize the Other is to give."[25] [26] The ethical "face to face retains an ultimate situation"[27] and "in it things figure not as what one builds but as what one gives."[28] This allows human sensitivity to pain, wounding, and suffering to be immediately ethically relevant. Ethics in this view is grounded in corporeality, in creatureliness, with a special marking because of pain, suffering, lapse, delay, and fissure. It is sensitive bodies in proximity that are the space of ethics, the fields of meeting. In my very hearing of the child's cries I am ethically claimed.[29] Face-to-face,

20. Caputo, *Demythologizing Heidegger*, ch. 8, 148–68.
21. Levinas, *Otherwise than Being*, 15.
22. Levinas, *Otherwise than Being*, 74.
23. Thus, Levinas worries that "Dasein in Heidegger is never hungry" (*Totality and Infinity*, 134).
24. Levinas, *Totality and Infinity*, 78.
25. Levinas, *Totality and Infinity*, 75.
26. "The-one-for-the-other is the foundation of theory" (Levinas, *Otherwise than Being*, 136).
27. Levinas, *Totality and Infinity*, 81.
28. Levinas, *Totality and Infinity*, 77.
29. Despite the considerable debt owed to Merleau-Ponty for his recovery of the agent body, John D. Caputo points out that his analysis, by overlooking improper and unbecoming, vulnerable and suffering bodies, "is still a form of idealism against which

flesh-to-flesh, I am wounded by the other's wounding—and responsible for it. Responsibility is prior to freedom. "This responsibility appears as a plot without a beginning, anarchic ... outside of all finality and every system."[30] There is no need for a reasoning process to discover or erect a rational reason to provide the moral force.

The other is experienced as an appeal, an absence, in that it creates in me a restlessness for contact that I don't have.[31] And the other is experienced as an excess in that the trace of Transcendence is inscribed in the face. "The Other is not the incarnation of God, but precisely by his face, in which he is disincarnate, is the manifestation of the height in which God is revealed."[32] "Strictly speaking, the other is the end; I am a hostage, a responsibility and a substitution supporting the world in the passivity of assignation, even in an accusing persecution, which is undeclinable."[33]

In *Against Ethics* John Caputo describes such views as "responsible" postmodernism because they answer a call from beyond our laws and principles, so that we can attend to the particulars, the lost, the different, the exceptions. This kind of ethic is not against laws, but is aware that laws and rules do not have authority in themselves. As Caputo puts it, with an allusion to Christ healing on the Sabbath, we need "to keep the law honest, to keep the eye of the law on the withered hand."[34] Indeed, to simply do what the law dictates is to fall short of doing justice. The law needs to be under justice, not justice under law. Such responsibility demands an exceeding of the demands of the law, incarnating a response to which laws intend to point the direction, but sometimes, in fact, obscure. Likewise, Edith Wyschogrod makes a plea for "excessive desire, a desire on behalf of the other that seeks the cessation of another's suffering and the birth of another's joy."[35] Similarly, although in his typically more dialectical fashion, Paul Ricoeur attempts to establish the primacy of the ethical aim (goodness) over morality by "granting rightful place to moral rules, without letting them have the last word."[36]

---

he always fought" (*Against Ethics*, 202). Whereas for Merleau-Ponty it is the resemblance between self and other, for Levinas it is the asymmetrical, unsurpassable difference that opens up ethics and discourse.

30. Levinas, *Otherwise than Being*, 135.
31. Not to forget or minimize the restlessness or unrest awakened on contact.
32. Levinas, *Totality and Infinity*, 79.
33. Levinas, *Otherwise than Being*, 128.
34. Caputo, *Against Ethics*, 221.
35. Wyschogrod, *Saints and Postmodernism*, xxiv.
36. Ricoeur, *Oneself as Another*, 171. Chapters 7, 8, and 9 describe how for Ricoeur the ethical aim needs to pass through the sieve of the norm, even as, when the norm

Asymmetry and Self-Sacrifice

All of this—the morality of corporeality, the spirituality of morality—finds deep resonance in my soul. Along with Levinas, I see ethics not as something later, to be fitted in, but as the nature of life itself. Indeed, for me it is of the highest import that life be seen as *conatus amandi* (evocation to love) rather than as *conatus essendi*. In this way, ethics—in the sense of responsibility to love—is as old as creation itself. Love is the quickening, the quivering[37] which evokes life and permeates life. The call to justice and love belong to the very fabric of everyday life, giving it shape and texture. In a world of violence, this call often arises most poignantly in the need of the neighbor and likewise is often discovered most acutely in the cry of suffering. Then the call comes as a summons: heal the wounds, bind up the brokenhearted. Being ethical is a primordial movement in the beckoning force of life itself. As gift and call, love is both the description of life and the prescription for life.

At the same time, I admit to a fluttering, sometimes throbbing, but always bothersome disquiet. For as much as I join with Levinas in his call to responsibility for the other, I am concerned that his emphasis on the priority of the other not give birth—albeit contrary to intention—to a guilting moralism calling for self-forgetfulness and self-forfeiture. For all its importance as a countermove to narcissism, calling for the ethical priority of the other not only has the feel of utopian impossibility about it,[38] but, more ominously, may inadvertently proliferate the very violence it sets out to counteract.[39]

And even though for Levinas the feminine is the other *par excellence*,[40] what are we, in a time when women are emerging from patriarchy with

---

leads to situations of impasse, we go back to the aim.

37. In contrast to the "anonymous rustling" of Levinas (*Otherwise than Being*, 3), the "incessant bustling" of the "there is [*il y a*], the horrible eternity at the bottom of essence" (*Otherwise than Being*, 176).

38. Levinas does admit that "there is a utopian moment in what I say: it is the recognition of something which cannot be realised but which, ultimately, guides all moral action" (Ainsley, Wright, and Hughes, "The Paradox of Morality," in Bernasconi and Wood, *The Provocation of Levinas*, 72).

39. In *Against Ethics*, by referring to a sentence of Derrida's in *Truth in Painting*, Caputo calls it "an impossible dream, even a dangerous dream, inasmuch as promises of what is absolutely unmediated are usually followed by the most massive mediations" (82). When legitimate self-needs are denied, they have a way of coming back with a vengeance, often in disguised, underhanded, and dangerous ways.

40. In *Totality and Infinity*, Levinas describes the importance of the "gentleness of the feminine face" (150) in establishing the intimacy of home, making space for hospitality to strangers, and thus establishing a subjectivity capable of ethical relationships.

agency and voice, to make of a view that sees subjectivity as dispossession and subjection? What, indeed, are we to make of Levinas's subsequent depiction of maternity as the paradigm of the behavior of a human subject toward the other?[41]

In his claim that being-responsible-for-the-other is the constitution of true selfhood, Levinas is calling—certainly first and last[42]—for disinterest in, if not repudiation of, all self-interest. For Levinas, I am expiation for the other, held hostage by the other, to whom I must give preference over myself. "The self, the persecuted one," is, in fact, says Levinas, not "in the state of original sin; it is, on the contrary, the original goodness of creation"[43] [44]

For Levinas an ethical relation is non-symmetrical because "I am responsible for the other without waiting for reciprocity, were I to die for it. Reciprocity is his affair."[45] "The face of a neighbor signifies for me an unexceptional responsibility, preceding every free consent, every pact,

---

The feminine other is also "the Beloved . . . an extreme fragility, a vulnerability" (256). Since traditionally the woman too often has been considered the other who needs to be put down by the man as same, Levinas's acknowledgment of the significant place of women contributes to a new ethics of respect for women. However, at the same time, in *Totality and Infinity*, his ambiguity in regard to the feminine emerges when, in relating the erotic to the feminine, he sees the erotic with its "return to the self" (266) as less than ethical, and when he talks of the "beloved," the feminine, as "without responsibility," fading into "ambiguity, into animality" (263). Moreover, it is not clear whether, for Levinas, a woman can also be an agent, the lover as well as the beloved. See Luce Irigaray's two essays on Levinas, "The Fecundity of the Caress," in Irigaray, *An Ethics of Sexual Difference*, 185–27, and "Questions to Emmanuel Levinas," in Bernasconi and Critchley, *Re-Reading Levinas*, 109–29. For a careful and nuanced discussion and critique of Levinas's portrayal of the feminine, see Brüeggemann-Kruijff, *Bij de Gratie van de transcendentie*. Chanter's *Ethics of Eros* is also an excellent discussion of Levinas's views of the feminine and Irigaray's critique.

41. Levinas, *Otherwise than Being*, 75–8. "Maternity, which is bearing par excellence, bears even responsibility for the persecuting by the persecutor" (75). Although it is clear that the feminine, as the trope for subjectivity, is at the heart of the ethical, I am deeply concerned about the felicity of employing feminine imagery for human subjectivity, which could, particularly by women, be heard not only as conflating being a woman with motherhood but also once more and once again glorifying their submission. Much better, it would seem, if one wants to emphasize the importance of committed caring for the other, the bearing of each other's burdens, to talk of paternity as well as maternity as ethical figures par excellence. See Joy, "Levinas: Alterity, the Feminine and Women—A meditation."

42. "But egoism is neither first nor last." (Levinas, *Otherwise than Being*, 128)

43. Levinas, *Otherwise than Being*, 121.

44. For Wyschogrod, "a saintly life is defined as one in which compassion for the other, irrespective of cost to the saint, is the primary trait," and "whatever the cost to the saint in pain and sorrow" (*Saints*, xxiii, 3).

45. Levinas, *Ethics and Infinity*, 98.

every contract."[46] The face is both my superior which demands my attention and my subordinate, because in his/her vulnerability she cannot compel me to give it.

In recognizing the dance of intersubjectivity as the crucial process in which the moral self is constituted, Levinas is, I believe, rightly claiming that my responsibility for my neighbor is not a function of or derivable from anything else than that they are my neighbor. But does this necessarily mean, on an ethical level, the indiscriminate acceptance of others regardless of their motives, an ethical "disinterestedness"[47] in my own welfare even "were I to die for it"?[48]

There can be no question about the need to avoid reducing the other to another self similar to me. The mystery of each unique identity means that there can be no question of having another person's experience. To the extent that I am a unique self, no one else can replace me in my responsibility. In that sense human experience is always asymmetrical.

Human uniqueness—and asymmetry—comes to the fore especially in the intimate ethical relationships of friendship, marriage, and family. In an economy of reciprocity and exchange, things and people have instrumental value in promoting one's interests and are thus replaceable or may be substituted by things or people who meet the need(s) equally well. However, in ethical relations of mutuality, persons are unique particulars and the beloved is different, incomparable, and irreplaceable (never a mere instrument). Each relation of mutual love is its own non-interchangeable relation. As opposed to a quantitative hierarchical scale of loves, we have a qualitative array of incommensurate loves in which "we love them all differently because they are incomparably different."[49] Thus, I express the "same" love to my children by loving them all "differently" because they are all unique individuals. You are my friend because you are you. That relation is incomparable with my relationship with anyone else, because nobody else is you.

The question is whether this asymmetry of experience calls for an ethical asymmetry in which the other normatively always has priority over me. Indeed, it seems to me that Derrida makes a good point when he asserts that "dissymmetry itself would be impossible without this symmetry" in which "I know myself to be other for the other. Without this, 'I' (in general: egoity),

---

46. Levinas, *Otherwise than Being*, 88.

47. Levinas, *Otherwise than Being*, 126.

48. It is clear that in actual life, due to the third party, Levinas is able to justify pragmatically self-defense in the face of aggression. The point is that he seems on the highest ethical level to disallow any and all self-interest.

49. Brümer, *The Model of Love*, 210.

unable to be the other's other, would never be a victim of violence."[50] That is to say, human intersubjectivity as mutual responsibility is an ethical symmetry of empirical asymmetries. From his side, Levinas is afraid of ethical symmetry-talk, not because he does not accept intersubjectivity, but because he is convinced that such talk willy nilly involves a generalizing (i.e., totalizing) insistence that the other be responsible in the same way that I am. That is—and remains, no doubt—a clear and present danger. But is it inevitably the case? Is the only alternative to egoism altruism? Is my ethical insistence on human co-responsibility for justice, for example, necessarily an imposition of my views on others? If I (we) take seriously the situatedness of our freedom and fallibility, my (our) insistence on justice will recognize that there will be differences of response to the common call. More importantly—as I will consider in more detail below—if we begin with ethical symmetry, another possibility opens up in which self and other are not irrevocably and inevitably locked in an economy of war, but in which there is a nonviolent economy of mutuality and love in which justice and care for the neighboring other is of one piece with justice and care of and for myself.

For his part, in insisting on ethical asymmetry, Levinas emphasizes the movement of the other to self (no responding self without an other summoning) at the cost of minimizing the corresponding movement of self to the other (no summoning other without responding self).[51] The result is that, ethically, instead of a two-directional interplay of mutuality, there is uni-directionality. For Levinas, prior to the ethical interruption of the other, the I (*le moi*) is fundamentally ignorant of, separate from, and closed off to the other. The other must storm the defenses of the self. There seems to be no room, ontologically, for the possibility of a self, of its own initiative, to reach out, attentive and open to the other. And when the ethical self is born ("awakened"), and is "hospitable," the self is, first and foremost, hostage to, and expiation for, the other. In Levinas's ethical asymmetry there is a necessary disinterest in self-concern and a corresponding complete non-indifference to others. "Subjectivity is not for itself; it is, once again, initially for another.... the other... approaches me essentially insofar as myself—insofar as l am—responsible for him."[52]

---

50. Derrida, "Violence and Metaphysics: An Essay on the Thought of Emmanuel Levinas," in *Writing and Difference*, 126. "That l am also essentially the other's other, and that I know I am, is evidence of a strange symmetry whose trace appears nowhere in Levinas's descriptions" (128).

51. In *Oneself as Another*, Ricoeur also voices his concern that Levinas one-sidedly emphasizes the relation of the other to self (335ff).

52. Levinas, *Ethics and Infinity*, 96.

It is true that in recognizing the other as higher (and lower) than myself, as an other for whom I am infinitely responsible, I avoid approaching the other as a rival whose power needs to be nullified. Granted, that is an enormous ethical advance over the modernist power-over mentality. However, one gets the idea that the only alternative to such imperialism is to recognize the other as higher than myself, one to whom I am hostage. Love of self seems to come down to forgetfulness of self and divestiture of all rights and interests. Aside from the impossibility of such divesting (which Levinas understands and accepts as the reality on the non-ethical level of ontology), that seems to be a dangerous message to pass on as the voice from on high. For the many who already struggle to believe that they have any right to have their own needs met and have little sense of their own power, this may encourage a further discounting of self and even self-effacement. On the other hand, for the many dedicated to the service of others who find such self-divestiture an impossibility, this may easily feed self-guilt or occasion escape into numbing diversions.

When we hear the paradoxical language ("obsession," "hostage," "substitution," even "occupation") which is descriptive of self for Levinas,[53] the questions multiply. What can it possibly mean that I am substitution for her/him? Does it mean that in being concerned with myself I am violently denying my true self? Doesn't being hostage to the other suggest a wholesale capitulation to the other? If so, is this not another version of the call to self-less agapic love in contrast to the self-interested love of *eros*? Moreover, what, on a practical level, does it mean to be totally responsible-for-the-other? How does one practice "substitution" for someone who has AIDS, or is unemployed, or is in an unhealthy relation? Suffering-with is one thing, but suffering-for? In general, it seems that the championing of the ethical priority of the other may in everyday life boomerang into a virtuous way of endorsing a demeaning submissiveness with the self-injury that inflicts and the potential backlash against others that it often invites. Don't such descriptions of self-extolling passivity, particularly from the viewpoint of women, First Nations, or Black people in North America, risk being understood as the glorification of victimization?[54]

Now, this is clearly not what Levinas intends or envisions. He wants to move beyond a self-as-power-over to a self-as-service. With Levinas I agree (in distinction from any modernist, rationally based ethic) that "it is not a matter of thinking the ego and the other together, but to be facing. The true

---

53. In a context of narcissistic male domination, the hortatory use of such phrases would strikingly make the necessary point.

54. Cf. Joy, "Levinas," 484.

union or true togetherness is not the togetherness of synthesis, but a togetherness of face to face."[55] Consequently, Levinas wants to move beyond the confining and totalizing categories of being as power-against by a discourse of a morality "otherwise than being" which comes "before" ontology.[56]

Insofar as Levinas wants us to face up to the unconditionality of moral responsibility for love of neighbor, his call can scarcely be gainsaid. He would then be describing the metaphysical or normative conditions for ethical activity, without describing a concrete ethical agenda. The difficulty is that, for Levinas, proximity, the ethical site, is "before," "beyond," "otherwise" than a place of power: the true self (*le soi*) is called prior to power relationships. The implication is that an activity is not ethical unless there is a complete lack of self-interest and self-concern, a complete passivity without power. Indeed, such concern for self is, in his view, the non-ethical ontological self inevitably closed in on its own self-interest. Disinterest, expiation, total subjection to the other regardless of his/her motivations is what it means to be ethical.

Power-Over or Power-With

Here is where the rumblings become louder. Is the exercise of agentic power always power-against neighbor, and thus unethical? Does non-indifference to the other need to mean disinterest in self? In contrast, I want to suggest the possibility of an ethical exercise of power as power-with.

Levinas insists that one cannot escape the perspective of one's own self. I couldn't agree more. What I disagree with is his contention that one's perspective inevitably and irrevocably can only totalize the other because that is what it means to have power. Power *qua* power is power-over, and that means war. For Levinas the "invincible persistence," the *conatus essendi*, is interest.[57] "Being's interest takes dramatic form ... in the multiplicity of allergic egoisms which are at war with one another." Through "calculation, mediation and politics" a "rational peace" of "reciprocal limitation and determination" is established.[58] Nevertheless, "interest remains" and "nothing is gratuitous."[59] Interest, enjoyment, calculation, and possessions make up an economy of reciprocal exchange in the domain of being which is ontologically non-ethical. Symmetry, interest, and reciprocity cannot avoid being egoistic, imperialistic, selfish. Consequently, to move beyond this means that, for Levinas, ethics

---

55. Levinas, *Ethics and Infinity*, 77.
56. Zygmunt Bauman reads this moral "before" as "better" (*Postmodern Ethics*, 72).
57. "*Esse is interesse*; essence is interest" (Levinas, *Otherwise than Being*, 4).
58. Levinas, *Otherwise than Being*, 4.
59. Levinas, *Otherwise than Being*, 5.

must be "otherwise than being," a "total gratuity, breaking with interest."[60] Indeed, the breakup of essence is ethics.

It is Levinas's view of power as inherently power-over that I see as highly problematic. Accepting that domination is indigenous to power and at the same time decrying such power-egoism leaves Levinas only one alternative: the ethical priority of the other.

Levinas is, in fact, accepting the long tradition[61] of envisioning power as fundamentally power-over.[62] He outlines his project in *Totality and Infinity* as developing discourse as a "non-allergic relation with alterity ... where *power, by essence murderous of the other*, becomes, faced with the other and 'against all good sense,' the impossibility of murder, the consideration of the other, or justice."[63] Again, in *Otherwise than Being*, Levinas asks "why should the other concern me? ... Am I my brother's keeper? These questions have meaning only if one has already supposed that the ego is concerned only with itself, is only a concern for itself."[64] Thus, although Levinas is very critical of this ontology of power, calling it in fact "a philosophy of injustice,"[65] his move beyond into an ethical metaphysics of alterity consciously builds on and is dependent on a recognition of an ontology of being-as-power-over. His insistence on the necessity of an ethics of deference to the other (because egoism is wrong) is concomitant with the recognition that it is ontologically impossible (because egoism is unavoidable).

Such thinking seems to take the basic opposition between closed selves, with all the ambiguity this involves for personal interaction, as a fundamental characteristic of human nature.[66] In this paradigm, given

60. Levinas, *Otherwise than Being*, 96.

61. For Levinas, "'I think' comes down to 'I can.' ... Ontology as first philosophy is a philosophy of power" (*Totality and Infinity*, 46).

62. Paul Tillich, for example, defines power as "the possibility a being has to actualize itself against the resistance of other beings" (*The Courage to Be*, 179). Paul Ricoeur claims that "[i]t is difficult to imagine situations of interaction in which one individual does not exert power over another *by the very fact of acting*" (*Oneself as Another*, 220, italics added). Derrida concurs: "if it is true, as I in fact believe, that writing cannot be thought outside of the horizon of intersubjective violence, is there anything, even science, that radically escapes it?" (*Of Grammatology*, 127). He considers "[s]uch violence may be considered the very condition of the gift.... *The violence appears irreducible, within the circle or outside it, whether it repeats the circle or interrupts it*" (*Given Time*, 147).

63. Levinas, *Totality and Infinity*, 47. (Italics added)

64. Levinas, *Otherwise than Being*, 117.

65. Levinas, *Totality and Infinity*, 46.

66. "But the moral priority of the other over myself could not come to be if it were not motivated by something beyond nature. The ethical situation is a human situation, *beyond human nature*, in which the idea of God comes to mind" (Levinas and Kearney, "Dialogue with Emmanuel Levinas," in Kearney, *Dialogues with Contemporary*

classic formulation in modern times in the work of Freud, Hegel, and Sartre, there are only two possibilities: dominate or be dominated. In this paradigm of violence, one either exercises power and becomes dominant and independent—that is, selfish—or one surrenders and becomes submissive and dependent—that is, other-directed.

In this model we have a world of ceaseless conflict and endless competition until one proves him/herself superior. But in such a world, when neither is able to surrender voluntarily, striving eventually becomes empty and meaningless because each person remains alone, disconnected, incapable of change and development. On the other hand, if we choose not to exercise our desire for power and subordinate our needs and interests, we have a relation with another person but at the cost of stifling our own needs and interests.

Within the confines of this paradigm, the route of self-sacrificial *agape* clearly has it all over the wiles of self-interested *eros*. *Agape*, as Nygren classically distinguished it in the Christian tradition, is supposed to be pure and disinterested love over against the egotistical and interested love of *eros*.[67] There is power without surrender (*eros*) or surrender without power (*agape*). Thus, for Reinhold Niebuhr, to take a modern Christian example, self-sacrifice is the end, goal, or ideal of history, and mutuality is a compromise ethic to accommodate fallen existence. "Sacrificial love (agape) completes the incompleteness of mutual love (eros)."[68]

My fundamental query is: how different, despite the details and complexities, is the position of Levinas? Levinas, it is true, does not ask us to deny or stifle our needs. Rather, acknowledging the needs and interests of the ego, we are then to interrupt them and put them out of play in accord with our higher ethical self. The questions return: Is there no legitimate ethical call to care of self and the needs of self? Is power of agency always self-interested, and therefore below the ethical plane?

Levinas is not unaware of the dangers. He exclaims, "But it is I, I and no one else, who am hostage for others." The "no one else" is important, for "to say that the other has to sacrifice himself to the others would be to preach human sacrifice";[69] indeed, he admits that the responsibility for the other "is troubled and becomes a problem when a third party enters."[70] Significantly,

Continental Thinkers, 25. (Italics added)

67. Nygren, *Agape and Eros*. "Eros is essentially and in principle self-love,. . . Agape, on the other hand, excludes all self-love" (216–17).

68. Niebuhr, *The Nature and Destiny of Man*, 86.

69. Levinas, *Otherwise than Being*, 26–27.

70. Levinas, *Otherwise than Being*, 157.

he even admits that "the relationship with the third party is an *incessant* correction of the asymmetry of proximity."[71] Faced with unlimited responsibility, the self can, because my neighbor is also a third party with respect to another, "be called upon to concern itself also with itself."[72] I am also another for the other and a third one. Thank God. Which is exactly what Levinas exclaims: "'Thanks to God' I am another for the others."[73] In this way, "there is also justice for me."[74] But, even then, he cautions that the "forgetting" of the "unlimited initial responsibility" is "pure egoism."[75] Nevertheless, in this way violence and evil may be resisted "when the evil he does to me touches also a third party, one who is likewise my neighbor."[76] Thus, Levinas does allow being for oneself, but always on the basis of a prior being for the other, and only as a function of this being for the other.

A basic question that emerges is whether there is in Levinas's thought, for all its hallowing of the other, the historical possibility of meeting an other, a neighbor, without distance or without fusion as Levinas desires. Not only is, ethically, the other always transcendent to me, but in "a history and politics," the asymmetrical ethical relation takes on "the aspect of a symmetrical relation."[77] "Separation is embedded in an order in which the asymmetry of the interpersonal relation is effaced, where I and the other become interchangeable in commerce, and where the particular man, an individual of the genus man, appearing in history, is substituted for the I and for the other."[78] In history, by means of the third party, the ethical priority of the other is transformed into a relation of equals. In history, it seems we at best have the balanced exchange of reciprocity as a welcome respite from the economy of war. But the exchange of "interchangeable" I's sounds more like a trading in sameness, rather than the meeting of unique, irreplaceable I's in difference. In the end, it appears that we have a chastened or corrected asymmetry in which equality and reciprocity[79] are possible, but not genuine mutuality.[80]

71. Levinas, *Otherwise than Being*, 158. (Italics Added)
72. Levinas, *Otherwise than Being*, 128.
73. Levinas, *Otherwise than Being*, 158.
74. Levinas, *Otherwise than Being*, 159.
75. Levinas, *Otherwise than Being*, 128.
76. Burggraeve, *Emmanuel Levinas*, 56. This is an exceptionally clear and concise exposition of Levinas's thought.
77. Levinas, *Totality and Infinity*, 225.
78. Levinas, *Totality and Infinity*, 226.
79. In my view, the equality and reciprocity of justice with the emphasis on balanced exchange differs from the mutuality of an ethical relationship (cf. below).
80. Levinas's recognition that there are always third parties and the necessary

Mutuality as Power-With

As an alternative to Levinas's model in which agency is inevitably and inescapably egoistic, I suggest a model of non-oppositional difference—an economy of love. Such an intersubjective model of mutual recognition, attunement, and empowerment, I believe, honors Levinas's intentions without some of the dangers which seem to haunt his position.[81] Here the movement of the other to myself is coincident with a simultaneous and voluntary movement of myself to the other. The desire of each evokes the desire of the other; mutual recognition, mutual yielding/receiving, mutual delighting, mutual empowering. There is the oscillating rhythm of giving and receiving, the dance of identity and intimacy called love. In giving to the other, I, paradoxically, in being received, am enlarged and enhanced—receiving, in the words of Levinas, "inspiration." In receiving the other, I expand, and paradoxically, through my receiving, give. Instead of power-over (with its corollary of power-under), or power-held-in-abeyance (to avoid domination), there is power-with and the dance of mutual empowerment.

The self is always intersubjective, either a connected (or a disconnected) self. Insofar as a human self is never an autonomous agent in splendid isolation but always a connective self, the intra-psychic and the inter-psychic need not always be in opposition to each other. Indeed, the formation and nurturing of self-identity is possible only in an intersubjective matrix. It is in being seen (or not seen) that I, as an infant, come to see (or not see) myself. It is in being loved (or not loved) that I come to love (or not love) myself—and others. Since my identity is a gift I receive from and with others, my connection with others is constitutive of my identity. Community is not the sameness of fusion, but the coming-into-connection of diverse identities. We live together, in genuine community, or we strive together, in the violence of war; but in any case there is no I without a We. In other words, otherness and difference are never wholly inside or wholly outside myself. I, or at least aspects of me, come alive and grow, or retreat and eventually die as I move in and out of relation with other selves. Mutuality assumes we cannot talk about response to and for others over and against response for and to self. In an intersubjective context of mutuality, self-desires are not fundamentally desires against the other. In fear and disappointment they often become fixated in that way—and mutuality is ruptured into hostility.

---

mediating structures again vividly raises the question of the practical viability of his ethics of priority.

81. Jessica Benjamin's *The Bonds of Love* is an articulate plea for "a new possibility of initial recognition between men and women" in which both are empowered and mutually respectful.

Mutuality is attunement of expression, recognition, and desire, a dance in which simultaneously the differing gifts and needs of each person are honored, recognized, and often met. From our places of irreducible otherness, each of us seeks a rhythm in the other without hierarchy and without abasement—beyond considerations of duty, balance, or advantage. We recognize each other, seek each other's good, identify-with each other—in the process loving the other as we love ourselves. In this interfacing, the giving over or yielding to the other is a voluntary move in which one retains his/her own individuality and difference. The dance between staying with one's self and reaching out is the interplay of difference that is life itself. The aim is not to eradicate, accommodate, suppress, or repress difference, but to allow contact with difference to move, enhance, and change us as we become more fully ourselves. Difference is not defect, deficit, or threat, but an otherness to cherish, connect with, be challenged by, learn from, and celebrate. Empowered through the giving/receiving experience, a positive spiral of mutuality begins to take shape in which we are inspired to recognize, reach out, and share more of ourselves with each other more often and more deeply. When it happens (the difficulties and fears are many, and there are no guarantees), we meet—graced with mutual recognition, mutual pleasure, and mutual empowerment—the fundamental ingredients of love. "The psyche is one open system connected to another, and only under those conditions is it renewable. If it lives, your psyche is in love. If it is not in love, it is dead."[82]

The dance of mutuality is always drenched in vulnerability and risk because it is a non-coerced meeting of two free subjects in the wild spaces of love. Timing and spacing are of the essence. Reaching out does not guarantee being met. The timing may be off, the partner may be otherwise occupied, not-at-home, angry, depressed, in a different space. Venturing out, but not meeting, leads to impasse, and brings with it hurt, grieving—suffering. When people learn to accept that the vulnerability of mutuality always includes moments of distance, pain, and suffering, impasses may be avoided or broken, and the suffering-from such non-meetings can even turn into suffering-with experiences of empathy, non-blame, and shared disappointment.

Opening to others may lead to indifference, negativity, rebuff, rebuke, assault—who knows? Indeed, it is that unknowing that makes us fearful, incessantly tempting us to try to guarantee the outcome or at least minimize the hazards through subtle or not so subtle means of control and manipulation. It is the fear of non-affirmation and disintegration feeding the urge to

---

82. Kristeva, *Tales of Love*, 15.

take advantage of the other, hidden in the recesses of every human heart, which closes our hearts, sets up defenses, and makes genuine meeting so difficult. The giving in such encounters is easily (if not consciously) counterfeit, a bribe, a come-on; the "giver" actually a taker. The receiving too becomes contaminated. Feeling a deep unworthiness, but, at the same time, being desperate for a gift, can lead to a feigned indifference, cloying "thankfulness," a guilt-ridden discomfort. Whether we are giving or receiving, insofar as we are deficient in self-esteem, our fears tend to get the best of us and opportunities for meeting degenerate into more or less calculated maneuvers of offense and defense, tugs-of-war of competition and resistance.

Since at every turn and in every moment the give-and-receive of mutuality threatens to degenerate into such strategies of manipulation, people often see no choice but to turn ethical relations into economic exchange relations with set demands for return and remuneration. That such degeneration is rampant in our skewed lives, however, need not mean, as is so often assumed, that all human relations are inevitably and finally only to be explained in terms of an economy of violence and sacrifice where giving necessarily implies taking from another. The mutuality model calls into question the assumption that appropriation (and the fear of expropriation) is intrinsic to human agency. Such an economy of love is not necessarily always already (although it often deteriorates into this) a zero-sum game in which giving to one is always a taking from the other. There is, instead, the possibility of a giving as an overflowing to the other which invites and often evokes (but neither demands nor coerces) a return. There is a return to the self (which would bother Levinas); but, since it is not at the cost of the other, it does meet Levinas's basic concern. In neither demanding responses nor being conditional upon them, mutual relations are not to be confused with or reduced to the reciprocities of market relations of exchange and contract. And there always remains the risk of violence. But in this model, as distinct from the Hegelian model of opposition, there is room for a genuine meeting of self and the other in a middle space, room for a giving in excess, without a why, which increases in its being given, transcending the economy of reciprocity and exchange. Love is the excessive gift that keeps on giving. The very possibility of betrayal and rejection—the risk of violence—is part and parcel of its "without-why"ness, making it a "beautiful risk" (Levinas), a risk worth taking. For when, in spite of the risk, a gift is given and received, both giver and receiver experience a miracle of unmerited grace, the kind that makes all the difference in life.

In genuine mutuality it is not that the other fills up or augments myself; nor do I lose myself in the other. In both these cases, it would seem, there is no alterity, only sameness—with its suspension of genuine risk! In the first case, I ingest or dominate the other into my sameness. In the second, my otherness is assumed or subsumed into the sameness of the other.

In maintaining that ethically I can make no demand on the other but rather that I give full priority to the other, Levinas seems to come dangerously close to this second situation despite his protestations to the contrary.[83] The problem seems to be that Levinas believes that expecting or seeking a response from the other necessarily means a tit-for-tat reciprocity, at best a contracted exchange of rights, duties, and goods, and at worst a manipulation. It is true, as I have just noted, that the risk and vulnerability of mutuality are often too much for us so we try to regain control either through covert manipulation or overt reciprocal contract.[84] In both cases, ethical relations take on an instrumental quality. But is an ethical asymmetry (with priority of the other person) the only alternative to either manipulative relationships (with the other as object) or the balanced exchange of economic transactions (with interchangeable selves)? If it is (as Levinas seems to assume), his approach would be my approach. However, as I have attempted to describe, the genuine mutuality of the ethical bears its own distinct mark, neither to be confused with or turned into the balanced exchange of reciprocal economies, nor confused with the priority of the other. Moreover, genuine mutual relations need to be clearly distinguished from their counterfeit, i.e., manipulative relations.

Genuine mutuality is not the calculation of reciprocal advantages in which I determine whether a neighbor treats me with equal regard, and then, if the conclusion is negative, I am absolved of my obligations. Levinas is right, I believe, to refuse to accept such calculation as the mark of the authentically ethical, even if, as we have observed, the difficulty of the ethical venture means that such exchange is often passed off as mutuality. In genuine mutuality both manipulation with its premium on control and reciprocity with its premium on balanced exchange are replaced with an ethics of being-with.[85] Genuine mutuality includes a self-love which is not self-aggrandizement or selfishness. It involves regard for self's own integrity, esteem for one's own worth, commitment to one's own convictions, and trust in one's own intuitions. Without such self-love, I fear, all relations with others, despite all protestations or pretenses to the contrary, will be efforts to gain a sense of belonging and worth at the expense of

---

83. "Contact with the other, . . . is neither to invest the other and annul his alterity, nor to suppress myself in the other" (Levinas, *Otherwise than Being*, 86).

84. For differences between manipulative, contractual (i.e., reciprocal), and fellowship kinds of relationships, see MacMurray, *Persons in Relation*, chs. 5–7, and Brümmer, *The Model of Love*, 56–73.

85. Olthuis, *The Beautiful Risk*.

the other—and thereby violent. Genuine love of other is as fundamentally impossible without love of self as love of self is fundamentally impossible without love of the other. That, indeed, is the great commandment: to love my neighbor as I love myself.

This model of mutuality also calls for a revisioning of the typical selfish *eros*/altruistic *agape* contrast. *Eros* is no longer the drive to unite, dominate, or fuse, returning everything to the Same which needs to be countermanded by an agapic drive to sacrificially give up self. *Eros* is *agape*, the intersubjective desire to connect in difference, the agapic power to interconnection (power-with) which is the meaning of life. *Eros* as be(com)ing-with is a mutual connecting which is neither indifferent nor disinterested, neither invasive nor domineering. Being-with is a power-with which respects, receives, and honors the other, and in so doing there is the mutual enrichment, mutual empowerment, and mutual pleasure of love. Without a self-other opposition, there is no longer a need to oppose *eros* and *agape*.

Suffering-With

However, as we all know too well, the mutuality of shared power—love—is too rare. *Eros* too often degenerates into selfish imperialism and defensive aggression. In fear, the power of love is warped into power-over: violence, hate, evil. The wild spaces of love are turned into the killing fields. In such circumstances the scourges of violence mean that the give-and-receive rhythms of mutual power-with often need to become exercises in suffering-with our neighbor—and in that sense a priority of the other. Suffering-with (as distinct from suffering-from) is a voluntary, gratuitous act of standing alongside, empathic listening, affirming, speaking, and acting on behalf of.[86] It is what Levinas calls the "suffering for the useless suffering of the other person."[87]

In other words, the reality of rampant inequality, disadvantage, and outright oppression in our world means that the ethical symmetry of mutuality often calls for a priority in meeting the needs of others. Exercising mutuality means taking into account the position and circumstances of the other. When the other is "widow, orphan, stranger" (i.e., disadvantaged, whether through accident, need, injustice, impairment, lack of resources, etc.), there is what has been called in liberation theology the "preferential option for the poor." At the same time, when the other is engaged in acts of domination and injustice, an ethics of mutuality calls for acts of resistance

---

86. See Olthuis, *The Beautiful Risk* for suffering-with in a psychotherapeutic context.

87. Levinas, "Useless Suffering," in Bernasconi and Wood, *The Provocation of Levinas*, 159.

and restraint. But this "asymmetry" is not an involuntary the-other-comes-first principle. Such "self-sacrifice" is not, I suggest, as with Niebuhr and Levinas, what it means to be quintessentially ethical. It finds its derivative place in an ethics of mutuality because of the brokenness and sinfulness of life. It is the compromise required by the breakdown of mutuality with the intention of making/restoring mutual partnerships. As Don Browning puts it, this makes "appropriate self-sacrifice as a transitional ethic on the way to restoring mutuality."[88] An ethics of being-with and suffering-with in this way also suggests that if maternity is to be the ethical metaphor *par excellence*, it would need to be recast not as the supreme problem of self-sacrifice but (with paternity) as paradigm examples of mutuality in which life is created, given, and shared.

In the end, my emphasis on "-am-with" (power-with) instead of Levinas's "-am-for" seems confluent with his (and my) intentions to envision a philosophy of non-violence. In his claim that the Face awakens me to responsibility, Levinas seems to assume that there is something in the ontological ego that urges or impels a journey into the exile of the "otherwise than being," giving rise to an awakening or birth of the moral self, not as "I am I," but as "I am for." Levinas stresses that this ethical "for" is not the social "with." However, "with" in my usage is not the social "being-with" of Heidegger. "With" carries the connotations of a humanity as a religious community-in-difference, gifted-with and called-to love, very similar to what Levinas calls "proximity"[89] as the religio-ethical place of responsibility, vulnerability, and non-violence.[90]

Co-responsibility, care, and compassion are the key terms in a postmodern ethic. Care goes back to the old Gothic word, *Kara*, meaning "to lament, to weep with, to grieve." Compassion comes from the Latin *com* and *pati*, meaning to suffer with. Suffering love as the voluntary willingness to suffer-with another person is required to restore genuine relations of mutuality. We may even have to suffer at the hands of the others for the cause of justice. In love we are moved from the center to the margins where the lame and ill are gathered. But such sacrifice of self is not done at whatever the cost to self, but is done in tune with and at the behest of a self who, in wholeness and integrity, wants to live out its convictions. In such circumstances, doing for the other may be for the self, and doing for self may be for the other. Thank God for such possibilities. I can come face to face with difference without effacement on my part or debasement on the

---

88. Browning, *Religious Thought and the Modern Psychologies*, 153.
89. Levinas, *Otherwise than Being*, 81–99.
90. Levinas, *Otherwise than Being*, 75–81.

part of the other. Inspired and inspiring faces, shining, glowing, not fused, not distant, but connected and connecting. In this broken world where violence is so often overwhelming, disfiguring, and dismembering, we are called to suffer-with, to sojourn together.

The poignancy and urgency of this call leads me to end this chapter with a spontaneous and forthright thank you[91] to Emmanuel Levinas for raising again the vision of the widow, orphan, and stranger in a world where compassion is too often in exile. May we all offer cups of cold water to the other, gifts which we offer and say, "Drink" (Bois)![92]

---

91. In the mutuality model I am developing, a free, unexpected, unsolicited, and uncoerced "thank you" escapes the economy of reciprocity and exchange. In contrast, since Derrida believes no gift can escape the economy of reciprocity and even the movement of gratitude returns to the Same, he ironically can thank Levinas only by being ungrateful and writing a faulty text. See Jacques Derrida, "At this very moment in this work here I am," in Bernasconi and Critchley, *Re-Reading Levinas*, 11–48. Simon Critchley incisively discusses Derrida's predicament in thanking Levinas in *The Ethics of Deconstruction*, 108ff.

92. "Bois" is Derrida's final word in his text of homage to Emmanuel Levinas, "At this very moment in this work here I am," in Bernasconi and Critchley, *Re-Reading Levinas*, 48.

CHAPTER 10

CROSSING THE THRESHOLD: SOJOURNING TOGETHER IN THE WILD SPACES OF LOVE

> In the wake of the eclipse of the divine, darkness . . .
> Sacred darkness lingers . . .
> lingers endlessly.
> Night
> Sacred night
> Night that is not day
> Night beyond
> Night
> Night
> From which we never
> Awake[1]

WE LIVE IN A "time between times," a "place which is no place,"[2] where, as Mark C. Taylor describes it, "sacred darkness lingers . . . endlessly." Like it or not, the Enlightenment dream of a world increasingly controlled by the light of pure rationality is fading fast over the horizon. Control through reason and science has left wide swaths of destruction in its wake: systematic violence, marginalization, oppression, suffering, domination of the "other." It is that sorry history that both lies at the root of the postmodern attack on the totalizing power of reason and gives shape to the postmodern ethical imperative to include the "other" and to make room for the "different." But what now—at the end of reason, after virtue, after philosophy, after God? What if there is neither a religion nor a morality within the bounds

---

1. Taylor, "Think Naught," in Scharlemann, *Negation and Theology*, 37.
2. Taylor, *Erring*, 6.

of reason alone? Was Taylor right when he recently exclaimed: "Though it continues, theology is as dead as the God for which theologians search"?[3] If the "sacred escapes the strictures of ontotheology,"[4] unattainable by either the *via positiva* or the *via negativa*, is the sacred beyond reach?

The questions are formidable. But they are also exciting, especially for those of us involved in the theological enterprise. The kinds of questions and queries about claims to certainty and warrants to power that postmodernism is raising are precisely the kinds of limit questions[5] that lie at the heart of the theological endeavor. In the modern era the declaration of human autonomy was also the announcement of God's death. But now, paradoxically, since postmodern voices are declaring that the death of God finds its completion only in the death of the self,[6] questions of how to talk of self and God are once more taking center stage. As I see it, new spaces are opening up for theologians to be once again relevant players and significant voices in the public realm.

I suggest that Jacques Derrida's emphasis on undecidability, the secret, and the *khôra* open the way to a new postsecular discourse about faith and God. However, Mark C. Taylor's figure of the erring, serpentine wanderer as a liberated being in carnivalesque release abandons us only to isolation, wounds, and tears, and asks that we give up on any possibility of meeting, healing, and mending. I therefore propose that we replace an ontology of being—with its question, "To be or not to be?"—with a vision of love—with its basic question, "To love or not to love?"[7] In the priority of love, agency returns, not as a self-construction but as a gift to be received and a call to be heeded. I conclude by intimating that sojourning (rather than settling or wandering) in the wild spaces of love is an apt metaphor for a genuine postmodern theology.

The House of Being: Power

In philosophical theology the concept of being has traditionally played a central role, and God has been considered the highest Being and the ground of every being. Since metaphysics needed a centerpiece, a keystone, in its house of being, it may be credibly said that the advent of "God" in

---

3. Taylor, "Think Naught," 36.
4. Taylor, "Think Naught," 37.
5. See David Tracy's discussion of "limit" in ch. 5 of *Blessed Rage for Order*, 91–119.
6. For Taylor the "death of God is at the same time the death of the self" (*Erring*, 20).
7. Although Jean-Luc Marion, in his *God without Being*, makes a similar proposal in respect to God, he continues (questionably, in my view) to see "to be or not to be" as "the first and indispensable question" for every creature (xx).

philosophy arose less from God than from metaphysics. As Heidegger has described, this concept of God finds its full formulation in the modernity of Descartes, Spinoza, Leibniz, and Hegel with the *causa sui*: "The Being of beings is represented fundamentally, in the sense of the ground, only as *causa sui*. "This is the metaphysical concept of God. . . . This is the right name for the god of philosophy."[8]

Heidegger concludes: "Man can neither pray nor sacrifice to this god. Before the *causa sui*, man can neither fall to his knees in awe nor can he play music and dance before this god."[9] In other words, the *causa sui* is only an "idol" of God, and so-called "god-less thinking is more open to him than onto-theo-logic would like to admit."[10] In another place Heidegger makes the same point: "[A] god who must permit his existence to be proved in the first place is ultimately a very ungodly god. The best such proofs of existence can yield is blasphemy."[11] In a 1951 seminar at the University of Zurich, Heidegger summarized: "If I were yet to write a theology—to which I sometimes feel inclined—then the word *Being* would not occur in it. Faith does not need the thought of Being. When faith has recourse to this thought, it is no longer faith."[12]

But the problem is not simply that as *causa sui* God becomes a prisoner of our concepts, metaphysically chained in the ontotheological abode of being.[13] The category of being itself as the institutionalization of reason, with its claims to full presence, is fraught with difficulty. For at least since Descartes set out to establish the ego as a point of absolute certainty, being has been characterized with what Spinoza termed the *conatus essendi*: "Everything, in so far as it is in itself, endeavours to persist in its own being."[14] Since for Spinoza all things are modes of God, this *conatus essendi* emerges by necessity out of the eternal and infinite essence of God. Since "God's power is identical with his essence,"[15] power becomes the

---

8. Heidegger, *Identity and Difference*, 106.

9. Heidegger, *Identity and Difference*, 72.

10. Heidegger, *Identity and Difference*, 72.

11. Heidegger, *Nietzsche*, 106.

12. As quoted in Marion, *God without Being*, 61, who gives the German text of Heidegger, 211–12. Derrida discusses it in "How to Avoid Speaking: Denials," in Coward and Foshay, *Derrida and Negative Theology*, 126ff.

13. Two discussions have been especially helpful: Marion, *God without Being*, chs. 2 and 3; and De Boer, *De God van de filosofen and de God van Pascal*, 49–58.

14. Spinoza, *Ethics*, Part 3, Proposition 6, 136.

15. Spinoza, *Ethics*, Part 1, Proposition 34, 74.

central concept of modern ontologies.[16] Here theology is the keystone in a theory of absolute power.

Even when the human ego replaces God as the apex of the system, the self-maintaining ontology of power takes center stage, whether as Leibniz's monads of power, Nietzsche's will to power, Freud's libido, Dasein's care (in Heidegger), or the striving for being (in Sartre). In other words, as Derrida and Levinas have argued, what has developed is a process of totalizing with reason as the instrument by which an ego or society of egos overpowers and totalizes, appropriates and disempowers anything that is "other" or "different."[17] Whatever the details and variety, Being is a system of maintenance, control, domination: power-over.[18] One either dominates or is dominated— as Freud, Hegel, and Sartre in particular emphasize.[19] Thus, Paul Tillich defines power as "the possibility a being has to actualize itself against the resistance of other beings."[20] To be a self is to have enemies. Implicitly, if not explicitly, one is always at war. This apotheosis of the self is seen to crest in the idealism of Hegel in which everything becomes itself in and through its own other. In the end, since the "other" has a utilitarian function in relation to the self, relationship to the other is, finally, self-relationship. When an "other" resists this role, failing to mirror the self, when it resists being used and consumed, it must be invaded and dominated.

There is one more telling aspect of this picture that needs to be noted before we continue with the deconstructionist critique. In the world of being-as-power, suffering has no legitimate place.[21] To recall some paradigmatic voices from the previous chapter, Spinoza again voices the dominant tradition: "Pain is the transition of a man from a greater to a lesser perfection."[22] Pain and

16. As we saw in previous chapters, "'I think' comes down to 'I can.'... Ontology as first philosophy is a philosophy of power... a philosophy of injustice" (Levinas, *Totality and Infinity*, 46).

17. In Derrida, *Positions*, 64. Derrida terms this totalizing "motif of homogeneity, the theological motif *par excellence*." As Kevin Hart points out, in Derrida's sense, a theological discourse need not involve God; it only needs something that functions as an agent of totalization (*The Trespass of the Sign*, 32).

18. In this context, I cannot resist alluding to Walter Wink's *Engaging the Powers*, where he insists that the heart of Jesus' life and message was challenging the "domination system."

19. For an excellent analysis of the "problem of domination," see Benjamin, *The Bonds of Love*.

20. Tillich, *The Courage to Be*, 179.

21. Theologically, I think this is one (perhaps *the*) compelling reason why the philosophical idea of the impassibility of God has historically often prevailed over the suffering love of God.

22. Spinoza, *Ethics*, Part 3, Definition 3, 174.

suffering are diminutions of being, Pain weakens the power of activity and suffering is powerlessness. Even Heidegger, an archcritic of the ontotheologic tradition, by considering that the essence of pain cannot be painful in a feeling sense, takes the suffering out of pain.[23] Strikingly, some postmodernists do the same. Deleuze and Guattari, for example, champion "the schizophrenic process" in its "potential for revolution"[24] without any attention to the actual psychological pain and suffering of schizophrenics.

Erring

In our day, prefigured by the masters of suspicion, Marx, Freud, and Nietzsche, the imperial self has also been declared dead. More precisely, the self as the child of enlightenment, fully present to itself, self-conscious, sovereign, absolute agent, given power over the world as object, is revealed to be itself a production of this very world and the processes it was said to master. All we have left is a decentered, deconstructed "self," the self as a product and effect of the crossings and interfacings of impersonal cosmic forces.

Mark C. Taylor has given in *Erring*[25] perhaps the fullest description of such a non-self self: postmodern persons are "transitory 'points' of intersection," "'sites' of passage," "erratic markings" (137). A human subject is a "wanderer" (15), and "errant trace" (144), a "drifter" (157) "attached to no home and always separated from father and mother" (156), "deindividualized" (135), "anonymous" (143). "Everyone becomes no one" (142), "always suspicious of stopping, staying, and dwelling" (156). "Rootless and homeless" (156), deprived of "origin, center, and conclusion" (156), "the subject is *always* both 'stained' and 'wounded,'" and the marks are "incurable" (139). The "life of erring is ... nomadic" (156) and the "serpentine wandering" (150) is "purposeless and aimless (endless)" (157). This "careless wanderer" yearns neither for "completion" nor for "fulfillment" (147), and therefore is not unhappy but free from "anxious searching" (157) and no longer preoccupied with past and future. Indeed, for Taylor, although such liberation means "self-dismemberment" (144), accepting that is "grace," which "arrives only when God and the self are dead and history is over" (157). "Extravagant expenditure" (142), "perpetual displacement" (156), "festive discharge, carnivalesque release" (161)... "endlessly" (143).

Let me offer four observations about such a description of the "non-self." First, along with Taylor, I do not believe there is any hope of

---

23. Heidegger, *On the Way to Language*, 181; and *Poetry, Language, Thought*, 205. See Caputo, "Thinking, Poetry, and Pain."

24. Deleuze and Guattari, *Anti-Oedipus: Capitalism and Schizophrenia*, 340.

25. All references to *Erring* in this paragraph are included in text.

resuscitating the Cartesian self or any of its remnants. But it is well to recognize that that is no real loss for it never existed in the first place; it was an illusory product of reason. Put in the language of psychotherapy, the self of reason is false self, defensively created out of fear,[26] that needs to be undone and broken through if I am to come to terms with my true self. This suggests that the death of the self of reason and the death of the god of reason reveals not the death of self and God, but the failure of reason. From this perspective, the death of God, and now the self, marks the dethronement of reason and the collapse of its house of being.

Second, the fact that the modern self of absolute agency is an illusion does not demonstrate that there is no such entity as a self. Indeed, I suspect the postmodern non-self will be shown to be as mythical as its predecessor, another adapted, false self. There is still room for an agent self that is not absolute, with no claims to self-authorization and full presence, but a gifted/called self, gifted with agency and called to co-agency by an *Other*. It is true that would demand breaking with the radical immanentism and autonomy of modern philosophy. But this is the very kind of thinking that is precisely being called into question by thinkers such as Emmanuel Levinas. I suspect that as long as postmodernism champions the non-self (as the negation of the modern self), it still, regrettably, is hostage to logocentrism.

Third, Taylor's erring wanderer is a scary, sad, desolate figure, nameless, impersonal, and incurably wounded. Can such a postmodern person, without home and without purpose, be called to responsibility? And is not such an anonymous person a difference that makes no difference—a difference that is the same, because there is no longer any uniqueness? Even more troubling, Taylor only has tears—tears and wounds. What about healing, mending, and hope? Taylor seems to collapse a healthy self/other tension (which includes mutually enhancing interactions as well as alienating ones) into a determinism of sorts, in which relations are unavoidably only wounding and tearing.

Fourth, it will not be easy to talk of self and God in new ways because talk of self and God, certainly philosophically and theologically, has been so tied to an ontology of being that to speak of self and God is almost unavoidably to invoke echoes of these illusions. Can nothing be said? Are we left speechless? Is silence the only answer? Echoes of Wittgenstein's "What we cannot speak about we must pass over in silence?" That also was Heidegger's

---

26. To take a classic example, we have discovered that Descartes's "ideal of the *cogito,* of the *mathesis universalis* means *denial,* a defense against the flesh because the flesh is synonymous with anguish; and the clean fission between mind and body is an *isolation,* a setting apart and rendering innocuous of all that which spells dread" (Stern, *The Flight from Woman,* 101).

response: "Someone who has experienced theology in his own roots, both the theology of the Christian faith and that of philosophy, would today rather remain silent about God when he is speaking in the realm of thinking."[27] But even then we need to say something, because silence bespeaks sometimes joy, sometimes contempt, sometimes pleasure, sometimes fear, sometimes consent, sometimes renunciation, sometimes impotence, sometimes honor. There is the ultimate silence of death. And there is the silence that has to do with God, with what Pseudo-Dionysius had in mind when he exhorted us "to honor the ineffable with a wise silence."[28]

Derrida: Remaining on the Threshold

Indeed, it is because of the recognized difficulties of the *via positiva* in talking about God, amplified in recent times by the deconstructionist critique, that there is today increased interest in the *via negativa*. The question is even being asked if deconstructionism itself is a form of negative theology. Does all negative theology have a "superessentiality"—a supreme being beyond being—or does it, at least in some versions, have a God who transcends all conceptions of being as presence? Does negative theology use language under erasure in a fashion similar to deconstructionism?[29] Though the verdict is still out, it does seem clear that deconstruction is atheistic in the sense that it de-centers and does away with God as the center of a system[30] (but as Kevin Hart makes clear, only in that sense).[31] In "How to Avoid Speaking: Denials"[32] Jacques Derrida directly addressed the supposed connections between his thinking of *trace* and *différance* and negative theology.

In the end, Derrida's denials, or denegations, as Taylor aptly translates,[33] seem neither to assert nor to deny. They circle around in a cacophony of sounds. However, strikingly, in and through the verbal clatter, there is the internal desert of silence. In Derrida's words, "We are still

---

27. Heidegger, *Identity and Difference*, 54–55
28. Quoted in Marion, *God without Being*, 54
29. See especially Hart, *The Trespass of the Sign*; and two other books of relevance: Scharlemann, *Negation and Theology*; and Coward and Foshay, *Derrida and Negative Theology*.
30. For Derrida, "God is the name and element of that which makes possible an absolutely pure and absolutely self-present self-knowledge" (*Of Grammatology*, 98).
31. Hart, *The Trespass of the Sign*, 29, 30.
32. Reprinted in Coward and Foshay, *Derrida and Negative Theology*, 73–142. See note 39.
33. Taylor, "nO nOt nO," in Coward and Foshay, *Derrida and Negative Theology* 174–75.

on the threshold."³⁴ That threshold is a "place of passage, this time, to give access to what is no longer a place,"³⁵ and seemingly he is unable to cross over with Eckhart to the "threshold that gives access to God."³⁶ On the threshold, he talks as if having no secret is the secret . . . "The name of God (I do not say God, but how to avoid saying God here, from the moment when I say the name of God?) can only be said in the modality of this secret denial: above all, I did not want to say that."³⁷

Derrida then proceeds to treat negative theology in terms of three paradigms—Greek, Christian, and neither Greek nor Christian. He does so, he notes, "to avoid speaking of a question that I will be unable to treat; to deny it in some way, or to speak of it without speaking of it"—the question of the relation of negative theology to Jewish and Islamic thought.³⁸ That this is an important void for Derrida is clear not only because he got out of his way to remind his readers of the omission two more times, but because Derrida is himself a displaced North African Jew. It is in this context that he talks of the "internal desert": "In everything that I will say, a certain void, the place of an internal desert, will perhaps allow this question to resonate. . . a resonant space of which nothing, almost nothing will ever be said."

Derrida pleads silence—almost. For then, in a telling footnote at precisely this point, he begins to self-disclose in a way that almost breaks the silence—but not without the hint of untold secrets and pain, even much pain:

> Despite this silence, or in fact because of it, one will perhaps permit me to interpret this lecture as the most "autobiographical" speech I have ever risked. . . But if one day I had to tell my story, nothing in this narrative would start to speak of the thing itself if I did not come up against this fact: for lack of capacity, competence, or self-authorization, I have never been able to speak of what my birth says should have been closest to me: the Jew, the Arab. This small piece of autobiography confirms it obliquely. It is performed in all of my foreign languages: French, English, German, Greek, Latin, the philosophic, the metaphilosophic, Christian, etc.³⁹

34. Derrida, "Denials," 96.
35. Derrida, "Denials," 21.
36. Derrida, "Denials," 128.
37. Derrida, "Denials," 95.
38. Derrida, "Denials," 100.

39. Derrida, "Denials," 135. Derrida wrote these words in 1987. After this speech was first delivered, I discovered that Derrida in 1991 surprisingly published a very moving, personal text—reflecting on his childhood and his mother's death and including also a commentary on St. Augustine's *Confessions*—called *Circumfession* as part of

Taylor, in commenting on this essay, perceptively notes: "For many years at least since *Glas*, and I suspect long before, perhaps even from the beginning—Derrida has been struggling with the question of autobiography. . . . I begin to suspect that Derrida's deepest desire is to write an 'autobiography.'" He concludes: "Derrida could (or would) no more write an autobiography than he could (or would) write a theology."[40]

To this point Derrida remains on the threshold.[41] No matter how strong his desire,[42] he cannot cross over and come home and tell his story.[43] He is the exile, the outsider, remaining always deliberately in/determinate and un/decidable. Do his constant deferrals on the threshold deliver us only to a gaping silence? Or does the work of Derrida perhaps open up a silent space before and beyond all metaphysical embarrassments, an interspace of in/finite im/possibility?

That this is a real im/possibility is clearly evident in his preoccupation, also in "Denials," with place and space. In his treatment of the Greek paradigm he treats at some length the "absolutely necessary space" that Plato in the *Timaeus* calls the *khôra*,[44] as the place making possible the formation of the cosmos. This *khôra*—place, spacing, receptacle—is not to be talked of "as of 'something' that is or is not, that could be present or absent, intelligible, sensible, or both at once, active or passive, the Good . . . or the Evil, God or man, the living or the nonliving."[45] *Khôra* is "radically nonhuman and atheological. . . radically ahistorical,". . . "nothing positive or negative. It is impassive, but it is nether passive nor active."[46] As "absolutely necessary space," *khôra* cannot be spoken of, but, at the same time, it cannot not be spoken of.

When Derrida moves on from the Greek paradigm to the Christian, he considers Eckhart, who conceives of Being as a place, "[s]olely a threshold,

---

a dual text written with Geoffrey Bennington under the title *Jacques Derrida*. "[T]he constancy of God in my life is called by other names" (Bennington and Derrida, *Jacques Derrida*, 155). See John Caputo's impressive, *The Prayers and Tears of Jacques Derrida*.

40. Taylor, "nO nOt nO," 195.

41. The threshold image is just one of the many un/decidability images which flood Derrida's work. Others include the hinge, breast, fold, valley, Plato's *pharmakon*, Mallarme's hymen.

42. In his "Post-Scriptum" (in Coward and Foshay, *Derrida and Negative Theology*, 318) Derrida sees a special connection between "desert" and "desire": "One has more and more the feeling that desert is the other name, if not the proper place, of desire."

43. My colleague Brian Walsh alerted me to the catchy line of Amos Wilder: "We cross the threshold into the story-world" ("Story and Story-World," 355).

44. Derrida, "How to Avoid Speaking: Denials," 104.

45. Derrida, "How to Avoid Speaking: Denials," 106

46. Derrida, "How to Avoid Speaking: Denials," 107.

but a sacred place, the outer sanctuary (*parvis*) of the temple,"[47] which gives access to God in what is beyond place. He suggests that Heidegger's viewpoint represents a paradigm neither Greek nor Christian. He calls attention to Heidegger's posing the question as to whether "a *wholly* other place" is a "place of Being" or is rather "*a place of the wholly other.*"[48]

Finally, in his *Post-Scriptum* to the Calgary Symposium, published under the title *Derrida and Negative Theology*, he raises the issue of place once more. In negative theology, "[t]here remains the question of . . . the place opened for this play between God and his creation."[49] Is it a place opened or created by God, by the name of God? Or is it "'older' than the time of creation, than time itself, than history, narrative, word, etc.," in order to make both God and his place possible? Is it a friendly place "opened by appeal" or is it a preceding space that remains "impassively foreign, like *khôra*, to everything that takes its place and replaces itself and plays within the place, including what is named God?"[50]

He asks whether we need to choose between the two. He wonders if it's even possible. But—and this heightens the stakes—he immediately adds: "But it is true that these two 'places,' these two experiences of place, these two ways are no doubt of an absolute heterogeneity. One place excludes the other, one surpasses the other, one does without the other, absolutely, without the other."[51]

Although faced with this un/decidability, ever wary of choosing, Derrida, ironically, precisely because his commitment to undecidability goes all the way down,[52] has to defer from the first space, which is primed in a certain way (I call it the with-space of creation,[53] the love-space), and opt for the un/primed second space, the without place, the "'something' without thing, like an indeconstructible *khôra*. . . as the very spacing of de-construction,"[54] the spacing of *différance*. The space is held to be more primordial, more neutral, a kind of nontemporal "abyss without bottom or

47. Derrida, "How to Avoid Speaking: Denials," 121.
48. Derrida, "How to Avoid Speaking: Denials," 123.
49. Derrida, "Post-Scriptum," 314.
50. Derrida, "Post-Scriptum," 314.
51. Derrida, "Post-Scriptum," 314. Derrida points out that "what still relates them to each other is this strange preposition, this strange with-without or without-with, *without.*"
52. At the same time, I admit to wondering if Derrida's "choice" for the second space does not precisely call into question whether undecidability can ever go all the way down.
53. In reference to the God-with-us (John 1) by whom all things were created.
54. Derrida, "Post-Scriptum," 318.

surface, an absolute impassibility (neither life nor death) that gives rise to everything that it is not."[55]

No doubt Derrida's staying on the threshold faithfully reflects his preference for un/decidability. At the same time, it may also leave him inadvertently under the bewitching spell of logocentrism. For, when all is said and done, if one tarries silent on the threshold because metaphysical claims to certainty and warrants for power are illusions to be overcome, have we really overcome them? To presume that we need to give up on any sense of a founded or grounded decision because the modernist tradition confuses/conflates giving logical reasons and grounding seems questionable. Grounding is much more and wider than logical grounding. Experiences of empathy, trust, and belonging, for example, are everyday sources of existential grounding.[56]

To repeat: I do believe that Derrida goes a long way in showing that language and metaphysics cannot provide privileged access to self-present meaning. But does that mean access to the mysterious, sacred desert place is impossible? Perhaps there are other ways and means to enter that space beyond or before. Can we agree with Derrida that another philosophy/theology will not help? Reason is im/potent. But what about an approach that sees access as a non-philosophical/non-theological gift[57] to be received rather than a way to be engineered?

As Derrida describes it, to cross the threshold is, for Meister Eckhart, to use the power of the eye as a sieve. This new eye, for the mystics, is the eye of love, an eye that opens up a place beyond words, where words are no longer necessary. There may be homecoming.[58]

But Derrida remains poised on the threshold: although he wants to come home and tell his story, he cannot. He remains on the outside, an exile, displaced, wanting to break through. In her summary comments at the

---

55. Derrida, "Post-Scriptum," 315. It is important to note that this does not mean ethical neutrality for Derrida. Undecidability is a kind of quasi-transcendental condition, calling for decision. Deconstruction is an intensification of responsibility, "a positive response to an alterity-which necessarily calls, summons or motivates it. Deconstruction is therefore a vocation—a response to a call . . . It is possible to see deconstruction as being produced in a space where the prophets are not far away" ("Deconstruction and the Others: An Interview with Derrida," in Kearney, *Dialogues with Contemporary Continental Thinkers*, 118, 119). See Olthuis, "An Ethics of Compassion."

56. For a valuable discussion of logical and existential grounding in the work of Richard Rorty and John Dewey, see Hart, *Grounding without Foundations*.

57. Derrida has emphasized that faith is presupposed by any deconstructive gesture. "I don't know, one has to believe" (*Memoirs of the Blind*, 129).

58. "Homecoming is not a return to the past but it is a becoming into the future" (Winquist, *Homecoming*, 9).

Calgary Symposium, Morny Joy touches the heart of the matter: "The eye of love is foreign to the forays of his deconstruction."[59] For Derrida it seems as if once Reason has been dethroned, there is no other possibility for providing direction and hope. So we remain wandering, sometimes dwelling in the threshold of the temple, but we can never cross over and enter.

But perhaps there is a new eye: a new eye of love that, with the death of the metaphysical concepts of god, espies a space open for God free from ontotheological apron-strings. It is a space prior to the theoretical space defined by metaphysical thought. However, it is also, as a with-space, the space of and for love, not the neutral "without" space of *difference*. The God that appears would have nothing to do with the god of the philosophers.[60] In this space (to play on Paul Ricoeur's famous phrase) "love gives rise to thought," discourse is reborn, not for purposes of mastery or limitation or hemming in with conditions, but for connection. Because God as love (and love as God) is an overflowing, an excess, an emptying going beyond its own limits, a letting go, life and discourse can be connective, celebrative, communicative.

Crossing the Threshold: A Vision of Love

Lingering in this space, and wending my way to a provisional end, I offer a few fleeting glimpses of the far-ranging implications of replacing an ontology of being, not with a deconstructed de/ontology, but with a (rediscovered)[61] vision of love.

In the first place, and of fundamental importance, "To be or not to be" is no longer the sum of the matter. Nor is the deconstructionist version on target: "to be *and* not to be, for to be is not to be, and not to be is to be."[62] Rather, the supreme question is: "To love or not to love." In other words, love replaces being-as-power as the highest category. For in the degree that one is not in love, one is deficient in being. God's love comes as a gift, an

---

59. Joy, "Conclusions: Divine Reservations," in Coward and Foshay, *Derrida and Negative Theology*, 263.

60. Marion, *God without Being*, 52.

61. Rediscovered, not only because it harks back to the love mysticism of St. Bernard, Meister Eckhart, John of the Cross, or Ruysbroeck the Admirable, but also because the important work of women mystics, such as the twelfth-century Hildegard of Bingen and the Rheno-Flemish Beguines of the thirteenth century, is coming to light. Eckhart's famous expression about the gratuitous nature of divine love, "without a why," appears for the first time in the work of the Cistercian nun Beatrice of Nazareth, and later in the writings of the Beguines. See Brunn and Epiney-Burgard, *Women Mystics in Medieval Europe*, xxxi.

62. Taylor, *Deconstructing Theology*, 56.

overflowing, an "excess," which calls us forth—luring, inviting, sustaining.[63] Being is liberated from its fixation on power and freed for love. As a result, in the phrasing of Jean-Luc Marion, "The fundamental ontic difference between what is and what is not becomes indifferent—for everything becomes indifferent before the difference that God marks with the world."[64]

Instead of the Cartesian self-grounding of "I think, therefore I am," beginning with God's love means "I am loved, therefore I am." The birth of a self and an identity is a bestowal of the love of others, birthed in and through the love shown by others. The human self is intersubjective: in the we there is the I: in the I there is the we. The self finds its center in mutuality. Consequently, the healthy decentering of the modernist self as self-centering need not lead to the postmodern non-self, but to a recentering of the self in relations of love in community.

The passive "am loved" also suggests that whether or not we are existentially able to love is inextricably related to whether we were first loved. Enfolded within the bosom of "To love or not to love?" is the question, "To be loved or not to be loved?" This pivotal interconnection between receiving love and giving love is one of the important emphases of all post-Freudian psychotherapeutic developmental theories since Erikson. Insofar as a child has not received what D. W. Winnicott calls "good-enough"[65] mothering, the child is handicapped in its ability to genuinely love and care for others. By the same token, healing, restoration, and empowerment of a fragmented self is best nourished in relationships of empathy and love.

The gift *of* love is also a gift *for* love; the gift is simultaneously a call. It is the birth of human agency as response-ability for the gift. Therefore, I love in order to be.[66] The process of receiving identity is at the same time a process of constituting one's identity in relation to others. A self is born not only in and through (receiving) love, but equally, reciprocally, in and through (giving) love to others. The two sides belong inextricably together. In this understanding of identity and agency, not as self-creation or self-certification but as a received empowerment, a call to live out and fulfill, it

---

63. Like Marion, I want to carefully distinguish between beginning with a gift given by God from Heidegger's impersonal *es gibt* in which the gift is the giving without starting from any giver. See Marion, *God without Being*, 102–7.

64. Marion, *God without Being*, 88. See Marion's discussion of Rom 4:17 and 1 Cor 1:28, where God calls "nothing to become beings. . . [and] calls the nonbeings as if they were beings" (88–95).

65. Winnicott, *The Maturational Process and the Facilitating Environment*, 145.

66. "*I am to the extent that I am loved, therefore I love in order to be.*" According to Julia Kristeva, this saying is "for the medieval thinker . . . an implicit definition of the subject's being" (*Tales of Love*, 171).

remains important to talk (in contrast to postmodernism) of a core self of continuity, coherence, and agency.[67] This core self—not, it is true, the Cartesian unitary self of reason—expands and contracts in the vicissitudes of its experience. It is crucial in helping us to make sense out of the multiplicity of experiences that both surround us and inhabit us. When we do not have a bounded core experience of ourselves, instead of being able to celebrate postmodern multiplicity, we suffer from fragmentation of self, sometimes to the point of psychosis or multiple personality.[68]

Indeed, I believe it is a fragmented sense of core identity, or even a lack of such a sense of core identity, that brings many people to therapy. Those who celebrate the fluid self as "effect" seem, as Jane Flax puts it, "self-deceptively naive and unaware of the basic cohesion within themselves that makes the fragmentation of experiences something other than a terrifying slide into psychosis."[69] Only when a person has some sense of core self can s/he/they enter the inter-space and reach out to a neighbor, not only with a sense of dread and fear of domination, but also with hope for connection, enrichment, and expansion.

Is it entirely coincidental that just when many women are attaining a sense of agency and selfhood, postmodernism, largely male and middle-class, questions the very existence of self?[70] It is even more disturbing, speaking psycho-therapeutically, to realize that the kind of multiplicity which certain forms of postmodernism champion results from the very patriarchal domination and abuse that it sets out to challenge. No wonder postmodern feminists such as Julia Kristeva and Luce Irigaray treat the issue of multiplicity with more sensitivity than many postmodernists.[71]

Those who think it best to abandon the subject altogether as a fiction, or who see the subject as a position in language or effect of discourse, may be adopting, wittingly or unwittingly, yet another strategy to avoid facing their deeper selves. Is it, asks Flax, yet another way "to evade, deny, or repress the importance of early childhood experiences, especially

67. In his groundbreaking clinical study, *The Interpersonal World of the Infant*, Daniel Stern concludes that infants between two and seven months form a sense of core self—self-agency, self-coherence, self-affectivity, and self-history.

68. In fact, James Glass, in *Shattered Selves*, critiques the postmodern celebration of multiplicity by demonstrating that for the many people who suffer from schizophrenia and multiple personality, multiplicity is unadulterated anguish.

69. Flax, *Thinking Fragments*, 218–19.

70. See Patricia Waugh, "Postmodernism," 344.

71. Toril Moi, in her introduction to *The Kristeva Reader*, 13, sees Kristeva doing a "balancing act between a position which would deconstruct subjectivity and identity altogether, and one that would try to capture these entities in an essentialist or humanist mould."

mother-child relationships, in the constitution of self and the culture more generally[?] Perhaps it is less threatening to have no self than one pervaded by memories of, longing for, suppressed identification with, or terror of the powerful mother of infancy."[72] Descartes, afraid of women and his body, retreated to the supposed certitude and splendid isolation of his ego. Is this postmodern espousal of the non-self a similar attempt to continue to repress, deny, or dull the pain? Perhaps the postmodern non-self is yet another version of the adapted or "false self" that needs to be abandoned in a dark night of the soul in order that the core or "true self" may emerge from hiding and begin the process of remembering and healing.

Beginning with love as an overflowing, an invitation (not a coercion) that is realized intersubjectively (not individualistically), opens up a new understanding of the spaces between self and other. In the big dichotomies that have defined the history of metaphysics since the Greeks, mind, culture, form, and intellect have been considered "male": body, nature, matter, and sentiment, "female." And, of special interest here, *techné*, time, and same have connoted the male; physis, space, and the other, the female.[73] The "only way to give language to Nature, to Space has been through *techné*—through techniques . . . . as the active, masculine aspect . . . giving a narrative to [female, passive] *physis*," says Alice Jardine.[74] The result has been the master narratives by which those in power dominate and exclude "the spaces of the *ensoi*, Other, without history—the feminine. . . [the] unknown, terrifying, monstrous,. . . the mad, the unconscious, improper, unclean, non-sensical, oriental, profane."[75] The breakdown of these master narratives has generated new ways of recognizing and renaming the other than ourselves—the space, now unbound, coded feminine, outside the logic of modernity, not made possible by its structures, and thus sacred, Kristeva, in fact, calls this sacred place "a place of passage, a threshold where 'nature' confronts 'culture.'"[76]

Buber names this sacred interspace the "the sphere of 'between.'"[77] I prefer the term the "wild"[78] spaces, to emphasize that it is a space as

---

72. Flax, *Thinking Fragments*, 232.

73. According to Kristeva, the connotations of space and the feminine go back at least to Plato's *khôra*, and "the 'other' is the 'other sex'" (*La revolution du langage poetique*, 326, quoted in Jardine, *Gynesis*, 114).

74. Jardine, *Gynesis*, 73.

75. Jardine, *Gynesis*, 72–73.

76. Kristeva, *Desire in Language*, 238. For Kristeva, the undifferentiated space shared by mother and child is called *khôra* (133).

77. Buber, *Between Man and Man*, 244.

78. I distinguish my use of "wild" in reference to interspace from Julia Kristeva's discussion in *Tales of Love* (1, 2) of a love "aptly called *wild* . . . a crucible of contradiction

free for love as it has been despoiled by control. "On the narrow ridge, where *I* and *Thou* meet, there is the realm of 'between.'"[79] It is a space "conceptually still uncomprehended... not an auxiliary construction, but the real place and bearer of what happens between ... [I]t does not exhibit a smooth continuity, but is ever and again reconstituted in accordance with [people's] meetings with one another."[80]

Love as gift creates a space-which-is-meeting, inviting partnership and co-birthing, and fundamentally calling into question the deconstructive idea that structures are necessarily always violent. It suggests a new thematization of meaning and truth as good connections, in contrast to both modernity's power, control, judgment and postmodernism's disruption and dissemination of any claim of entitlement to meaning and truth. Narratives are possible, not as grand control devices, but as tales of (broken) love coauthored in community. There are countless narratives of endless suffering and horror, but there are also wonderful tales (small, subversive stories)[81] of meeting, healing, and suffering love in the midst of and in spite of suffering.

This is not an encouragement to retrench and build fixed residences in the domesticity of modernity. Neither does it, in postmodern rejection of the modern, need to mean exile in the desert (expulsion and wandering), perpetual homelessness. Rather, we have an invitation to meet and sojourn together in the wild spaces of love as alternatives both to modernist distancing or domination and to postmodern fluidity and fusion. Connection rather than control is the dominant metaphor. In the interstices of love, Nygren's antithesis of *eros* and *agapes* notwithstanding, mutuality can be a sojourn together in which loving self and loving other need not be in opposition but may be mutually enriching. Together, in all we do, sojourning on our way *ad amorem*: to a homecoming in and with God in a new creation as a house of love.

I am making room for a mutuality ethos, a vision of love that re-envisions *eros*, not as the urge to unite, but as the urge to connect. Therefore, *eros* would no longer be a nostalgic but feared wish to return to a primal, undifferentiated state, as it is with Freud (and even Heidegger). For Freud, both individual and social history moves from undifferentiation (birth)

---

and misunderstandings." For me, love is the primal force both gifting to and calling for good ordering (i.e. good connections). Kristeva's wild, semiotic love is over against and subversive of the symbolic rule of the law of the Father even as it is subject to it.

79. Buber, *Between Man and Man*, 246.

80. Buber, *Between Man and Man*, 244–45.

81. De Boer contrasts the Grand Stories of domination with the "small story ... of Abraham, Isaac, Jacob and Jesus Christ" (*De God*, 152). Brian Walsh works out the idea of the gospel as subversive in *Subversive Christianity*.

to differentiation and back again to undifferentiation (death). In this way *eros* (love) and *thanatos* as the realization of *eros* is the death of the individual self.

With the focus on *eros* as the desire to connect, as the passion for mutuality and right relation, we have the possibility for non-possesive, non-competitive (i.e. non-violent) connecting, co-partnering, co-birthing, in the interspaces of love and creativity. Tragically, such spaces are often the abysses of the wounded, the labyrinths of the lost. But they can also be places of healing and meeting. Tears, no doubt, but also laughter: tears, but also mending.

The priority of love, with its impulse for mutuality over being, with its focus on survival and power, does not mean there will be no conflict; nor does it suggest a resigned toleration of whatever demons of oppression and domination are afoot. In fact, when we begin from a self created in, with, and for love, choosing not to resist injustice further injures and diminishes the self. Acts of resistance against injustice are acts of love. Beginning with a vision of love means that dominations and alienation need not be inevitable. There is also the possibility of mutual recognition, empowerment, and pleasure. Transformation is possible. Healing can be as real as rending. Power need not always be meted out as power-over or power-under. Power relations can be transformed into power-with relations, relations of love.

If I read Foucault correctly, this belief goes along with his treatment of power, and then goes a step farther. For Foucault, when power relations are fixed and no longer in constant struggle, there is no power but violence and slavery. Power relations always imply the possibility of reversal. In my view this possibility of reversal, when seen through the eyes of love, can become not only a continual reversal of who is in control, but also a transformation of the power dynamics of conflict to one of shared connection. Power-with as an alternative to hierarchical power-over also opens up the possibility of ecological partnership with the earth and all its creatures, co-partnership in the cosmic family so that the cosmos may become a house of love, a hospitable home for all its creatures and peoples.

Love is the difference that matters. And suddenly suffering has a different place, a legitimate place. It is no longer a diminution of being, a suffering-from which detracts from who we are, but a very different suffering-with, a voluntary being-with that comforts and heals, enriching and transforming everyone and everything it touches.[82] Love as excess—without a why—overflows onto the plains and meadows of life as a celebrating-with. It seeps into life's cracks and fissures as suffering-with.

---

82. According to Rom 8:17, suffering-with goes along with being an heir of Christ.

Beginning with love as a creative power (making something out of nothing) gives new place to love as forgiveness (making nothing out of something). In the experience of forgiveness there is release, a letting go, a freeing to new starts and new creations. Love turns us to the other, not as diminution of being, but as enrichment, hospitality, and celebration.[83]

Letting be (*Gelassenheit*) is the way of God. Since the way of God is love, this letting be is not simply a Heideggerian releasement to things; nor is it a meditative waiting for and remaining open for the miracle of Being's advent. It is a proactive being-with, especially with those who suffer, and, when appropriate, a robust pursuit of justice for the oppressed and a planetary ecological ethic for all creatures. In other words, such letting be is not ethically neutral, as it is with Heidegger, in which both the "hale" and the "evil" appear equally in the clearing of Being.[84]

At the same time, since love cannot be controlled, the *Gelassenheit* of love eschews control. And giving up control demands faith and trust, in spite of. *Gelassenheit* is a surrender of our will to control, a giving over, an Eckhartian abandonment to the cosmic wave of God's love. Such surrender is not forced. It is a voluntary movement of empowerment that releases to the energies alive in other people, in the world, and in God.

In closing, I trade on two of Julia Kristeva's titles. We do not simply have the "powers of horror": we have also "tales of love." Instead of a Heideggerian *Dasein* facing the otherness of death, we have persons facing each other

> crossing the threshold, despite . . .
>
> taking the risk, despite . . .
>
> not trying (always to counter),
>
> not (always) fusing or fleeing,
>
> but sometimes meeting-in-the-middle spaces of love,

---

83. In "Post-Scriptum," 317, Derrida notes: "To let passage to the other, to the totally other, is hospitality."

84. "With healing, evil appears all the more in the lighting of Being. The essence of evil . . . consist[s] . . . in the malice of rage. Both of these, however, healing and raging, can essentially occur only in Being, insofar as Being itself is what is contested" [Heidegger, "Letter on Humanism," in *Basic Writings*, 237). For Neutrality as a property of traditional ontologies of being, see De Boer, *De God*, 49–52. In contemporary philosophy Levinas, in particular, protested that such neutrality is in fact oppressive. Paul Ricoeur's *Oneself as Another* is also an eloquent plea against ethically neutral ontologies. I want to emphasize again that Derrida intends his principle of undecidability to intensify ethical responsibility. See Caputo's *Radical Hermeneutics*, chs. 9 and 10, and *Against Ethics* for a Derridean ethics of dissemination that contrasts with Taylor's more Nietzschean approach. See also Critchley's *The Ethics of Deconstruction*.

not always wandering in labyrinths,
or falling into abysses,
yet not smugly settled, serenely ensconced,
but journeying together . . .
sojourning in the wild spaces of love, despite and in spite of
 Zarathustra's laughter,
  in spite of the killing fields . . .
Faith is always despite . . .
We sojourn not alone.
God tents, tabernacles—sojourns—with us.[85]

The ways of Love are strange,
As those who have followed them well know,
For, unexpectedly, She withdraws Her consolation.
 He whom Love touches
  Can enjoy no stability.
  And he will taste
  Many a nameless hour.
Sometimes burning and sometimes cold,
Sometimes timid and sometimes bold,
The whims of Love are manifold.
 She reminds us all
  Of our great debt
  To Her lofty power
  Which draws us to Herself alone.
Sometimes gracious and sometimes cruel,
Sometimes far and sometimes near
He who grasps Her in faithful love
 Reaches jubilation.
 Oh, how Love
 With one sole act
 Both strikes and embraces!
Sometimes humble, sometimes haughty,
Sometimes hidden and sometimes revealed;
To be finally overwhelmed by Love,

---

85. Lev. 26:11, Rev. 21:3, John 1:14.

>   Great adventures must be risked
>   Before one can reach
>   The place where is tasted
>   The nature of Love.
> Sometimes light, sometimes heavy,
> Sometimes somber and sometimes bright,
> In freeing consolation, in stifling anguish,
> In taking and in giving,
> Thus live the spirits
> Who wander here below,
> Along the paths of Love.[86]

---

86. Hadewijch of Antwerp, most of thirteenth-century Stanzaic Poem V, quoted in Zum Brunn and Epiney-Burgard, *Women Mystics*, 113–14.

CHAPTER 11

TOWARDS A RADICAL POLITICS OF LOVE: ON THE INTERFACE BETWEEN PERSONAL INTEGRITY AND SOCIETAL RENEWAL

SOMETHING NEEDS TO CHANGE in our global village—for the sake of survival, for the survival of the earth itself. We are running out of the basic stuffs necessary for life: clean air, good food, energy, stable currency, warm families, good friends, hospitable communities. Demagogues are thriving. Millions of people, displaced by violence, live in crowded refugee camps. Democracies are in crisis, reflected in increasing disparities of wealth, income, criminal justice, health care, etc. Systemic racism is rampant in social and political institutions. And there is more. The world at present is in the grip of the Covid-19 pandemic. Climate change is endangering the earth and all its living creatures.

We are all victims surrendering our humanity. Faced with the threats and the uncertainties of the present, with multitudes throughout the world amplifying their calls for justice, while the powers that be entrench themselves in their positions of wealth and entitlement, what now? That is the question. Justice demands the very transformational changes that many privileged people of power, wearing blinders in their fear, resist and denounce. The pathos of this juncture in world history cannot be underestimated. For the first time in the history of the earth, through the wonders of video and other social media, we are able in virtual moments to listen in and see what is transpiring wherever in the world. We are almost first-hand ear and eye witnesses. A classic case in point: the traumatic video of the killing of George Floyd revealed for all to see the brutality of the very police officers called to protect their citizens.

This is the immediate context of this last chapter. What does the championing of Love as the oxygen, fire, and flame of existence mean socio-politically and globally? What is the fallout of the conviction that love carries all things, hopes all things, bears all things, and promises all things—not only for us as individuals, but politically—for society at large, for the earth itself? Needed: Love as the motor and drive for politics.[1]

The first (as well as last) thing love says is: Lead with love. Reach out, listen . . . and then listen again and again, openly, attentively . . . to the sounds of others, to the sounds of the earth, and to ones's own internal sounds. Listening is a primary gesture of love. Loudly and clearly, the silence of listening declares, "I am available, I am eager to hear your story. Let me know who you are, what you feel and think. Before I reflect, before I act, I wait for a word from you." Availability gives birth to hope, the hope that our stories will be heard, that conversations may break out, connections transpire, and "we" moments happen.

With the ears and eyes of the heart, we listen to each other's dreams and hopes, sorrows and hurts. Rather than the between-spaces as arenas of combat, listening intently to each other's stories creates a space for meeting-in-the-middle, suffering-with and celebrating-with together. Talking-with rather than talking-at each other gives birth to hope and working-with each other.

The challenge for a politics of love is enacting this rhythm in the much bigger forum of politics. Love's full-throated Yes, Yes to life is, at the same time, an emphatic No, No against anyone or anything that poisons, curtails, or destroys life. As private citizens, in priestly fashion, we can attend to the victims of trauma, standing with the marginalized, abused, and disenfranchised. But politically, love also calls for resistance and protest against unjust policies, programs, and procedures. Love calls for a public standing-with all who are victimized by cruelty, starvation, abuse, racism, genocide, exclusion, etc., and a confronting call-to-repentance-and-letting-go-of-hate to all doers of injustice. Indeed, today, in grief with the earth, it means calling to account all those who ravage rather than care for the earth.

1. Needed: A Marriage of Personal Maturity and Social Justice

All of this is to say that loving relationships and just societies call for compassionate, healthy, and mature people living in open and caring societies. That is my focus in this chapter. There is an integral, ineluctable interlacement between personal wellbeing and institutional, socio-political flourishing. Just nations and thriving institutions are the work of healthy, dedicated individuals pooling concerns and resources for the good of the commonwealth as a whole. At the same time, wholesome people are best able to come into

---

1. See Hardt and Negri, *Multitude*, 351–52, for a similar plea.

their own in supportive communities and equitable societies. The personal is political and the political is personal. Societal renewal only happens in tandem with personal maturity. Like a horse and carriage, personal integrity and social justice flourish together or flounder together.

Neglect of the needs of society and retreat to private islands, as well as all-out involvement in socio-political causes with inattention to personal dynamics, are both recipes for disaster. In positive terms, love of self is of one piece with love of neighbor and love of neighbor is one with love of self. Humans are not monads of self-interest. Humans are selves-with, selves-in-relation. The way to a more just, equitable society will misfire, derail, and inevitably fail unless it is the fruit of personal integrity and maturity.

To understand that personal growth and societal renewal entail each other means rejecting the individualist-collectivist, self-society dilemma that still too often holds us captive. On the whole we still act as if the overarching question is how little or how much self-interest is permissible for a viable, prosperous society, as if commitment to society and its institutions can only take place at the expense of personal freedom. Breaking this dilemma of social collectivism or individualistic self-interest is the knowledge that the needs of the person and the needs of society are not at odds, but inextricably and integrally interwoven. Not only do we belong together, in and with all our differences of ethnicity, race, sex, culture, faith, but we, both individually and in our diverse groupings, can only flourish when these differences are fully recognized, honored, and celebrated. True community is not a fusion into sameness, but a communion-of-and-with-differences.

In the individualistic tradition, self-interest is enshrined as the primary virtue. Personal possessions and individual performance—what each of us has and the career success we attain—are supreme measures of success. Attention to public duty and the common good require compromise in that they involve curtailment of self-interest and curbs on individual rights. In contrast, in the collectivist tradition, the rights of the individual give way to group goals and interests. Conformity to the group with the reining in of individual desire is the norm.

Individualism and Collectivism saddle us basically with only two possibilities: self-satisfaction at the expense of society, or self-denial for the good of society. This dilemma has not served humanity well. Individualism tends to see the government not as the integrating agency coordinating the disparate sections and diverse needs of its citizens in pursuit of a just society, but in minimalist terms with its main task of protecting individual freedoms which always seems to mean protecting the freedom of the Market. On the other hand, collectivism tends to see the government as the overarching authority in charge of arranging and administering all the different areas of society for the good of all its citizens.

Both traditions share the underlying assumption that humans are fundamentally monads of self-interest in opposition to and in competition with each other. The disastrous implications of this shared misunderstanding is dramatically and tragically ever more obvious today. Whatever collectivist government we look at, say, China, Russia, or North Korea, we see Xi Jinping, Vladimir Putin, Kim Jong-un and their cohorts, foisting and enforcing their own particular self-aggrandizing policies as the Common Good for all citizens. Likewise, in many democracies in the individualist tradition, we observe something similar. Presidents, say Recep Erdogan of Turkey, Donald Trump of the United States, and Jair Bolsonaro of Brazil, supposedly having put self-interest aside as servants of the people, are acting as authoritarian autocrats.

In our pluralistic, multi-faith society, the greatest challenge is the respectful embrace of difference. A viable alternative to individualism and collectivism begins with the development of a model of non-oppositional difference, an economy and politics of love in which power-over opposition is replaced with the mutual recognition of power-with. Love of self at one piece with love of others. Loving the other enhances self, degrading the other diminishes self. Freedom is not freedom-from (autonomy), but freedom-with (mutuality). Freedom is being free-to-love, and loving-to-be free. Working-with others is not the curtailment, but the avenue of freedom.

Such a vision of humanity (detailed in chapter 5) lies at the heart of any search for personal-societal *shalom*. Avoiding such false oppositional constructs between love of neighbor and love of self is, and always has been, no easy matter. Who we are as co-members-in-a-community-of-differences is not a ready-made given. As a gift to be received, it is a calling to fulfill. In a world broken by sin and evil, the other and different often become objects of fear rather than of embrace. Difference is considered inherently oppositional in structure and nature, threatening, hostile. Afraid of being dominated, there lurks in all of us the impulse to control, dismiss, even eliminate difference. Fear and the suppression of difference it evokes is (and has been) devastating for the practice of compassion that the world so desperately needs. In contrast, a politics of love begins with embrace of difference.

2. Healthy Self-Identity Is the Key

Paradoxical as it may seem, the best preparation for involvement in the multi-faceted, multi-layered, multidimensional ins and outs of societal and socio-political life is the formation and nurture of a robust self-identity on the part of each of us. Unless we know who we are, at ease with ourselves, at home in our skin, we will not have the surety and soundness of self-presence to give unstinting and ungrudging attention to the concerns of others and the needs of the community at large. It is the strength of character, the uniqueness of self-sense, which affords continuity amidst change to which others appeal and upon which they rely. It is that "myself," steady and secure of spirit, which reaches out to others seeking connection without deep anxiety or aching desperation.

Knowing oneself calls for an inward journey of self-acceptance, discovering and owning our strengths and gifts, realizing and admitting our limitations, owning our hurts, facing our fears, illusions, foibles, and failures. Crucial to this journey is whether or not we have a bodily, felt-sense of being loved, cared for, and esteemed. For when we feel wanted and unconditionally loved, a safe space opens up inside for us to invite others in, to connect, to discover our giftedness freely together. In the mutual giving and receiving, a sense of self-love and self-trust, in tandem with a desire-to-love-and-trust-others, takes root and germinates. With a sense of inner flow, present-and-available to self, we are present-and-available to others. The more I enjoy being me, the more easily I enjoy the mystery of another. Identity (love of self) and intimacy (love of another) go hand in hand. In the process, developing our giftedness as persons, connecting with others, a dynamic develops awakening interest in joining with others to attend to the problems and needs of the public at large, its people, its institutions, its commerce.

There is a rhythm to this inward-outward movement: increased inner wholeness promotes societal concern, and societal renewal encourages and promotes inner growth. However, that being true, the reality we too often face is the negative side of this same two-directional dynamic. Personal trauma and emotional wounding can give rise to socio-political agendas of hate and anger, even as socio-economic wounding and lack of opportunity stunt personal growth and foster a pathology of hate. In their hurt, fear, anger, and shame, people with fragile egos scramble to secure an identity base to shore up their self-esteem, to belong and feel worthy. They tend to either over-inflate or under-inflate. Self-inflaters puff themselves up, posturing as fearless, strong, having it all together, looking for ways to take center stage. Self-deflaters, devaluing themselves, disheartened, feeling powerless, set about carving out an existence without causing too much of a stir. When inflaters, often beneath a masquerade of self-less public service, portray themselves as champions of the common people to achieve attention, deflaters are naturally drawn to such causes; for, in identifying with the cause and its leaders, they too gain a sense of power and of belonging. The dovetail is perfect, two illusions powerfully feeding each other. We over-inflate, dominating others to receive adulation and cover over a deep fear of being unlovable losers. And we under-inflate, allowing ourselves to be taken in and co-opted, covering over a deep fear of being powerless nobodies. This scenario has repeatedly played itself out in a variety of forms throughout history with disastrous results. A particularly telling example—one we will look at in some length—is the populism currently awash in the United States.

3. Personal Growth

But we are getting ahead of ourselves. What is personal growth? It is realizing and actualizing our individual, integral uniqueness with other fellow members of the human community. It is achieving an awareness of self as subject, as an agent active on its own behalf, owning often fragmented and unbalanced sides of self, working through deep hurts and disappointments, taking responsibility for hurts inflicted on others. It means working out what it means to be an I of a We: giving and receiving, rather than giving and taking, working-with as opposed to working-against. It is about the mutuality of doing-with, rather than the subservience of being done-to/lived-through, or the machismo of doing-to, putting down to pump oneself up.

No human is like a layer cake (an edible concoction topped with a special "personal" icing), nor like a football (a leather pigskin "body" filled with the soul of "air"). We are human throughout. There is a wholeness to us humans with every dimension of ourselves integral to our humanity. We do not have bodies; we are our bodies. Whatever upsets or affects a person, upsets and affects the whole person he or she is/they are. When my body imbibes too much liquor, I am drunk. To concentrate all one's efforts on making a person "spiritual" is in fact to dehumanize that person, just as to stress emotional health or physical wellness above all leads to one-sidedness. The truly spiritual person is at the same time the more human, the healthier, the more fully developed, the more bodily alive, the more in-touch person. To grow emotionally, artistically, physically, faith-wise, in whatever way, a person grows humanly. Physical health alone does not make a whole person. Nor does emotional health. Health in each area of life makes for and is conducive to total health. Human well-being is an integrated affair: one's faith life is inextricably interwoven with one's physical life, the emotional with the social, the analytical with the ethical, and so on.

However, two dimensions in their mutual two-way interaction play particularly unique and crucial roles in personal integration: the ultimate commitment, conviction, or faith dimension and the feeling or emotional dimension. Personal identity, open and yet grounded, calls for an orienting perspective, a guiding commitment or ultimate purpose to give frame, structure, and contours to one's existence in terms of which to live out and integrate self-experience. At the same time, a person needs to be in touch, having a robust bodily sense of self-esteem, safe to feel what one is feeling, emotionally sensitive, open to others, with the passion, energy, and oomph necessary to take one's place responsibly in society. The two-way interplay between these dimensions is complex and dynamic.

4. Commitment and Conviction: The Role of Faith

Commitment and conviction are the keys both to personal integrity and wholeness as well as the way to openness requisite for connection. Committed, one is dedicated, orientated, having a directional GPS which points the way. Convicted, one is inspired, empowered by enthusiasms that encourage connection and communication. A person of faith has a guiding vision *for* life in the world which is also a perspective *of* the world, a window on the world through which the world opens up. On the one hand, worldviews describe what we see: "this is the way the world *is*." On the other hand, they stipulate how we want the world to be: "this is the way the world *ought* to be." A worldview is a human formation, shaped, formed, streamlined in terms of our insights, knowledge, location, imagination, reaching as far as we can see. It is both the window through which we view the world, and the window through which the world impacts us. The way reality registers is framed by the lens, the eye-glasses through which we see the world. If our glasses are rose-tinted, we see the world in pink—even if the world is rather grey. On the other hand, if our glasses have a grey tint, our world will look grey—even if the world is more colorful.

To say this makes for a complex state of affairs is an understatement. The "glasses" metaphor makes clear that, while we cannot see without a vision, what we see is unavoidably framed by that vision, by the "glasses" we wear, glasses we put on, glasses ground by us or for us in terms of our history, needs, and desires. Near-sighted, far-sighted, or 20/20, we see things against a horizon, on a horizon. But the horizon itself we never see, it is always disappearing, always beyond. This is crucial. No vision can claim to be a God's-eye-view, "the" all-seeing vision of and for the world. Human horizons are always limited, continually changing, expanding as history moves on and things constantly develop. Our visions are always provisional and partial, products of a certain time and particular place, requiring periodic adjustments, recalibrating, regrounding.

Wholesome worldviews—always in-process, open to revision, fine-tuning, open to learning from the insights of others—are positive, inclusive, life-affirming visions. Such visions offer perspective, delineating what we see in its similarity and difference, mapping out the topography and network of interconnections, giving each its due without overplay or underplay, without fusion and without isolation.

It is the new and strange that are particularly challenging and unsettling, often leading to worldview crises. We find ourselves in uncharted waters. What now? We need to recalibrate and redraw our maps. Our uneasy caution can quickly escalate into fear. Instead of seizing the opportunity to expand our horizons, we get defensive and color the world in black and white. We are drawn to worldviews that allow us to "see" reality in ways that make it easier to cope, not only mitigating risk, but justifying both our fears and our negative response.

Instead of providing an open perspective on the world, worldviews and their core beliefs can become myopically narrow, defensive, and toxic, visioning the world in ways that inhibit growth, promote immaturity, and foster division. When a worldview declares itself to be *the* perspective, *the* horizon, *the* worldview, it has become an ideology: a closed system of thought giving a false sense of security and superiority. The watermark of an ideology is baptizing a certain understanding of truth as the Truth—period. Ideologies with their absolute truth-claims act as eye-blinders, predetermining sightlines, in effect discouraging, eclipsing, and closing down the possibility of seeing things differently and remaining open to learning from others. In the grip of an ideology, people are brain-washed to believe that their "glasses" allow them to see the world with undoubted certainty as the way the world really is. Ideologies then become disguises for ulterior motives, projections of unacknowledged fears, blinders hiding us from reality.

Ideologies are—make no mistake about it—dangerous. They absolutize certain time-conditioned human perceptions as the infallible blueprint for life. They discourage and undermine giving serious consideration to the insights of others. They vitiate the possibility of authentic negotiation with those of different persuasions. And, perhaps most damaging, they conveniently absolve their adherents, not only of the need to constantly test and recalibrate their worldviews, but to acknowledge, understand, and own their reasons for holding the views they do with unquestioned loyalty.

The dangerous impact that ideologies can and do exert is painfully evident in the pernicious grip that Trumpism (a populist ideology) had and still has on so many Americans, including millions of white evangelical Christians. Despite being morally challenged in the extreme, Donald Trump, trading on their fears and hurts, succeeded in recruiting millions to his alt-right, xenophobic, white supremacist views to the point that they became promoted as a Christian nationalism. Trump became God's appointed Cyrus, "the standard-bearer of the Christian Right."[2] And Trumpism was and is presented as the real thing, the Truth. The fact that so many people, aided and abetted by conspiracy theories, continue to remain firm in their belief that the 2020 US Election was without doubt rigged is a stark reminder, not only of how an ideology's blinders narrow one's range of vision, but also of how ideological views are virtually unamenable to revision in spite of the truth that this election was the securest in the history of the U.S. How is this possible, and how does it work?

5. Emotional Life Is Foundational

To achieve a deeper understanding of the inner dynamics and seductive draw of populism and other ideologies, it is necessary to pay attention to the foundational role of feelings and emotions in human development. While we all experience the important role feelings play in our personal lives, more attention needs to be given to the pivotal role they play in the process of worldview choice and political stereotyping. That is to say, emotional attitudes, in particular, emotional anxieties, have everything to do with the kind of worldviews and political credos we create, are drawn to, and adopt. As young children, we touch, feel, hear, smell, taste, and see our way through the world. An intuitive sensorium—a panoply of senses—develops which aids and abets us as we make our way. We see the world, not first of all in terms of what we think about the world; rather, we see and think about the world in terms of how we sense and feel. Feelings and emotions are our alarm clocks telling us how we feel about what is going on in us and around us. Feeling sad helps us deal with the depth of loss, excitement keeps us with the task at hand, anger is energy for change, joy brings us close. The feeling of being loved elates us, and we hum with expectation. Fear brings us up short, puts us on alert, and up go the walls.

An emotionally healthy person experiences the full gamut of emotion, expressing feelings in ways appropriate to the situation. Having good feelings about ourselves gives us the desire and confidence to reach out to others and to genuinely like them. Feeling cared for ourselves, we are moved to care for others and together engage in efforts to build a just society. Good-enough emotional development for people as individual persons equips them with the self-esteem, courage, desire, and resolution to participate in the public arena with its socio-political projects for the public good. Citizens with a felt sense of anger are energized and emboldened to push hard for redress when aware of injustice.

---

2. Du Mez, *Jesus and John Wayne*, 263.

Central to all this is the acknowledgement of the monumental role of feelings in human life. If we don't own our feelings, our feelings own us. And that is not only troublesome, it is dangerous. Being angry, for instance, is a positive, healthy response when a person is injured, harmed, wounded, or abused. However, anger doesn't go away on its own, and working through anger is not easy and takes time. We can easily be tempted to hold it down in denial, pretending nothing is amiss; or we can let the anger engulf us, holding us hostage. When unattended or harbored, anger builds what Carl Jung called a "house" of anger, imprisoning us. Anger takes up "residence" in our "basements," knotting our stomachs, stiffening our backs, clenching our fists. Whatever the specifics, unowned anger not only saps energy and quashes delight but threatens to erupt for no apparent reason or at the slightest inconvenience. Or, nursing anger, we roam the streets unleashed, ever ready to let loose on whomever crosses our path. In contrast, healthy people own their anger, fear, joy, or sorrow, and act appropriately.

If, however, the incurred emotional wounds and hurts of childhood are not recognized, dissolved, and worked through, we remain emotionally "stuck," living our adult lives according to a deficient childhood script. Not feeling loved, we become haunted by an ever present need to be cherished and adored. When our wounds and hurts are not worked through, thus allowing the fear and anger to discharge, we go on high-alert. Fear becomes the immediate default response to everything, triggered especially by the new and different. The fear can feed on itself, becoming a pervasive anxiety about everything and nothing. Unworked through anger, often a cover for fear, slowly thickens and clots, hardening into hate. Hate is frozen anger. Meanwhile, even as people try to deal with their fear and anger, the specters of hopelessness, depression, and despair can begin to raise their ugly heads. Some people withdraw, turning off inside, falling into deep depression. Others, walking on eggshells, set themselves to get through life by settling for less. Still others, determining that they never again will be traumatized, hurt, humiliated, or shamed by others, harness their anger by devoting themselves to becoming the kind of dominating intimidators that others fear. In the brokenness of human existence, all of us, as R. D. Laing graphically expressed it, are called to go through our own hidden forms of madness in order to promote emotional maturation.

These very early ways of orienting ourselves give rise to emotional meaning patterns—psychologists refer to them as expectancy filters— which become second nature to us. They predispose how we experience the world. We are aware *that* we experience, but we are not aware of the filter or frame *through which* we experience. This is crucial for our discussion. These emotional meaning patterns function as *implicit* worldviews, as the "glasses" which "frame and color" the world we see. Outside of our conscious experience, unawares, we approach life with *implicit* biases. If in early childhood we feel seen and heard as lovable and precious, unconditionally loved, we develop a sense of security and trust, both in ourselves and of our surroundings. We see the world as a safe, welcoming place; and we are eager to explore. Psychologists call this a *Secure* attachment filter with low anxiety about abandonment and low avoidance of intimacy. However, if things developmentally do not proceed in "good enough" fashion (if we are put down, even abused, and do not feel seen, heard, loved), defensive filters take shape. Psychologists talk of three kinds of negative filters: *Preoccupied* (in efforts to get their needs met, inattentive to the needs of others, with high anxiety about abandonment), *Dismissing* (expect nothing, disconnected from self and others with high avoidance of intimacy), and *Fearful* (need closeness, afraid of closeness, with high anxiety about abandonment and high avoidance of intimacy).[3]

6. Toxic Worldviews: Ideologies

All of this means that as we are schooled, come of age, and take up our role as citizens in communities at large, we come with our expectancy filters in full operation. These *implicit biases* play an indispensable and inextricable role in the kind and type of *explicit* worldviews we adopt and promote. If our expectancy filters are "secure," we will be attracted to open worldviews that encourage and promote inclusion and solidarity with an emphasis on care, respect, and justice for all. If, on the other hand, our early life experience was not "good enough," our expectancy filters are "fearful," "preoccupied," or "dismissing." We look at the world with apprehension, suspicion, on high alert. Consequently, we will quite naturally, as a matter of course, be attracted to defensive worldviews, policies, and practices that not only give voice to and justify our fears and anger, but also serve to excuse and legitimize whatever it takes to defend them.

These emotional dynamics then play themselves out, compounded exponentially on a macrocosmic political level. Politically, people with welcoming, caring worldviews will be drawn to political parties, programs, and strategies that emphasize inclusion, generosity, impartiality, and justice. On the other hand, people with defensive worldviews will be drawn to political parties and policies that self-protectively legitimize exclusion, division, and discrimination. It is well to note that there is nothing easy or automatic about how this all works. In the rough tumble of ordinary life, citizens with a "good enough" emotional upbringing may end up in

---

3. Coe and Hall, *Psychology in the Spirit*, 240–49.

support of discriminatory policies just as people with a "less good" emotional history may find themselves in the ranks of those with more open and inclusive policies.

A particularly striking historical example of how this complex framing dynamic between implicit bias and explicit worldview typically plays itself out, both personally as well as more broadly in culture at large, is the infamous *cogito, ergo sum* (I think, therefore, I am) of René Descartes. Descartes was of sickly disposition and ill at ease with women. By shutting down "all my senses,"[4] he relieved his emotional anxieties toward his body and women through the fabrication of a mind/body dualism in which the thinking-ego is separate from the body. This "ideal of the cogito" in which "thinking" is the essence of being human served as his "defense against the flesh because the flesh is synonymous with anguish . . . rendering innocuous of all that spells dread." Psychiatrist Karl Stern concludes his study of Descartes by observing that "the raw material of suffering is assimilated by genius."[5] Although, in Descartes's view, rationality and knowledge are claimed to be neutral and "sexless," "sexless knowledge" is, as Genevieve Lloyd has shown, illusory, a covert way of privileging maleness, and toxic for women.[6]

The relief and privileging, on the one hand, and reprisal and discrimination, on the other, is a typical mark of toxic worldviews, ideologies, and the political policies and practices they generate and justify. We put down the other to insure our safety but also to declare our superiority and justify our reprisal. For centuries women were proclaimed to be "emotional" and, therefore, rightly confined to the domesticity of home and excluded from universities or politics and the universal demands of "rationality." We have portrayed different others as in some way questionable, whether inferior, uncouth, primitive, savage, pagan, barbarian, or uncivilized. We considered it morally permissible to vanquish or confine to "reservations" the Indigenous peoples of North America. After all, they are "only (uncultured) Indians." Similarly, since Black people were seen to be "lesser," their second-class status as slaves was seen as no great problem, but even an asset (to whites). Centuries later, women, Indigenous peoples, and people of color still tragically suffer daily and often dearly from the hidden and not so hidden after-effects of the sexism and racism built into the structure of society.

The monumental question that comes out of all of this: Why is fear of difference so virulent and widespread? Why are racism, sexism, -isms of all kinds, so endemic? What is going on? Here—and this point calls for

---

4. Descartes, *Meditations and Other Metaphysical Writings*, 30.
5. Stern, *The Flight from Woman*, 101.
6. Lloyd, *The Man of Reason*.

underlining—I suggest that the actual fear is not fear of the new and the different as such. Rather the strange and the different give occasion for rekindling an already present anxiety: The loss of control. And the fear of loss of control is, as we have recounted, the result of not having sufficiently worked through internally the pain of earlier wounds and hurts. We remain unsettled, ill at ease, troubled, wounded, not in charge, afraid—despite everything we have done, all the rituals and habits we have installed and employed to suppress the fear, forget, and move on. Meeting the strange and different sets us off again, our emotional anxieties once again begin to rumble and percolate. Strangers, immigrants, people of a different class, sex, faith, or color are immediately seen with suspicion. They are threatening. Once again, we project our fear and anger outward.

We defensively skew and disavow the reality of the different. We spin tales, embroider stories, set up stereotypes to justify and reinforce our fears. Rather than seeing the world in its multicolored richness, we see the world in the simplified categories of fear-fed stereotypes. Others, the different, are (portrayed as) primitive, pagan, uncultured, second-rate, inferior, substandard . . . dangerous, out to get us, untrustworthy, bad, evil, whatever. We rationalize and project. Out of sorts, our internal terror of being out of control takes over. Not only do stereotypical stories in this way justify our fear, but when they function ideologically, they justify measures of control, marginalization, persecution, and even elimination. Until we come to terms with our original woundings, we stubbornly, aggressively, hold on to our stereotypes. We fool ourselves even as we are fooled.

The various forms of populism that are currently springing up across the world graphically illustrate both the seductive and the destructive power of ideological skewing of reality. Populism is a defensive compensatory political stance of citizens who justifiably or unjustifiably feel insufficiently recognized, whether unfulfilled, "left out," "left behind," or "wronged." Struggling with fear of losing out, proactive types are attracted to toxic policies, programs, and strategies which enact policies and practices that not only disadvantage others and advantage themselves, but also allow themselves to feel self-righteously justified in enjoying their privilege and superiority. That such practices are discriminatory or racist is brushed aside and whitewashed. The proactive types prop themselves up in their desire for admiration, recompense and revenge by backing and joining campaigns to elevate themselves and keep certain others down and in place.

Many others of the more passive sort slowly become more and more disillusioned; in their pain, anger and frustration deepens. Fearful, feeling unfulfilled, powerless, forgotten, as if they are nobodies, some settle for less, others take the road of addiction or completely withdraw. However, all of these people—the disillusioned, the disempowered, the disenfranchised, like all of us—long to be-long. This makes them susceptible to being drawn in by the proactive types, especially flamboyant, authoritarian figures promoting baneful populist socio-political policies and programs. Assured that they are right to feel aggrieved, that the problem is the stranger, the immigrant, the people of color, the women, etc., who are taking their jobs, whatever, they feel heard and seen. Their rage and fear is felt to be justified! They jump on the bandwagon—even if it is racist, unjust, and divisive, even if in actuality it disadvantages themselves. No matter! They are recognized. They feel a sense of power. They belong, they count, and that's all that counts. It's worth any sacrifice. Basking in the glow of the leader is everything! In return, populist leaders do whatever is needed—acting the strong man, spewing lies, feeding the rumor mill—to trade on, incite, and harness the underlying fear to keep their followers worked up and in line. The inflation of the groups' self-importance goes hand in hand with conspiracy thinking about secret evil activities of others.

Along these lines, we get a good sense of why populist movements like Trumpism are such a potent mix. Leaders acquire the admiration that is their obsession, acolytes the sense of belonging they have longed for. Followers pumped up by the full-of-themselves confidence of leaders. Leaders, feeding on the adulation, posturing as messiahs. In their reciprocal interaction, autocratic pandering then becomes self-aggrandizing for those in power, and self-tranquilizing for those who follow. When leaders act out their unresolved childhood scripts ("I will never again be humiliated, abandoned, abused, whatever") in the guise of particular programs and policies, they foment societal turmoil and discord everywhere and on multiple levels.

Moreover, populist movements have staying power. Trumpism did not go away with the defeat of Trump. Under attack, fidelity to populist causes is often exacerbated rather than diminished. They, the "righteous," feel unjustly wronged, underappreciated and betrayed, all of which reinforces their sense of being threatened by others. Their fear takes on a paranoiac quality, "group narcissism" (Eric Fromm) morphing into its twin, "group paranoia." Their fear remains very real—even if sorely misplaced. The reality of such paranoia[7] was brought home to me with a jolt when, shortly after President Biden's inauguration, I received a text-message from a friend taken in by Trumpist demonization of the Democrats. "Pretty soon, Jim, talking about the Truth of the Lord Jesus Christ is going to be deemed hate talk." Which brought to mind an earlier experience of the traumatic effect on the national and international

---

7. With the unmitigated disaster of Putin's invasion of Ukraine, we are at present witnessing the tragic, horrible, utterly destructive impact of group narcissistic paranoia.

consciousness of an out-of-control president. One morning as I was working in Starbucks, a distraught and disheveled man began a loud tirade about everything and nothing. Everyone, myself included, tried to pretend not to notice, even as we were annoyed and slightly frightened. Then, another man, who turned out to be the manager, entered the room. Instantly, the first man ceased his jabber, and, looking around, declared in no uncertain terms: "If the President of the United States can rant and rave, so can I." In one sentence, a scruffy-looking person called out the hypocrisy of our time: Why am I not allowed to disturb the peace of a few people, when Trump's presidential rants which disturb the world are given free rein?

7. Embracing Difference: Societal Justice

The personal and the social operate in bidirectional intertwinement. The personal trauma of unworked through emotional wounding is compounded exponentially both interpersonally and socio-politically. And, socio-economic traumas of poverty, unemployment, and lack of education precipitate personal and interpersonal crises of despair and desperation. Personal trauma goes contagious, precipitating rampant, cultural crisis; and socio-economic crises go contagious, infecting and aggravating personal dis-ease. Personal distrust, fear of loss of control, transfixed into fear and disdain of the other, result in an inflamed, partisan politics of rancor, hate, and division.

If, as I am claiming, it is fundamentally the fear of loss of control that is the prevailing dynamic playing itself out in fear of difference, what does this entail politically in our time of emerging pluralism and rising populism with its growing dilemmas of differences? For most of human history, there were neighbours and there were faraway strangers, often feared enemies. Neighbours were the people who, despite real differences, we lived with in greater or lesser familiarity and sameness. Strangers were aliens from other regions about whom we heard and told fearful and sometimes exotic tales but were people we seldom met. When strangers met strangers, these encounters were usually affairs of trade and commerce or, often, on a tribe to tribe, country to country, nation to nation basis, battles and wars.

Gradually, and dramatically, with the dawn of what we now call modernity, this all began to change. With continually advanced means of technology, transportation, and communication, strangers came and stayed. "Strangers stay and refuse to go away (though one keeps hoping they will in the end)—while, stubbornly, escaping the net of local rules and thus remaining strangers."[8] Strangers seem to be neither neighbours nor aliens. But

---

8. Bauman, *Postmodern Ethics*, 152.

then who are they? They don't go away, so they are not visitors. But they are not really aliens either. They live amongst us, we see them every day on the streets, their kids go to the same schools as ours, they work hard—but they remain different. What are we to make of this?

The dominant culture in the West with its modernist theory of impartial reason developed stratagems of toleration of the strange and different which in effect bracketed, denied, ignored, or dismissed the very characteristics—color, gender, ethnicity, class, faith—which constitute the uniqueness of the different. In what became known as "liberalism," differences were tolerated, provided they were kept personal and private, out of public spaces. "Strangers" either assimilated or were marginalized.

At present, the modernist synthesis has largely unraveled. The bodiless, sexless, historyless subject of modern moral philosophy has been itself unmasked as a dangerous illusion not only by Marx, Freud, and Nietzsche, but also by social movements for justice: justice for women, black people, indigenous people, people of color, workers, the LGBTQ+ community, and others. Marginalized peoples are not only taking pride in asserting their difference, but they are unmasking the so-called "neutrality" of society as actually the institutionalization of white male privilege, structurally discriminatory and oppressive to those who are different.

However, challenged by Black Lives Matter to own society's built-in racism, many members of culturally dominant groups, backed by others who also for whatever reasons feel disenfranchised and betrayed, resent and resist programs instituted to remedy injustices. Faced with calls for comprehensive health reform, elimination of socio-economic inequalities, prison reform, restructuring of the police, they themselves feel victimized, crying "All Lives Matter." Throughout the world, similar unsettling and unnerving scenarios are being replicated. Groups and nations, under the pretext of risks to national security, entrenched in fear of losing control, continue to stereotype others, enacting xenophobic policies and practices.

So the challenge is clear. Working towards a radical politics of love calls for the negotiation of civic covenants of inclusion which, honoring and embracing difference, undo systemic racism and redress injustice. To negotiate these tangled and agonizing scenes without dissolving into internecine conflicts or harsh autocracies will require what Soren Kierkegaard, in reference to Abraham, called "humble courage."[9] Courage to put ourselves on the line, developing, nourishing, and promoting positions and approaches open to and embracive of diversity and difference. Humble, recognizing that our views are partial and limited, waiting, expectantly,

---

9. Kierkegaard, *Fear and Trembling*, 41.

for response, input, and correction from others. Humble courage provides the forthrightness, compassion, and sensitivity of spirit needed to give shape to an inclusive socio-political ethos that celebrates and respects difference—the only viable alternative to exclusionary policies of hegemonic domination, marginalization, and oppression.

But more is required. In terms of the argument of this chapter, we especially need the humble courage to do the journey inwards, the hard work of facing and owning our personal wounds, implicit biases, and demons. Humble, aware that we are wounded, finite, and limited, single persons. Courage, in conviction that we are agents-of-and-for-love, gifted and called to become each in our own way unique partners in a global ministry of love.

That means, for the good of the world and for the good of each of us, it is not less sense of self that is needed, but more. Not too much self-identity is our problem, but too little. Lacking a robust sense of self, as we have remarked, a person either self-inflates into an intimidator or self-deflates into being submissive. When, however, we have a fulsome and wholesome sense of self, we are able to give each other space. I do not need to pull neurotically on you for acceptance and affirmation, nor do I need to pull back from you, fearing engulfment, when you are needy and reaching out.

Without healthy self-awareness, any campaign of social renewal will be undercut, derailed, sabotaged, and devolve into a battle between competing interest groups on the backs of those who are of different color, class, or religion. While dueling power-brokers orchestrate ways to hide, excuse, and rationalize their actions in their drive to remain in control, minorities of all sorts find themselves stereotyped and marginalized, their needs shelved. The result: justice denied and compassion exiled.

Without the journey inwards of personal growth, our submerged personal anxieties and agendas, rather than the good of the commonwealth, will ineluctably motivate and determine political maneuverings. We will not have the collective heart, the humble courage, to stand firm in the struggle for justice, not "just us," nor will we have the proper motives that make for true healing and authentic shalom. Without the dark night of the soul (as Christians in the mystic tradition have graphically described it), without the self-knowledge gained in self-examination, struggle, repentance, and growth, people will inevitably get in their own way in working for societal renewal. They will engage in causes for all kinds of (mainly wrong) reasons: for power, money, applause, acceptance, attention, escape. In fear of being taken advantage of, defensively projecting their inner rage hyper-critically on certain groups in society, scapegoating those who are other and different, their causes will be, at critical junctures, betrayed and misled by their own hidden, unresolved fears and needs.

No wonder that society so urgently needs renewal and transformation. For if people are not in touch with their deepest selves, aware of their own emotional proclivities and wounds, their societal involvement is bound to be more about their own power and position, more about winning and personal fame than about justice and the plight of others. Power-struggles and partisan bickering will trump bipartisan compromise, equitable sharing of wealth, and open-armed embrace of difference. The tumult and pandemonium that the world is experiencing at present with the rising threat of populism is a particularly distressing case in point.

On the other hand, healing societal transformation starts with a proper esteeming of every human person as a love-worthy "other"—a unique other to esteem, to dance with, to learn from, to love—a person not to be regarded as an "other" of indifference, deviance, fear, and disdain, an other to put down, imprison, or eliminate. Then, the welfare and well-being of our fellow humans, rather than personal neuroses, become the compelling motivation for transformational, communal, socio-political action. In and through which we all grow and prosper together in mutuality. For an economy of love is not a zero-sum game in which, if one person or one group wins, the other loses. Spending yourself in acts of love does not bankrupt or weaken you. Rather, in the radical paradoxical logic of love, it strengthens you and you are enriched.

Despite risks, challenges and threats, love-of-other-at-one-piece-with-love-of-self empowers us to look evil and injustice right in the face. Inward healing ripples and radiates outward. Compassion takes shape in a variety of communal forms: public investments in universal healthcare, education, recreation, employment, the arts, housing, public space, transportation, parks, libraries, places of worship, etc. Compassion inspires policies and projects confronting racial, ethnic, sexual, and religious discrimination, combating poverty, addressing climate change. In turn, such health-enhancing societal programs and installations serve to create the life-affirming spaces and conditions for individuals to thrive and flourish. To repeat the main thrust of this chapter: neglect of the needs of society is as detrimental for the flourishing of individual selves as neglect of the needs of self is for the society at large.

Working towards a political praxis of love is a team-project calling for team-work, engaging in specific projects that excite us the most as we co-partner for the common good. We are called to stand in solidarity with and in support of the crushed in spirit, the broken-hearted, the marginalized and disenfranchised, the very planet itself. Such suffering-with is wit(h)nessing-with, an exercise in speaking the truth—the "way of faithful relationality in which we are called to walk and talk."[10] Speaking truth to power calls for people of compassion banding together, raising voices of concern and protest in heartfelt distress about the needless and useless suffering of fellow human beings. It means getting into what Congressman John Lewis so aptly called "good trouble." Witness to power needs to be an insistent: "This is not right. This is not the road to blessing. It is intolerable. For the sake of all the family of the earth's creatures, including the earth itself, this must stop." Such wit(h)nessing is especially challenging, joining voices with the oppressed without speaking *for* them and, at the same time, suffering-*with*, as love demands, the very people, factions, and forces responsible for the atrocities.[11]

When, as too often happens, justice is trampled underfoot, we need to keep the faith, working and waiting, remembering that love carries all things, bears all things, and hopes all things. We do this encouraged, with hope, given heart, for the God who *ex amore* created the world remains with us and in us. In receiving the Gift of life from the Creator, we receive ourselves as gifted, as loved. In receiving the Call of life from the Creator, we receive ourselves as called, to love.

We are called to do compassion politically—suffering-with those who suffer, weeping with those who weep, celebrating with those who celebrate. We compassion not to win or succeed, not for acclaim or renown, but to remain true, waging love, not war, listening to the cries of the oppressed and hurting. We can do nothing else. We do this in hope. To be human is to love and to love is to hope. To hope is to put aside the fear which isolates and closes down new possibilities. It is to open ourselves to the promise of the healing empowerment of love, creation's lifeblood. A trusting hope in the Promise of Love's invigorating abundance (both initiating, and fulfilling) as opposed to the "less than nothing" antagonism of the abyss. "For God did not give us a spirit of cowardice, but rather a spirit of power and of love and of self-discipline."[12]

We dare to hope boldly and love deeply. For the hope of love is the promise of the world. This hope is, as Paul Ricoeur reminds us, "not a theme that comes after other themes, an idea that closes a system, but an impulse that opens the system, that breaks the closure of the system; it is a way of reopening what was unduly closed."[13] In contrast to ideological control and exclusion based on fear, the Spirit of Love is the creative and

---

10. Keller, *On the Mystery*, 211
11. See my essay, Olthuis, "The Wit(h)ness of Suffering Love."
12. 2 Tim 1:7 (NRSV).
13. Ricoeur, *Figuring the Sacred*, 211.

recreative stirrings which revive hope, giving rise to a spirituality of love open to others, to surprise, to healing, to adventure ... to "the power [of love] made perfect in weakness."[14]

> *May God bless us with a restless discomfort*
> *about easy answers, half-truths, and superficial relationships,*
> *so that we may seek truth boldly and love deep within our hearts.*
> *May God bless us with holy anger*
> *at injustice, oppression, and exploitation of people,*
> *so that we may tirelessly work for justice, freedom,*
> *and peace among all people.*
> *May God bless us with the gift of tears*
> *to shed for those who suffer from pain, rejection, starvation,*
> *or the loss of all that they cherish,*
> *so that we may reach out our hand to comfort them*
> *and transform their pain into joy.*
> *May God bless us with enough foolishness*
> *to believe that we really can make a difference in this world,*
> *so that we are able, with God's grace,*
> *to do what others claim cannot be done.*[15]

---

14. 2 Cor 12:9 (NRSV).
15. Traditional Franciscan prayer.

BIBLIOGRAPHY

Adams, Marilyn McCord and Robert Merrihew Adams, eds. *The Problem of Evil.* Oxford: Oxford University Press, 1991.
Anderson, Nicole. *Derrida: Ethics Under Erasure.* New York: Continuum, 2012.
Anselm, *St. Anselm: Basic Writings.* Translated by S. N. Deane. La Salle: Open Court, 1962.
Ansell, Nicholas. *The Annihilation of Hell: Universal Salvation and the Redemption of Time in the Eschatology of Jürgen Moltmann.* Eugene: Wipf and Stock, 2013.
———. "The Call of Wisdom/The Voice of the Serpent: A Canonical Approach to the Tree of Knowledge." *Christian Scholar's Review* 31/1 (Fall, 2001) 31–57.
Aristotle. *The Complete Works of Aristotle.* Volume 2. Edited by Jonathan Barnes. Princeton: Princeton University Press, 1984.
Bernasconi, Robert and David Wood, eds. *The Provocation of Levinas: Rethinking the Other.* London: Routledge, 1988.
Allen, Prudence. *The Concept of Woman.* Volume 1: *The Aristotelian Revolution, 750 B.C.–A.D. 1250.* Grand Rapids: Eerdmans, 1997.
Bachelard, Gaston. *The Poetics of Space.* Translated by Maria Jolas. Boston: Beacon, 1994.
Barbour, Ian and John Russell, eds. "David Bohm's Implicate Order: Physics, Philosophy and Theology." Special Issue. *Zygon: Journal of Religion & Science.* 20:2 (June 1985).
Bardwick, Judith M. *Psychology of Women: A Study of Bio-Cultural Conflicts.* New York: Harper & Row, 1971.
Barrett, William. *Death of the Soul: From Descartes to the Computer.* New York: Doubleday, 1986.
———. *Irrational Man: A Study in Existential Philosophy.* New York: Doubleday, 1958.
Barth, Karl. *Church Dogmatics.* Vol. III/1: *The Doctrine of Creation.* Edited by G. W. Bromiley and T. F. Torrance and translated by J. W. Edwards, et al. Edinburgh: T & T Clark, 1960.
Bateson, Gregory. *Steps to an Ecology of the Mind.* San Francisco: Chandler, 1972.
Bauman, Zygmunt. *Postmodern Ethics.* Oxford: Blackwell, 1993.
Benjamin, Jessica. *The Bonds of Love: Psychoanalysis, Feminism, and the Problem of Domination.* New York: Random House, 1988.
Bennington, Geoffrey. *Interrupting Derrida.* New York: Routledge, 2000.
Bergson, Henri. *Creative Evolution.* Translated by Arthur Mitchell. New York: Dover, 1988.

Berman, Morris. *The Reenchantment of the World*. Ithaca: Cornell University, 1981.
Bernasconi, Robert. "Seeing Double: Destruktion and Deconstruction." In *Dialogue and Deconstruction*, edited by Diane P. Michelfelder and Richard E. Palmer, 233–150. New York: SUNY, 1989.
Bernasconi, Robert and Simon Critchley, eds. *Re-reading Levinas*. Bloomfield: Indiana University, 1991.
Berry, Thomas. *The Dream of the Earth*. Berkeley: Counterpoint,1988.
Blum, Lawrence. *Friendship, Altruism, and Morality*. London: Routledge & Kegan Paul, 1980.
Bohm, David. *The Search for Meaning: The New Spirit in Science and Philosophy*. Edited by Paavo Pylkkanen. Northamptonshire: Crucible, 1989.
———. *Wholeness and Implicate Order*. London: Routledge and Kegan Paul, 1980.
Bonzo, Matthew J. *Indwelling the Forsaken Other: The Trinitarian Ethics of Jürgen Moltmann*. Eugene: Wipf and Stock, 2009.
Brock, Rita Nakishima. *Journeys by Heart: A Christology of Erotic Power*. New York: Crossroad, 1988.
Brooks, Daniel R. and E. O. Wiley. *Evolution as Entropy: Toward a Unified Theory of Biology*. Chicago: University of Chicago, 1986.
Brown, William P., M. P. Graham, and Jeffrey Kuan, eds. *History and Interpretation: Essays in Honour of John H. Hayes*. Sheffield: JSOT, 1993.
Browning, Donald. *Religious Thought and the Modern Psychologies*. Philadelphia: Fortress, 1987.
Brüeggemann-Kruijff, Atie Th. *Bij de Gratie van de transcendentie. In gesprek met Levinas over het vrouwelijke*. Amsterdam: VU Uitgeverij, 1993
Brümer, Vincent. *The Model of Love: A Study in Philosophical Theology*. Cambridge: Cambridge University Press, 1993.
Buber, Martin. *Between Man and Man*. Translated by Ronald Gregor Smith. London: Collins, 1947.
———. *I and Thou*. Translated by Walter Kaufman. New York: Scribners 1970.
Burggraeve, Roger. *Emmanuel Levinas: The Ethical Basis for a Humane Society*. Leuven: Center for Metaphysics and Philosophy of God, 1981.
Butler, Judith. *Gender Trouble: Feminism and the Subversion of Identity*. London: Routledge, 1990.
———. *Undoing Gender*. London: Routledge, 2004.
Buytendijk, Frederik Jacobus Johannes. *Prolegomena to an Anthropological Physiology*. Pittsburgh: Duquesne University, 1974.
Capra, Fritjof. *The Turning Point: Science, Society and the Rising Culture*. New York: Simon and Schuster, 1982.
Caputo, John D. *Against Ethics: Contributions to a Poetics of Obligation with Constant Reference to Deconstruction*. Bloomington: Indiana University Press, 1993.
———. *Demythologizing Heidegger*. Bloomington: Indiana University Press, 1993.
———. *Hermeneutics Facts snd Interpretation In the Age of Information*. UK: Penguin Random House, 2018.
———. *The Insistence of God: A Theology of Perhaps*. Bloomington: Indiana University Press, 2013.
———. *The Prayers and Tears of Jacques Derrida: Religion without Religion*. Bloomington: Indiana University Press, 1997.

———. *Radical Hermeneutics: Repetition, Deconstruction, and the Hermeneutic Project*. Bloomington: Indiana University Press, 1987.

———. "Thinking, Poetry, and Pain," in *Southern Journal of Philosophy* 28, Supplement (1990) 155–81.

———. *The Weakness of God: A Theology of the Event*. Bloomington: Indiana University Press, 2006.

Caputo, John D., and Jacques Derrida. *Deconstruction in a Nutshell: A Conversation with Jacques Derrida*. New York: Fordham University, 1997.

Carroll, Sean. *The Big Picture: On the Origins of Life, Meaning, and the Universe Itself*. New York: Dutton, 2016.

Cassirer, Ernst. *An Essay on Man: An Introduction to a Philosophy of Culture*. New Haven: Yale University Press, 1972.

Céline, Louis-Ferdinand. *Journey to the End of the Night*. Translated by Ralph Manheim. New York: New Directions, 1983.

Chanter, Tina. *Ethics of Eros: Irigaray's Re-writing of the Philosophers*. New York: Routledge, 1995.

Chodorow, Nancy. *The Reproduction of Mothering: Psychoanalysis and the Sociology of Gender*. Berkeley: University of California Press, 1978.

Claremont de Castillejo, Irene. *Knowing Woman: A Feminine Psychology*. New York: Harper & Row, 1973.

Cockburn, Bruce. "Lovers in a Dangerous Time." Track 1 on *Stealing Fire*. True North Records, 1984.

Coe, John H. and Todd W. Hall, *Psychology in the Spirit*. Downers Grove: IVP Academic, 2010.

Cohen, Leonard. "Anthem." Track 5 on *The Future*. Columbia Records, 1992.

Commoner, Barry. *Science and Survival*. New York: Viking, 1967.

Critchley, Simon. *The Ethics of Deconstruction: Derrida and Levinas*. Oxford: Blackwell, 1992.

———. *Ethics-Politics-Subjectivity: Essays on Derrida, Levinas, and Contemporary French Thought*. New York: Verso, 1999.

Crockett, Clayton. "Entropy." In *The Future of Continental Philosophy of Religion*, edited by Clayton Crockett, Keith Putt, and Jeffrey Robbins, 272–282. Bloomington: Indiana University Press, 2014.

Coward, Harold and Toby Foshay, eds. *Derrida and Negative Theology*. Albany: SUNY, 1992.

Davis, Stephen D., ed. *Encountering Evil: Live Options in Theology*. Atlanta: John Knox, 1981.

De Beauvoir, Simone. *The Second Sex*. Translated by H. M. Pashley. New York: Knopf, 1953.

De Boer, Theo. *De God van de filosofen en de God van Pascal*. 's-Gravenhage: Meinema, 1989.

Deleuze, Gilles and Felix Guattari. *Anti-Oedipus: Capitalism and Schizophrenia*. Translated by Robert Hurley, Mark Seem, and Helen R. Lane. London: Athlone, 1977.

Derrida, Jacques. *Acts of Literature*. Edited by Derek Attridge. New York: Routledge, 1992.

———. "Circumfession: Fifty-nine Periods and Periphrases." In Geoffrey and Jacques Derrida, *Jacques Derrida*. Chicago: University of Chicago Press, 1993.

———. *Dissemination*. Translated by Barbara Johnson. Chicago: University of Chicago Press, 1981.

———. "Force of Law: The Mystical Foundation of Authority." Translated by Mary Quaintance. In *Deconstruction and the Possibility of Justice*, edited by Drucilla Cornell, Michel Rosenfeld, and David Gray Carlson, 3–67. New York: Routledge, 1992.

———. *The Gift of Death*. Translated by David Wills. Chicago: University of Chicago Press, 1995.

———. *Given Time: I. Counterfeit Money*. Translated by Peggy Kamuf. Chicago: University of Chicago Press, 1992.

———. *Glas*. Translated by John P. Leavey, Jr. and Richard Rand. Lincoln: University of Nebraska Press, 1986.

———. *Limited Inc*. Translated by Jeffrey Mehlman and Samuel Weber. Evanston: Northwestern University Press, 1988.

———. *Memoirs of the Blind: The Self-Portrait and Other Ruins*. Translated by Pascale-Anne Brault and Michale Naas. Chicago: University of Chicago Press, 1993.

———. *Of Grammatology*. Translated by Gayatri Chakravorty Spivak. Baltimore: John Hopkins University Press, 1976.

———. *Of Spirit: Heidegger and the Question*. Translated by Geoffrey Bennington and Rachel Bowlby. Chicago: University of Chicago Press, 1989.

———. *On the Name*. Edited by Thomas Dutoit. Translated by David Wood, John P. Leavey, Jr., and Ian McLeod. Stanford: Stanford University Press, 1995.

———. *Points . . . : Interviews, 1974-1994*. Edited by Elisabeth Weber. Translated by Peggy Kamuf et. al. Stanford: Stanford University Press, 1995.

———. *Positions*. Translated by Alan Bass. Chicago: University of Chicago Press, 1981.

———. *The Post Card: From Socrates to Freud and Beyond*. Translated by Alan Bass. Chicago: University of Chicago Press, 1987.

———. *Psyche: Inventions of the Other*. 2 vols. Edited by Peggy Kamuf and Elizabeth G. Rottenberg. Stanford: Stanford University Press, 2007–2008.

———. "Remarks on Deconstruction and Pragmatism." In *Deconstruction and Pragmatism*, edited by Chantal Mouffe, 77–88. New York: Routledge, 1996.

———. *Rogues: Two Essays on Reason*. Translated by Pascale-Anne Brault and Michael Naas. Stanford: Stanford University Press, 2005.

———. *Spectres of Marx: The State of the Debt, the Work of Mourning, and the New International*. Translated by Peggy Kamuf. New York: Routledge, 1994.

———. *Spurs: Nietzsche's Styles/Éperons Les Styles de Nietzsche*. Translated by Barbara Harlow. Chicago: University of Chicago Press, 1979.

———. *The Work of Mourning*. Edited by Pascale-Anne Brault and Michael Naas. Chicago: University of Chicago Press, 2001.

———. *Writing and Difference*. Translated by Alan Bass. Chicago: University of Chicago Press, 1978.

Descartes, René. *Meditations and Other Metaphysical Writings*. Translated by Desmond Clarke. London: Penguin, 2003.

Dettloff, Dean. "Žižek's Ruptured Monism: A Comparative Typological Reading of *Less Than Nothing*." *Philosophia Reformata* 83/2 (2018) 177–203.

Dinnerstein, Dorothy. *The Mermaid and the Minotaur: Sexual Arrangements and the Human Malaise*. New York: Harper & Row, 1976.

Dooyeweerd, Herman. *A New Critique of Theoretical Thought*. 4 vols. Translated by David H. Freeman, William S. Young, and H. de Jongste. Philadelphia: The Presbyterian and Reformed Pub. Co., 1956–1958.

Dudiak, Jeffrey. *The Intrigue of Ethics*. New York: Fordham University Press, 2001.

Du Mez, Kristin Kobes. *Jesus and John Wayne: How White Evangelicals Corrupted a Faith and Fractured a Nation*. New York: Liveright, 2020.

Eckhart. *Meister Eckhart: The Essential Sermons, Commentaries, Treatises, and Defense*. Translated by Edmund Colledge and Bernard McGinn. Mahwah, NJ: Paulist, 1981.

Ehrlich, Paul and Richard Harriman. *How to Be a Survivor: A Plan to Save Spaceship Earth*. New York: Ballantine, 1971.

Falk, Richard. *This Endangered Planet: Prospects and Proposals for Human Survival*. New York: Random House, 1971.

Firestone, Shulamith. *The Dialectic of Sex: The Case for Feminist Revolution*. New York: Bantam, 1970.

Flax, Jane. *Thinking Fragments: Psychoanalysis, Feminism, and Postmodernism in the Contemporary West*. Berkeley: University of California Press, 1990.

Foucault, Michel. *Power/Knowledge: Selected Interviews and Other Writings: 1972-1977*. Edited by Colin Gordon. Translated by Colin Gordon, et al. New York: Pantheon, 1980.

Fowler, James. *Stages of Faith*. San Francisco: Harper & Row, 1981.

Fox, Matthew. *Original Blessing*. Santa Fe: Bear & Co., 1983.

———. *A Spirituality Named Compassion*. Minneapolis: Winston, 1979.

Fox, Matthew, ed. *Hildegard of Bingen's Book of Divine Works*. Santa Fe: Bear & Co. 1987.

Fretheim, Terrence E. *Creation Untamed: The Bible, God, and Natural Disasters*. Grand Rapids: Baker Academic, 2010.

———. *The Suffering of God: An Old Testament Perspective*. Philadelphia: Fortress, 1984.

Freud, Sigmund. *The Standard Edition of the Complete Psychological Works of Sigmund Freud*. 24 vols. Edited and translated by James Strachey, et al. London: Hogarth and the Institute of Psycho-Analysis, 1953–1974.

Fuchs, Gotthard and Hans Hermann Henrix, eds. *Zeitgewinn: Messianisches Denken nach Franz Rosenzweig*. Frankfurt am Main: J. Knecht, 1987.

Gadamer, Hans-Georg. *Truth and Method*, 2nd ed. Translated by Joel Weinsheimer and Donald G. Marshall. New York: Crossroad, 1989.

Gasché, Rodolphe. *Inventions of Difference*. Cambridge: Harvard University Press, 1994.

———. *The Tain of the Mirror: Derrida and the Philosophy of Reflection*. Cambridge: Harvard University Press, 1988.

Gilkey, Langdon. *Message and Existence: An Introduction to Christian Theology*. New York: Seabury, 1981.

Gilligan, Carol. *In a Different Voice: Psychological Theory and Women's Development*. Cambridge: Harvard University Press, 1982.

Glass, James. *Shattered Selves: Multiple Personality in a Postmodern World*. Ithaca: Cornell University Press, 1993.

Goiten, S. D. "YHWH the Passionate: The Monotheistic Meaning and Origin of the Name YHWH." *Vetus Testamentum* 6 (January 1956) 1–9.

Goldberg, Steven. *The Inevitability of Patriarchy*. New York: Macmillan, 1973.

Gould, Stephen Jay. *Ever Since Darwin: Reflections in Natural History.* New York: Norton & Company, 1977.
Greer, Germaine. *The Female Eunuch.* New York: Bantam, 1972.
Griffin, David Ray. *God, Power, and Evil: A Process Theodicy.* Philadelphia: Westminster, 1976.
Grosz, Elizabeth. *Sexual Subversions: Three French Feminists.* Sydney: Allen and Unwin, 1989.
Guntrip, Harry. *Psychoanalytic Theory, Therapy and the Self.* New York: Harper & Row, 1971.
Habermas, Jürgen. *Moral Consciousness and Communicative Action.* Translated by Christian Lenhardt and Shierry Weber Nicholsen. Cambridge: MIT, 1990.
Hafiz. *The Gift.* Translated by Daniel Ladinsky. New York: Penguin Compass, 1999.
Hardt, Michael and Antonio Negri. *Multitude: War and Democracy in the Age of Empire.* New York: Penguin, 2004.
Hart, Carroll Guen. *Grounding without Foundations: A Conversation Between Richard Rorty and John Dewey to Ascertain Their Kinship.* Toronto: Patmos, 1993.
Hart, Hendrik. *Understanding Our World: An Integral Ontology.* Lanham: University Press of America, 1984.
Hart, Kevin. *The Trespass of the Sign: Deconstruction, Theology, and Philosophy.* Cambridge: Cambridge University Press, 1989.
Hauerwas, Stanley and L. Gregory Jones, eds. *Why Narrative?: Readings in Narrative Theology.* Grand Rapids: Eerdmans, 1989.
Hector, Kevin W. *Theology without Metaphysics.* Cambridge: Cambridge University Press, 2011.
Heidegger, Martin. *Basic Writings.* Edited by David Farrell Krell. New York: Harper & Row, 1977.
———. *Being and Time.* Translated by John Macquarrie and Edward Robinson. New York: Harper & Row, 1962.
———. *Identity and Difference.* Translated by Joan Stambaugh. New York: Harper & Row, 1969.
———. *Nietzsche.* Vol. II. Translated by David Farrell Krell. New York: Harper & Row, 1984.
———. *On the Way to Language.* Translated by Peter D. Hertz. New York: Harper & Row, 1971.
———. *Pathmarks.* Edited by William McNeill. Cambridge: Cambridge University Press, 1998.
———. *Poetry, Language, Thought.* Translated by Albert Hofstadter. New York: Harper & Row, 1971.
Heilbroner, Robert. *Inquiry into the Human Prospect.* New York: W. W. Norton, 1974.
Herman, Judith. *Trauma and Recovery.* New York: Basic, 1992.
Heyward, Carter. *Touching Our Strength: The Erotic as Power and the Love of God.* San Francisco: Harper and Row, 1989.
Hines, Melissa. *Brain Gender.* Oxford: Oxford University Press, 2005.
Hobbes, Thomas. *Leviathan.* New York: Penguin, 2017.
Hobson, Marian. *Jacques Derrida: Opening Lines.* New York: Routledge, 1998.
Hocking, Jeffrey. *Freedom Unlimited: Liberty, Autonomy, and Response-ability in the Open Theism of Clark Pinnock.* Eugene: Wipf and Stock, 2010.

Holliday, Laurel. *The Violent Sex: Male Psychology and the Evolution of Consciousness*. Guerneville: Bluestocking, 1978.
Horney, Karen. *Feminine Psychology*. New York: W. W. Norton, 1967.
Irigaray, Luce. *An Ethics of Sexual Difference*. Translated by Carolyn Burke and Gillian Gill. Ithaca: Cornell University Press, 1993.
———. *The Forgetting of Air in Martin Heidegger*. Translated by Mary Beth Mader. Austin: University of Texas Press, 1999.
———. *In the Beginning, She Was*. New York: Continuum, 2012.
———. *i love to you: Sketch of a Possible Felicity in History*. Translated by Alison Martin. New York: Routledge, 1996.
———. *Key Writings*. New York: Continuum, 2004
———. *This Sex Which Is Not One*. Translated by Catherine Porter. Ithaca: Cornell University Press, 1985.
———. *Sexes and Genealogies*. Translated by Gillian Gill. New York: Columbia University Press, 1993.
———. *to be two*. Translated by Monique M. Rhodes and Marco F. Cocito-Monoc. London: Routledge, 2001.
———. *the Way of Love*. Translated by Heidi Bostic and Stephen Pluhácek. London: Continuum, 2002.
Irigaray, Luce and Michael Marder. *Through Vegetal Being*. New York: Columbia University Press, 2016.
Irwin, Alexander C. *Eros Toward the World: Paul Tillich and the Theology of the Erotic*. Minneapolis: Fortress, 1991.
Iser, Wolfgang. *The Act of Reading: A Theory of Aesthetic Response*. Baltimore: John Hopkins University Press, 1978.
Jardine, Alice. *Gynesis: Configurations of Woman and Modernity*. Ithaca: Cornell University Press, 1985.
Jaspers, Karl. *Philosophy*. Vol. II. Translated by E.B. Ashton. Chicago: University of Chicago Press, 1970.
Johnson, James Weldon. *God's Trombones*. New York: Viking, 1927.
Joy, Morny. "Levinas: Alterity, the Feminine and Women—A Meditation," in *Studies in Religion/Sciences Religieuses* 22/4 (1993) 463–85.
Jung, Carl. *Modern Man in Search of a Soul*. Translated by W. S. Dell and Cary F. Baynes. New York: Harcourt, Brace & World, 1933.
———. *Two Essays on Analytical Psychology*. Translated by R. F. C. Hull. New York: Meridian, 1956.
Kahn, Herman. *On Thermonuclear War*. Princeton: Princeton University Press, 1960.
Kearney, Richard. *The God Who May Be: A Hermeneutics of Religion*. Bloomington: Indiana University Press, 2001.
Kearney, Richard, ed. *Dialogues with Contemporary Continental Thinkers*. Manchester: Manchester University Press, 1984.
Kegan, Robert. *The Evolving Self*. Cambridge: Harvard University Press, 1982.
Keller, Catherine. *Cloud of the Impossible: Negative Theology and Planetary Entanglement*. New York: Columbia University Press, 2014.
———. *The Face of the Deep: A Theology of Becoming*. London: Routledge, 2003.
———. *From a Broken Web: Separation, Sexism, and Self*. Boston: Beacon, 1986.
———. *On the Mystery: Discerning Divinity in Process*. Minneapolis: Fortress, 2008.

Kierkegaard, Søren. *Fear and Trembling*. Translated by Steven Evans and Sylvia Walsh. Cambridge: Cambridge University Press, 2006.

Kingsolver, Barbara. *Small Wonder*. New York: Harper Collins, 2002.

Kohlberg, Lawrence. *The Philosophy of Moral Development: Moral Stages and the Idea of Justice*. New York: Harper & Row, 1981.

Kohut, Heinz. *The Analysis of the Self: A Systematic Approach to the Psychoanalytic Treatment of Narcissistic Personality Disorders*. New York: International University Press, 1971.

———. *The Restoration of Self*. Chicago: University of Chicago Press, 1977.

Konner, Melvin. *The Tangled Wing: Biological Constraints on the Human Spirit*. New York: Harper & Row, 1982.

Krabbe, Silas C. *A Beautiful Bricolage: Theopoetics as God-Talk for Our Time*. Eugene: Wipf and Stock, 2016.

Kristeva, Julia. *Desire in Language: A Semiotic Approach to Literature and Art*. Edited by Leon S. Roudiez. Translated by Thomas Gora, Alice Jardine, and Leon S. Roudiez. New York: Columbia University Press, 1980.

———. *In the Beginning Was Love: Psychoanalysis and Faith*. Translated by Arthur Goldhammer. New York: Columbia University Press, 1987.

———. *The Kristeva Reader*. Edited by Toril Moi. New York: Columbia University Press, 1986.

———. *Revolution in Poetic Language*. Translated by Margaret Walter. New York: Columbia University Press, 1984.

———. *Tales of Love*. Translated by Leon S. Roudiez. New York: Columbia University Press, 1987.

Lacan, Jacques. *The Seminar of Jacques Lacan Book II: The Ego in Freud's Theory and in the Technique of Psychoanalysis, 1954–1955*. Translated by Sylvana Tomaselli. New York: W. W. Norton & Company, 1991.

———. *The Seminar of Jacques Lacan Book XI: The Four Fundamental Concepts of Psychoanalysis, 1964*. Translated by Alan Sheridan. New York: W. W. Norton & Company, 1981.

———. *The Seminar of Jacques Lacan Book XX: Encore, On Feminine Sexuality: The Limits of Love and Knowledge, 1972–1973*. Translated by Bruce Fink. New York: Norton, 1998.

LaCugna, Catherine Mowry. *God for Us: The Trinity and Christian Life*. New York: Harper Collins, 1991.

Lasch, Christopher. *The Minimal Self: Psychic Survival in Troubled Times*. New York: W. W. Norton, 1984.

Lawlor, Leonard. *Imagination and Chance: The Difference Between the Thought of Ricoeur and Derrida*. Albany: SUNY, 1992.

Levenson, Jon. *Creation and the Persistence of Evil: The Jewish Drama of Divine Omnipotence*. Princeton: Princeton University Press, 1988.

Levinas, Emmanuel. *Basic Philosophical Writings*. Edited by Adriaan Peperzak, Simon Critchley, and Robert Bernasconi. Bloomington: Indiana University Press, 1996.

———. *Entre Nous: Essays on Thinking-of-the-Other*. Translated by Michael Smith and Barbara Harshav. New York: Columbia University Press, 1998.

———. *Ethics and Infinity: Conversations with Philippe Nemo*. Translated by Richard Cohen. Pittsburgh: Duquesne University Press, 1985.

———. *The Levinas Reader*. Edited by Sean Hand. Oxford: Blackwell, 1989.

———. *Otherwise than Being or Beyond Essence*. Translated by Alphonso Lingis. Hague: Martinus Nijhoff, 1981.

———. *Totality and Infinity: An Essay on Exteriority*. Translated by Alphonso Lingus. Pittsburgh: Duquesne University Press, 1969.

Lloyd, Genevieve. *The Man of Reason: "Male" and "Female" in Western Philosophy*. London: Routledge, 1984.

Loevinger, Jane. *Ego Development: Conceptions and Theories*. San Francisco: Jossey-Bass, 1976.

MacIntyre, Alasdair. *Three Rival Versions of Moral Enquiry*. Notre Dame: University of Notre Dame Press, 1990.

Macquarrie, John. *In Search of Humanity: A Theological and Philosophical Approach*. London: SCM, 1982.

MacMurray, John. *Persons in Relation*. Atlantic Highlands, NJ: Humanities, 1979.

———. *The Self as Agent*. New York: Harper and Brothers, 1957.

Malabou, Catherine. "Post-Trauma: Towards a New Definition?" In *Telemorphosis: Theory in the Era of Climate Change*, Vol. I, edited by Tom Cohen, 226–238. Ann Arbor: Open Humanities, 2012.

Marion, Jean-Luc. *Being Given: Toward a Phenomenology of Givenness*. Translated by Jeffrey Kosky. Stanford: Stanford University Press, 2002.

———. *The Erotic Phenomenon*. Translated by Stephen E. Lewis. Chicago: University of Chicago Press, 2007.

———. *God without Being*. Translated by Thomas A. Carlson. Chicago: University of Chicago Press, 1991.

———. *Prolegomena to Charity*. Translated by Stephen E. Lewis. New York: Fordham University Press, 2002.

May, Gerhard. *Creatio Ex Nihilo: The Doctrine of "Creation out of Nothing" in Early Christian Thought*. Translated by A. S. Worrall. Edinburgh: T & T Clark, 1994.

May, Rollo. *Man's Search for Himself*. New York: Dell, 1953.

Mead, Margaret, *Male and Female: A Study of the Sexes in a Changing World*. New York: William Morrow & Co., 1949.

Merleau-Ponty, Maurice. *Signs*. Translated by Richard McCleary. Evanston: Northwestern University Press, 1964.

Micks, Marianne H. *Our Search for Identity: Humanity in the Image of God*. Philadelphia: Fortress, 1982.

Middleton, Richard. *The Liberating Image: The Imago Dei in Genesis 1*. Grand Rapids: Brazos, 2005.

Milbank, John. "Can a Gift Be Given? Prolegomena to a Future Trinitarian Metaphysic," *Modern Theology* 11/1 (January 1995) 119–61.

Miles, Angela and Geraldine Finn, eds. *Feminism in Canada: From Pressure to Politics*. Montreal: Black Rose, 1982.

Milhaven, J. Giles. "A Medieval Lesson on Bodily Knowing: Women's Experience and Men's Thought." *The Journal of the American Academy of Religion* 57/2 (Summer 1989) 341–72.

Mines, Samuel. *The Last Days of Mankind: Ecological Survival or Extinction*. New York: Simon & Schuster, 1971.

Moltmann, Jürgen. *The Coming of God: Christian Eschatology*. Translated by Margaret Kohl. Minneapolis: Fortress, 1996.

———. *The Crucified God: The Cross of Christ as the Foundation and Criticism of Christian Theology*. Translated by R. A. Wilson and John Bowden. London: SCM, 1974.

———. *God in Creation: An Ecological Doctrine of Creation*. Translated by Margaret Kohl. London: SCM, 1985.

———. *The Trinity and the Kingdom: The Doctrine of God*. Translated by Margaret Kohl. San Francisco: Harper & Row, 1981.

Money, John and Patricia Tucker. *Sexual Signatures: On Being a Man or a Woman*. Toronto: Little, Brown & Co., 1975.

Montagu, Ashley. *The Natural Superiority of Woman*. New York: Macmillan, 1953.

Naas, Michael. *Derrida From Now On*. New York: Fordham University Press, 2008.

Niebuhr, Reinhold. *The Nature and Destiny of Man*. London: Nisbet, 1943.

Nygren, Anders. *Agape and Eros*. Translated by Philip S. Watson. Philadelphia: Westminster, 1953.

Olthuis, James H. *The Beautiful Risk*. Grand Rapids: Zondervan, 2001.

———. "An Ethics of Compassion: Ethics in a Post-Modernist Age." In *What Right Does Ethics Have: Public Policy in a Pluralistic Culture*, edited by Sander Griffioen, 125–46. Amsterdam: VU University Press, 1990.

———. "A Hermeneutics of Suffering Love." In *The Very Idea of Radical Hermeneutics*, edited by Roy Martinez, 149–65. New York: Humanities, 1996.

———. "Afterword: A Radical Ontology of Love: Thinking 'with' Radical Orthodoxy." In *Radical Orthodoxy and the Reformed Tradition*, edited by James K. A. Smith and James H. Olthuis, 277–293. Grand Rapids: Baker Academic, 2005.

———. "Testing the Heart of *Khôra*: Anonymous or Amorous." In *Cross and Khôra: Deconstruction and Christianity in the Work of John D. Caputo*, edited by Neal DeRoo and Marko Zlomislic, 174–86. Eugene: Pickwick Publications, 2010.

———. "The Wit(h)ness of Suffering Love." In *A Sort of Homecoming: Essays Honoring the Academic and Community Work of Brian Walsh*, edited by Marcia Boniferro, Amanda Jagt, and Andrew Stephens-Rennie, 145–60. Eugene: Pickwick Publications, 2020.

———. "On Worldviews." In *Stained Glass*, edited by Paul Marshall, Sander Griffioen, and Richard Mouw, 26–40. Landham: University Press of America, 1989.

Olthuis, James H., ed. *Knowing Other-Wise*. New York: Fordham University Press, 1997.

Palmer, Richard E. *Hermeneutics*. Evanston: Northwestern University Press, 1969.

Pannenberg, Wolfhart. *Anthropology in Theological Perspective*. Translated by Matthew J. O'Connell. Philadelphia: Westminster John Knox, 1985.

———. *Basic Questions in Theology*. Vol. I. Translated by George H. Kehm. Philadelphia: Westminster, 1971.

Peacocke, Arthur. *Cosmos as Creation*. Edited by Ted Peters. Nashville: Abingdon, 1989.

———. *Theology for a Scientific Age: Being and Becoming—Natural, Divine and Human*. Minneapolis: Augsburg Fortress, 1993.

Peperzak, Adriaan. *Ethics as First Philosophy: The Significance of Emmanuel Levinas for Philosophy, Literature and Religion*. New York: Routledge, 1995.

Phillips, D. Z. *The Problem of Evil and The Problem of God*. Minneapolis: Fortress, 2005.

Piaget, Jean. *The Moral Judgment of the Child*. Translated by Marjorie Gabain. New York: Free Press Paperbacks, 1932.

Pirovolakis, Eftichis. *Reading Derrida and Ricoeur: Improbable Encounters Between Deconstruction and Hermeneutics*. Albany: SUNY, 2010.

Placher, William. *Narratives of a Vulnerable God*. Louisville: John Knox, 1994.
Plantinga, Alvin. *The Nature of Necessity*. Oxford: Oxford University Press, 1974.
Plato. *Theaetetus*. Trans. Harold North Fowler. Cambridge: Harvard University Press, 1921.
Pool, Jeff B. *God's Wounds: Hermeneutic of the Christian Symbol of Divine Suffering*. 2 vols. Eugene: Wipf and Stock, 2009–2010.
Pseudo-Dionysius. *The Divine Names*. In *Pseudo-Dionysius: The Complete Works*, translated by Colm Luibheid, 47–132. New York: Paulist, 1987.
Putt, Keith B., ed. *Gazing Through a Prism Darkly*. New York: Fordham University Press, 2009.
Reynolds, Thomas E. *Vulnerable Communion: A Theology of Disability and Hospitality*. Grand Rapids: Brazos, 2008.
Reynolds, Vernon. *The Biology of Human Action*. San Francisco: W. H. Freeman & Co., 1976.
Ricoeur, Paul. *The Conflict of Interpretations: Essays in Hermeneutics*. Edited by Don Ihde. Evanston: Northwestern University Press, 1974.
———. *Evil: A Challenge to Philosophy and Theology*. Translated by John Bowden. New York: Continuum, 2007.
———. *Fallible Man*. Translated by Charles A. Kelbley. New York: Fordham University Press, 1986.
———. *Figuring the Sacred: Religion, Narrative, and Imagination*. Edited by Mark I. Wallace. Translated by David Pellauer. Minneapolis: Fortress, 1995.
———. *Hermeneutics and the Human Sciences*. Edited and translated by John B. Thompson. Cambridge: Cambridge University Press, 1981.
———. *Interpretation Theory: Discourse and the Surplus of Meaning*. Fort Worth: Texas Christian University Press, 1976.
———. *Oneself as Another*. Translated by Kathleen Blamey. Chicago: University of Chicago Press, 1992.
———. *The Symbolism of Evil*. Translated by Emerson Buchanan. Boston: Beacon, 1967.
Rifkin, Jeremy. *Entropy: A New World View*. New York: Viking, 1980.
Rosenzweig, Franz. *The Star of Redemption*. Translated by William Hallo. Notre Dame: University of Notre Dame Press, 1970.
Roszak, Theodore. *Person/Planet*. New York: Doubleday, 1978.
———. *Unfinished Animal*. New York: Harper & Row, 1975.
Royle, Nicholas. *The Uncanny*. Manchester: Manchester University Press, 2003.
Rousseau, Jean-Jacques. *Discourse on Inequality*. Translated by Maurice Cranston. New York: Penguin, 1985.
Rubin, Lillian. *Intimate Strangers*. San Francisco: Harper & Row, 1983.
Sanford, John. *Evil: The Shadow Side of Reality*. New York: Crossroad, 1982.
Scharlemann, Robert, ed. *Negation and Theology*. Charlottesville: University of Virginia Press, 1992.
Scheler, Max. *Man's Place in Nature*. Translated by Hans Meyerhoff. Boston: Beacon, 1961.
Schell, Jonathan. *The Fate of the Earth*. New York: Knopf, 1982.
Schumacher, E.F. *A Guide for the Perplexed*. New York: Harper & Row, 1977.
———. *Small is Beautiful*. New York: Harper & Row, 1973.

Segundo, Juan Luis. *Evolution and Guilt*. Translated by John Drury. Maryknoll: Orbis, 1974.

Singer, June. *Androgyny: Toward a New Theory of Sexuality*. New York: Anchor, 1977.

Sloan, Douglas. *Insight-Imagination: The Emancipation of Thought and the Modern World*. Westport: Greenwood, 1983.

Sloterdijk, Peter. *Spheres*. Vol. I: *Bubbles: Microspherology*. Translated by Wieland Hoban. Cambridge: MIT, 2011.

Smith, James K. A. *The Fall of Interpretation: Philosophical Foundations for a Creational Hermeneutic*. Downers Grove: Intervarsity, 2000.

———. *Jacques Derrida: Live Theory*. New York: Continuum, 2005.

Smith, James K. A., and Henry Isaac Venema, eds. *The Hermeneutics of Charity: Interpretation, Selfhood, and Postmodern Faith*. Grand Rapids: Brazos, 2004.

Smolin, Lee. *Einstein's Unfinished Revolution: The Search for What Lies Beyond the Quantum*. New York: Penguin, 2019.

Spinoza, Benedict de. *Ethics*, in *The Chief Works of Benedict de Spinoza*. Translated by R. H. M. Elwes. New York: Dover, 1955.

Spitz, Rene. *The First Year of Life: A Psychoanalytic Study of Normal and Deviant Development of Object Relations*. New York: International Universities Press, 1965.

Steiner, George. *After Babel: Aspects of Language and Translation*. London: Oxford University Press, 1975.

Stern, Daniel. *The Interpersonal World of the Infant: A View from Psychoanalysis and Developmental Psychology*. New York: Basic, 1985.

Stern, Karl. *The Flight from Woman*. New York: Farrar, Straus and Giroux, 1965.

Swimme, Brian. *The Universe is a Green Dragon: A Cosmic Creation Story*. Sante Fe: Bear & Co., 1985.

Tabin, Johanna Krout. *On the Way to Self: Ego and Early Oedipal Development*. New York: Columbia University Press, 1985.

Taylor, Mark C. *Deconstructing Theology*. New York: Crossroad, 1982.

———. *Erring*. Chicago: University of Chicago Press, 1984.

Thomson, William Irwin. *At the Edge of History: Speculations on the Transformation of Culture*. New York: Harper & Row, 1979.

Tillich, Paul. *The Courage to Be*. New Haven: Yale University Press, 1952.

———. *Systematic Theology*. Vol. I. London: James Nisbet, 1953.

Toffler, Alvin. *Future Shock*. New York: Bantam, 1970.

———. *The Third Wave*. New York: William Morrow, 1980.

Tracy, David. *Analogical Imagination: Christian Theology and the Culture of Pluralism*. New York: Crossroad, 1981.

———. *Blessed Rage for Order: The New Pluralism in Theology*. New York: Seabury, 1975.

———. *Dialogue with the Other: The Inter-Religious Dialogue*. Grand Rapids: Eerdmans, 1990.

———. *Plurality and Ambiguity: Hermeneutics, Religion, Hope*. New York: Harper and Row, 1987.

Trible, Phyllis. *God and the Rhetoric of Sexuality*. Philadelphia: Fortress, 1978.

Uhlein, Gabriel. *Meditations with Hildegard of Bingen*. Santa Fe: Bear & Co., l982.

van der Hoeven, Johan. "The Problem of Evil—Crucible for the Authenticity and Modesty of Philosophizing: In Discussion with Paul Ricoeur." *South African Journal of Philosophy* 5/2 (1986) 44–52.

Van Peursen, Cornelis Anthonie. *Body, Soul, Spirit: A Survey of the Body-Mind Problem*. London: Oxford University Press, 1966.
Venema, Henry. *Philosophical Anthropology, and the Problem of Evil: An Interpretative Analysis of Paul Ricoeur's Philosophy of Will*. Toronto: Institute for Christian Studies, 1986.
Verny, Thomas. *The Secret Life of the Unborn Child*. Toronto: Collins, 1981.
Walsh, Brian. "A Critical Review of Pannenberg's *Anthropology in Theological Perspective*." *Christian Scholar's Review* 15/8 (1986) 247–59.
———. *Subversive Christianity*. Bristol: Regius, 1992.
Waugh, Patricia. "Postmodernism." In *Feminism and Psychoanalysis: A Critical Dictionary*, edited by Elizabeth Wright, 341–45. Oxford: Blackwell, 1992.
Webb, Stephen H. *The Gifting God: A Trinitarian Ethics of Excess*. New York: Oxford University Press, 1996.
Westphal, Merold. *Overcoming Onto-Theology: Toward a Postmodern Christian Faith*. New York: Fordham University Press, 2009.
Whitford, Margaret. *Luce Irigaray: Philosophy in the Feminine*. New York: Routledge, 1991.
Wilder, Amos. "Story and Story-World," *Interpretation* 37/4 (1983) 353–364.
Wink, Walter. *Engaging the Powers: Discernment and Resistance in a World of Domination*. Minneapolis: Fortress, 1992.
Winquist, Charles. *Homecoming: Interpretation, Transformation, and Individuation*. Missoula: Scholars, 1978.
Winnicott, Donald. *The Maturational Process and the Facilitating Environment*. New York: International Universities Press, 1965.
Wohlleben, Peter. *The Hidden Life of Trees: What They Feel, How They Communicate—Discoveries from a Secret World*. Translated by Jane Billinghurst. Vancouver: Greystone, 2016.
———. *The Inner Life of Animals: Love, Grief, and Compassion—Surprising Observations of a Hidden World*. Translated by Jane Billinghurst. Vancouver: Greystone, 2017.
Woodruff, Sue. *Meditations with Mechtild of Magdeburg*. Santa Fe: Bear & Co., 1982.
Wyschogrod, Edith. *Saints and Postmodernism: Revisioning Moral Philosophy*. Chicago: University of Chicago Press, 1990.
Žižek, Slavoj. *Absolute Recoil: Towards a New Foundation of Dialectical Materialism*. New York: Verso, 2014.
———. *The Fragile Absolute: Or, Why Is the Christian Legacy Worth Fighting For?* New York: Verso, 2000.
———. *Less Than Nothing: Hegel and the Shadow of Dialectical Materialism*. New York: Verso, 2012.
———. *The Parallax View*. Cambridge: MIT, 2006.
———. *The Plague of Fantasies*. New York: Verso, 2009.
Zum Brunn, Emilie and Georgette Epiney-Burgard. *Women Mystics in Medieval Europe*. New York: Paragon House, 1989.

SUBJECT INDEX

addiction, 47–48
air, 83–85, 152n67
alienation, 110–14
Allen, Prudence, 103n29
Angelus Silesius, 18, 150
anomos nomos, 72
Ansell, Nik, 67n32, 68n33
Anselm, 22
Aquinas, Thomas, 22, 191
archi-love, 27–29, 35, 38
Aristotle, 59n3, 76n10, 104
assymetrical ethical relation, 186, 191, 193–202, 206, 208
attending-to, 169–72
Augustine, 22, 68

Barrett, William, 93–4
Barth, Karl, 10,
Bateson, Gregory, 99
be(com)ing, 27–28, 32, 35, 168
be(com)ing human, 68, 99–117, 138
Bergson, Henri, 38,
Bernasconi, Robert, 178n63
the "between", 40, 76, 79–85, 152, 162n18, 167, 224–25
birthing, 170, 177–79
the body, 95, 99, 101, 110–11, 191–92, 235
Bohm, David, 37, 97–98
Brock, Rita Nakashima, 156, 162n18, 165
Brown, William P., 11
Browning, Don, 208

Buber, Martin, 51, 114, 156, 162n18, 167, 191, 224–25
Burrell, David, 188
Buytendijk, F. J. J., 99

Caputo, John, 35, 52, 150, 155, 182n72, 192n29, 193, 194n39
  on God, 13, 60, 62, 73
the caress, 86–90
Carroll, Sean, 27
Cassirer, Ernst, 93
Céline, Louis-Ferdinand, xiv
chance/necessity, 126–27, 130–35, 139
chaosmos, 48, 126, 139
climate change, 33, 230
Cockburn, Bruce, 7
compassion, 39, 208, 247–48
conatus essendi/amandi, 28, 50–51, 69, 164–65, 194, 212
creation, 27–30, 35–39, 57
  ex amore, xvi, 3–10, 13–18, 20, 69–70, 90, 139
  ex nihilo, 4, 9–10
  as God's risk, 70–71
  and trauma, 44, 54
Crockett, Clayton, 38
the crucifixion, 12, 71

Davis, Stephen D., 62
death, xx-xxi, 12, 49, 71
deconstruction, 141–42, 158, 163–64, 174–75, 216, 220n55

265

SUBJECT INDEX

Derrida, Jacques, 9, 36, 72, 116, 119–20, 130–32, 137–38, 156, 161–65, 174–75, 185, 200n62, 209n92
   on the gift, 140–51
   on God, 58–60, 216–20
   on *khôra*, 37, 147–50
   on self/other, 52–53, 145–46, 157, 162, 196–7
Descartes, 7, 104, 241
desire, 57, 80–81, 87–88
difference, fear of, 233, 241–42, 244–45
   hermeneutic mediation of, 156–57, 160–61, 165–66, 173, 178
   interpretation of, 159–61
   non-oppositional, 17, 76, 132–35, 154, 157–59, 203–4
   oppositional, 50–56, 64–65, 84–85, 145–46
   respect for, 233
   sexual, 76–7, 80–82, 103–7
   theological, 21–22
différance, 148–49, 161
disclosure, 177, 179, 182
discontinuities, 133–34
Dooyeweerd, Herman, 36–37
domination, xvi, 112, 166, 200–201, 210, 213, 226
doxology, 23–5
dualism, 16–7, 53, 158
   male/female, 103–7
   mind/body, 97, 99
Dudiak, Jeffrey, 51n67

ebullitio, 13–15
economy
   of exchange, 140–45, 151, 157, 196, 199, 205–6, 209n91
   of love, 140, 144, 151–55, 157, 205
ecstasy/enstasy, 81, 86, 89, 152
egocentric/exocentric, 111–13
emotional life, 47, 238–40
   and politics, 240–43
Empedocles, 81n42, 82
eros, 81, 157, 225–26
   and agape, 50, 102, 110, 146, 186, 198, 201, 207, 225
   to connect, 164–66, 168

ethics, xvii, 151, 220n55
   of Levinas, 51–52, 186, 190–202, 206–8
   modernist, 187–90
   and ontology, 190–94, 199
   quantum, 79
evil, xv, xvi, 13, 31, 39, 41–49, 54–57, 61–67, 71, 110–14, 134–36, 176, 202

the face, 190–3, 195–96, 199, 208
faith, 21, 212, 220n55, 236–38
the Fall, 12, 42, 54, 135, 162
fear, 46–47, 51, 239, 241–45
Flax, Jane, 158n3, 223–24
Foucault, Michel, 226
Fox, Matthew, 95
freedom, 13–15, 50, 61, 63–68, 70, 186, 193, 233
Fretheim, Terrence, 63
Freud, Sigmund, 50, 78, 126–31, 136–37, 225–26
friendship, 9

Gadamer, Hans Georg, 170, 174, 178
gap/rupture, 55–7
Gelassenheit, 31, 227
gender, 103, 105
the gift, 140–47, 151–55, 205
gift/call, xiii, xv, 32, 36, 66, 68–69, 114–15, 248
ghosts, 137–9
Gilligan, Carol, 189
Glass, James, 223
God
   as causa sui, 212
   conceptualization of, 15, 17, 22–25, 212
   and creation, 3–4, 6, 8–17, 27–30, 57, 65–66, 98, 222
   death of, 58, 81, 211, 215
   in Derrida, 58, 60, 216–21
   and evil, 13, 39, 42, 46, 48, 61–66
   and humanity, xiii, xvi, 5, 20, 30, 114–15
   and/as love, xiii, 10–5, 16, 18, 20, 25–26, 28–29, 57, 62, 65–66,

68–70, 73, 89–90, 114–15, 138, 157, 221–22, 227
omnipotence of, 11–13, 42, 58–62, 65
self-limitation of, 63–6
suffering of, 15–16, 39–40, 59–60, 71
Trinity of, 6, 14, 68–70
vulnerability of, 5, 10–12, 39, 58–60, 62, 66, 70–71
word of, 12, 68
"yes" of, 18, 36, 68, 71, 164
Goiten, S. D., 18
Gould, Steven Jay, 27
Griffin, David Ray, 60

Hadewijch of Antwerp, 228–29
Hafiz, xvii, xviii, 19
Hart, Henk, xvii, xix-xxii
Hauerwas, Stanley, 188
haunting, 137–39
Heidegger, Martin, 23, 27, 29, 32, 77, 85, 114, 137–38, 147–48, 212, 216, 227
Heraclitus, 81n42
Herman, Judith, 133
hermeneutics, 156–62, 164–68
fourfold spiral of, 157–58, 168–82
mastery mode of, 157–59, 166–67, 171, 173–74, 176, 179, 181
two-way dance of, 165–68
as violence, 158–59, 162–63
Heyward, Carter, 165
Hick, John, 61–62
Hildegard of Bingen, 6, 12
Hobbes, Thomas, 50
Hocking, 68n33
hope, 231, 248
humanity, 56–57, 93–96
and God, xiii, xvi, 5, 20, 30, 114–15
multi-dimensional complexity of, 96–117
as part of nature, 96–98
humble courage, 245–46

identity, 79, 101, 105–6, 118–19, 178, 203, 233–35
ideology, 237–38, 240–44

il y a (there is) 9, 27–28, 37, 77, 155
khôra, 37, 144, 147–50, 153
l'amour/Liebe, 28, 37, 155
matrix, 149–50, 153
imago dei, 57, 98–99, 103, 114
incarnation, 16, 31–32, 39, 69–70, 72, 86, 89
individual/collective, 101–2, 232–3
interpretation, 156, 159–62, 164–82
Irigaray, Luce, 40, 75–90, 103, 117, 151–55, 165

Jardine, Alice, 224
Johnson, James Weldon, 3–4
journeying with, 169, 172–77
Joy, Morny, 221
Jung, Carl, 106
justice, 193, 197, 231–33, 244–49

Kearney, Richard, 13
Kegan, Robert, 108
Keller, Catherine, 8n13, 10, 11, 15
khôra, 37, 147–50, 218–19
Kierkegaard, Soren, 245
kindom/kingdom, 7, 73
Kingsolver, Barbara, 33
knowledge, 166–67
Kohut, Heinz, 100n25
Kristeva, Julia, 35, 68–69, 156, 164, 204, 222, 224

Lacan, Jacques, 44, 80, 129–30
LaCugna, Catherine, 22–23, 70
Lasch, Christopher, 94
law, 72, 193
let there be's, 6, 11–12, 32, 36
Levenson, Jon, 10
Levinas, Emmanual, xiv-v, 7, 15, 28, 51–52, 163, 166–67, 185–87, 190–202, 205–9
listening, 231
Lloyd, Genevieve, 104, 241
love, x, xix-xx, 20, 90, 139, 149, 151, 228–29
agents of, 20–21, 29–30, 49, 73, 114, 125
and being, 7, 16–18, 25–26, 68–69, 114–15, 138, 221–23

love *(continued)*
  conditioned/unconditioned, 72
  and connection, 164–65, 225
  and creation, xiii, xv, 3, 8–10, 14, 20, 26–29, 32–33, 35–41, 65–66, 90, 194
  economy of, 140, 151–55
  and ethics, 194
  and evil, xiv, 41–46, 48–49, 56, 73–74
  eye of, 221
  and freedom, 67–68
  and/as God, 4, 10, 12, 14–15, 17–18, 25–26, 28–29, 35, 57, 62, 65–66, 68–70, 73, 115
  and hermeneutics, 164–65, 167, 182
  interpersonal, 30–31
  and khôra, 149–50
  and knowledge, 78, 167
  and politics, 230–33, 245–48
  and power, 53, 60–61, 69, 72–73, 226
  of self/other, 50, 78, 102, 115, 146, 148, 232–34, 247
  sexual, 80–88, 102
  wild spaces of, 79, 149, 161, 204, 207, 211, 224–28
  the without-why of, 28, 38, 44, 221n61
  wisdom of, 75–76

MacIntyre, Alisdair, 189–90
MacMurray, John, 114
Malabou, Catherine, 129
Marion, Jean-Luc, 26, 72
May, Gerhard, 10
meaning, 37
Mechtild of Magdeburg, 6
Meister Eckhart, 14, 31, 218–20
me/myself/I, 96, 116–25
metaphysics, 17, 23, 26, 158–59, 161, 211–12, 220, 224
Middleton, Richard, 8, 11
modal theory, 34–36, 100
modernity, 93–94, 187–90, 244–45
Moi, Toril, 223n71
Moltmann, Jürgen, 10, 64n27

morality, 185
  rational foundations of, 187–9
mucous, 85–86
mutuality, 101–2, 153, 166, 168, 186–87, 196, 203–9, 225–26, 235
mystery, 23–24, 28–35, 37, 83

Naas, Michael, 60
Neibuhr, Reinhold, 201,
Nietzsche, Friedrich, 41–42
Nygren, Anders, 50, 102n26, 201n67

ontology
  of antagonism, 54–56
  and ethics, 190–94
  of Levinas, 190–99
  of love, 16–18, 54, 211, 221–22
  of power/violence/control, 15, 26, 50–52, 69, 146, 200–201, 211–13
  relational, 15–17, 40,
openness, 48, 96, 168, 170–72, 175, 179, 204–5
  cosmic, 40–43
  the other, 51–53, 76–77, 82–87, 156–57, 160–62, 165–66, 171, 178–80, 197–98, 204–6, 210, 242, 247
  ethical priority of, 191–95, 200–202

pain, 191–93, 213–14, 215n26
Palmer, Richard, 174
panentheism, 15
part/whole, 95–96
personal growth, 235–36, 246
Pannenberg, Wolfhart, 23, 109, 111–12
Peacocke, Arthur, 9, 63
Plantinga, Alvin, 61
Plato, 49, 76n10, 104, 146
Plessner, Helmuth, 110
pluralism, 185–86
politics, 231–33, 245
Pool, Jeff, 59, 63, 65, 133n23
populism, 235, 237–38, 242–43
postmodernism, xiv, 157–59, 185–86, 190, 192–93, 210–11, 214–15
power, 226
  of God, 13, 49–50, 58–66, 69–70

over/with, xiv, xvi, 12–13, 49–53, 60–62, 64–65, 67, 70, 73, 146, 187, 199–208
presence/mediation, 161–62
Pseudo-Dionysius, 147, 216
psychoanalysis, 128–31

quantum physics, 34–35, 79

racism, 242, 245
rationality, 78, 100, 104, 185, 187–88, 191, 210–11
the Real, 29, 32, 54, 57, 129–30
realism/antirealism, 33–5
relationality, 39–40, 70, 97–98
resistance, 231
responsibility, 113, 193, 196–98
the resurrection, 12
Ricoeur, Paul, 50, 110, 113, 134, 159n5, 170, 193, 200n62, 248
Rosenzweig, Franz, 150
Rousseau, Jean-Jacques, 50
Royle, Nicholas, 127n1, 136n35
Ryle, Gilbert, 99

sacred interstices, 162–63
Scheler, Max, 93, 97, 99, 11
self, 99–102, 116–17
    apotheosis of, 213
    caring, 98
    Cartesian/Kantian, 94–95, 97–98, 222–23
    as decentered non-self, 214–15, 223–24
    deflator/inflator, 234–35
    development of, 107–9
    and evil, 111–13
    as gift/call, 114–15, 222–23
    and God, 215–16
    as house, 118–19, 121–25, 239
    me/myself/I faces of, 116–25
    and other, 50–52, 144–46, 152, 154, 180, 197–99, 205–7, 213, 215, 224, 232–33
    and politics, 231–35, 246
    in Levinas, 198–201
    sexual, 102–7
    and trauma, 46–47

self-interest, xv, 147–48, 186–87, 198–99, 201, 232–33
self sacrifice, 145, 186–87, 194–99, 201, 208
sensible transcendental, 81–82
sexuality, 80–88, 102–7, 241
shalom, 233
sin, 31
Sloterdijk, Peter, 70
Smolin, Lee, 34
social transformation, 230, 247
sovereignty, 58–62, 72–74
space/time, 5–7, 40–42, 78–80, 132, 219–20
Spinoza, 49, 50, 191, 212–13
spirit, 100–101
Steiner, George, 173–74, 179–81
Stern, Daniel, 100n25, 108–9, 223n67
Stern, Karl, 241
strangers, 244–45
subjectivity/intersubjectivity, 83–84, 88, 100–102, 145–46, 151, 162–63, 166–67, 178, 196–97, 203
suffering, 41–42, 49, 71, 213–14, 226
    of God, 15–16, 39–40, 59–60, 71
suffering with, 15, 39, 182, 207–9, 226–27
superstition, 131
Swimme, Brian, 97n15
sympathy, 97

Taylor, Mark C., 210–11, 214–16, 218
theodicy, 13, 42, 61–66
theology, 13, 21, 58, 61–62, 211–13, 216
    in Derrida, 216–21
    in the mode of doxology, 24–25
    positive/negative, 22–23, 216–17, 219
    primary/secondary, 21–22
    strong/weak, 62
theopoetics, 24–26, 28, 70
Tillich, Paul, 50, 101, 200n62, 213
touch, 86, 88
Tracy, David, 159, 171, 178
transforming, 170, 179–82
trauma, 43–44, 46, 55, 126–30, 133–39
    and politics, 234–35, 243–44
Trumpism, 73–74, 237–38, 240–44

trust, 170–72, 174, 176

the uncanny, 136–39

violence, 51–53, 135, 157–59, 188, 201, 205, 207
    of the gift, 140, 144–45
    hermeneutics of, 158–59, 162–63
vulnerability, 132, 171, 204

Weil, Simone, 7
the weself, 101–2
Whitford, Margaret, 77

wisdom, xiv-xv, 26, 67n32, 75–76
with-ing, xvii, 28, 30–31, 44, 87, 147, 187
Wohlleben, Peter, 33n33
wonder, 76–78
worldviews, 236–37, 239–40
Wyschogrod, Edith, 193, 195n44

the "yes", 18, 36, 68, 71, 74, 150–51, 155, 163–64

Žižec, Slavoj, 44, 53–57, 135–36

SCRIPTURE INDEX

Genesis

1:1	35
1:28	98n21
1:30	98
2	31
3	67
3:9	4–5, 12
4:7	46
4:10	33
6:6–7	71

Leviticus

26:11	228n85

Deuteronomy

30:11–16	30

Job

12:7–8	33

Psalms

19:1	27
24:1	27
33:5	28

Habakkuk

2:11	33

Matthew

25	49, 74

Luke

6:36	20, 74
19:40	33

John

1:14	66, 228n85
1:16	27
3:8	138
3:16	71

Romans

8:17	39, 49
8:18	16

1 Corinthians

13:7	39

2 Corinthians

11:14	48
12:9	248

Colossians

1:24	31
1:27	16, 31
2:9	27

2 Timothy
1:7	248

1 Peter
5:8	46

2 Peter
3:12	7

1 John
3:14	67
4:7–8	25, 89
4:12	xiii
4:16	xiii, 18

Jude
21	75

Revelation
2:17	117
21:3	228n85